AF506236

Nobody's Boy and His Pals

Nobody's Boy & His Pals

THE STORY OF JACK ROBBINS
AND THE BOYS' BROTHERHOOD REPUBLIC

Hendrik Hartog

The University of Chicago Press

Chicago and London

The University of Chicago Press, Chicago 60637
The University of Chicago Press, Ltd., London
© 2024 by The University of Chicago
All rights reserved. No part of this book may be used or reproduced
in any manner whatsoever without written permission, except in
the case of brief quotations in critical articles and reviews. For more
information, contact the University of Chicago Press, 1427 E. 60th
St., Chicago, IL 60637.
Published 2024
Printed in the United States of America

33 32 31 30 29 28 27 26 25 24   1 2 3 4 5

ISBN-13: 978-0-226-83435-1 (cloth)
ISBN-13: 978-0-226-83437-5 (paper)
ISBN-13: 978-0-226-83436-8 (e-book)
DOI: https://doi.org/10.7208/chicago/9780226834368.001.0001

Library of Congress Cataloging-in-Publication Data

Names: Hartog, Hendrik, 1948– author.
Title: Nobody's boy and his pals : the story of Jack Robbins and the Boys'
    Brotherhood Republic / Hendrik Hartog.
Other titles: Jack Robbins and the Boys' Brotherhood Republic
Description: Chicago ; London : The University of Chicago Press, 2024. |
    Includes bibliographical references and index.
Identifiers: LCCN 2023051395 | ISBN 9780226834351 (cloth) | ISBN
    9780226834375 (paperback) | ISBN 9780226834368 (ebook)
Subjects: LCSH: Robbins, Jack, –1958. | Robbins, Jack, –1958—Will. |
    Boys' Brotherhood Republic (Chicago, Ill.) | Social reformers—Illinois—
    Chicago—Biography. | Boys—Illinois—Chicago—Societies and clubs. |
    Social work with children—Illinois—Chicago. | Social work with
    teenagers—Illinois—Chicago. | Juvenile delinquency—Illinois—
    Chicago—Prevention.
Classification: LCC HV878 .H378 2024 | DDC 362.7/7569092 [B]—
    dc23/eng/20231212
LC record available at https://lccn.loc.gov/2023051395

♾ This paper meets the requirements of ANSI/NISO Z39.48-1992
(Permanence of Paper).

Contents

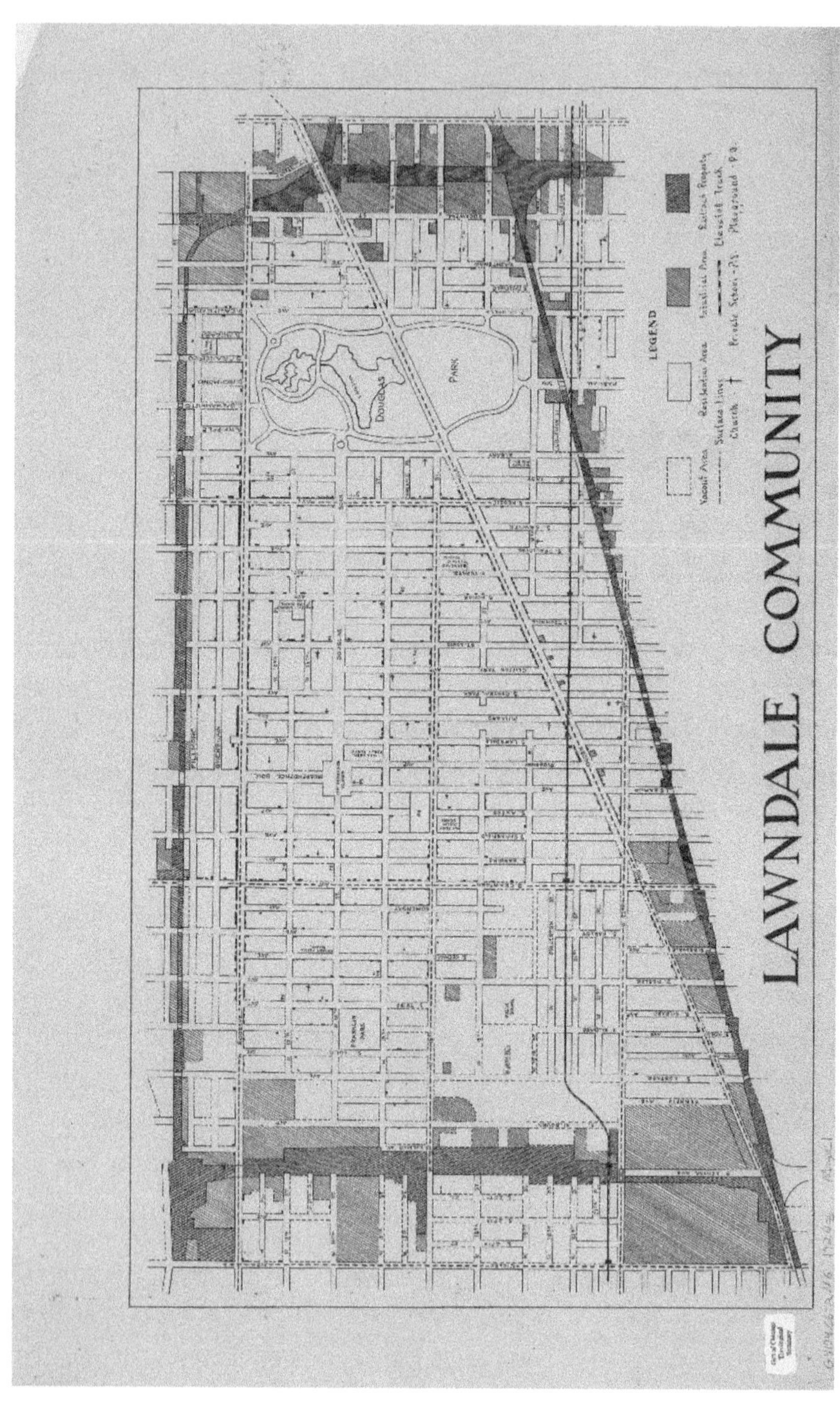

Map 1: Lawndale, Chicago, in 1920. University of Chicago Department of Sociology.

Map 2: Chicago motor coach pictorial map of Chicago, 1920. Clason Map Co., John R. Borchert Map Library, University of Minnesota Libraries, Minneapolis, MN.

Introduction

It was in 1913 that Jack Robbins first became the "big brother" to "chanceless waifs." Newspaper readers soon learned much about how he befriended boys living on city streets and how he advocated for them.

In 1914, he and a group of Chicago boys he worked with created the Boys' Brotherhood Republic, an alternative institution that challenged conventional understandings of boyhood and citizenship. He and the boys imagined a boyhood in which they might live as free citizens of an empowering and rights-based and self-consciously legalist republic. The boys governed themselves, democratically and with care for one another, without parents or parent substitutes—indeed, mostly without any other adults at all.

The constitution they then drafted for the Boys' Brotherhood Republic denied that boys who did wrong, "bad boys," or, we might say, juvenile delinquents, needed to be separated from other boys. The group's mantra was, "So long as there are boys in trouble, we too are in trouble." It resisted the prevalent notion that adolescent boys were "dependent," in need of adult care. At a time—in America's Progressive Era—when reformers were arguing about whether the answer to the "boy problem" lay with parents or with creating alternative structures, run by adults, that would replicate what parents ought to have offered, Jack Robbins and his adolescent collaborators imagined a republic where boys would be "pals" to one another. The goal was to ensure that a boy had "pals" who would be there to care for and to support him, regardless of the trouble the boy found himself in.

The Boys' Brotherhood Republic would inevitably negotiate with an adult world of powerful and sometimes violent institutions, with juvenile courts and reform schools and with the police, among others. But it did so as one republic dealing with another. As such, the Boys' Brotherhood Republic became a part of Chicago's landscape of reform institutions, controversial and singular but also integrated into its public life.

And so it survived for the better part of thirty years.

After his death in 1958, Jack Robbins left a will that included a trust that promised care for a particular subset of troubled children: "the Negro child or children" of men and women convicted of and imprisoned for political crimes. The terms of his will, drafted in explicit rejection of the norms of Cold War America, produced a 1962 California judicial decision that, in its own small way, challenged the legal conformity of the era and looked forward to the social disruptions of the later 1960s.

Robbins's will concluded with a kind of credo, one that underlay the provisions that he had just set out and that looked back forty years and more to a time when he had been a prominent, even a notorious, figure in American culture. "Unorthodoxy or lack of conformity" he wrote, had never been a "governing factor" in his life. Beyond that, he had always believed in "full, complete, and unabridged freedom of expression in a democratic society." He wished to preserve the right to be "different." And that is why he drafted the will that he had.

The particular "difference" that Jack Robbins had worked to preserve, one that had animated him and had gained him a great deal of public attention forty years before, was the right of adolescent boys to live in republican freedom and to care for one another, extracted from adult control and from the coercive institutions of a repressive state. The Boys' Brotherhood Republic he had worked to create would stand apart as a legal entity. It embodied a countercultural identity, one not controlled by the state or by parents or by reformers, and a site where free speech, debate, and argument were valued.

* * *

Jack Robbins's story begins with the "boy problem." It ends with an uncelebrated episode of late Cold War litigation in the early days of the civil rights movement. Neither the beginning nor the ending has any place in familiar constitutional and legal histories of American freedom and of American criminality.

Place is also significant, as the story begins in one famous and emblematic location, Progressive Era Chicago, and it ends in midcentury Los Angeles, another site of famous and infamous conflicts. In the early twentieth century,

Chicago was the paradigm of a city gripped by "the boy problem." It was where what today is called "juvenile justice" was modeled and first institutionalized. But Chicago was also where some reformers imagined new ways of understanding boyhood and of supportive care and citizenship. Los Angeles was where the anti-communist crusade of the Cold War, the Red Scare, had many battles and victories. The city was notorious for the violence of its policing, the conservatism of its leading newspaper, and the docility of its major industries, in the face of the "inquisitions" of the Cold War. It was noteworthy, too, for the resistance of its power structure to African American aspirations. But as we will see, Los Angeles also was a site for novel legal strategies that responded to a changing America.

This book charts one American story, held together by the life and words of one odd individual, Jack Robbins. It is about how Robbins thought about American freedom and care and responsibility and criminality—and how he was thought about by others. Jack Robbins was of his time, involved with other radicals and reformers, some prominent and some obscure. He was one of several "boy workers" in early twentieth-century America, all of whom were then absorbed by the "boy problem." Across a half century of American history, across a changing America, Jack Robbins adjusted his thinking and his expressed political commitments—and he told many lies, especially to newspaper reporters. Yet he remained doggedly focused on the needs of and the harms experienced by adolescent children. The institution he had helped to create in 1914 and that, for the next thirty years he "supervised," the Boys' Brotherhood Republic, articulated ways of understanding boyhood and care and criminality that have not received the attention they deserve. The will he drafted in the late 1950s suggests that he continued to think about and to worry about uncared-for children, even as the political and legal contexts that shaped children's lives changed dramatically.

Telling this story has required particular research strategies. Jack Robbins left no archive of personal papers. Nor is there an archive for Chicago's Boy's Brotherhood Republic. All that survives are fugitive notes and files and documents and images in scattered libraries, a few reports by potential funding agencies, and a large number of journalistic accounts and descriptions. Much of the early story can be told because, for a time, between 1913 and the early 1920s, Robbins and the boys he worked with fascinated a national public of newspaper and magazine readers. American journalists met that demand by writing and publishing hundreds of articles about him and the Boys' Brotherhood Republic (BBR).[1] Yet, once the fascination passed, once urban America stopped worrying about "the boy problem," once his particular kind of radicalism no longer seemed interesting, no longer "news," Jack Robbins mostly disappeared from public view.[2]

And today both Jack Robbins and the Boys' Brotherhood Republic are long forgotten.

Still, it has been possible to reconstruct aspects of a life and, even more, of the projects that animated him and that made him "news," to tell a story about a way of being that may seem lost to us.

My ambitions for this book are both modest and grandiose. Jack Robbins may remain a sideshow to predominant legal histories of Progressive reform, of childhood, of criminality, of repression, of race and ethnicity, and of free speech, although he may have had a marginal impact on larger narratives, and though he certainly had interesting things to say about those themes. I don't imagine that I have produced a new version of *Law and the Conditions of Freedom*, or of *The Transformation of American Law*, familiar titles that signify general histories of law and of how Americans, mostly those with resources and capacity, have managed to use and to understand law. His story, or my version of his story, remains a small and particular story, even as it taught me to see aspects of modern American history in new ways.

Still, I believe this book models one way to go beyond the conventional wisdoms that have had determinative weight in American constitutional and legal history, particularly the focus on economically competent, mostly white and mostly middle-class participants in the legal culture, those adults who were sometimes capitalist producers and always consumers in the economy. How should legal historians make space for others—for the diverse and strange lives, words, and legacies of women and men like Jack Robbins, and for the adolescent boys of the Boys' Brotherhood Republic, some among the many nonelites who have embodied relatively underground streams in American legal culture? How are we to treat both him and the boys as living complex but free lives both in and against the law, and as the creators of forms of participatory citizenship, of resistance to subordination, and of community responsibility? That is the project that became this book.[3]

And along the way I found a story, one that uncovered episodes of American history and culture, and one that engaged themes of childhood and adolescence, state power and violence, care, community, race and ethnicity, sexuality, wealth, radical politics, and civil liberties, across much of the twentieth century, a period sometimes called the American Century.

ONE

The Big Brother

I first found Jack Robbins by way of the 1962 California case that tested his will. I was reading property law casebooks in order to discover how the Cold War shaped property law as a law school subject. *In Re Robbins' Estate*, the case, appears in one obscure 1981 law school casebook. It was not then, and it is not today, a standard case in property law lore. It is not a case familiar to most property law teachers.[1]

In that casebook, the case led or introduced a section that explored, in the awkward language of the casebook editors, "claims questioning the compatibility of the donor's objectives with overriding community policies." *In Re Robbins* exemplified the conflict between the freedom of the individual to do what she or he willed with what was her or his own, on the one hand, and the demands of the "community," on the other. Did one have the right to do as one pleases with what one possesses? Must one limit uses of property to those the state approved of? Could a donor, a Jack Robbins for example, create a will that disposed of his small wealth in a way that countered or challenged laws identified with McCarthyism, with the anti-communist crusade? Especially as those laws had, by the time of the decision in the case, mostly been held constitutional and enforceable by compliant courts?[2]

What students (and I) learned from the excerpted text in the casebook was that someone named Jack Robbins died in 1958. His will divided his estate into two parts. One part, worth around ten thousand dollars, went as gifts to a sister in Canada, to her son, and to Chicago's Multiple Sclerosis Foundation. This part raised no legal issues. The second part, the part that produced litigation, consisted of the proceeds from the sale of two small parcels of real estate in

Los Angeles. Those lands, worth then a bit more than twenty thousand dollars, were given in trust to three trustees, with full discretionary power to use in support of the trust's purpose. That purpose: "to provide for the care, comfort, support, medical attention, education, sustenance, maintenance or custody" of a "Negro child or children," whose father or mother, "or both," had been convicted and imprisoned for having committed "a crime or misdemeanor of a political nature." The rest of the will text, as edited in the casebook, explained what Robbins meant by "political nature," which included many of the standard crimes identified with postwar anti-communism.

Lee Mishkin, a grandnephew of the testator, of Jack Robbins, challenged the creation of that trust. Irvine Robbins, a nephew, was named as administrator of the estate. Lawyer members of the Southern California branch of the American Civil Liberties Union were involved on both sides of the litigation.

In Re Robbins came to the California Supreme Court on appeal because the lower California courts, both the Los Angeles Superior Court and the intermediate California District Court of Appeal, held that a trust that encouraged the commission of "political crimes" was an illegal trust. A trust that provided care for the children of convicted criminals would reward those criminals for their criminality by softening the effects of imprisonment and by offering support to the criminals' children. The trust, those courts held, thus created an incentive to commit crimes. Therefore it was illegal and unenforceable.

The opinion for the California high court, written by the eminent Justice Roger Traynor, reversed, meaning that it allowed Robbins's trust to be enforced. Thus trustees could find and support a "Negro child or children" of someone who had been convicted of having committed a political crime.

Traynor's opinion moved in two directions. First, it acknowledged an argument made by the lawyers who represented Jack Robbins's estate. That is, the "political" crimes that the will set out—including refusal to name names, membership in the Communist Party, failure to disclose Communist Party membership, refusal to sign loyalty oaths, and trade union activism—involved "areas where the lines between constitutionally protected activity and illegal activity" were "vaguely defined." These "political crimes"—their relative illegality—were not as settled *as crimes* as they seemed to be. All were constitutionally controversial. Had the parents of Robbins's beneficiaries done anything that should really be understood as criminal wrongdoing?

The lawyers interpreted Jack Robbins's will as intending to support only those who had been "unlawfully" or wrongfully "convicted for engaging in" what in the end would be recognized as "constitutionally protected activity." Those parents of a "Negro child or children" had been engaged in constitutionally protected protest and law reform, just as those involved in the civil rights movement, a continuing presence at that moment in 1962 when Traynor drafted his opinion, were involved in constitutionally protected protest and law reform. Through his will, he, Jack Robbins, was helping to challenge laws that would eventually be overturned as constitutionally flawed.

Thus, the lawyers argued, the question of encouraging illegality could be avoided. The parents could be reinterpreted as engaged in activities that revealed their respect for law, for the rule of law. They were not really criminals.

But Traynor went further. He silently rejected the lawyers' argument, even as he came down on their side. He assumed "the testator," Jack Robbins, "might have intended to benefit the children of those convicted of even valid laws." Robbins might well have been something more than a genteel and law-abiding reformer. He intended to encourage those who violated even valid laws. And yet, for Traynor it didn't matter that the laws the parents had violated would remain enforceable and enforced, as would their convictions. It didn't matter that their convictions might not have been constitutionally flawed. Why didn't it matter? Because "assistance to the minor beneficiaries of the trust," that is, to the "Negro child or children," was itself a "valid charitable purpose." Period. The risk that offering funds encouraged crimes was "remote." And the benefit to society of assistance to a discrete category of children who would otherwise not be supported transcended "whatever criticism there may be of his [Robbins's] motives, which have died with him."

One can imagine the casebook lesson as either being that a testator's freedom—the freedom to give and to use one's resources for nearly any purpose one chose—trumped all else, or that the competing "community" good of supporting otherwise unsupported children, the "Negro" children of those serving time for political crimes, transcended or modified the good of enforcing "political crimes." It did not matter that the testator's motives were inconsistent with recognized norms or policies. It did not matter that Jack Robbins might have wanted to encourage lawbreaking. According to Traynor, it was not the business of courts to challenge the freedom of the property owner to dispose of her or his resources as she or he chose, especially when the end result was support for "innocent" children.[3]

But who was this Jack Robbins? The will and the opinions in the case told nothing, other than that Jack Robbins apparently had lived in Chicago, because that is where the will was drafted, and where the named trustees lived, and that he owned property in California. Nor did the briefs that survive in the Los Angeles County Law Library and in the California State Archives tell much more. A newspaper that covered the case called him a "Chicago philanthropist." The same paper, after the decision in the case was announced, called him a "Los Angeles philanthropist." The *New York Times* quoted his lawyer, who called him "a humanitarian interested in civil liberties."[4]

Could I find more, using the vast digital resources available today? There were, as one might expect, several possible "Jack Robbins," each of whom left traces in online records.[5] The Jack Robbins I was looking for was hard to pin down in the formal genealogical records. He was in ceaseless motion, although he mostly lived in Chicago until sometime in the late 1940s, when he moved to California.[6] According to the 1940 census, this Jack Robbins (recorded by the census worker as Cobbins) was then fifty-eight, which meant he was born around 1882. His social security application in the 1950s identified his place of birth as Deretzin in Poland (now Belarus). He was naturalized. His first language was Yiddish. He lived on Hamlin Street in Chicago, in Lawndale, a part of Chicago that had once been almost entirely populated by Eastern European Jewish immigrants but would after World War II become largely African American. And he worked as a "superintendent." He lived alone, and he was divorced. Assuming that Irvine Robbins and Lee Mishkin were his nephew and grandnephew, as they were identified in the will litigation, one would conclude from following their traces at Ancestry.com that the family name of the particular Jack Robbins I was after had been Rabinovitch or Rabinovitz before it was anglicized, and that some of his family lived in Canada before coming to the United States.[7]

This Jack Robbins's 1942 draft card added one crucial detail. He worked for Chicago's Boys' Brotherhood Republic. That organization is what he then "supervised." And that detail opened up the story, made it possible to find a thread through the records.

* * *

Who was Jack Robbins? If the genealogical records for this Jack Robbins were sparse, the journalistic ones were full, at least in the years just before and during World War I. According to the reporters and editors who retailed the stories he told them, he had been raised in an orphanage in New Jersey until early adolescence. Then he spent several years in the Glenwood Manual Training School outside Chicago. How he got from New Jersey to Illinois was never described. Then he lived on the streets of Chicago (or perhaps it was New York according to some accounts), until he made his way back to New Jersey, where a friend of his absent father may have given him a job. He succeeded in that work. Eventually, he became a tobacco salesman with several employees. Of his early life and his parents, and of how and why he ended up in an orphan-age in New Jersey, if that is where he spent his early life, I can find no trace. He talked constantly about the failures of mothers and fathers but never about his own. None of the published accounts of his early life tell how or when he came to the United States.[8]

Jack Robbins, the Jack Robbins I was in search of, suddenly became a well-known figure in newspapers around the country in Progressive Era America. By 1913, according to the *New Orleans Times-Democrat* as well as many other newspapers, he was "known the country over as the 'big brother' to friendless waifs." Or, as one much reprinted 1919 article put it, he was an artist, a sculptor, who put the soul into "human clay," who carved "fine men" out of "bad boys. . . . Taking them from the gutter of sin, from penal institutions and the streets[,] Jack Robbins moulds them into boys who will be men, husbands, fathers, citizens, an honor to their country and a living monument to their sculptor." He was, the article continued, a greater genius than Michelangelo, producing something that was of "greater value to the world" than "all the marble statues in niches and upon pedestals."[9]

He first appeared in American newspapers in 1906. He was living in Perth Amboy, New Jersey, an industrial and commercial center, a railroad terminal, and a coal shipping point. In July, the Socialist Party organized in the city, electing him as "secretary," a position that—the *Perth Amboy Evening News* noted—came with what the paper called "full charge," as the socialists had no office of president. In early 1908, the paper found him at the head of a tenants' committee organized to fight high housing costs. Rents had increased three to four dollars over the previous four years in the large tenements. A rent strike had begun. A few days later, the newspaper asserted he was "in hot water." At least one landlord had complained to the mayor that Robbins was an "undesirable citizen" who should be ordered to leave town.[10]

On January 14, 1908, the same newspaper reported that Robbins had invited the socialist labor agitator Big Bill Haywood to come visit the city. Haywood began his answer to Robbins's invitation, "Dear Comrade," and the article identified Robbins as a "socialist leader." Two days later, a listing of "city briefs" in the Perth Amboy paper noted that "socialists" were meeting that night in Jack Robbins's rooms in Fayette Street to arrange a reception for Haywood. At that meeting, the Italian "branch" argued unsuccessfully for an admission fee, but all agreed that they would probably need a larger meeting hall than originally planned. Robbins was appointed to go to Grand Central Station in New York City to arrange things with Haywood. He did so the next day.[11]

In early February, another speaker came and spoke at Perth Amboy's

Braga Hall, on the subject of "Hard Times, their Cause and Cure." Jack Robbins chaired, and eleven men came forward at the end to give their names to become Socialist Party members. That same day Robbins abandoned the rent strike he had instigated, to devote his full time to the growth of the local Socialist Party.[12] In March and April, though, he placed notices in the paper soliciting "agents" to come work for him in the field of "horse insurance," the "only business" not affected by "the panic." There was "big money" to be made, as local horses were suffering from distemper. He needed another "good man" to work with him, to meet the demand. He was not feeling "the panic" that businesses were experiencing at the time.[13]

But in October 1908, Jack Robbins wrote from Anamosa, Iowa, to the Perth Amboy paper. Anamosa was the home of the Iowa State Penitentiary, although I can find no evidence that he was either serving time there or working for the prison. Why had he left "his beloved homeland?" Why had he abandoned Perth Amboy? Perhaps because he was being sued for having violated New Jersey's insurance laws, which is not what he wrote to the paper. Instead, he wrote that he had reverted to what his "friend," the famous novelist and socialist Jack London, called the "Call of the Wild." He promised he would soon return, though. At a meeting Robbins had attended in Chicago, he had unsuccessfully tried to convince Socialist Party officials to bring the "Debs Red Special" to Perth Amboy, "so that some of you may learn the truth of politics." He feared, though, that there was no support in Perth Amboy for Eugene Debs, the Socialist Party candidate for president. But where he was now, in Iowa, was not much better. Everyone there was for William Jennings Bryan, the Democratic Party candidate.[14]

Then, Jack Robbins mostly disappeared from the newspapers, for almost five years.[15]

* * *

On February 19, 1913, he reappeared, under a headline, "Jack Robbins Secures Fame." The Perth Amboy paper described how this "former local man" had gained new renown in Chicago. While still working as a tobacco salesman and also serving as the president of the Glenwood Alumni Association, the alumni association of the Training School where he had once been a student or "inmate," he had discovered that "advertising pays." As soon as he had found an apartment in Chicago where he could leave his suitcase, he "rushed" to place an advertisement in all the papers: "Personal—Any boy, good or bad, who wants advice or 'eats,' see Jack Robbins." He had already found jobs for more than twenty boys, and there were twelve more on his list. It cost no more than $2.50 to outfit a boy for employment, he said, and "no boy should go hungry."[16]

These ads appeared in papers nationally, spread with the help of news services. Editors noticed, and they assigned and printed articles about Jack Robbins and his Chicago project. For the most part they reprinted copy from the news services, but they individualized their headlines. The *La Crosse* (Wisconsin) *Tribune* headlined the story with "Ex-Waif Brother to Lonely Boys." It continued: he knew what it was to be a "hungry boy," because he had once been one himself. "I never had a home of any kind until somebody put me into the Boys' home at Glenwood, and if it had not been for that I never would have had a chance." That is why he wanted "other youngsters [to] get at least a footing." Iowa's *Keokuk Daily Gate City* headlined, "Hungry Boys' Friend is Big Hearted Jack." And it described what he was doing as a "side line" to his work as a tobacco salesman. According to the subhead to the article, the ad brought him "good results right away." The *Washington* (DC) *Times* headlined, "Salesman Aids Hungry Youngsters as Sideline." The Stockton, California, paper led with, "Only a Drummer, but He Is the Big Brother to Homeless Boys." The Knoxville, Tennessee, paper declared: "Once a Waif Himself Will Help Other Boys to Look Out for Themselves." And the *Grass Valley* (California) *Morning Union*: "Traveling Man Offers Advice and Eats Free."[17]

What led him to place these ads? That is a mystery. The only explanation that the stories offered was his sense of indebtedness to the Glenwood Manual Training School, where he had spent some of his adolescence. And yet that detail alone tells little. What did he hope to accomplish? Whom did he expect to impress? Why this way of securing "fame" or of repaying the Glenwood school for what it had once done for him? Was there any connection between placing these ads and his self-identification as a socialist? What did he want from the boys who responded to what he offered?

And why did the newspapers regard his ads as newsworthy? A second mystery.

But Jack Robbins had become a national figure. And his travels continued.

In July 1913, Jack Robbins, by then settling into this new identity as the famous "big brother," was in Detroit. There he promised to establish a "last chance" club for boys otherwise headed to the reform school. He had, he said, created similar clubs around the country. Seven had been built already and were "successful and effective institutions." At the Pontchartrain Hotel he met with prominent men and women who might contribute capital, and Henry Ford had assured someone at the meeting that he would give some support. The new home would have everything "to hold a boy and interest him." It would offer "a comfortable home, wholesome amusements[,] and pleasant surroundings." 108 boys were apparently ready to enroll as soon as it could be built. A month later Detroit's Workingman's Circle received a telegram from Mother Jones, the famous radical labor agitator, who was organizing workers in the copper country in northern Michigan. She wrote: "By all means get into touch with Jack Robbins, 'Chicago's big brother.' . . . [G]et him to come and be a big brother to the boys here. Am informed he is in Michigan." Efforts were then made to find him.[18]

Five days later, Jack Robbins returned to Detroit from wherever he had been. An article expanded on what Robbins hoped would result from a Last Chance club, and on his credentials as a big brother. "As a species of animal," boys were "very interesting to Robbins." He had. the article continued, "delved far into the minds and psychology of the young chaps who are potentially the men of the future." He had given a questionnaire to sixty-seven boys living on the streets of Detroit.

Here is what their answers revealed. The Detroit boys he interviewed averaged about sixteen years of age. All were workers, with wages ranging from five to fourteen dollars a week. Fifty-one did not save any of the money they earned. Eight had bank books, six saved money at home, and one had sixty dollars laid aside for a motorcycle. Of those who did not save, thirty-one were being helped by parents or others. How much had those boys "laid by" for a rainy day? Forty could not last a week without a job. Twelve were flat broke. Thirty-eight had only one suit of clothes. Eighteen were behind in their "board" bills, meaning they were probably not living at a parental home. Thirteen owed money to friends. Seventeen boys had both parents living at home. Twelve had one surviving parent, and thirty-eight boarded with relatives or outsiders. Of the sixty-seven boys interviewed, fifty-one smoked. Mostly cigarettes. Only two were entirely free from the tobacco habit. "Big Brother Jack," still apparently a tobacco salesman, "evidently does not consider smoking a very bad thing." According to the article's author, "13 of the boys were faultless, although only two did not smoke." Four drank, "and five were too much interested in women." Twenty-one stayed out late, twelve played cards for money, and fourteen went to dances. Forty-three did not go to church. Home influences were "very bad" for thirty-five boys, "not good" for thirteen others, and only "fair" for the remaining eighteen. What that meant was not explained. Many had, Robbins reported, unwholesome companions. Nine belonged to notorious gangs, twenty-seven followed bad chums, fourteen belonged to clubs, eight belonged to secret societies, and nine were unattached. Nineteen boys spent much of their leisure time in the poolroom, twelve preferred baseball, eleven spent most of their spare time in the movies, eight spent time playing cards, two were prizefighters, two frequented saloons, two enjoyed time at clubs, and eleven stayed at home. Forty-six boys didn't shave, and one boy had no neckties at all. Five went to barbers; others shaved themselves. One boy had twelve neckties, nine had six, eleven had four, nine had three, and thirty had one. Eighteen boys had been arrested, seven had been twice behind bars, and two of them had been jailed three times. Fifty-one were learning no trade, and only four were studying (that is, in school). Five were at their original jobs, but two had changed jobs seven times. Fifty-two were dissatisfied, and only six really liked their work. Intellectually, Robbins found only eleven who were above average. Nineteen were just ordinary thinkers. Thirty-four seemed to be entirely devoid of ambition. Three had no thoughts at all. "It is to reach boys of this sort, not only those who do not think and are without ambition but those who are handicapped by unfavorable surroundings, that Mr. Robbins wants to build his home."[19]

In August, to the *New Orleans Times-Democrat*, he identified himself as the founder and the president of the Glenwood National Fellowship Boys' Club, made up of alumni of the Glenwood Manual Training School. Once again he conducted a survey, this time of graduates of the Glenwood school, to see what had happened to them. According to the Louisiana paper this was the "most human and personal investigation" ever made of the lives of boys "of the type that takes to the streets naturally." He asked thirty questions sent to one hundred former students, all of whom had left the school before 1909. Fifty-four answered, and the results revealed that many of them were still living on the edge of destitution (or over the edge). Robbins took pride in the fact that only twelve had been arrested once, and only three arrested twice. But over twenty spent their leisure time playing pool. The article finished by noting that Upton Sinclair, the famed author of *The Jungle*, was a graduate of the school. Like everything else in the story, that "fact" came from Jack Robbins.[20]

Jack Robbins had found a calling: big brother to chanceless waifs. Or, as the Perth Amboy paper put it, this "former local man" had found a "vocation . . . to take care of hungry boys and find jobs for them." But it would take time before he learned how to exercise, how best to practice, that calling. What it meant to be the "big brother" was still unsettled, still in process. In the meantime, he would stay on the move, apparently still a traveling salesman for a tobacco company, and at the same time a denizen of newspaper editorial offices and places where boys could be found. And he would play at several possible ways of being what he had decided he was called to be.[21]

It should be added, as well, that the newspapers and the news agencies found him and used him. He offered a way to give voice to a deep anxiety experienced everywhere then in urban America, about how to solve the "boy problem." Newspapers and readers could not ignore the presence of unemployed or underemployed adolescents, who "swarmed" on the streets of American cities, who were uncared for, who seemed to and sometimes actually did threaten adults and other children. Some of those children were understood to be or to be becoming criminals. Many of them were in gangs, which could mean many different kinds of groupings, some of them dangerous, none of them controlled by adults. Boys out in public challenged the norms that ought to have governed American urban life. And some Progressive reforms, like child labor laws and unenforced and mostly unenforceable compulsory education laws, were not helping and may have been making things worse.[22]

* * *

By October 1913, Jack Robbins was traveling around the country with a new project: on the hunt for the worst of the worst boys. In Milwaukee, according to an Atlanta, Georgia paper, he had spoken at a national Big Brothers' Association meeting. Milwaukee boys, he announced, were the third worst in the country, just behind those in Toledo, Ohio, and in Erie, Pennsylvania. To reach that conclusion he had interviewed fifty-three local boys, forty-one of whom smoked cigarettes, four of whom smoked a pipe, and one of whom chewed tobacco. Three played pool when they had money, fourteen played cards, and four went to the movies. Twenty-nine used their leisure to read, six were interested in baseball, and forty-two liked prizefighting.[23]

In early November 1913, so the papers reported, he was back in Detroit, where he ("known the world over as the 'Big brother of the Boys,'") met with Upton Sinclair ("famous poet and author") and Robert Hunter, another socialist writer (author of *Poverty* and *Socialists at Work*, a study of the international movements), to formalize a plan for the reform of boys. This reform was to be an "interesting sociological experiment." Jack London, the famous author of *The Call of the Wild* and *White Fang*, among many other works, was unable to attend the meeting, but was said to have sent a telegram of support. These men had decided to take twelve boys "of admittedly evil reputation" and to reform them at a Nevada "Last Chance Ranch," or "Last Chance Boys Club." This place would be a "home" without corporal punishment or physical restraints. Or, as the subheading in the Detroit paper put it, the reformers would "experiment with [one] dozen bad kiddies." And they hoped "to revolutionize [their] method of dealing with delinquents."

These men, all socialists, were described as "long interested" in the problem of the "bad boy." They had made a "systematic study of his problems."

Their conclusion: "kindness" was the only cure for "viciousness." What today are called carceral institutions—that is, juvenile courts and reform schools, not to mention jails and prisons and policing—the coercive spaces of violent state power—did not work. Indeed, these institutions reproduced "viciousness," and they made bad boys incorrigible. Five boys had already been identified as among the worst of the worst, according to the Perth Amboy paper, which noted that Robbins had formerly lived in the city and was "well known" there. Each boy selected would be given the opportunity to become a "good man," no matter how tough he had been up to that point.[24]

At the "Last Chance Ranch," in Nevada, purchased with an "enormous" fund raised from "many prominent and wealthy men who were [once] not good boys," the boys would "be treated with the utmost kindness, given every liberty, unhampered with rules and regulations and given every opportunity to repeat their old habits after they arrive[d] at the home, whether stealing or any other crime." And then "the new experiment—kindness" would be used "in an effort to bring them out of the life and make them fit for a place among men of standing."

Robbins, who admitted proudly and unapologetically that he had once himself been "an incorrigible," noted that officials in many of the cities he had visited declared they had no such boys. Invariably, those cities offered him the best field. As of late November, six of the twelve boys had been chosen.

In late November, as "the hunt for the toughest boys" continued, he was in Pittsburgh, where he contacted juvenile court officials and truant officers. "Can Pittsburgh produce the meanest, toughest, most no-account, most dishonest, most evil, vicious, wicked—in fact, the worst boy morally, mentally[,] and physically in the State of Pennsylvania and one of the 12 most dishonored boys in the United States?" That was the question Jack Robbins "of Chicago," known "the world over" as "Big Brother of the Boys," was asking, according to one of the local papers. The Anaconda, Montana, paper headlined a story about the Pittsburgh search, "The Toughest Boy in Town Is in Demand Right Now." The Grass Valley, California, paper noted that a place was reserved in Nevada for a Pittsburgh boy considered sufficiently immoral.[25]

But Pittsburgh failed to provide Jack Robbins with a bad enough boy. The city was not fertile ground. The headline of the Harrisburg paper concluded, "The Boys in Smoky City Good." Pittsburgh lacked any "real bad urchins." So Robbins had learned, after having inspected forty-five boys. There followed another of his lists. Among the highlights: Twenty-one were working; nine had jobs; and fifteen went to school. Five "lads" went to church on Sunday, and seven went "once in a while." Nine came from "fairly . . . good homes, seven bad homes[,] and sixteen very bad homes." Mentally, twenty were "ordinary" and eight were "above the average." Thirty-seven had only one suit of clothes. Twenty had never been arrested. "On the other hand," five attended dances regularly, three played cards for money, seventeen were night owls, and one frequented saloons. Thirty-three had never been to church, ten belonged to gangs, thirteen had bad companions, two belonged to secret societies, twenty-seven were not following a trade, ten had been arrested once, and seventeen were devoid of ambitions. Thirty smoked cigarettes. Twenty-nine had "no guidance at all." Still, with all these faults, not one of them was "considered bad enough for the purposes wanted." According to the *Newark Evening Star*, there was "not one really truly bad boy in all Pittsburgh."[26]

While he was in Pittsburgh, Robbins was also back in touch with the Perth Amboy paper, which identified him as "a former resident . . . who startled the community a few years ago with an announcement that he was going back to nature." (What was "nature"? Iowa?) According to the article, he had become successful organizing clubs for boys in Chicago, and his search for the twelve worst boys had become a matter of national notoriety. He promised to organize a boys' club in Perth Amboy. The police would welcome such an initiative, the journalist thought, since they found it difficult to deal with juvenile crime. The boys were too young for prison, but parents claimed they could do nothing with them. Robbins reported, once again, that he had once been a boy without a chance, who had spent five years in an orphan asylum. He had been "sent out to dig for himself when fifteen years old." The lesson he drew from that experience: "Boys without parents or guardians need attention in a kind and gentle manner."[27]

After his "failed" search in Pittsburgh, he moved on to Harrisburg and then to Erie. In Erie, he had heard, a real "terror" lived. In Harrisburg, he interviewed eighteen boys. One told thirty-one lies in just twelve minutes, although, after a quarter of an hour, Robbins had so won his confidence that the boy began to tell the truth. Three were practically "faultless," although they had never had the chance to show their good qualities. Thirteen came from "bad homes." Only two went to school. None of them were bad enough to qualify for the Nevada ranch. But Robbins thought they all needed more care. This, according to the *Harrisburg Telegraph*. The *Harrisburg Courier*, another paper in the city, heard Robbins differently, however. Its headline crowed that Harrisburg's boys were the best in the state. Not nearly bad enough to go to Nevada. The worst boy in Harrisburg had a score of 78 percent bad, by Robbins's calculations. The average boy in Harrisburg was "independent" and did not want help. He wanted kindness, and what he needed were "friends" who would look after him and assist him in building a path to "good citizenship." Robbins, the *Courier* reported, did not believe in reform schools or houses of detention. He described a "Big Brothers' League," which had an "army of followers" in Chicago. He looked forward to setting up a branch in Harrisburg.[28]

Of the cities he had inspected for its boys, Erie was the second worst, possessing one of the worst of the worst boys. And that "terror" boy, who actually lived in Windber (not at all close to Erie), was much more "bad" than any child in Harrisburg. A truant who broke windows, robbed eleven different houses, and stole thirty-two dollars and a ring from an aunt who had befriended him and cared for him while his mother went to work. He ran away from home almost weekly. He sounded false alarms, and he stole a bicycle. He hit his teacher with slates three times, pulled a little girl's hair, and spilled ink on the school room floor. He was often caught smoking cigarettes. For all that, he had a ranking of 87 ½ percent bad by Robbins's measures. The worst boy in the country was 91 percent bad. Still, 87 1/2 percent bad was bad enough to gain admission to the Nevada Last Chance Ranch.

Back in Perth Amboy, the *Evening News* announced that Jack Robbins would be making a return visit to the city on December 5 and 6, 1913. He did not expect to find one of the worst boys while he was in town. He knew there were many boys there who just needed a talking-to. "Jack," as he wanted to be known, loved Perth Amboy, and he wanted to share with the boys of the city some of his experiences while traveling across thirty-four states in the years since he had left the town. He had never before had a mass meeting with boys in Perth Amboy, though he had, he claimed, held many such meetings elsewhere, attended by thousands of boys, in nearly every city of the union. (He claimed that the previous Saturday he had conducted such a meeting for 307 boys in Greensburg, Pennsylvania.) Aside from his work with Upton Sinclair and Jack London on the "experiment" of the Last Chance Ranch, and aside from continuing to work as a tobacco salesman, Robbins had "done wonders," he said, with the establishment of boys' homes in several large western cities. In each he had convinced men and women with capital to invest in such homes, and "encouraging results" had "been secured." The boys had learned that kindness "is the best cure and perhaps the only cure for viciousness." They became "young business men."[29]

The platform that underlay the homes he had established went as follows:

Any homeless or friendless boy will be cared for.
Boys over fourteen years of age will be employed only when there
    is a fifty per cent chance for advancement.

Brotherly advice, motherly love, a clean bed, clean underwear and
  three meals a day will be offered to homeless boys, employed
  for a nominal sum a week.
Boys over fifteen act as big brothers to smaller boys.
Big brothers will be held responsible for the actions of their
  little brothers.
Bad boys (so-called) will be given another chance.
Boys whose past will not stand investigation, will be given
  another chance to rebuild.
Business men will be made out of errand boys, professional men
  out of street urchins, merchants out of clerks, managers out
  of cash boys and firemen out of bench hands.[30]

That same day, the *News-Herald* of Franklin, Pennsylvania offered a critical commentary on the Last Chance Ranch project. The anonymous writer noticed that all four of the men involved were socialists, although, the author conceded, they were not acting as socialists in this project. The main goal of the experiment was to demonstrate that the penal system was "wrong." And they hoped to show that kindness was better. But the author disagreed. The author believed that weakness before temptation was largely the result of an organic defect, a lack of physical support for the nervous system. It took "a certain nerve vitality" to stand up to temptation. And most "bad boys" suffered from malnutrition or lack of enough good food when they needed it. "All the kindness in the world" and all the "science" could not make such a boy stand up to temptation. "The boys being experimented upon will need years to get into good nerve health. They can be made to want to do right in a little while, but the ability to control their desires is something which cannot so easily be gained." In the meantime, the writer concluded, they surely needed to be physically controlled.[31]

The search continued. On December 4, Robbins also decided to pass on Philadelphia, which had no boys more than 87 percent bad. The worst of them only "smoked, chewed, swore [,] and drank."[32]

Ten days later, in Buffalo, his search there for the worst boys ended "tragically," according to the *Buffalo Courier*. Buffalo's worst boy was not bad enough for the experiment of these "sociologists." New York's worst lived in Brooklyn, not Buffalo, and the Brooklyn authorities were notified of the victory of their bad boy. Buffalo's worst boy was only 78 percent bad, far below the threshold. That boy may have been arrested four times and convicted each time, and he may have spent most of his life in reformatories and the penitentiary, since emerging from an orphanage. Still, he was not bad enough. Brooklyn had "the

Baddest Boy," went the headline. Indeed, Robbins, when interviewed at his hotel, pronounced Buffalo remarkably free from delinquents, as compared to other cities where he had interviewed many boys. On the other hand, both the superintendent of the truant school and the head of the juvenile court probation office insisted that they had never been contacted by any "Jack Robbins." Nor had the local "detention home." Another Buffalo paper celebrated: "We Aren't Eligible."[33]

Back in Detroit, Jack Robbins identified one more boy for the farm or ranch in Nevada. Frank Bologh had ascended or descended to become the third worst, "one point" behind a Racine, Wisconsin boy. Frank, according to the paper, had made trouble for the police for several years, had been arrested twenty times. His parents were dead. Once in a while he showed up at the home of his aunt. His depravity was discovered because Robbins had studied the local juvenile court records.[34]

By January 10, 1914, the winning dozen boys, the worst of the worst, were brought together in Chicago, before beginning the voyage to the nine-acre ranch twenty-seven miles from Reno. There the work to turn them into good citizens would begin. In the group were seven "Americans, three Hungarians, one Jew [,] and an Italian." "We do not believe," Jack Robbins announced, here identified as the president of the Glenwood National Fellowship Club, "in anything of a police nature in the reformation of boys." Police methods only made the bad worse. The plan would take several years to unfold. But at the end it would stand as the "greatest bad boy reclamation project ever known." According to *the Dayton Herald*, Sinclair, Hunter, London, and Robbins were "social workers," trying a new experiment in the ongoing struggle to find ways to "wean the bad boy" from habits that made him a threat to society.[35]

But barely a month later, on February 17, 1914, came tragic news. Papers reported that Upton Sinclair, who had taken on the task of being the warden of the Last Chance camp in Nevada, had telegraphed Robbins that he wanted to quit. (The *St. Joseph Daily Press* headlined the story as "Sinclair Tires of Utopia.") Eleven of the twelve "incorrigibles" were in a state of rebellion. One of them, John Gargo (or Fargo), had escaped with two camp ponies and all of the camp funds. Sinclair had abandoned the chase after he discovered that the boy had boarded a train going east. The *Stockton Evening Mail* commented that the organizers of the camp had learned to their cost that "there is no last chance; that chances happen along every few minutes and that a boy of 14 possesses the faculty of making chances." The article ended by regretting that a beautiful theory had been ruined. "Perhaps if London and Sinclair had incorporated a few of the eugenic theories into the scheme it would have worked."[36]

In June, Harriette N. Dunn, identifying herself as an American citizen and a patriot, and along with her brother a prominent critic of the Chicago juvenile court, wrote a critique of such "child-saving" methods, as a letter to the editor. Were the boys that Robbins had removed to Nevada wards of the state or the municipality? Who had the right to authorize their removal? Was the removal done with the permission of parents? She wanted a law that no child could be taken from any jurisdiction without parental permission. A few days later, S. R. responded to Dunn's critique in the same paper, Chicago's *Day Book*, under the heading, "The Bad Boy Problem." What Dunn wrote was "nonsense," S. R. said. Dunn had asked whether the children were taken with the consent of parents or kin. Neither were they arrested with the consent of parents or kin. According to S. R., Jack Robbins and the others he worked with were the "sanest of humanitarians." They were trying to turn "scum into humans," something no law could do. It was a pity, S. R. concluded, that such men were misunderstood.[37]

* * *

What Jack Robbins hoped to accomplish in identifying himself with uncared-for and often homeless young boys, in making himself into their imagined big brother, must be left to our imaginations. What gave him a sense of moral and political mission, a calling? As several readers have noted, something was strange about his behavior. And, if one wanted to imagine oneself as Robbins's therapist, one would want to learn what he hoped to find in his search for the worst of the "bad boys." One would want to know both what drew boys to him and what lack, or perceived lack, he was trying to fill by attending to and searching for troubled boys.

But to continue with his travels across America . . .

After the end of the search for the worst of the worst boys, Jack Robbins found new ways to live the life of the "Big Brother" to boys. Starting in March 1914, he worked to gain the release of Herman Coppes, the youngest "lifer" in the Joliet, Illinois, state penitentiary. Coppes had killed a mother and her child or children on a farm west of Elgin, Illinois. (The story varied in different papers; some wrote that one child had been killed, while others wrote that two were killed.) Coppes had been identified as "degenerate" by testifying physicians. According to Robbins, on the other hand, "that boy never intentionally did any wrong. He never had a fair chance in his life, but if there is such a thing as justice he will get a new start now." Robbins promised to help Coppes "make a man of himself," and he found a farmer who said he would care for the boy if the governor pardoned him. "Gee—that'd be fine," said the young prisoner, who would be turning fifteen the next week.[38]

Robbins failed to secure Coppes's pardon in March. But in October 1914, he tried again. On October 9, the *Joliet News* reported that Robbins had made a study of the boy. But he did not make much progress in his plea for a pardon. According to the paper, Coppes, the boy lifer, had been placed into the St. Charles Reform School by his parents when he was ten. But he had been paroled into the care (foster care) of Mrs. Manny Sleep. He had murdered Mrs. Sleep and her two daughters on their farm. Robbins wanted to send him to the ranch in Nevada (assuming it still existed). He believed that doing so could make a man of him. "The boy's downfall is due to society," Robbins was quoted as saying. And "society should help him rise." Robbins said his interest in the boy was purely "humanitarian." A day later, according to the Champaign paper, Robbins mobilized one hundred boys to march with him to the capitol in Springfield. The boys ("good boys, bad boys, street boys, friendless boys, lonesome boys, and needy boys, . . . the kind of boys who know the adverse side of life"), were to appear before the governor to plead for a chance for the "little lad." That is, for Coppes in Joliet Penitentiary. This article added to the previous accounts of the boy's life that Coppes had been treated inhumanely by Mrs. Sleep. He was overworked and repeatedly beaten. He killed her after he was cornered in a room by her and was receiving a beating with a broom handle.[39]

We will soon return to Herman Coppes. But for the moment, let us continue to follow Jack Robbins. In April 1914, Robbins was again in Detroit, accompanied by the head of Chicago's Jewish Big Brother clubs, and they expected to be joined by Upton Sinclair. They planned to gain pledges from two thousand prominent business and professional men to start such a club in Detroit. Detroit was, Robbins said, the largest city in the country with no such club. He knew of at least 1600 boys in the city who were in need of a "big brother." With a little attention, all of them could develop into "good men." Such clubs were not intended to assist the "upper class." They attended "to lads of the lower strata of society."[40]

At the same time, while in Detroit, he advocated for the release of Harold Ullery, another young boy murderer sentenced to life imprisonment. According to the *Detroit Times*, Ullery had killed Mrs. William Dayhuff, a storekeeper in Fairland, Michigan. The boy had gone into the store where he made some trivial purchases. As she turned to get his change, he shot her, "stepped over the body and robbed the cash drawer and cigar case." When asked why, Ullery said he did it "just for excitement." Robbins promised to take Ullery to the Last Chance Club camp in Derby, Nevada, where the boy could, with care, become a useful and honest citizen. In five years, Robbins would bring Ullery back to Michigan, "a manly man[,] one with a new and proper sense of his relations toward society." Robbins was willing to sign a bond for $15,000 for the return of the boy on the demand of the state. He had, he claimed, investigated the case, and Ullery was "a lad who did not realize just what he was doing when he shot the woman." He was a boy without "proper training for the affairs of life." Life incarceration of such a boy was "an even greater crime against society than that which he [Ullery] committed" when he killed the woman.

A few days later Robbins traveled to Lima, Ohio, to look for Ullery's records. While there he hoped to start a "big brother movement" in Lima, a place that had, he thought, many "bad boys." Indeed, he was shocked to discover that there were at least 250 boys there in need of guidance. There were gangs and secret societies. Children went home when they pleased. Only a big brother movement could counter the influence of the gangs. One boy Robbins had interviewed was ashamed to acknowledge his mother when he saw her on the street. Nine boys to whom he had spoken did not remember their mothers. He considered this one of the "saddest facts" he had confronted.[41]

Around the same time, Jack Robbins spent a day in Chicago working as a Western Union messenger boy. He wanted to see what the work was like, since it was the kind of job that many boys held. He found it so exhausting (and had such bad blisters on his feet) that he resigned after one day, "by telegraph." This story was reproduced in papers everywhere in the country. A year later he testified before the Commission on Industrial Relations about the plight of messenger boys. He testified that he had made "a personal study of the life of a messenger boy." He continued: "I do not believe that there is an institution in this country that abuses boys more than the Western Union Telegraph Co. Whenever you see a natural boy—a rosy-cheeked boy—delivering messages, you can be sure this boy has only been on the job a week or two. They are generally overworked; they have no chance for advancement; they have nothing to look forward to; and the only time a boy becomes a messenger boy is after he searches all over for another position, perhaps for weeks and can not find one."[42]

On May 25, 1914, Jane Whitaker, a columnist in Chicago's *Day Book*, a Progressive and reform-oriented daily paper run experimentally, without advertisements, wrote a long column about Jack Robbins, the "big brother" of "chanceless boys." She was the only regular woman writer for the paper, and most of her articles concerned the conditions of working women and girls.[43] Jack Robbins, though, captured her attention and her sentiments. He was, she declared, an authority on boys. He had long "loved" and "helped" and "guided" them. He was a student of psychology who knew that there were no "bad boys." When they were bad, when they did something that society condemned, society was to blame. She contrasted Robbins's perspective with the conventional understanding of boys as "ever-hungry, tousled-head, freckle-face creatures, usually mischievous, and sometimes bad. When they were bad, their parents and society felt 'affronted.'"[44]

Whitaker asked Robbins how far he would carry his notion that there were no bad boys. She tried to get him to admit that the boy who murdered should be seen as a "menace." But Robbins refused the bait. All boys, he acknowledged had "a streak of savagery." But such boys also "hunger for companionship." Companions or pals would save them from the savage "moment." Mothers were no help, for they focused on dirt, rather than what was in the head or in the heart.[45]

He shared a letter from a thirteen-year-old, a letter so full of "affection and loyalty" that it brought a lump to the journalist Whitaker's throat. This was a boy, according to Robbins, who had "gone bad" in a week. He had "shot" at the gas globes of streetlights. His mother was afraid of him and threatened to call the police. With other boys, he held up a store. And then he was arrested. Robbins appealed to the judge not to send him to the reformatory. Instead, he should go to a Jewish home, inasmuch as he was Jewish. And the judge agreed.[46]

Robbins insisted that it did not take long for him to gain a boy's confidence. "I just get him by himself, and I say, 'Kid, what's the trouble?'" He claimed he talked to a boy as one brother to another. A boy would then want to make Robbins proud of him. Robbins continued by describing the Last Chance Club in Nevada as a place to send such boys, skipping over its apparently unfortunate last act.

He showed Whitaker a second letter, from a boy who was a "lifer," for having killed an Italian woman while robbing her store. The boy wanted no "charity," and no "threats," which is all he had ever gotten from reformers.[47]

Robbins was, according to Whitaker, no reformer, which she defined as someone who said, "I am good, and you are bad, and I want to make you as good as I am." He had none of the "smug complacency" that one finds in reformers. Instead, he carried the lines on his face of someone for whom life had been rough. He was, she thought, "unconscious" of his power. He acknowledged that he had once been a street kid, and he knew what it was not to have a chance. But boys would get a chance from him. And they were going to be "pals," because they were alike.[48]

Also, Robbins drew no "fat salary," as reformers did. He continued to work as a tobacco salesman. Robbins emphasized that boys were future citizens. The "chanceless boy" was his "hobby." Doing what he did, he said, took the place of other "amusements."[49]

That same day, again in the *Day Book*, Robbins published a "letter" of advice to boys who might read the *Day Book*: Don't become a soldier. This was 1914, and World War I was on the horizon. But Robbins was thinking about the use of troops to suppress labor and dissent. A soldier, he wrote, does not think or reason. He is "like a tool. . . . When he is told to shoot down men in a crowded street, men who are poor and who are clamoring for bread, he does it without thinking, and sees the gray-haired old woman stained with blood, but he feels no sympathy." He continued: "All the manhood, all the good in him, all his sympathy, he has sworn away when he enlisted in the army; his body, his mind and his soul are owned by his officers." Your "Big Brother," he concluded, "does not believe in killing institutions."[50]

On a weekend in June 1914, he mobilized more than one hundred boys to picket in front of the Standard Oil building in Chicago in support of the Ludlow strikers. The Ludlow strike or "massacre" occurred during the Colorado Coalfield War, which began when the United Mine Workers went on strike against the coal mines controlled by John D. Rockefeller Jr. Soldiers from the Colorado National Guard and private employees attacked a tent colony in April 1914, killing perhaps twenty-one people, including miners' wives and children. At the end of April, the strike ended after President Woodrow Wilson sent in federal soldiers.

At the June event, Chicago boys marched silently in front of the offices of John D. Rockefeller Jr., in a "death march" for the "men, women[,] and children slain in the Colorado industrial war." So Upton Sinclair reported, reading from a letter he had received from Robbins. According to the Perth Amboy paper, "some discouragement was caused because the police did not interfere" as they had at a similar event in New York. Just before the "promenade of grief" was abandoned, Robbins, identified as the head of the Last Chance Boys' Club, silently handed a scribbled note to a reporter. It read: "We begin again," after the weekend. "Not enough people downtown today."[51]

And on June 20, in another letter to the *Day Book*, Robbins advised "Last Chance Boys" to fear nothing, not even the police. They should demand their rights. "Whatever you desire of good is yours, you have to stretch forth your hands and take it." Stop at nothing. This letter was followed on June 25 with another letter in the paper, to the parents of Last Chance Boys. Robbins counseled them not to expect a boy to be truthful if his parents did not "keep faith" with him. Boys who have been disappointed will no longer follow parental guidance. Boys learned by example. Don't promise what can't be performed. "Be real if you want your boy to be real."[52]

In early July, a letter by Herman Harris, who identified himself as the secretary of the Glenwood National Club, an organization of six thousand members, announced in the *Day Book* that it was "strong" for Jack Robbins, "the Big Brother." As the head of the club, Robbins had worked tirelessly "in support of homeless boys." The club worked to "materialize" Robbins's "theories and practical teaching to better conditions of friendless boys." Harris asked any readers aware of "needy" boys to get in touch with him.[53]

At around the same time, Robbins wrote another letter in the *Day Book*, this time to challenge the conclusions of the prominent psychologist and eugenicist Dr. Herman Hickson, who had been quoted as proving "statistically from personal observation" that criminality was a disease. Eugenics was, of course, the racist theory of "racial improvement" and "planned breeding" that held that criminality was one of several inheritable conditions identified with particular identities. Robbins regarded Hickson's conclusions as "absurd." He asked the reader to imagine how Hickson might have "secured his data." A "kid" had done something wrong, caught by the police, and been brought before a judge. The child found himself "among strangers," in a scary and "unfriendly" environment. He was being questioned about something, which he knew, if he answered honestly, would only bring him punishment. "He becomes afraid, distraught." At that moment, the boy would be taken to be cross-examined by Hickson about his mental condition. Under those conditions, few adults would be able to "answer in what a psychologist would call a lucid manner[;] [n]o boy would." But those were the conditions that Hickson used to produce his statistics.[54]

By way of contrast, Robbins then turned to "the recent nation-famous 'Last Chance Boys' Club.'" He described how he had taken one boy from each of twelve states, "the most so-called criminally hopeless from each state." Then, "with the permission of the penal authorities" (here was an answer to an earlier critique that he ignored courts and probation officers), he and his associates gave them another chance on a "farm" in Nevada. Today, he claimed, eleven of the twelve were "perfectly normal," less than a year since they had been "considered irretrievable criminals" and hopeless. Was "there any difference, except one of degree, between the five-year-old kiddie in the good home who sneaks to the pantry shelf and becomes involved with the forbidden jam, and the twelve-year-old slum boy who raids the corner fruit stand? How can a sane man allow himself to be so perverted by words and figures on a sheet of paper?" And then he returned to Hickson: If the eugenicist ever allowed himself to be questioned by another psychologist as he questioned the children, "his batting average" might declare him to be "criminally insane."[55]

Three days later, on July 27, Robbins wrote another letter to the editor in *the Day Book*, with "a problem to solve." A "bad" boy, a longtime "terror of his neighborhood," had been sent to the St. Charles Reform School by Judge Merritt Pinckney of Chicago's juvenile court. Others feared the boy, and "mothers instructed their boys to keep away from the bad boy." Some ran when they saw him coming. Gossiping women called him the "wild boy"; little girls called him the "bum"; big, strapping men feared him, not for his strength, but for his viciousness. Boys who were known as bad called him the toughest guy in the city. Every police or probation officer on the west side of Chicago knew him. He had been arrested nine times in thirteen months, once for shooting at a butcher who "objected to a hold-up on the part of this lone boy." And then he had been sent to reform school.[56]

The boy, identified by Robbins with the pseudonym Harold Wray, had escaped from the reform school by tying bedsheets together and sliding down from the roof. He had walked the many miles back to Chicago. Then he lived on the streets of the city for three days "almost starving to death." On the fourth day he had found Jack Robbins. He knew of Robbins, because Robbins had taken his part once in juvenile court and had left him his card.[57]

That was eight days before. Since then Harold Wray had been fed and housed by the "Last Chance Boys' Club" (one evidently located in Chicago). The police were looking for him, and if caught he would go back to the reform school. "And he knows what is waiting for all runaway boys there."[58]

But what should Robbins do with him? The "club" had no funds. Last night Harold came to see him, "with a cigaret in his mouth, though he knew that I object to it, but what Harold does, he does it in front of you." Robbins lectured Harold about the evils of smoking. Harold promised he would "never smoke cigarets again. I will do everything you ask me to do," he continued, "if you will promise not to stop loving me." Robbins noted that he had written to eleven institutions and about as many "so-called" reformers, telling this "history." He asked each if they would take Harold Wray and take a chance on him. So far he had received twelve answers, all refusals. Wray's mother was dead, and his father was in the Joliet penitentiary. Wray had spent his life in orphanages and reform schools. "He never knew right from wrong. He never had a real chance. He was kicked and pinched all his life. And now, at the age of fifteen and three months, society had cast him aside as a hopeless case."[59]

Robbins added a PS: Seven of the twelve answers he had received suggested that he turn Harold over to the police. This he would not do. Never. But what then should he do?[60]

Three readers responded to Robbins in letters in the *Day Book*. O. J. S. noted that he himself once had been one of the worst boys in his own neighborhood, but, given a chance (his parents having given him the opportunity to finish school), he was able to stay employed. O. J. S. and Louis Perlman, another letter writer, agreed that the refusal of the seven officials and reformers who responded was "heartless" and offered "a sad and tragic commentary" on "the hellish system under which we exist, and some of the ignoramuses . . . responsible for it." Perlman regarded Harold Wray's story as emblematic of the situation "thousands of boys and girls" found themselves in, "perverted from their natural selves and human impulses by the environment in which they live." What Harold Wray needed was "corrective influences," which meant schooling and work and a "private home," where someone would take the place of a mother for him. "As the rose unfolds to the sun, air and water, so this boy will unfold and expand to the good influences of congenial surroundings." Perlman also added a PS: Obviously, a lawyer, he advised Robbins that before doing anything for the boy, "in order to protect him as well as yourself," Robbins should have him paroled or discharged by juvenile authorities.[61]

The third letter was from a member of a boys' club. The letter had been read and discussed at a club meeting, and the club decided to help Harold Wray get a job and to buy him a suit of clothes. He could pay them back later. Harold was lucky he had run into Robbins instead of a reformer or a preacher. He, the club member, had once been like Harold Wray. He too had once attended St. Charles, the reform school, and he didn't blame Harold for escaping. He used to have to go without dinner when he was there because he laughed while standing in line. "Now I can laugh at them all I want." The club he now belonged to was available for boys from thirteen to sixteen. They had no place to meet. So they met in a house, and each boy paid dues of five cents weekly.[62]

On August 18, 1914, according to a Fort Wayne, Indiana, paper, Robbins and Upton Sinclair met there to plan a permanent organization for the "Big Brother" and the "Last Chance" clubs of the town. Two well-known Fort Wayne women had promised to back the "movement." Apparently, Mother Jones, the famous radical labor leader, was coming to join them as well and speak to a mass meeting. Three days later, however, the Fort Wayne paper reported that the plans had been called off when Sinclair and Robbins failed to acquire the proper spirit of cooperation from local businessmen. The mass meeting was canceled. Mother Jones never appeared.[63]

Jack Robbins's travels continued. October 10, 1914, found him in St. Louis, where he planned to organize a club for "down-and-out" boys. He was scheduled to hold a meeting with society women. And he would try to arrange for support from two hundred businessmen. His hope was to get each one to commit to look after one boy. He wanted to reach the boy who had no mother, the boy who was not reached by the YMCA. He called his clubs the "Last Chance Boys' Clubs." Judge Hennings, the head of the local juvenile court, disagreed with Robbins's plan. The children of St. Louis were already well taken care of by several "big brothers" societies, run by various religious organizations. Any boy who was not receiving the proper attention was at fault himself, Hennings thought. And there was no room in St. Louis for Robbins and his plan.[64]

Two weeks later Robbins was in Oklahoma City. The headline for the story in the local paper (the lead article in the issue, positioned above news about the war in Europe) ran: "War against Jail for Juveniles Now Is Started Here." He and Mother Jones and the journalist Charles Edward Russell, "a formidable trio," were there to conduct a "whirlwind campaign," accompanied by helpers and "experienced" social reformers.[65] They came at the invitation of local club women. One of the club women had already committed to pay for half the cost of a clubhouse for boys. A mass meeting would be held in three days, on Tuesday, October 27. The local club was expected to be a branch of the Big Brothers club that Jack Robbins had set up in Chicago in 1906. There would also be a "Last Chance Club" created. This would be a separate club for those boys who had already gotten into trouble. The club women would join together to form an "auxiliary" that worked with both clubs. The goal was to create a "stone wall" between boys and reform school. "No longer will small boys be placed in the city and county jails." According to Jack Robbins, "Murder is committed every time a boy is sent to your reform school . . . If you don't murder the boy by sending him there, he will murder somebody after he is released. Perhaps he may murder three or four. . . . I have never known a boy who was reformed at a school like that." They are "Siberias for Boys," and "training school[s] for criminals."[66]

He continued: The stone wall to be created had to be one that cannot be "moved or shattered" by politicians, who imagined juvenile work as a way to gain jobs for supporters. Boys who committed mischief were placed in institutions where their "self-respect" was taken. . . . youthful ideas and hopes . . . shattered." Boys were "made . . . hunted, shrinking, fear-crazed." The work Robbins was doing was "fought by politicians. . . . If the people knew what these blood-suckers, that sap the life's blood of the future citizens of the country, were doing, the cry to arms would be heard; people would rise up and do away with them."[67]

Boys needed not just one last chance, but a dozen, even one hundred chances. "How many times do you think a mother forgives her erring boy?" No boy was criminal, Robbins continued. "A boy is nothing else than mischievous." Robbins had nothing but contempt for a juvenile worker who would label a boy a criminal. Doing so revealed the "mean, dried-up, ungodly soul" of such a man. "When a boy is declared hopeless, that boy is the one that society and humanity should make the greatest effort to save." That was the goal that lay behind the Last Chance Boys' Club. Such clubs now existed in thirty-two cities, he said. He also insisted that the bad boys sent to a western ranch (here described as located in Utah) were "entirely changed," once given a chance.[68]

A week later an odd column in the Lincoln, Nebraska, newspaper wondered whether Mother Jones and Jack Robbins were in the city. Robbins had telephoned the paper to announce they were both there, but it turned out that only he was at the hotel. And the "whirlwind campaign" he had promised did not begin. Robbins caught the next eastbound train, having discovered that Lincoln was not a "fertile field" for his efforts. The journalist wondered if announcing Mother Jones's presence was simply a way for Robbins to advertise himself.[69]

Back in Chicago in early December 1914, Robbins put a notice into the *Day Book* asking for a job for a boy who would otherwise be sent to the St. Charles Reform School by Judge Pinckney of the juvenile court. Robbins was identified in the notice as the "Big Brother" of the "Last Change Boys Club," located at 1138 Ashland Boulevard in Chicago. The boy had been told to find employment within thirty days. But now the boy, who had been walking the streets of the city unsuccessfully "hunting work," had only one more day to find work.[70]

Two days later, on December 5, Jane Whitaker published a second article about Jack Robbins, under the headline "What Do We Want Our Chanceless Boys to Be—Men or Muckers—Answer Is Ours." She had read a magazine story about a "mucker," defined as someone "with no respect for women," and none for property. A mucker "had no regard for human life." Then Jack Robbins called her on the telephone to ask her to make an appeal for chanceless boys. He told her a "pitiful" story about a boy who had been in the "Home for the Friendless." He was now at Allendale Farm, a school for homeless children, and he had lived for a time in the Deborah Boys' Club, where boys were boarded for a nominal sum. But the sum had to be paid, and when it wasn't, the boy was evicted. The boy had lost his job, and he had left the Deborah Club three weeks ago. Since then he had been "wandering around, hunting work, going hungry, . . . and sleeping where he could." While a municipal dance went on in Dreamland Hall, this boy "huddled in the alley back of the hall." He slept there all night after a day of starvation. Then he went to find Robbins, to ask for one "last chance."[71]

According to Robbins this was one of eighty boys he was trying to help at that time. The boys were not asking for charity. They wanted work. Institutions like the St. Charles Reform School and the Glenwood Manual Training School turned boys away when they turned sixteen, telling them "to get along the best they can." They might get ten cents carfare and no work. Whitaker quoted Robbins, who described one such boy. His mother had died when he was a baby, and his father was killed two years ago, leaving him "homeless and adrift." The boy was nearly twenty, though his psychological age according to the "psychopathic laboratory" placed him as a nine-year-old.[72] The boy had been to New York, where he found no work. Then he rode the rails back. "We talked together like boy to boy," Robbins said. The boy said he was going to get drunk. Robbins told him that would not help his situation. Boys like him were pleading for "a last chance." Whitaker concluded: "Can we afford to let them drift? They are the material we depend on for our future citizens. Are they to be men or have we decided to let them be muckers?"[73]

Five days later Robbins visited the Joliet penitentiary to make another appeal to commute the sentence of Herman Coppes, the youth given a life sentence after having killed his foster mother and her daughter or daughters. While there Robbins attacked the St. Charles Reform School, arguing that it was a place that only offered training in crime. It taught them that the "whole world" was "against them." The journalist who wrote the article balanced Robbins's viewpoint by talking to St. Charles residents. They watched "the work" of the institution (and probably worked there), and they were "incensed" by Robbins's attack. They felt "a great work for boys" was "being done" at the school.[74]

In May 1915, to skip ahead for a moment, unparoled and with sentence uncommuted, Herman Coppes wrote his own statement about how he had come to commit murder. He did so at the request of Jack Robbins, and the story was printed by Jane Whitaker in *the Day Book*. At the age of nine, Coppes had been attending school in Plano, Illinois, and living with his parents. He wanted to have a bicycle, and he borrowed those of others without permission, riding them during recess. But his parents could not afford to buy him one. This lack got him into trouble. During vacation he was working on a cousin's farm. He stole a bike from the rack at the local factory. And then he wrecked it, and he was arrested and sent to the county jail. He was kept in jail for two months. He was then ten years of age. Later he stole $2.45 from his teacher, which he used to buy candy and an air rifle. Once again he was arrested. He was then given the "choice" of working three years on a farm or one year at St. Charles

Reform School. He chose St. Charles, which he regarded as the mistake "of my life." After eighteen months there he was paroled to "Mr. Sleep" to work on Sleep's farm. There he was "beaten, kicked, cursed[,] and abused." When he complained, the family threatened to return him to St. Charles. He had to do "a man's work, milk six cows, and brush and attend to nine horses every day, haul manure and hay." He was forced to "bolt" his food, because Mr. Sleep could not bear to see anyone sit down for five minutes at the dinner table, not even his wife or daughter. He was allowed to go home for Thanksgiving. But he got lost on the way back to the farm. When he finally got back there, he was abused for being late. Mr. Sleep beat him, but a hired man interfered, and they had a fight.[75]

About that time, Herman found a revolver and a box of cartridges on a pantry shelf. He had always wanted a gun, so he took it and hid it. A teacher heard he had it. So he decided that he had better put it back. When he got to the pantry for that purpose, Mrs. Sleep was in the next room. The gun discharged (accidentally, so he wrote), and Mrs. Sleep screamed, and he saw her fall. In his fright, he must have kept his finger on the trigger. She and the little girl were dead. He carried them to the cistern and put them in. He told Mr. Sleep they had gone away. He kept on working. A week later Mr. Sleep discovered a bullet hole in the pantry floor. This discovery led him to search, and he soon found the bodies. Herman was asked if he had a grievance against Mrs. Sleep or the little girl. He said he had none, but he did not love the little girl. He soon made a complete confession. Whitaker concluded: "Jack Robbins believes this boy should be given another chance. . . . What do you think?"[76]

A year later, to skip still further ahead, to February 1916, Mother Jones joined up with John D. Rockefeller Jr. to advocate for Coppes's release. According to the *St. Louis Post-Dispatch*, the *Washington Herald*, and many other papers, all of whom loved the notion of the strange bedfellows, Mother Jones and John D. Rockefeller Jr., working together, Mother Jones had first heard about the Coppes case through her "friend" Jack Robbins. She contacted Rockefeller, explaining that he could make up for the death of a young man killed by guards at Rockefeller's Ludlow mine in Colorado by "redeeming" another. And apparently, Rockefeller decided to work with her on this mission (see figure 1).[77]

Unfortunately, the Jones-Rockefeller team failed to convince the Illinois governor, just as Jack Robbins had failed. Coppes's sentence was not commuted.[78]

On December 24, 1914, Christmas Eve, *the Day Book* published another case study of a boy who needed help, apparently penned without acknowledgment by Robbins. The headline was "Boy Called 'Impossible Case' Will Jump

Can the Rockefeller millions give a "life for a life?"

John D. Rockefeller Jr. thinks so. He is trying to obtain the freedom of Herman Coppes, branded the "worst boy in the country" and under life sentence in Joliet penitentiary. Rockefeller would educate the boy convict and offer him to society in restitution for the life of Harry Snyder, victim of the Ludlow mine plots—called the "best little lad in Ludlow."

A bullet a state militiaman sent into the heart of the 12-year-old Snyder boy at Ludlow, April 21, 1913, may be the force that will open prison doors to Coppes, a farm lad, in Illinois, who on the day of Snyder's death confessed to a triple murder.

Coppes, at 14, was convicted for the murder of Mrs. Maude Sleep, the woman for whom he worked on a farm at Plano, Ill. The two Sleep children shared their mother's fate and died at the hands of their playmate. Herman was convicted on his own confession.

On the Plano farm Coppes toiled from 5:30 in the morning until 8 o'clock at night. Medical experts say he was not very bright, that he inherited bad tendencies.

The boy whose life the "Money King" would gain never heard of the lad who died at Ludlow; Rockefeller never heard of either boy, but "Mother Jones," "mother of miners" and friend of the oppressed everywhere, knew the history of both.

When the "best little lad in Ludlow" was murdered "Mother Jones" openly charged the fuel interests with responsibility for the murder; she later told John D. Jr., himself that he ought to help reimburse society with a "life for a life."

Now "Mother Jones" is to supervise the reclamation of Herman Coppes, to give the boy murderer a chance to live the life the Ludlow boy might have lived. Young Rockefeller has told her to spare no expense in the education of the boy.

The Machinery at Work.

"Mother Jones," with Rockefeller's aid, has started the official machinery in Illinois which she hopes will liberate Coppes before February 27, his seventeenth birthday anniversary.

If Governor E. F. Dunne signs Herman's pardon, "Mother Jones" will send him, at Rockefeller's expense, to a farm in Nevada. He will be in charge of a teacher who will study his mental and moral possibilities and limitations with a view to directing his activities according to his capacity.

"Mother Jones'" experiment, it is said, is the first practical "dollars and cents" effort to establish the new social law that will give a "life for a life."

Herman Coppes, the boy who may be pardoned from Joliet penitentiary and educated at the expense of the Rockefellers, to take the place in the world of a boy killed during a mine strike; pen picture of his career.

Figure 1: John D. Rockefeller Jr. and Mother Jones work together to free Herman Coppes, 1916. Omaha Daily News, March 5, 1916, 29.

at 'a Chance.'" Jane Whitaker picked up the story two days later, reframing it in more moralistic and mother-centered terms. "Who will give a fair chance for 'Nobody's Boy'?" She was "gripped" by the story of a motherless and fatherless boy. "Boys love their mothers, but they adore their fathers." What made the boy an "impossible case"? His father was imprisoned; the boy was said to have been genetically determined to become a criminal. When he was little, according to Whitaker, he had already roamed the streets "trying to amuse himself" while his mother scrubbed office buildings. And then he did steal, and he did learn "viciousness." He was caught, and he paid the price. "They had shattered his idols, they had broken his dream, they had left him nothing that was beautiful to keep an ideal alive, and then they shut him away from the one thing he had possessed, freedom. . . . Can you not understand the rebellion that was in him that caused him to run away?" But he was caught repeatedly and sent back to the reform school. But now he was again free. But "his freedom means to him only that he is out of an institution." He was homeless but for the help of Jack Robbins. He did not know "how to keep a job" if and when he could get one. He was the product of the "evil" he had learned in institutions. He was "afraid to be on the streets" because he had been "picked up so many times." He was, to coin a phrase that Robbins would reuse often, "Nobody's boy." Would no one help him?[79]

In early January 1915, a Kansas paper noticed that Jack Robbins was trying to organize a "juvenile" Socialist club in Chicago. A few days later he was in Milwaukee and Racine, Wisconsin, looking once again for the worst boy in the state. According to the article, Robbins came yearly to the state, where he picked the worst boy he could find, in order to take him to a ranch in Arizona where he would be converted into a "model citizen." Richard Tucklowsky of Racine was a good candidate. But Richard had "put one over" on "the Big Brother." He was now living with adopted parents, going to school, and he no longer took "delight in doing things as they shouldn't be done." Robbins would therefore be disappointed. Still, Robbins's declaration that Milwaukee was the third-worst city in the nation in terms of its boy problem was picked up by several Wisconsin papers. And apparently the label of third-worst city caused much outrage in Milwaukee.[80]

In March, in Coshocton, Ohio, Robbins told a reporter from the local paper how shocked he was that boys were playing pool in pool halls on both sides of the town's main street. The headline was "'Big Brother' Man Finds Mere Boys Play Pool." And the "saddest thing" was that the boys did not have another place to go. No club existed in the town. One had, Robbins emphasized, to move beyond "don'ts." Instead, one ought to give boys something productive to do.[81]

He came once again to Pittsburgh, later that month, at the request of "a wealthy woman" in the city, who wanted the Western Union messengers investigated. He had planned to wear a messenger's uniform once again and report to work at their offices. But the head of the office refused to allow him to proceed with an "inside" inquiry.[82]

In April 1915, he was in Richmond Virginia, ostensibly to set up a "last chance" club there. Mother Jones was supposed to join him, though she was not to be found. The paper, though, focused on Robbins's challenge to Billy Sunday, the celebrated evangelical preacher. Both he and Sunday were going to be addressing gatherings in Paterson, New Jersey, the next week. Before then Robbins wanted a test of whether Sunday was sane or insane. He had organized a committee of men and one woman who would give ten thousand dollars to any charitable organization if three reputable physicians would declare Billy Sunday sane. "I do not care to criticize the man," Robbins said, "for unquestionably he is insane. He has amassed a great fortune working under the cloak of religion. I stand for almost anything but insincerity. Billy Sunday is not sincere."[83]

Around the same time, there was a plan to build a movie "paradise" for boys in the Chicago Loop. The theater would have a seating capacity of 4,100 and six reels of pictures would be shown for one cent. John Coleman, the financial secretary of a Big Brothers' organization, said that this theater would take the boys away from the shows that were "injurious to their morals." No crime pictures, nor any "questionable love films," would be screened. Jack Robbins, identified as the "head" of the Big Brothers and a "well known sociologist," had submitted "final plans," although there was need for help from the city council. Robbins, the story noted, had recently gathered twelve of the toughest boys in the country and sent them to a farm near Reno. Soon, it concluded, "Chicago will have the first strictly children's moving picture theater in this country."[84]

* * *

Chicago's Boys' Brotherhood Republic may have begun as one more improvisation, one more way for Jack Robbins to perform and to be recognized as the "big brother to chanceless waifs." In March 1916, Robbins described to a journalist how two years earlier, in April 1914, he had watched as police arrested a boy for having stolen a woman's purse. In the crowd that gathered to watch the scene, he noticed another boy, who kept signaling to the arrested boy. Robbins whistled to the friend, who came over. "I told him I had just seen his friend pulled [over] and that I was anxious to help the kid get out of trouble. . . . 'No use,'" the friend said. "He'd be pinched again soon." Robbins said he still wanted to try, but more importantly, he made an appointment to talk with his "new friend." The friend came early, and they talked about the arrested boy, Pete. Once again the familiar narrative: father in prison, and mother dead. The boy had been sent to a home (unidentified) at age six, then to the Glenwood Manual Training School. He ran away from there and was next sent to the St. Charles Reform School. He ran away again and was then sent to the John Worthy School. Ran away and then sent back to St. Charles. He was then "paroled" to a farm. Ran away from there back to Chicago, where he joined a gang. Robbins told the second boy that he was "interested in the gang." And one month later, on May 8, 1914, he met with seven of the gang members in his apartment.[85]

The purpose of the meeting was to organize a club, a gang alternative. A few days later they met again, along with five more gang members. At that second meeting they decided that instead of a club they would found a "republic." They voted, and seven of the twelve agreed. Robbins told them that it would take a long time to draft a constitution, and he didn't think they could do that and also, at the same time, work "to give boys a chance to make good." But, according to Robbins, one of the boys said, "We can learn the constitution and take care of the kids at the same time." And they decided to try it. The boys at the meeting then voted to divide into two committees. One went to the library to get books on city government, in preparation for drafting a constitution for the republic. Another investigated a few cases of boys in trouble with the police and the juvenile courts.[86]

By January 1915, there were sixty-five "citizens" of the republic. At first they met every other week, but that soon changed to weekly meetings. As of March 1916, there were 132 citizens of what had become the Boys' Brotherhood Republic (BBR).[87]

The rest of the 1916 article described in detail, almost ethnographically, what a meeting of the republic was like, all the committees and governance structures, and how the boys worked together. The author was struck with the fact that Robbins was present "to supervise," but not to do much else. He concluded: "The most unique feature of the Boys' Brotherhood Republic is that it is work for boys by boys. Left alone to devise their own methods, the citizens are the leaven in the lump, doing their part to remove the much-discussed 'boy problem' and achieving convincing results."[88]

An article by Jane Whitaker in November 1915 offered a similar narrative about how the Boys' Brotherhood Republic had begun. It had the headline, "'And a Bunch of Boys Shall Lead Us'—Or at Least We Can Get Some Pointers." There were several other, slightly competing, origin stories. Ralph Goodman, who became the first mayor of the republic, and who spent much of the rest of the rest of his life involved with the Boys' Brotherhood Republic, told one in 1927. He described himself as having been in 1914 the head of a "near-outlaw gang" that became the nucleus of the "club." Jack Robbins, whom he called the "guiding spirit," suggested that he and his gang form a club for which he would provide baseball uniforms. There were about thirty-five of them, though only seven joined at the beginning, not enough for a baseball team. "I remember how I came back at Jack and made him understand that if we did go in for it, there would be just one boss in the outfit, and I would be that boss. . . . [H]e agreed to that and it has always been governed by the boys themselves." In 1935, at a celebratory event held for the original members, it was said that Jack Robbins, "a lonely young man, a graduate of an orphan school, used to watch the nightly gatherings of the 'boundary line gang.'" The gang was filled with "tough kids," nuisances to the police and to the neighborhood. "But th[r] ough Jack Robbins, they needed only a helping hand to swerve them to a life of usefulness." Other articles claimed that Robbins established the Boys' Brotherhood Republic after witnessing the trial of seven boys for a minor offense.[89]

By August 1915, in a notice in the *Day Book*, Jack Robbins wrote: "If Chicago were placed on trial before a judge and jury of boys of the Boys' Brotherhood Republic, it would be found guilty of nearly every crime against boyhood." He continued: "The above is the spirit of 143 boys, citizens of the Boys Brotherhood Republic and future citizens of Chicago." And it was signed, "Jack Robbins, Supervisor." And that is how he would continue to be identified for the next thirty years.[90]

What it meant to be the "supervisor" of the BBR was left deliberately vague. Most decisions would be made by the boys, who performed all the roles of an adult city government. At the same time, Robbins's political values were internalized into the Boys' Brotherhood Republic. To take one early example, in September of 1915, he, as "supervisor," wrote to the *Day Book* that he had been instructed to announce that the Republic would no longer meet at the Hebrew Institute, where it had been meeting since it was first organized. The leaders of the Institute were acting in ways that were contrary to the "belief and opinion" of the citizens of the BBR. What had happened? The Institute had "stopped a peaceful gathering of men and women" who were protesting the actions of Jacob Loeb, the president of the Hebrew Institute. Loeb, a prominent financier, was also the head of the Chicago School Board, and he had just promulgated what became known as the Loeb Rule, which meant that no teacher in the Chicago schools could be a union member. At about the same time, Alexander Berkman, a famous anarchist who had once tried to assassinate Henry Frick and who had been the lover of Emma Goldman, had been invited to speak at the Institute. He came to gather support and funds for those who were on trial in Los Angeles for the bombing five years earlier of the *Los Angeles Times* building. But the Institute, led by Loeb, refused to allow Berkman to speak. The

BBR stood, according to Jack Robbins, "for a free voice for all men and partiality for none," and it would not remain where those values were rejected.[91]

He and the boys then moved into temporary quarters at the Workers' Institute on Halsted Street. (This from a December 1915 *Tribune* article about how the boys in the Republic were attending once again to the fate of poor Herman Coppes, the boy sentenced to life imprisonment in Joliet. The article described the boys as motivated to become "Good Fellows" to as many boys in "reform institutions" as they could take care of.) The Workers' Institute, like the Hebrew Institute, was located in Lawndale, an area of Chicago on the west side of the city that was almost entirely Jewish. And on January 1, 1916, they moved into larger quarters at 1727 (or 1725) West 12th Street, still in Lawndale, where they remained until they moved in September 1916 to 839 South Ashland. The Ashland space, leased (though available for sale for six thousand dollars), included a meeting hall, committee rooms, a library, and four rooms (dormitories) to be used to house homeless boys. There they would remain until the later 1920s when they were given a permanent building at 1530 Hamlin Street, built as a memorial to the banker Edmund Hulbert, an early supporter.[92]

A few days after leaving the Chicago Hebrew Institute, two boys from the Boys' Brotherhood Republic went to the Maxwell Street police station to defend five boys arrested for larceny. They gave the captain a circular they had written on the subject "Why Chicago Boys Are Bad." The circular was picked up and reproduced by newspapers around the country. It began: "There are 55,000 boys uncared for in Chicago." It continued:

> Ninety percent of all the murderers convicted went to work before the age of 15.
>
> Every year 500 boys are sent to farms by the Juvenile court where they work from eleven to sixteen hours a day without pay, in Chicago.
>
> Nine hundred boys are discharged from orphan homes with instructions to go out and make a living; 45 percent of them wind up in reform schools or in jail, in Chicago.
>
> Twenty thousand boys go to bed hungry at night, in Chicago.
>
> Thousands of boys are forced to steal for an existence, in Chicago.[93] (see figure 2)

At about the same time, a "member" of the BBR wrote to the *Day Book*: When so many were worrying about "bad boys," why not "give a thought to the homeless boy, the subnormal boy, or, in other words, the boy without a chance?" The goal of the BBR was to give such boys a chance. If boys were or-

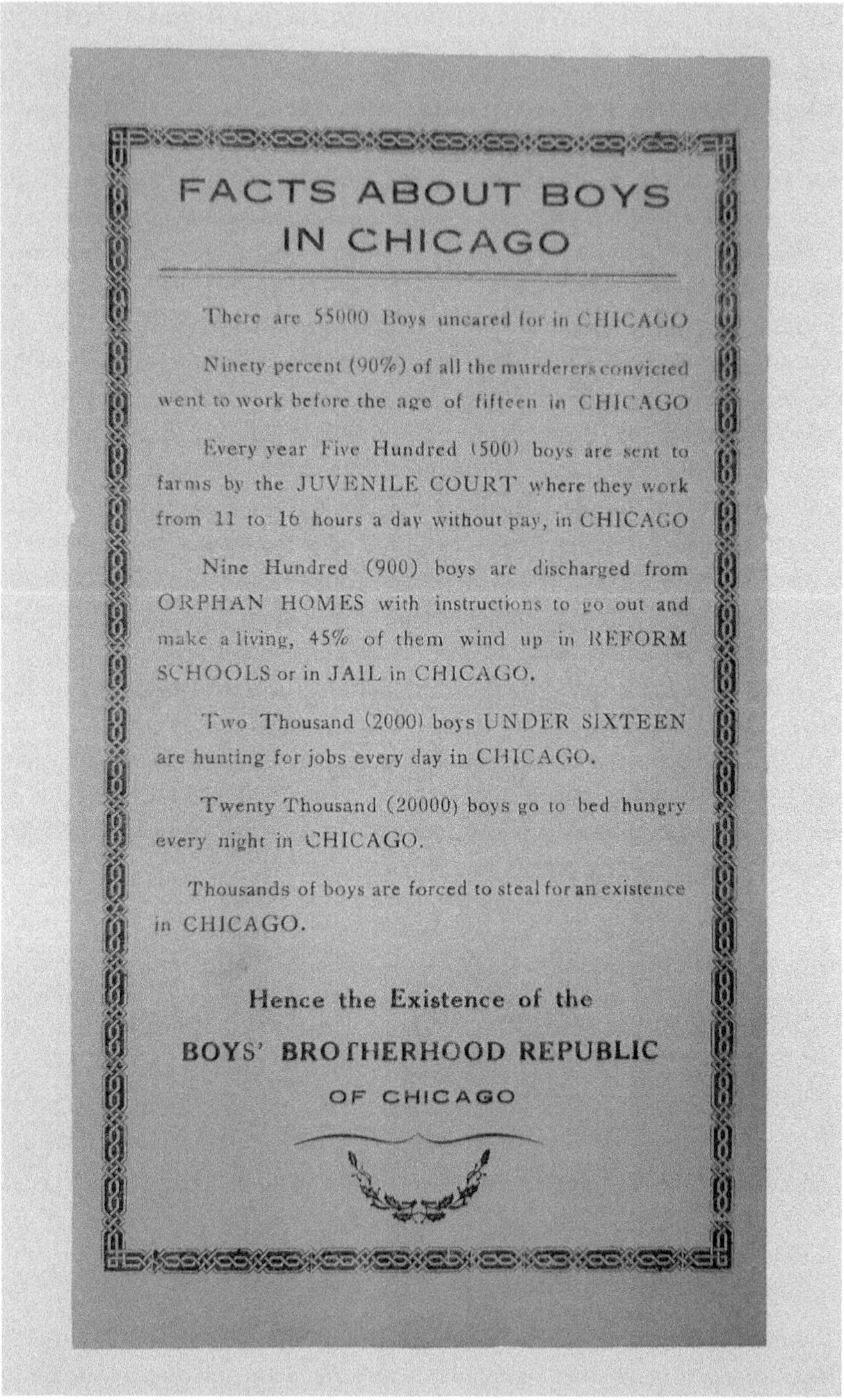

FACTS ABOUT BOYS
IN CHICAGO

There are 55000 Boys uncared for in CHICAGO

Ninety percent (90%) of all the murderers convicted went to work before the age of fifteen in CHICAGO

Every year Five Hundred (500) boys are sent to farms by the JUVENILE COURT where they work from 11 to 16 hours a day without pay, in CHICAGO

Nine Hundred (900) boys are discharged from ORPHAN HOMES with instructions to go out and make a living, 45% of them wind up in REFORM SCHOOLS or in JAIL in CHICAGO.

Two Thousand (2000) boys UNDER SIXTEEN are hunting for jobs every day in CHICAGO.

Twenty Thousand (20000) boys go to bed hungry every night in CHICAGO.

Thousands of boys are forced to steal for an existence in CHICAGO.

Hence the Existence of the

BOYS' BROTHERHOOD REPUBLIC

OF CHICAGO

Figure 2: "Facts about Boys in Chicago," Boys' Brotherhood Republic flier, 1916. Van Lieu Minor Papers, folder 24, box 2, Clarke Historical Library, Central Michigan University, Mount Pleasant, MI.

ganized into such clubs, where they could enjoy themselves at night, "instead of running the streets or being in poolrooms," perhaps the recidivism of the reform schools would decline. There were, he continued, "millions of dollars spent to prevent cholera among the hogs, yet not a cent for the betterment of conditions of boys." Those who did want to see progress should visit the BBR's space at West 12th Street.[94]

TWO

On the Boy Problem

What made Jack Robbins good copy? What made him and his boys interesting to newspapers and journals across America?

The answer is that he embodied "the boy problem." He had lived it, and he embraced it. And he seemed to have solutions for it as well.

This chapter steps largely away from Jack Robbins to offer something of a prospectus of the boy problem. It provides a congealed and condensed portrait of what journalists and worried readers of American newspapers would have known and seen, both what they took for granted and what they investigated and explored. It sets out the basic assumptions and the common language they used to understand the problem. It focuses on the situations Robbins confronted and that produced an audience for him and for the Republic.

I understand the boy problem as a description of what adults then saw on the streets of American cities and also, at the same time, as the occasion for the creation of novel institutional responses. It was both a problem and an opportunity for some, as social problems often are. Those situations were new and old. Those situations were also both national and distinctively local. Chicago in the Progressive Era, the primary site for this part of Robbins's story, was an explosively growing city that was also defined by the presence of two generations of impoverished recent immigrants and their children, as well as of more elite women and men who were creating new disciplines and identities, making the boy problem their work. As such, Chicago was both a representative and a distinctive site of the boy problem.[1]

* * *

But what was the boy problem? At least, what was the distinctive boy problem of the 1910s in urban America?

In part it was an experience of presence, the presence of poor boys out in public. They swarmed. They were an inescapable feature of an urban landscape. They annoyed. Sometimes they did actual harm. In part, though, it was also an experience of absence, of boys not where they ought to be, away from the home and the workplace and the farm, where most observers expected they should be. Boys could be scary. Some were violent, and more trespassed on and sometime stole what adults regarded as sacrosanct private property. Boys formed gangs, some of which preyed on other children and on adults. Boys and their "problem" also offered opportunities for adults to create new institutions, including public parks and courts and reform schools and clubs and settlement houses. The boy problem led, too, to the passage of laws—and some of those new institutions and laws perhaps fueled distinctive features of the boy problem of the 1910s. Progressive reforms, particularly child labor laws and compulsory school laws, did not reduce or solve the boy problem. Indeed, it was a plausible inference that they were making things worse, at least in the short run.[2]

The boy problem was not new in the 1910s. Every American city had long confronted the presence of undisciplined and apparently uncontrolled boys—of gangs and young toughs, of "bad boys" who assaulted notions of middle-class propriety, who exercised a rude freedom on streets and other public spaces that were not imagined as properly available to the young. For the early Chicago sociologist Robert Park, the boys he studied exemplified extreme "immigrant demoralization," a phrase that combined two meanings of "demoralization." Immigrant boys, by which he meant both first-generation Americans and new migrants, became demoralized. That is, they lacked confidence in their prospects in life. And, as well, they also lost their traditional morality, a morality he identified with their traditional ethnic cultures. Girls, fallen or falling, and sometimes uncontrolled and having fun, were also seen as a problem on city streets, but to a far lesser extent. Boys were a discordant presence, an assault on the gentility and order that Gilded Age reformers believed ought to characterize a republican city. They were at one with the dirt and disorder—the matter out of place—that reformers understood as a moral, a political, a cultural, and a religious problem. They were one measure of America's failures.

The boy problem bore a complex relationship to changing understandings of "childhood." As we will see, and as Jack Robbins well knew, boys out in public, particularly adolescents, were sometimes understood as children, often not. From earlier in the nineteenth century onward, the difficulty was that poor boys on the streets were not "performing" as children were expected to perform, or at least not as middle-class reformers imagined such children ought to perform.[3] Their boyhood was itself the problem, and it was produced through a complex array of performances. And yet the liminal character of "bad boys"—the ways such children or adolescents were and were not like other children, were and were not understood as "innocent"—had long been present as a dark underbelly to nineteenth-century romantic and sentimental portrayals of innocent childhood.[4]

Before there were "boy workers," there had been "child savers." "Child saving" had been an aspiration and a set of practices for more than half a century, shaped by evangelical Christianity and by increasingly outdated notions of penology. Late nineteenth-century child saving saved a white child. (It said little about African American children or the children of Native peoples.) But from what? First of all, and above all else, from a sinful life of crime. That belief is what justified reform schools and other child-saving institutions, institutions that took in children, mostly boys. Most of those institutions were affiliated with religious denominations. They were supposed to be distinguished from prisons and jails. The goal was, in the words of Enoch Wines, to "deplete" penitentiaries of convicts "by saving the young from vicious and criminal courses." Along the way, late nineteenth-century child savers discovered and rediscovered the evil seductions of public life. To quote Wines in the late 1870s, using phrases that presaged Robbins's lists a generation later, though with distinctive emphasis on the neglect of "church and Sunday-school," unsaved boys became

> frequenters of theatres, and more than a third habitual chewers or smokers of tobacco; a moiety had been arrested more than once; a large proportion were homeless, or otherwise out of the normal family relation, not simply by orphanage, but by having step-parents or parents who had been separated or were in prison; and almost all were the children of neglect, of ignorance, of poverty, of misery of the street, of the dock,—in a word of evil surroundings and evil influences whose name is legion, and their power well-nigh omnipotent. What a catalogue of exposures, temptations, and perils![5]

But men like Wines mostly saw child saving as a corollary of or a complement to the problem of imprisonment, although there was also a new "child protective" movement that identified child saving with the regeneration of the family, as well as with the protection of the relatively helpless.[6]

Looking out over two centuries of a changing political economy, it is possible to characterize the early twentieth-century boy problem as an accompaniment of structural transformations of American society and American political economy. Where once boys were necessary farm labor, that had become less the case, certainly for white boys. Where once boys could be situated in apprenticeships, those were of declining significance in producing adult work lives. Boys, unlike girls, were no longer understood as essential labor in homes or farms. Families relied less on them, either as direct labor or as resources or sources of family wealth. And the freedom of boys to move and to move around, often to run away, had provided, ever since the time of Benjamin Franklin, a model for what it was to lead a free life. Boys were both emblematic of American free labor and, also, of the capacity to escape from labor and schooling and control. They were Ben Franklin, but they were also Huck Finn. And the railroads and the roads and the waterways and the growing presence of the internal combustion engine opened up the whole country to young men who were not cabined by the household or by parents. Changing technologies of work and enterprise and transportation, changing cultural conceptions of childhood and boyhood, and the recognition of the weakness of parental power all played a part.

The story of the BBR and of the early twentieth-century boy problem then unfolds against a background of changing ideas of work and leisure. "Should children be working?" is a question that in itself implicates and implicated transformations in the nature of work and of dependency (including Taylorism and Henry Ford's conceptualization of his employees). It likewise calls attention to changing notions of the "family wage," the view that properly situated and disciplined and employed fathers should be able to earn a sufficiency for their families—without the need for the remunerative labor of other family members. Boys' work, once intrinsic to working-class family survival, was becoming identified with an archaic work culture. To what extent should boys—adolescent boys—be understood as belonging to their families, at least for the purposes of the work they did?

But to leave the boy problem as a structural problem, as a bland expression of sociological generalizations and metahistorical forces, is to rob it of its experiential features. And it also may underplay the distinctive and even novel intensity of the boy problem in the 1910s, as it was felt by several publics. It may underplay, too, the breakdown of older, often religiously based, understandings, of what boys needed.[7]

Where should boys be? Where to put them, so that they would not be swarming and annoying and stealing? How to control the uncontrollable? How to impose or to reimpose adult authority on resistant youths? What to do in a city like Chicago, a city identified with reform, with settlement-house workers, and with new and innovative legal institutions, and also an explosively growing city where well over half the population was made up of recent immigrants or the children of those recent immigrants? "Boy workers," that is, those adults who worked with boys, who made the "boy problem" their work, struggled to find answers. How to deal with the "swarms" of children and with the overwhelmed parents of those children? Their "boy problem" was a burden, but it also offered an opportunity to create new professional identities.[8]

Settlement workers and early social scientists studied and tried to intervene, in part to identify and to distinguish the more bad from the less so, and to figure out ways of working with (and often against) parents. There were gangs, some of which were like clubs, and some of which were criminal enterprises. It may be that there were at that moment genuinely more boy criminals, or a greater breakdown of adult (or elite adult) authority, though the reality behind the statistics mobilized by various interested parties, including Jack Robbins, is largely unrecoverable. There were shifting groupings of boys at various sites around the city: on the streets, in movie theaters, in pool halls, on the railroad yards, in parks. There were also vagrant boys or tramps who moved in and out of cities like Chicago, finding work some of the time. The policing problems were, one might imagine, overwhelming.

By the early twentieth century, the adults who made solving the "boy problem" their business, Jack Robbins's contemporaries, had discovered that it was hard to distinguish the "delinquent," the incipient or potentially criminal, from the "dependent," and from the merely poor. The mass or swarm of boys on the streets (or in public) was understood to contain an inadequately differentiated variety of types: some criminals or "juvenile delinquents," many under-cared-for boys, living entirely or mostly or occasionally on the streets, some who were probably tourists who would live in and be cared for within parental households (and perhaps even went to school), some tramps, and many working boys. To reforming (or child-saving) adult eyes, many of them needed care. But what kind and how? The older categories of "child saving" were understood as inadequate to the problem.[9]

The Illinois legislature had, through a variety of statutes, empowered courts to define children as "dependent" and in need of what their families were not offering. And "dependent," was differentiated from "delinquent," in theory if not in practice. Dependent on whom? Answers varied. But always the answers returned to a defense of institutions and practices that legitimated the dependence of the young, including adolescent boys. In a constitutional culture that marked "dependence" as violative of republican citizenship, children constituted, in fact children embodied, the modal example of a legitimately "dependent" population. That is, they were understood as members of a group for whom a hostile attitude toward dependence was inappropriate. Paternalism and state care were what the dependent young needed, so that they could, eventually, but not yet, become full citizens and independent—unlike adult free laborers, who should be neither subjected to nor given the benefits of a dependent identity.

It was uniformly understood as a kind of progress when juvenile courts and probation officers removed the label "criminal" from the rap sheet of a young miscreant and replaced it with the label "dependent." Children ought to be in dependence, in a dependent relationship with an adult or within an institution run by adults who served as parental substitutes. Sometimes, the goal was to return or reintegrate a dependent child with improved, that is reclaimed or reeducated, parents; sometimes reformers pinned their hopes on new public and private institutions and officers: reform schools and probation officers, but also settlement houses and boys' clubs. All such reformers justified themselves in their insistence that boys were dependents and in need of a caring hand, one coming from above, a hand that would be metaphorically if not actually parental.[10]

By the 1920s, Chicago school sociology would work to identify the distinctive identities of juvenile delinquents, in part to separate them out from the mass of more or less innocent boys. That distinguishing schema is what "positive criminology" would eventually offer. But that development lay at least a decade in the future. In the years between 1900 and 1920, however, the legal categories—dependent, delinquent, incorrigible, etc.—did not do a good job of sorting out the members of the "swarm," marking off the criminal from the precarious needy. As Judge Merritt Pinckney of the Chicago Juvenile Court testified in 1911 to the Cook County Civil Service Commission: "I found . . . after I had been there less than six months, that there were a great number of what I call semi-delinquent boys and girls, not bad enough to be sent to a delinquent institution and yet too bad to be sent to a dependent institution." His testimony continued, and it continued to swirl around his discomfort with applying the categories.[11]

Sophonisba Breckenridge's early study of delinquent children, that is, of those brought up on charges before the Chicago juvenile court, illustrates the conceptual swarm, the confusion of the categories. She began with an examination of the charges that brought boys into court. "Stealing" covered 50 percent of the "offenses," of the charges she counted between 1899 and 1909. ("All offenses which involve either the taking or the attempt to take property" were grouped together under the term "stealing.") But 45 percent of the charges were grouped around a variety of offenses, all of which referred to behaviors identified with boys on the streets: "incorrigibility," "disorderly conduct," "malicious mischief," and "vagrancy." Breckenridge acknowledged that these terms were, given the equitable powers of the juvenile authorities, "misleading" in their imagined specificity. She gave an example of four boys who "broke a till" and then divided the money. One, a ten-year-old boy, was charged with "larceny." Two of those who received a share (aged ten and thirteen) were labeled "incorrigible." The fourth (fourteen years old) was called "disorderly." Not that it mattered in terms of consequences. All four were put on probation. She also added an elaborate note that listed and explained the "real offenses," we might say, the facts, that lay behind apparent "charges." So, to take the first three boys on a five-page list of offenders in the note: a Norwegian twelve-year-old was really guilty of having followed a six-year-old boy home and taken one dollar from his pocket. He had previously stolen from parents. An Irish thirteen-year-old had stolen a bicycle valued at $20 from a man's home. He claimed to have bought it for $3 from a boy. And a German fifteen-year-old had run away and was found sleeping in buildings downtown at 12:30 a.m. He would not obey his father. All three were charged with "incorrigibility."[12]

Consider the definition of "incorrigibility" drawn from the 1905 revision of the 1899 Illinois Juvenile Court Law:

> Any boy under seventeen or girl under eighteen who without just cause and without the consent of its parents, guardian or custodian absents itself from its home or place of abode . . . knowingly frequents a house of ill-repute; or knowingly frequents any policy shop or place where any gaming device is operated; or frequents any saloon or dram shop . . . or patronizes or visits any public pool room or bucket shop; or wanders about the streets in the night time without being on any lawful business or lawful occupations; or habitually wanders about any railroad yards . . . or uses vile, obscene, vulgar, profane or indecent language in any public place or about any school house.[13]

An incorrigible child was a resistant child, one who did not submit to parental authority or the authority of parent substitutes. Such children were everywhere. And the "acts" that produced "incorrigibility" were manifold. All those acts were defined by the fact that the child had gone somewhere and done something "without the consent of its parents, guardian or custodian."

As with so many terms in what became the field of juvenile justice, the label "incorrigible" carried ambivalent meanings. The inability to correct, or the refusal to be corrected, suggests the need for coercive methods and separation. Yet, at the same time, optimistic Progressives assumed that, given the right conditions, the incorrigible might become corrigible. Incorrigibility was a constant theme in the reporting on Jack Robbins. He often identified himself as having been an incorrigible, and his work focused on the "successful reclamation" of those labeled incorrigible. "There is a great deal of knowing how to manage the bad boy and to deflect his misdirected energies into proper and wholesome channels. Not all incorrigibles can be reclaimed. But if only one success resulted from one thousand attempts, the efforts in this direction would be abundantly justified."[14]

At the same time, the physical presence of "incorrigibles" and other boys in public also remained an inevitability. Many reformers had long believed that removing such boys—putting them into schools or shipping them out to healthier rural environments; situating them elsewhere, often in substitute families, whether loving or not, but off the streets—was a prerequisite for the creation of a more godly and virtuous America. But in spite of all those efforts, such boys remained on the streets—mostly because they were needed. Even as many apprenticeship structures broke down, boys' work remained enmeshed in American economic life. Boys were crucial in making a city work. Some positions, some jobs, newsboys and messengers among others, were identified as distinctively boys' work. And of course, outside the cities, boys were still understood as essential labor for the farm economy: cheap but necessary labor. A 1915 Chicago crime report noted that as of September 1914, employed formerly delinquent boys filled thirty-six different occupations: ninety-three errand boys, fourteen office boys, twenty-four messenger boys, sixteen machine workers, ten farm boys, and ten teamsters. The rest were distributed among the other occupations. Presumably nondelinquent boys, by which I mean, of course, boys not labeled or not yet labeled as "delinquent," would have added still more variety to the list of occupations.[15]

Not working was a greater problem than working. One common measure of recurrent depressions and other dips in the economy was the presence of groups of boys lounging around or riding streetcars or trains, with nothing to do, without work. They were not working but making life unpleasant for others. They were there because there was no longer work for them, at least temporarily. And no one imagined that they should properly be at home. Schooling was a wish but rarely a reality. Some of them would soon become identified as "delinquent" or "dependent" or incorrigible. That is, they might fall into the coercive hands, the institutions, of a coercive state.[16]

Why were so many boys "free" on the streets, whether working or not? One answer, an uncomfortable one for reformers, was that the streets were where they wanted to be. Not at school and not at home. A generation earlier, Jacob Riis had already noted that what boys wanted was not integration or reintegration into domesticity. They loved life outside in public. Being out and about was "fun." If they had to vote or choose between "their old life with its drawbacks, its occasional starvation, and its every kicks and hard knocks," and domestic life, "the street would carry the day by a practically unanimous vote."[17] And by "the street," one necessarily included the railroad yard and the pool hall and the theater and any number of other public places.

But beyond that, most of them had to be there, in public places, hopefully working. They were not wanted in their overcrowded homes. (Here was an important difference between adolescent boys and girls, since girls were expected to be useful at home and to remain there.) And no one other than a naive reformer really expected them to be at school.[18]

Few things, then, marked the boundaries between classes so thoroughly as the divide between the schooling of middle- and upper-class boys, disciplined and controlled at least through high school, and the identities and the presence of working-class boys, as workers or as ruffians or as louts. Or as delinquents. Those boys who made life unpleasant or dangerous for the genteel were not in school. Indeed, for many adolescents the only time they would spend in school would be when they would be committed by a court to a reform school or to a manual training school. And when reformers and critics of reform talked and argued about compulsory education, there was a constant slippage between public schools as we would understand them and coercive reform schools and training schools to which bad boys were committed. The questions Jack Robbins asked of the boys on the street in his early surveys, as he traveled around America, paid only the slightest attention to conventional schooling. There would have been little point in doing so. Well into the twentieth century, most adolescents had completed what schooling they were going to get before the age of fourteen. According to the national census, in 1890, only 3.49 percent of all seventeen-year-old young people finished high school. By 1900 that percentage would grow to 6.38 percent; by 1910 it would rise to 8.6 percent, and in 1920, 16.3 percent. In 1920, only 29.1 percent of those Chicago adolescents between the ages of sixteen and seventeen were still in school.[19]

Boys who could work and play and move about in public spaces were hard to keep in school, even more so than girls. And although a Progressive state like Illinois passed laws requiring children to stay in school until the age of fourteen, boys of ten and up were a palpable presence on Chicago's streets. Our notion that children were kept in safe and secluded spaces, at least by day, because they would be "in school," did not fit the experience of most working-class young people, certainly not for those who had reached adolescence. Many families still depended on those children as essential economic resources. Working-class children were not "priceless," to use Viviana Zelizer's apposite label. Rather, parents hoped they would provide necessary economic value, often survival, for their families, though elite reformers found that notion appalling. And the ordinary expectation remained that adolescent boys needed to be working. The 1915 crime study, while suggesting that much might be solved if compulsory education laws were enforced and if required schooling were increased to the age of sixteen or even eighteen, explained that of 436 delinquent boys on probation in Chicago on September 1, 1914, 242 were employed and 194 were unemployed. The study writers ascribed such high unemployment to the fact that those delinquent boys had to compete with the "army" of nondelinquent boys looking for work (and also to the fact that so many boys on probation were "subnormal"). Schooling was treated as an irrelevance.[20]

And working boys were themselves participants and consumers in the local economy. As an editorial comment in the journal *Work with Boys* put it, working boys were both a "neglected class" and an "extravagant class. . . . They eat enough candy and smoke enough cigarettes to buy a Ford peace ship. And they pour into the tills of the pool room magnate and the show house potentate a regular argosy of wealth."[21]

Truants went truant not just because parents needed their labor, although that was part of the story, but also because schooling was easy to escape from, and young men and women found better places to be than the "dismal, overcrowded places" that were urban public schools. Compulsory education laws were close to a nullity. The truant officer was a presence, but a laughably inadequate presence. And the streets and stores and movie theaters and railroad yards, along with the companionship of other boys and girls, beckoned. "One could not understand schools . . . without understanding how they competed with the media, families, church, and gangs for boys' affections and imaginative energies."[22]

Work with Boys, a journal for "boy workers," that is, for adults who worked with boys, mostly in "boys' clubs," embodied the mainstream professionalism of the early twentieth century. It had been published since 1900. Early on, in the years 1900–1905, when it was called *How to Help Boys*, the editorials written by the first editor, William Forbush, emphasized the importance of Sunday School. In 1902, he placed at the front of the issue a revised "Apostle's Creed" that emphasized religious instruction. Its "I believe"s included faith in "Nature, Pets, and Treasure-Boxes," in the "absolute supremacy and essentialness of the Home," and all "sincere, simple, and persistent endeavors to help boys." It also believed "in the Gang, wisely chaperoned." "I BELIEVE," the creed concluded, "that a Helper of Boys must be to them as nearly as possible what God is to himself."[23] Whatever that meant.

By the 1910s, however, the magazine had shifted to target a more secular and professionalized audience, and to a recognition of the situations of the boys they were supposed to be serving. After 1914, it had become *Work with Boys: A Magazine of Methods*. And beginning with volume 17, the motto of the journal, pasted into the front of each issue (where the "New Apostle's Creed" had once gone), went as follows: "This Magazine stands for a square deal for the boy who works and his younger brother. There are millions of such boys, and they need the help of sympathetic, farseeing men and women. This magazine aims to help the worker with boys to do better work; and to arouse and stimulate those who [could] do more."[24]

The ambivalence at the heart of the journal, implicit in its title, and explicit in this motto, was whether its concern was with the work that boys did or with those who worked with boys. But those two themes or tasks were reconciled in the editorial pages of the journal, which increasingly emphasized how boys' work (as well as its absence) produced the need for attentive work by professionals. So, in January 1917, the following editorial comment appeared, one that reflected on the success of Progressives in passing legislation that limited the workday: "The shortening of hours of labor is a strong reason for more activity in boys' club lives. It does not only mean that the boys will have more time for rest and fun. It means rather that the boys will have more leisure time in which to go to the mischief—that is to say, to the deuce, to the bad, to the old Nick, to the devil, in short—if no better form of occupation is provided or no better route is mapped out for them." The editorial continued: "Idleness is not a crime in itself. But it leads to crime. . . . By no means do we urge a 14-hour day in order to keep people out of mischief." But there was a "vast danger in idleness." And it was the job of boys' clubs and boy workers to fill boys' time with things that were "good," if they were no longer to be found hard at work.[25]

The passage of Progressive legal reforms that privileged schooling and worked to exclude children from the workforce may have been one part of the problem, at least as perceived by boy workers and other reformers. As the editor of *Work with Boys* noted, one of the unplanned effects of a changing, legally restricted workday might be that more boys would be lounging and hanging about on the streets and the railroad yards. A discussion of "methods of discipline in a boys' club" included the comment: "Boys who have interesting *work* to do need no discipline, especially if they are responsible for their own government."[26]

The relationship of boyhood to work and to schooling was changing and would change, although haphazardly, depending on where a child lived and what his family's and his community's expectations were. Slowly, but only slowly, schooling was becoming a normal expectation for many relatively poor adolescents. Starting in 1915, "Employed Boy's Brotherhoods" were set up by some YMCAs around the country, evidently as a way to deal with the distinctive, increasingly singular, problems of boys still in the workforce, not in school. These clubs tried to offer some of the activities that were available to other non-working boys at YMCAs (including games and socials, father-son dinners, and occasional sightseeing trips), within the time constraints of employment. And "Employed Boy's Brotherhoods" continued into the 1920s, at least in a few cities. But by then, employed boys were understood, at least by those who ran the YMCA, as a residual and presumably declining category of boys. In a Chicago study based on records from 1917 to 1923 (but not published until the end of the 1920s), truancy, not attending school, was by then understood as a primary conduit toward a criminal career. By then, not going to school marked a boy off from his peers as taking a distinctive course, at least for the sociologists doing the study.[27]

* * *

What produced "the boy problem"? Over the course of the late nineteenth century and on into the early twentieth century, elite urban reformers who worried about the "boy problem" usually placed responsibility for the disorder on lower-class parents. Working-class homes were failing their children or had failed. Fathers disappeared or abused children or went to prison. Housing had no spaces for boys after infancy, and boys, unlike girls, were sent out onto the streets. Working mothers, mothers who had to work outside the home and become "breadwinners," often because of the death or absence or imprisonment of husbands, were a newly discovered presence. In the words of Julia Lathrop, a prominent child saver, into a mother's "lap ill fortune has poured calamities that have crowded out her children. . . . The children . . . 'get ahead of her' because there is no one to look after them in the hours when they are not in school." And, Lathrop continued: "In the selected histories of the families of boys, . . . who have been obvious failures and who are now in . . . places of detention, we find drunkenness, poverty, indecency, cruelty, demoralizing childish work at selling papers and at other unskilled, irresponsible occupations, sickness, insanity, nagging and beating, coarse bullying, fathers' and mothers' quarrels—in brief, there is no phase of family misery which is not illustrated in this fearful picture of a bad child's progress."[28]

In the late nineteenth century, parental failures or absence had been imagined as often solvable by moving improperly cared-for children away from parents, if parents there were, usually moving them out of the city. Rural farm life was imagined as the solvent to the corruptions that accompanied an urban childhood. Thus came into being "orphan trains" and other mechanisms that imagined that the care offered by farm families would naturally rectify the evils of the city. Children would be fostered (and occasionally adopted) within farm families, and put to work doing farm labor, which was itself often understood as a healing experience for the needy child.[29]

But by the twentieth century, moving "lost" or "bad" boys to the farm had become a less effective or attractive option. Mechanization, particularly the mechanization of agriculture, reduced the demand for unskilled boy labor.[30] The notion that placing boys on farms was a good idea, both for their moral development and as training for their adult lives, made less and less sense. As we have seen in several of the stories about boys who Jack Robbins worked with, city boys hated the work, and they felt abused by the farmers, male and female. And the ease of movement of the time meant that they were less stuck. They could leave and come "home" to the city. They could hop on trains or hitch rides, and they could sleep in movie theaters or in parks. And then they would be back on the streets of the city.

Judge Pinckney of Chicago's Juvenile Court, testifying in 1911 before the Cook County Civil Service Commission, reported that when he made an order of commitment, placing a dependent or delinquent child on a farm, he always instructed the boy, "Under no circumstances run away." But saying that did not make it so, and he knew that many would ignore what he said. Much of his testimony was devoted to the ways he changed his orders in an effort to keep boys from running away from the farms to which they were assigned. But still, they "escaped."[31]

Gilded Age reformers had also created a variety of enclosed institutions for the distinctive care of bad boys (and bad girls), including reform schools and manual training schools. Often these institutions were prisonlike; sometimes they aped the boarding schools or military academies that served more elite children. All of them were intended to separate the vulnerable but reclaimable bad child from the evils attached variously to the streets and temptations of the city, from "delinquency" as well as from inadequate or failed homes. And the goal remained to prepare them for lives as workers. Often those who ran the institutions provided religious instruction and socialization. Most such institutions were defined by ethnicity and by religious identities. The Glenwood Manual Training School, for example, was understood by Judge Pinckney to be a Protestant institution. Many administrators created spaces that were expected to be "homelike." Children committed to a place like the Glenwood Manual Training School might be assigned to a "house" space or a "cottage" that was imagined as offering a simulacrum of a nonexistent or no longer existing parental home. However, those institutions were also understood as breeding grounds for criminality, in which older boys sometimes socialized and abused younger ones and prepared them for delinquent, that is, for criminal, lives. And all of them were also, as several of the stories told by and about Jack Robbins and the boys demonstrated, relatively easy to escape from.[32]

In 1914, Leo A. Philips, the head of the Glenwood Manual Training School, wrote a short defense of "institutional care of the normal dependent child." Philips was a liberal "boy worker," and a prominent figure in social-reform circles. In 1914, his report captured many of the contradictions that shaped the institutional responses to the "boy problem."[33]

He began by acknowledging that the private family was really the only "satisfactory" place to rear a child, "with the loving care of a natural mother, the wise guidance of a real father and the happy companionship of brothers and sisters." Unfortunately, he continued, "through poverty, misfortune, drunkenness, crime, neglect, incompetence, ignorance, the death of parents, the divorce courts, the home is often disqualified." And then "society" had to find a "satisfactory substitute." He quoted from a clause in Illinois's 1899 juvenile court law that mandated that what the state should do was try to approximate what parents—the right parents—ought to have done. Often, he continued, foster care failed at that. The families that took in children were only looking for a hired boy or a hired girl "to do the drudgery of the home without the inconvenience of having to pay wages." Institutions sometimes did better.[34]

The standard for institutional care at a place like Glenwood remained "the normal family home." And thus those in charge worked to make sure the atmosphere was homelike. Two themes then took precedence in his discussion of home governance at Glenwood. One was about the training the boys would receive and how they would be compensated for their work. He described a Wage Earners' League, made up of honor boys who had served a limited apprenticeship in one of the "industrial departments." Those in the league could be paid a "wage" or allowance, which varied from fifty cents to two dollars a month, if they took a pledge to become "self-supporting," meaning they would provide their own spending money and their own clothing. They promised to lay aside 10 percent of each dollar earned in reserve for when they left the school. They promised not to escape before finishing their studies, and they acknowledged that money earned would be forfeited if they violated the rules of the Wage Earners League or if they left Glenwood prematurely. That is, if they "escaped." The second theme Philips marked was about punishment. He characterized himself as a critic of corporal punishment. "Corporal punishment has its place," he averred, "but it is usually administered as a soothing balm to the wounded feelings of the giver." And it failed as a deterrent, since it almost always arrived "too late." He referred, glancingly, to his own unhappy memories of having been beaten. Yet, like most reformers, he left corporal punishment as an available possibility. He was no abolitionist. But he shifted the discussion to monetary and community incentives, the rewards for good behavior. "An appeal was made to the boy's self-respect, and desire for fair play." These, he thought, worked best within Glenwood.[35]

He concluded his defense of the Glenwood Manual Training School with a worry that too many boys were being sent to the wrong institutions. Some were sent to reform schools because doing so was to the financial advantage of the county. Delinquents cost the county less in reform schools than dependent children cost when sent to manual training schools. Some delinquents were really dependents, and vice versa. There were "feeble minded" children being sent to reform schools. Some children came to Glenwood who were too young for the training that it offered. These misdirections and misassignments were "unfair" to the child, as well as to the institution.[36]

* * *

The 1899 creation of the juvenile court was once understood as a monumental expression of Progressive Chicago reform, one of the markers of Chicago's status as the "home" of Progressivism. The juvenile court signaled the amelioration of a rigid criminal law system that had failed to distinguish the hardened criminal from the reclaimable and reformable child. It embodied the "socialization" of law that Roscoe Pound and other Progressive legalists called for. Into the historically received understanding that criminals were free moral beings who, when they did wrong, confronted the legitimate violence of state power—as adjudged by "the law" and by a relevant community (the jury)—the makers of the juvenile court interjected the notion of a caring and rehabilitative institution (or institutions). Evil adult men, dangers to their communities, would still be disarmed and punished behind prison walls. But children who did wrong, at risk of becoming evil criminals, could be cared for by specialized courts and specialized "schools." Cured, instead of punished.[37]

The juvenile court and its related institutions, according to Judge Julian Mack, the second judge of Chicago's juvenile court, reinterpreted and rearticulated the historically received understanding of equity jurisdiction. Equity gave the juvenile court what was called the parental state power (parens patriae), to do for the miscreant but not (yet) criminal child what his parents had failed to do. It made the state—or state agencies—a protective and caring space. As one of the lawyers who helped draft and interpret the laws that underlay the juvenile court announced: "The child . . . henceforth shall be viewed as the ward of the state, to be cared for by it, and not as an enemy of the state, to be punished by it." Or as the feminist and early juvenile court official, Miriam Van Waters, put it in a canonical formulation: "Recognition of the offender as a juvenile delinquent . . . subjects him to administrative authority or direct judicial control rather than to the processes of criminal law. He is placed under the legal disabilities and immunities of infancy."[38]

The juvenile court, as it was imagined, also played off changing notions of criminal responsibility, evolving notions that ever since the late eighteenth century had become central to the enterprise of law reform, if not criminal law practice. No longer would the child be understood as a fallen sinner who had chosen to do wrong. That "free will" understanding of criminality may have remained fundamental to the justifications for the prosecution, conviction, and sentencing of adults, even as much legal and philosophical and psychological writing of the time challenged the salience of free will throughout the criminal law. The residual presumption of the adult offender's moral freedom, of his capacity to choose to be good or bad, law abiding or criminal, was increasingly understood as remarkably out of date but hard to change.[39] In the juvenile court, though, children were to be treated using a different modality of judgment, a protective modality. The juvenile court would produce novel environments that would make children good or prevent them from doing evil. In theory, a child brought before the juvenile court and subjected to the coercive power of its agents was not going to be punished at all. He would be "saved" by the court from becoming a criminal. Everything the court did was supposed to be educative and reclamatory. The "child savers" were doing for the child, helping the child,

in ways that substituted for (perhaps improved on) what parents were supposed to have done for him.[40]

Juvenile courts tried to work with children in what its administrators and
judges understood as a parental manner. The courts embodied the supervis-
ing authority of the state under the parens patriae doctrine. That meant that
children who had been caught doing wrong would be dealt with using fuzzy
standards and the nearly unlimited discretionary authority of a juvenile
court judge, who could make decisions that would be absolute and usually
unreviewable. Just as, so they imagined, a good and responsible parent could
and would. And the not-yet-criminal but "dependent" child found on the
streets, unparented or parented improperly, could be subjected to the same
judicial authority. As Judge Pinckney and Sophonisba Breckenridge and others made clear, under the parens patriae standard it became unnecessary
(and actually impossible) to draw sharp lines between "dependent" children needing state care (because of the apparent inadequacies or failures
of parents) and "delinquent" children needing state care (again, because of
parental inadequacies and failures). All were, so they imagined, children in
need of care.

But how to provide needed care without labeling one child or the other
as criminal raised difficult and constitutionally uncertain issues, even in
the early days of the juvenile court.[41] As legal historian Thomas Green and
other students of the criminal law have shown, it was difficult to escape an
underlying belief in free will as foundational to criminality (to the assess-
ment of guilt). And it was even harder to justify the loose processes of an
"equitable" juvenile court, whose determinations would result in subjecting
a child to what was still, in the end, experienced as imprisonment. And the
resources that a truly "caring" set of institutions would have required were
never forthcoming.[42]

Constitutional issues lurked. Long-standing precedents, in Illinois law
and elsewhere, affirmed the authority of fathers (and secondarily of mothers)
and challenged on due-process grounds the deprivations of liberty that child
savers advocated for. A controversial early case, *People v. Turner*, had in 1870
held unconstitutional the statute authorizing the police to take and commit
to Chicago's Reform School, without the need for a conviction for crime, children found to be "vagrant . . . destitute of proper parental care or . . . growing
up in mendicancy, ignorance, idleness or vice." The opinion in the case was
written by Justice Anthony Thornton, a Democrat who had sympathized with
the South during the Civil War. And yet, his opinion mobilized the language
of the Thirteenth Amendment to challenge what would have been understood

at the time as characteristically Republican forms of coercive reform, that is, of reform schools and other institutions that limited the paternal or parental freedoms of white immigrants.[43]

Thornton's opinion countered the loss to the father of parental rights that resulted from committing a son to the Illinois reform school. In that sense, one can understand the opinion as reinforcing what might be understood as a patriarchal constitutionalism, the right of a father to control and to educate his child. And so it is often read. But a second theme in the opinion focused on the rights of the boy, fourteen-year-old Daniel O'Connel, to his own liberty. "In our solicitude to form youth for the duties of civil life, we should not forget the rights which inhere both in parents and children. The principle of the absorption of the child in, and its complete subjection to the despotism of, the State, is wholly inadmissible in the modern civilized world." And a few paragraphs further down, Thornton challenged the "uncontrolled discretion" of state officials, who kept an "imprisoned boy, unconvicted of any crime, from breathing "the pure air of heaven outside his prison walls, and to feel the instincts of manhood by contact with the busy world."[44]

Later decisions by the Illinois courts limited the significance of the *Turner* decision. In 1882, an Illinois Supreme Court decision distinguished a law that had committed a nine-year-old girl to an industrial school from the law held unconstitutional in *Turner*, where an adolescent boy was sent to a reform school. Later courts often found ways to cabin the Turner precedent. But one has to understand the defense of the equitable jurisdiction of the early juvenile court, by Judge Mack and others, as having had a defensive and reactive quality. The relationship of the juvenile court and its attendant institutions to parental identities and power (as well as to the liberty interests of adolescent boys) remained fraught and constitutionally unsettled.[45]

From early on Progressive reformers understood themselves as confronting a dilemma. To what extent was it really possible to create caring and parent-like state institutions? Wouldn't the resources be better spent on prevention? Or, as the criminologist Sheldon Glueck put it in his early 1920s lecture notes, "The need for keeping young people away from the hardening influences of the police station, patrol wagon, [and] court hearings, . . . was paramount in the minds" of reformers. What was necessary was treatment for "the children who will probably become delinquent, before they become delinquent enough to be brought into Court or even before they present any behavior problems at all and are seen only as unhappy, maladjusted, peculiar or neurotic children." And that meant focusing on "problems of children rather than with problem children." Glueck went on to advocate for an "experimental approach" responsive to local conditions. He paid some attention to institutional alternatives, including the BBR. But he gave particular attention to programs focused on the education of parents.[46]

No one still regards the creation of the juvenile court as a triumphant achievement. That perspective is long gone both from the historiography and from our contemporary understanding of juvenile justice. And a general sense of malaise and of failure quickly became part of how educated opinion understood the court and what it offered as a solution to the "boy problem." Jack Robbins was hardly alone in his sense of it as both repressive and inept, an inadequate set of institutions that offered little that distinguished it from adult carceral power, that served neither children nor their parents nor the larger society. As Anthony Platt concluded, in language that Jack Robbins would have agreed with, the programs of the child savers from early on "diminished the civil liberties and the privacy of youth. Adolescents were treated as though they were naturally dependent, requiring constant and pervasive supervision." The makers of the juvenile court were more concerned with "restriction than with liberation."[47] Nor did they talk very much about the citizenship of the young. The resources needed, if the institutions of the state were to become effectively "parental," as the reformers wanted, if those offices and officers and institutions were going to prepare problem boys for useful adult lives, never came.

Indeed, already in 1915, the city of Chicago's "Committee on Crime" noticed that for the roughly one thousand boys on parole from the St. Charles Reform School, there was one untrained parole officer. And the boundary between prison and "reform school" always remained porous and unsettled. By the time of the Illinois Crime Survey of 1929, the general conclusion of the authors of the chapter on juvenile delinquency was of a sad and sclerotic set of bureaucratic institutions staffed by the time-serving and the unimaginative (exactly as Jack Robbins always claimed). When the superintendent of a reform school was asked about the very large number of escapees, or "informal departures," he answered that it was "natural for the boys to want to run as soon as they are released from the atmosphere of force and coercion to which they are subjected by police and court." The teaching program at the school, its curriculum, was labeled by the chapter's authors as "uninteresting and inadequate." When they turned to the still-high numbers of truants in 1920s Chicago, they explained the figures as inevitable given the "hopeless" inadequacy of the office of the "division of compulsory education." The sociologists who drafted the chapter thought it unlikely that merely adding more staff to the office would change that inadequacy.[48]

When historians and others try to characterize the early history of the institutions of juvenile justice, and their failures, two interpretations predominate. On one side stands what was once called the social-control perspective. The reforms that produced the juvenile court—whether understood as generated by upper-class or middle-class values, by hegemonic white Protestantism, by a capitalist ideology concerned with making productive and docile workers, or by professionalizing social workers, sometimes feminists—all were intended to destroy a resistant and dangerous and archaic working-class culture. Reformers hoped to impose elite or middle-class norms on parents, who were understood to have failed as parents, and whose failures constituted a threat to a virtuous republic. Families that had been overwhelmed by industrialization and modernity would be disciplined. Or, to put it still more baldly, the values and practices of poor parents needed to be crushed. On the other side stand "revisionist" historians and others who took more seriously the language of the Progressives, those who created the court and its attendant institutions. According to the revisionists, the institutions identified with the juvenile court (reform school, probation, parole, foster care, etc.) were actually created to return power to parents and to the home. Parents had lost control of errant boys because of the seductions and attractions of the streets of the city. The juvenile court would, it was hoped, return control to them. In any event, the goals of the reformers were to work with parents. One side saw a more or less cynical and more or less conscious intentional plot; the other side gave more credence to the values expressed by the reformers, and to unintended consequences. Often this second side then emphasized the failure of good intentions or of "the best laid plans."[49]

Both sides, or nearly all sides, participants and critics and scholars alike, have shared an intuition or a commitment that the proper focus of attention should stay on parents and their failures. At bottom, the "boy problem" was a parenting or familial problem. How to create practices and caring institutions that would replicate what parents provided, or promised to provide, if only they were able to do so? Adequate parents were the missing ingredient in the lives of problem boys. Or inadequate parents were the too-much-present ingredient. Or the not-quite-enough-present ingredient. All might have been well, if only parents had not lost control or had failed to regain control. Or had disappeared. Could parents be made to retake control of the uncontrolled and troubled child, who had become a threat to society? And if and when parents failed at that task, or were adjudged to have failed to have taken proper or appropriate control, could the officers and bureaucrats of the juvenile court and its related institutions become the substitute parents that those children needed? As one historian put it, "The juvenile court flunked parents just as the public schools flunked children." And a few paragraphs later: "In the juvenile court of the Progressive era, parent and child were on trial together. The parents' ability to provide future care for the child lay at the heart of the court's decision-making process."[50]

As we will see, Jack Robbins and the Boys' Brotherhood Republic fundamentally disagreed with the presumption that the "boy problem" could only be solved by parents or by institutions that substituted for parents. There were other ways for young men to grow up to be competent adults and citizens than to be forced back into parental homes, or into institutions that, so the fantasy went, would substitute for the domestic, private home. What boys needed, both in their present lives, and as preparation for lives as competent citizens, was something else. He and they would offer a different diagnosis and a different prognosis and a different remedy.[51]

The boy problem also provided an opportunity for new professional identities. Adults profited, one might say, from the problems boys confronted, as well as from what was increasingly understood as the breakdown of the formerly solid private family. And those adults did so in new ways. Jack Robbins complained that the institutions meant to deal with "bad boys" were mostly just spaces that provided jobs for time servers. But they were also opportunities for new professionals, including many women, who could exercise professionalized care.[52]

Those professionals, those women and men who profited from these new institutions, devoted attention to the fact that boy criminality, the boy problem, was a problem of group behavior. "Delinquents" became delinquents in groups, in gangs, a fact that the reformers and later students of the court found difficult to reconcile both with the drumbeat of blame for parents and with the traditional focus on individual moral responsibility identified with the criminal law. As Sophonisba Breckenridge, the leading analyst of the early juvenile court and the problem of delinquency, put it, "The presence of a gang in any neighborhood is always offered as an adequate explanation of the delinquency of any of its members; and it becomes customary for the mother of every member to blame her own boy's badness upon the badness of the other mothers' sons." And a few paragraphs later, writing in the bland social science of the day: "The impression made by a study of the actual reasons for bringing boys into court is that the delinquency is in many instances distinctly one of a social character and is due to the organization of a little group whose purpose may be harmless enough but whose social effort is misdirected."[53]

Thus, to add one more stream to the several that shaped the particular dimensions of the "boy problem" of the 1910s, one should add the "discovery" of adolescence as a distinctive stage of life. Adolescence, social scientists discovered, was marked by a search for solidarity with contemporaries, and it was, more importantly, marked both by the legitimacy of separation from parents and family and resistance to adult authorities. Adolescence added one more problem to the raft of problems that contributed to "the boy problem" of the early twentieth century. Not only were parents failures, but worse yet, adolescent boys were joining together, often into "gangs," in ways that kept them away from parents and other adult authorities.[54]

The boy problem produced a universe of agencies. It also generated a complex discourse and conversations about what to do with those boys in trouble, as well as with those likely to get in trouble, and also, though never attentively enough, what to do with them after they had been in trouble. The boy problem became life work for a variety of adults. And imagining programs and policies for the young were what those adults did.[55]

* * *

Jack Robbins was, as we have seen, a participant in those conversations. And the boy problem certainly became his life work. Without it, he would not have had a calling.

What the boy problem meant for him and for the organization he founded, the Boys' Brotherhood Republic, and how he and they meant to solve the problem, will be the subjects of the next two chapters.

But here is how, at one relatively early moment in his life as "the big brother," he imagined the "problem." I draw it from a letter he wrote to Jack London, the famous novelist, in January 1915, although I focus more on the letterhead that he had printed at that time than on the letter itself.

The letter invited London, identified as "Comrade London" and as a humanitarian, to become a founding member of the "National Committee" in the movement to organize "Last Chance Boys Clubs" around the country. Last Chance Boys' Clubs were, according to Robbins, ones that served boys that had been turned out of reform schools or orphanages, "with instructions to go out and make a living." 63 percent of those boys, Robbins asserted, would end up in jail, if they were not properly supported. "Several" such clubs were already in existence. But the goal was to have one in every city that needed one. And each such club would have a local "advisory board." But standing over or above those advisory boards, there should be "a national body" that would provide "a moral interest" in all of the clubs. Participation in the National Committee, Robbins assured London, would require "little if any time and no outlay of money." Robbins wanted Jack London's name on the masthead, not his labor or his funds.[56]

The contents of the letter, as described in the last paragraph, are interesting and worthy of attention. But the core of Jack Robbins's approach to the boy problem appears in the printed letterhead of the letter. And it is Robbins's printed letterhead that marks the distinctiveness of his approach to the boy problem. It is as if he created a letterhead that could provide a contrast to predominate understandings of the boy problem, as mainstream reformers would have posed it.

To begin at the top of the page, above Jack Robbins's name and address and telephone number, there was a bold headline in large type: "A FAIR CHANCE FOR NOBODY'S BOY." Where almost all varieties of reform emphasized the somebodies who should have been taking care of the boys, meaning parents or institutions that substituted for parents, Robbins began by acknowledging that there was nobody. That is to say, the boy belonged to himself. To belong to the Last Chance Boys' Club meant that one was "nobody's boy." Neither families nor the state owned those boys or cared for them—at least, not until they found themselves "in" the club.[57]

Along the left margin of the letter were three clumps of text, each typographically distinguished from the others (and apparently not well proofread). One clump stated the facts that gave him a sense of mission. The second gave him his identity. The third invited "chanceless" boys to join this new organization.

So, first came one of his characteristic listings of the harms that were visited on the boys.

> *Thousands* of well meaning boys are badly fed—badly clothed and badly housed.
> *Thousands* of friendless boys die every year from preventable diseases.
> *Thousands* of boys go to bed hungry every night.
> *Thousands* of bad boys (so called) develope [*sic*] criminal tendencies in a natural fight for existance [*sic*].
> *Thousands* of bad boys (so called) are victims of police persecution.
> *Thousands* of boys are send [*sic*] to reform schools because of lack of guidance.
> *Thousands* of delinquent boys never had a human chance.

To prevent those "conditions," one should be a

Big Brother
                To the
        Street Boys
            Hungry Boys
                Friendless Boys
                    Lonesome Boys
                        Needy Boys
                            Poor Boys
                                Bad Boys
                                    Good Boys.

Third, Robbins made an appeal to the boys themselves:

Chanceless boys, the kind who have been cast off by society as hopeless cases, or when you are in trouble[,] join the

        Last
            Chance
                Boys
                    Club[58]

* * *

Jack Robbins was part of the swarm of adults who dealt with the boy problem. The boy problem made possible his identity as the "big brother." But he was also distinctive, if not singular. Like other reformers of the time, he believed that children were to be understood as "fundamentally in relationship to others, rather than as autonomous individuals who could be held solely responsible for their acts or could be solely burdened by the neglect of their parents or guardians." Unlike most others, he did not believe that the parent-child relationship offered any model for the relationships that adolescent boys needed. For him, parents were not the problem; nor were they the solution, metaphorically or really. As we will see, parents were fundamentally irrelevant.

Instead, what was needed, according to Robbins, was a different understanding of the boy and of the relationships through which he would flourish. What boys needed were "big brothers." And even more they needed pals, and they needed ways to mobilize their own energies. As a 1918 Perth Amboy editorial put it, in praising Robbins and the Chicago Boys' Brotherhood Republic, "the way to reform a bad boy" was "to let loose his boyish energy and pent-up enthusiasm in ways wholesome and up-building." And achieving that aim meant that adults had to give up the illusion of control and to allow for boys' self-government.[59]

THREE

Jack Robbins, Supervisor, and the Boys' Brotherhood Republic

Jack Robbins was a braggart and a fabulist. A teller of tall tales. He lied constantly to newspapers, relying on their inability to check up on him and on their need for copy and for good storylines. He exaggerated, and he inflated. There were, according to him, six thousand members of the Glenwood Manual Training School alumni association. It is not even clear that there was then a Glenwood alumni association when he made that claim. (One did come into existence later.) He insisted he had spoken often to crowds of three hundred. Whether he was close to Mother Jones or to Upton Sinclair or to Jack London remains a mystery, although there is a photograph of Mother Jones with the boys of the BBR. Certainly, the letter to London quoted in the last chapter reveals nothing that suggests prior connection or friendship. The Last Chance Boys' Clubs, wherever they were located, whatever they were, disappeared into the ether. No evidence of that "ranch" or "club" remains, in Nevada or anywhere else.[1]

The time he spent in a New Jersey orphanage appears to be unrecoverable, as is, for the most part, his time at the Glenwood Manual Training School. He never talked about his own family, although he must have had contact with his sister and her son, who both lived in Canada and who each received bequests in his will, and probably with other relatives.

In 1913 and 1914, when he was already in his thirties, he created a singular persona ("self-fashioning" is the term historians use) as the "Big Brother" to "chanceless" boys. Sympathetic journalists suggested that he understood, as others did not, what it was to be an uncared-for boy in a cruel urban world. They portrayed him as offering a solution for the ubiquitous social disease of the "boy problem": for the absent parents, the inadequate schooling and disappearing apprenticeships, the brutal policing and criminal justice institutions that pretended but failed to offer a substitute for those parents. Jack Robbins promised a cure for a malady that harmed every American city (see figure 3).

But how uncared-for were the boys he drew into his orbit? Did the struggles parents and "boy workers" confronted justify their turning to this uneducated tobacco salesman? And what did he really offer boys—at a fantastic "Last Chance Ranch," or later at the somewhat less fantastic Boys' Brotherhood Republic, or at the innumerable clubs he told journalists in one place that he had started in another? What were the remedies that he was selling? The national organization of Last Chance Boys' Clubs that he described in his letter of solicitation to Jack London never went anywhere, and, so far as one can tell, Jack Robbins quickly let it die. There is a blur of Last Chance Clubs, Big Brother Clubs, and more, always organized successfully and serving great numbers of boys, just out of sight of the writers and editors who listened to him describe them. (This is, of course, a world without Google or other internet searches. And journalists were always writing on deadline.)

One has to wonder what psychic needs were satisfied by Jack Robbins's assertion and presumption that he had become a "big brother" to chanceless waifs. Looking backward from a time today when we know too much about men who prey on young boys, about men who abuse the young, it is impossible to read about Robbins's projects—what he was said to do and whom he did it with—without suspicion and anxiety. Was he a sexual predator? Or was he "merely" looking to fill a need to have and sustain connections with poor adolescents? What was he doing? I cannot answer the questions. I do not know. Yet what I do know is that, at a time when there were numbers of reformers and journalists who disliked him and his projects, who wanted him to fail, one cannot find any intimations in any accounts of improprieties on his part or of what would then have been referred to as perversion. Those questions were never raised.[2]

He was, in any event, flighty, ceaselessly on the move. And it is remarkable how little the newspaper authors and editors knew about the man whose remedies they momentarily celebrated, whose stories they eagerly reproduced. Constantly in motion from one city to another, from one newspaper office to another, and talking to boys and to newspaper editors wherever he went. It was as if he could not sit still in one place. And he was constantly trying out one idea after another. Was he a kind of confidence man? It is never made clear where the money came from that he needed to survive. For how long did he

Figure 3: Jack Robbins in 1918 (publicity photograph). Author's collection.

actually continue to work as a tobacco salesman? However he was "working," he was selling all the time, playing on his apparent friendships with prominent individuals, usually radicals, hawking a cure for what was at the time a pressing social disease.[3]

There are hints in the journalism of more critical understandings. Sometimes an editor or reporter would catch him in a lie, in producing what we today call "fake news." A few realized or discovered that Jack Robbins was making things up, was bullshitting. A columnist in the December 12, 1913, issue of the *Geyserville* (California) *Gazette* used his stories about the search to find the worst of the worst boys "to illustrate how some kinds of news are manufactured for the diversion of the public." After quoting from the Pittsburgh papers about the plans for Nevada's Last Chance Ranch, the columnist noted that the story was "possible—even plausible." But then the writer turned to the *San Francisco Post*, which had asked Jack London, supposedly Robbins's collaborator and friend, what he knew about the plan to build a ranch in Nevada. "Darned if I know anything about the matter," was London's response. "And so another dream goes a glimmering," the column concluded. "The worst boys of Pittsburgh and Chicago will have to take their last chances in the slums of those delectable towns, while that ranch near Reno will remain the home of the lonesome sage brush."[4]

Under the headline "Sinclair's 'Worst' Boy Colony 'Lost' in Nevada," the *Inter Ocean*, a Chicago paper, reported that Reno's postmaster had been unable to locate "this colony of incorrigibles." The postmaster was stuck with about thirty letters addressed to the camp. He had "diligently" advertised but received "not a rumor of a bad boy for miles around." The postmaster had written to Robbins, asking *him* to point out the spot on the map where the "bad boys" lived, so he could deliver their mail. Robbins declared that he was disappointed that the boys of the Last Chance Camp were not "live enough to wake up the whole state of Nevada to the fact that they were there." He identified the location of the camp as twenty-two miles from Derbuy, which was the nearest railway point. Reno was twenty-seven miles away, and mail should have been addressed to Derbuy instead. Not Reno. He added that he was going to "rake" Chicago to find a "worst" boy, to replace John Fargo, of Racine, who had had the designation, but who had run away from the colony or camp because he disliked the vegetarian diet prescribed by Sinclair.[5]

A columnist writing in the March 18, 1914, issue of the *Colusa* (California) *Daily Sun* did further research, drawing on stories from the news services. His article began by drawing on a story about the famous writer Upton Sinclair vacationing in Bermuda with his wife, playing tennis. It then retold the story of the end of the Last Chance Ranch in Nevada, once again highlighting Upton Sinclair's role and his vegetarianism. Why had the boy, John Gargo or Fargo, done what he had done, stealing the horses and the supplies? The boy, the worst of the worst (of the worst), who had been before the juvenile court already nineteen times, was by then at large with two stolen ponies and several days of provisions, "somewhere in the Middle West." He was "consumed with a desire to realize the dream" of being "a real pistol and dagger outlaw, with a trail of extinct Sheriffs and Constables behind him." In Nevada, however, the "reformers" (that is, Robbins and Sinclair) had given him ranch work and fed him "nuts, vegetables, cereals[,] and other things that form Upton Sinclair's ideas of diet." The diet and the routine had soon grown "tiresome. . . . Young Fargo yearned for excitement and beefsteak." According to the columnist, he was likely to get both.[6]

The story in the *Colusa Daily Sun* continued. Upton Sinclair had set out in pursuit of Fargo on the Last Chance Ranch's one remaining pony. The Colusa paper then quoted from a story in the *Milwaukee Free Press*. Sinclair had arrived in Derby, Nevada, "saddle-worn and hungry," on a "scrawny Mexican pony." Sinclair had been in the saddle all day, and his supply of peanuts, "his chief article of diet," was nearly exhausted. "As soon as the famous poet-novelist-vegetarian-reformer arrived[,] he made for the principal restaurant, where he ordered a beefsteak smothered with mushrooms." Then, "after taking a bath and securing a goodly supply of peanuts and canned baked beans, Sinclair again mounted his pony and started for the Indian reservation."[7]

The problem with the Derby story in the *Milwaukee Free Press*, if one juxtaposed it with stories from other news services, as the columnist for the *Colusa Daily Sun* had (and putting to the side the fact that there was never a town of Derby in existence, with or without a "principal restaurant"), was the inconvenient fact that the Upton Sinclair was also reported to be vacationing in Bermuda at the same time. "The ability to be in two places at the same time" was "a most useful gift." The tennis-playing Upton Sinclair, according to "Bermuda Colonist," would not admit "a predilection for peanuts or that [writing] *The Jungle* had ever spoilt his appetite; neither had he ever founded a colony for bad boys, at Reno or anywhere else." So, who then was the mysterious or fantastic Upton Sinclair on horseback in Nevada?[8]

But none of that really mattered. Jack Robbins knew how to use the news services and the newspapers' unending need for copy. Most papers continued to reprint whatever he offered the news services to run. And they interviewed him when he arrived in their cities and made his way to their editorial offices. Few ever checked his stories or his numbers for accuracy. Some articles called him a "sociologist."[9] But he was a shallow pretense of a social scientist, with fantasies of numerical precision. What it meant that a boy was 87 ½ percent or 91 percent bad was never explained. And remarkably few journalists or columnists ever questioned his qualifications or his methods. He understood that what journalists wanted were good stories and explanations and solutions for the crisis, for the boy problem. One suspects that many of the journalists were drawn as well to his criticisms of mainstream liberal reform. His radicalism, his apparently sincere challenge to the juvenile courts and the reform schools and to all the other remedies that had been presented as solutions to the boy problem over the previous decades, was itself attractively newsworthy. It seems he was a superb storyteller, seductively so, particularly to female reform-minded journalists like Jane Whitaker.

Throughout the early years of the Boys' Brotherhood Republic, his socialist commitments were open, unhidden. His heterodox radicalism extended to antiwar statements and to animal cruelty initiatives. A piece he wrote for the *Day Book*, written without the "supervisor" moniker, decried the Boy Scouts. Scouts were strikebreakers. To take boys out into the woods and to arm them with guns did not encourage "woodcraft"; it only stirred up the "hunting spirit" and "blood-lust." A boy scout was "not a real boy." Instead a boy scout "talks and thinks continually of guns or bullets." A "good" scout was the one who had become the most "brutal." He concluded with advice to parents: "To allow your boy to become a boy scout is to put his head into the military noose. . . . Beware."[10]

Robbins's hatred of mainstream authority and of the criminal justice system, of what today would be called the carceral state, shines forth from many of his statements, and it is present as well in the public expressions of the BBR. He wanted to "save" children from the reform schools and juvenile courts and the other coercive "child-saving" institutions. He and the BBR would save boys from the "child savers." He hated conventional reformers. In an article in the *Day Book*, also signed under his own name, without the addition of the office of "supervisor," Robbins decried the religiosity of so-called reformers. Such men and women were "too much taken up with church, religion, heaven, and kindred impractical ideas ever to achieve great results among the down-and-out boys." Such reformers lacked the "true heart spirit" needed to win over the delinquent. "Less bible and more helpful fellowship should be the unwritten motto of our reformers." If they wanted to be useful, they ought to show the bad boy how to be "clean, honest, and straight." Give him food to eat and clothes to wear, and "play the Big Brother to him." Then he would become a good citizen. "Personally," Robbins continued, he was "against reform schools, truant institutions, juvenile courts, probationers and all that scents of forced corrective methods, officer, courtroom scenes." These all made "a boy more criminal and obstinate." But, he concluded, rather than spending a few hours each day looking after a boy, it was "more convenient" for reformers to send him to a reform school or to lock him in a detention home.[11]

Many reformers and others in institutional roles reciprocated Robbins's antipathy. He was widely disliked. Philip Seman, a lawyer and social worker, and for many years the head of the Chicago Hebrew Institute (which would later become the Jewish People's Institute), hated Jack Robbins. Eventually, Seman would start a rival boys' organization in the same part of Chicago. The dimensions of his dislike are apparent in a report he prepared in the early 1920s that reflected back on his interactions with Robbins in 1914 and 1915.[12] Seman thought Robbins lacked "almost every qualification very essential in the boy-leader." Robbins was uneducated, and uncouth, without culture and refinement. He lacked personality. He did "not possess the qualities that one would want the normal American boy to emulate." And Robbins encouraged the boys in an inappropriate socialist activism, Seman felt. How much Seman's dislike was shaped by the disdain educated upper-class German Jews often felt about an Eastern European recent immigrant, who probably spoke English with a Yiddish accent, has to be left to our imaginations.

Another report, prepared around the same time by the acting director of the National Information Bureau, an investigative bureau created during World War I to provide information to large charities about agencies and institutions asking for support, summarized how much those in charge of other Chicago social welfare organizations distrusted and disliked Robbins and his methods. This report dismissed the fact that there were rich, charitably minded individuals who supported Robbins and his work. They did so, according to the writer, because they relied on "sympathy" rather than on "scientific knowledge of boys' work." And a somewhat less hostile third report, prepared by the head of Chicago's YMCAs, concluded that Robbins was "of very limited intelligence; . . . unprepossessing in appearance and rather uncouth in manner." Such a man was "liable to make unwarrantable statements, not because of a deliberate intention to deceive anyone, but because of his mental and spiritual limitations." Robbins was "very unpopular" among nearly all social workers. They spoke of him in "caustic terms."[13]

A typical exchange with a critic occurred in December 1916, after the *Day Book* once again gave Robbins space. His article led with the claim that 35 percent of those who emerged from Chicago's orphan asylums became criminals and reformatory inmates. At fifteen, they had become "ripe victims of conditions and environment that soon guide them in the ways of evil." The men who ran orphan asylums were "job holders" and political appointees, seldom "humanitarians." Robbins conceded that the boys might be physically well cared-for in the orphanages, but not so in a way that built "up their mentality or moral courage." They were not made ready to "fight the battle of life. . . . Organized institutional charity" failed them because it lacked "humanity." They needed "something more than a full stomach and a clean bed, something more even than a good education . . . to enable the lads to go into the world and fight a good fight." Boys from orphanages could not compete against boys from the country and from the city who had the advantages of "home training. . . . Broken in purse and spirit," the orphans fell "in with bad boys or designing men and the course is short until it runs into a courtroom." He concluded the article by condemning the obvious tactics of "asylum superintendents," to "shunt" boys into "factories, stores, poorly-paid trades and even the army, just . . . to get them out of the way."[14]

A. E. Lonston responded in the next issue, defending the orphan asylum staff that Robbins had critiqued. Lonston was a young alumnus of the Marks Nathan Jewish Orphan Home, an exclusively Jewish orphanage recently opened in Lawndale.[15] He called Robbins's statistics "bunk." More importantly, he said, Robbins's critique ignored the moral training and teaching that the orphanages offered, training and teaching that emphasized the "great men" that had "made good." The teachers were "humanitarians," though Lonston acknowledged he had not been "petted" while there. Boys who came out of the asylum had more "spirit" than any others, in part because they had been guided by "governors" who knew them better than anyone else. Those governors understood when boys were suited for a particular position, or even for the army. They made such decisions not to get the boys out of the way but rather for the benefit of the boys and "of the community at large. . . . [W]ho is Jack Robbins to dictate to men who have made taking care of boys a life work?" When businessmen refused to employ asylum graduates, it was not the fault of those who ran the asylums. Only those on the "inside" could know what went on in an orphan asylum. Yet, Robbins knew nothing. And Robbins knew nothing, Lonston added, because he had twice applied unsuccessfully to be an asylum superintendent, but he had been rejected "on account of his teachings." Robbins's article was, as a result, merely his attempt at "vengeance."

In the middle of the piece, Lonston's critique took a more personal tone. "Now let us be frank. Jack knows he can kick, if you please, and be destructive, but Robbins has never been constructive." Lonston continued: "If you tell a boy of evil men, no matter where the man ends his days, this boy will think of evil things, and this has been his teaching so far as I know him, and I know him well." (I have no idea how they knew each other.)[16]

A week later, two letters to the *Day Book* defended Jack Robbins against Lonston's charges. They suggested that Lonston's critique had been dictated by the "jobholders" who ran the asylums and orphanages. Robbins's description of the orphanage was, the writers insisted, perfectly accurate.

A third letter came two days later, from a boy "citizen" of the Boys' Brotherhood Republic. He invited Lonston to come to the republic's headquarters and speak with orphan boys who had got into trouble, but who then were rescued. The writer held the office of chairman of the "investigating" committee, which took responsibility for helping such boys. He defended Robbins's claim that 35 percent ended up in the criminal justice system. He described a particular case of a boy released from the orphan home (presumably the same orphan home Lonston had graduated from) who had been arrested as a "baby automobile bandit." The members of the investigating committee had come to his trial, where they told the judge that the boy had never had a chance to "make good." The Boys' Brotherhood Republic, the writer continued, had 350 members, 65 percent of whom had bankbooks, and none of whom had been arrested. In case there were any question, "When I speak of the republic, I speak of Jack Robbins," who had "taught" the boys and "guided" them for the past three years.[17]

* * *

In spite of his radicalism and his hatred of the institutions of the carceral state and those who staffed them, the institution Jack Robbins "supervised," the Boys' Brotherhood Republic, would also have to work closely with those officials and institutions. The police, the courts, the reform schools, and other institutions connected to juvenile justice supplied many of the boys who would become citizens. And he was apparently always soliciting the financial support of businessmen and clubwomen in Chicago, as well as in the towns to which he traveled. He and the Boys' Brotherhood Republic would have to live the complexities and contradictions of dependence and autonomy.[18]

Robbins was an enthusiast for several radical causes. He had, early on, identified himself as a socialist. Yet it was his identification with the boys on the streets that defined him. The core of what he stood for was his certainty that adult society had failed those boys. (In spite of his socialist identity, he never used the word "capitalism.") In later years, he would celebrate the business successes of the alumni of the organization. He knew, as we will see, that the future of the BBR depended on finding jobs for the boys in it. His radicalism was fluid and changeable, never extreme, and it always focused on the existential situations that boys confronted.

Much that Jack Robbins told newspapers he did and created was fictional. He is, one might say, the epitome of an unreliable narrator. At the same time, unlike the Last Chance Boys' Clubs for which he tried to solicit the support of Jack London, and unlike the Last Chance Ranch in Nevada that never existed, the Chicago Boys' Brotherhood Republic (BBR) was not a fiction. By 1915 the BBR was a registered nonprofit corporation.[19] The Boys' Brotherhood Republic eventually became a Chicago institution. A chronology of historical events in Chicago published in 1937 listed the 1914 founding of the Boys' Brotherhood Republic as one of the significant events that shaped the city, along with the founding of the Glenwood Manual Training School (1887) and the establishment of the first specialized juvenile court (1899), among other events and institutions. According to the National Humane Review in 1918, Chicago, identified as "a very enterprising city," had many unique institutions "but none more so than the Boy's Republic." The BBR was real, and it remained so for the next forty years. By the mid-1920s, it had a permanent building as headquarters, named after an early supporter. It also had an office address in the Old Republic Building, near City Hall. By 1946, when Lawndale, the still largely Jewish though quickly changing area of Chicago where the BBR was located, celebrated its seventy-fifth anniversary, Hulbert Hall, the BBR headquarters on Hamlin Street, was identified as one of its monuments. The building still stands (see figures 4 and 5). The BBR was listed as one of the sites to see in the Depression-Era *WPA Guide to Illinois*.[20]

By 1916, articles about the organization and its growth and its singular identity as a self-governing republic were ubiquitous in papers and journals around the country. And yet, as Clara Laughlin, whose writings we will return to, noted, mainstream Chicago institutions still paid it as little attention as they could:

Some day (soon!) "Chicago boosters" will doubtless be heard, on platforms or on printed pages, proudly saying that in no other city but Chicago could an institution of this sort have had its genesis and growth. Mebby so. But Chicago as a corporate entity has given the Brotherhood as little as any city could have given it; and Chicago organizations (with two or three notable exceptions) have been as successful in overlooking the boys as the organizations of Berlin or Baghdad could have been. The boys "got away with" the thing almost in spite of Chicago rather than because of Chicago.[21]

Figure 4: Hulbert Hall, 1530 South Hamlin, in the 1920s. DN-0080378, *Chicago Sun-Times* / Chicago Daily News collection, Chicago History Museum.

Figure 5: Doorway of 1530 South Hamlin, in 2022. Author's photo.

An undated and haphazard listing of "Organizations Which Affiliated Themselves with the Boys Brotherhood Republic Very Recently," found in the papers of the Chicago Home and Aid Society, the city's primary Protestant foster-care organization, produced probably in the fall of 1916, revealed that many Chicago agencies had already come to depend on the BBR. This was a three-page list of the many boys being "turned over" to the BBR by a variety of agencies and groups, presumably because they were not being served by more conventional organizations. To take just the first items on the list, the Immigrant's Protective League, headed by Grace Abbott, turned over a "colored boy" who had recently arrived from Columbus, Ohio, with his mother. The Immigrant's Protective League found a position for the mother in Winnetka, while the BBR "guided" the boy. Another boy was turned over to the BBR from the Illinois Training School for Nurses. The boy had been a patient at the Cook County Hospital. And further on down the list, the YMCA sent the BBR a boy who was in the detention home awaiting trial. The Anti-Cigaret League turned over a boy who was "homeless and friendless." And a large number of boys were "turned over" both from the Marks Nathan Jewish Orphan Home and from the Glenwood Manual Training School. What it meant that boys were being "turned over" to the BBR was not explained. In most of these instances, one imagines that the BBR saw the situation differently. As we will see, the BBR understood itself as taking in boys as a consequence of proactive action by the BBR's "investigative committee." Who initiated action remains uncertain. But the important point is that already by then, barely two years after it was founded, the BBR was more or less integrated into the world of services and agencies that tried to deal with the "boy problem."[22]

What the BBR offered was distinctive. It neither reduced the boys to potential criminals nor insisted on their innocence. It took adolescents where they were, doing the work they did, living the lives they did, even if they were in trouble or troubled. And it found a way to grant them a kind of democratic citizenship. Its survival depended on the capacity of the boys to work together, and, so far as the records permit us to judge, the boy citizens did continue to work together and create a functioning "republic."

And apparently adult "boy workers" in Chicago soon realized that the BBR could not be ignored, that it offered services that other agencies did not, or failed at. Those adult "boy workers" needed to work with it.[23]

So, in December 1916, Wilfred S. Reynolds, the head of the Children's Home and Aid Society, called a meeting. He gathered together the heads of many of Chicago's prominent social welfare organizations for a conference. The meeting included representatives from the Boy Scouts, the Chicago Juvenile Court, the YMCA, the "Big Brothers," the Chicago Boys' Club, the Cook County Sunday Schools, the Association of Commerce, and the Chicago Commons. The purpose of the conference was to settle on the "wisest course to pursue in cooperating with the Boys Brotherhood Republic and in 'conserving' the results of the work done with this group of boys by Jack Robbins." That is to say they worried how they should deal with him.[24]

The conference produced and articulated seven "conclusions," and one less formal understanding. The formal conclusions began by diminishing the originality of the BBR. The ideas behind the republic were not new, they wrote. And, second, it was not an entity in itself. Rather, it represented one "phase" of "work with boys." It was part of the larger mosaic of agencies that served boys throughout the city. Either the BBR should be enlarged, or it should be integrated with "already existing agencies." Clearly, the members of the conference preferred the second alternative. Third, the BBR needed a more conventional organization, including a functioning board of directors. It was "not wise or safe" for the BBR to continue "long centered about one personality." Here the conference report got to what was clearly the core concern of these boy workers. They worried about the centrality of this one odd and discordant individual, Jack Robbins. But fourth, the group also realized that Jack Robbins was "an inseparable part" of the "problem." That is, he could not be ignored or be easily removed. He was "the one binding force" that kept the group together. He was "jealous of the prerogatives and independence" of what they called "the Club." And he would "certainly resent any intrusion." There was no BBR without him. And those at this meeting knew they needed to have his cooperation. Fifth, they went on to recommend that the BBR affiliate with an existing institution. (Other documents in the folder in the Children's Home and Aid files make it clear that they wrote to Minnie Low, Jane Addams's close associate, sometimes identified as the "Jane Addams to the Jews," hoping that Hull House would make space for the BBR.) Sixth, they recommended a study of "a representative group" of boys at present in the BBR. They hoped to discover the "object" of the boys in joining and participating. But more they meant to explore whether there was "an unwholesome element in the manner in which the present Club is conducted." What they meant by "unwholesome element" was a worry about "the danger" that the boys were gaining "an impression of their [own] importance; also that the narrow scope of the Club" was "apt to lead them into a purely political groove and into a destructive socialistic tendency." That led to their seventh and final conclusion: that Jack Robbins needed to be "cultivated" by other boy workers. He needed "education as to the breadth and scope of boy life; as to up-to-date methods." He needed to be socialized.

That assertion then led to the group's less formal conclusion. Some boy workers, some of those at the meeting, ought to "cultivate the friendship of Jack Robbins in an informal way." Not just to study his relationship to the BBR, but also "to try to bring out the strong qualities which are his and to tactfully suggest to him how he can best use his natural influence which he has over boys."[25]

The group recommended, as such groups often do, that a new committee be formed to pursue those goals. Yet, for reasons that will soon become apparent, other than a letter to Minnie Low, the files of the Children's Home and Aid Society reveal no further steps taken. And nothing suggests that the group was able to take control of the organization of the BBR, or to discipline or socialize Jack Robbins, as they had clearly hoped to do.[26]

* * *

Even as he was celebrated as the inventor of the republic, the creation myth Jack Robbins told and retold, about how boys met in his apartment and decided to bring this gang substitute into being, focused attention on the creativity of the boys, and on their determination. He diminished his own role, and he emphasized theirs. When he talked with journalists and others, he always gave credit to the boys as the creators. He had simply brought them together. They had decided they would create an alternative to the gang they were all already members of. That alternative would both "save" boys in trouble and, at the same time, create a constitutional republic. When he said to them at that first meeting that they should not try to do too much at one time, they overruled him. He called himself only a "supervisor." His goal was to identify and support the power and the capacities of the boys, as well as their ability to work together.

In all this he was quite different from William George, whose institutions were always identified as "George Junior Republics," and to whom Robbins was often compared. Implicitly, Robbins denied adults the control or the capacity to create a sheltered childhood. The BBR was the boys' organization, not his. And he denied that his boys were playacting at adult life. Their citizenship was not a pretense.[27]

The Boys' Brotherhood Republic really became an institution run almost solely by boys, without much of an adult presence—and successfully so. When, in early 1917, Wilfred Reynolds of the Children's Home and Aid Society wrote to Minnie Low to inquire about the possibility that the BBR might affiliate with Hull House, he provided a crude budget that must have been given him by

Robbins or by some of the boys. The BBR's monthly budget was said to be $277.50, not counting $45 a month for rent for the BBR's "present quarters," which was being paid for directly by the Children's Home and Aid Society. $75 a month went to a Miss Carpenter, Myrtle Carpenter, who was working half time, and who Reynolds acknowledged was a "guiding force" for "constructive work." $125 a month went as salary for Jack Robbins. No other adults were mentioned. Most of the funds expended came from "taxes" paid directly by the boy citizens to the Republic.[28]

What Jack Robbins did as "superintendent" stayed vague, although he was also ever-present. And it should be added that Myrtle Carpenter's presence and labor remained almost entirely unmentioned and unexplained, except in one unpublished source that portrayed her as a quietly saintly but powerful force for good: "How much the BBR owes to her no one will ever be able to compute, but it is a very great deal."[29] When in 1915 he testified before an Industrial Relations Commission about the conditions of messenger boys, Robbins said that he was still employed by "a tobacco factory in the East." And he described himself as conducting several boy's clubs. When asked how he was compensated for his services to the BBR, he claimed that he did it gratis, and "only . . . when I have time—evenings and Sundays."[30]

The constitution he and the first group of boys drafted in May 1914 devoted "Article 13" to the duties of the supervisor. (Unsurprisingly, it said nothing about Myrtle Carpenter, who held no constitutional role.) The supervisor would, in theory, be chosen by election, from three names submitted by the BBR's city council. He would hold office for a two-year term. His duties included having "full charge of all committees, . . . at all meetings in order to supervise and guide same." But he had no vote, although he was entitled to express opinions. At meetings, he had the right to "speak, advise, and supervise, at will." Any "business" transacted "outside" the doors of the Republic had to be passed on by him. He had the power "to create publicity . . . using his own methods." (This stipulation was obviously important to Robbins, the salesman.) He had "full charge" of all legal matters. He had the power to dismiss a citizen who had become "a detriment" to the Republic. But he had to notify the "city clerk" of what he had done. And he had the theoretical power to appoint "assistant supervisors." Those would be drawn from the ranks of the BBR alumni.[31]

Not marked in the constitution, but clearly among the gifts that Robbins gave to the boys in the BBR, was instruction in how to promote and to advertise, which may also have meant how to fabulate.[32] When, in later years, alumni of the early BBR gathered to celebrate him, they called Jack Robbins their "boss." And newspapers sometimes identified him as being in "active charge."[33]

What did the boys know about Robbins? A reminiscence by Harry Slonaker, who had been an early member, noted that they knew nothing about his past. But they had "no desire or inclination to question him about his past or motives. . . . [W]e as recipients were happy to have a meeting place and participate in the many activities—amen." In an unpublished memoir, Herbert K. Abrams, one of the named trustees of the trust Robbins created in his will, and a member of Chicago's BBR in the late 1920s, wrote of how Robbins, the "free thinker" and the apparent friend of Jack London, Upton Sinclair, Emma Goldman, and other "writers and social activists[,] . . . fascinated" the boys with reminiscences of his life as a "hobo." [34]

When the new organization first produced letterhead, Robbins was listed as "Founder and Supervisor," along with photographs of two boys and the phrase "An Organization for the Benefit of Future Citizens of Chicago." And a promotional pamphlet, probably produced in 1916, included a statement about "service" written by a boy "citizen." "All we need," the boy wrote, is a "city hall of our own, . . . [t]he tools to work with, . . . [a] little friendly counsel—mixed with plenty of patience, . . . And last, but best of all, JACK ROBBINS, with all his time, free to guide us."[35]

What struck everyone who wrote about the BBR was both the relative absence of adults, other than Jack Robbins, and the assertion by boys of governing authority. At least early on, and well into the 1920s and 1930s, adults played only peripheral roles, primarily as fundraisers and as voluntary teachers in the night classes that the BBR held. A 1937 report on "Youth-Serving Organizations," prepared by the American Youth Commission of the American Council on Education, found that the Chicago BBR served 1,100 boys (the New York City BBR at that time served 410). By then, the Chicago BBR had two full-time paid employees, two part-time employees, and one part-time unpaid worker. In 1915 when he testified before the Industrial Commission about messenger boys, Jack Robbins was asked if he was associated with other men and women in "this work." He answered "I am doing this work alone. We have what is known as the Boy Brotherhood Republic. There are seven men and women who have charge of this particular organization [as fundraisers?], and I happen to be one of them. All this other work I do myself." (No published source attended to the silent presence of Myrtle Carpenter, ubiquitous but mostly unacknowledged, as a kind of wife.)[36]

As Robbins told the story to a journalist in 1924, early on, in 1916, the growth of the BBR was so rapid that Robbins had needed to ask for help from an unnamed social service organization. The organization set up an advisory board of professionals and other adults, each member of which was to supervise some aspect of the life of the BBR. It is likely or at least plausible that this group was the same group of "boy workers" that came together in December 1916 under the aegis of Reynolds of the Children's Home and Aid Society, and that produced the "conclusions" already discussed. But, as Robbins remembered it eight years later, they had met at his request. And what happened next, as he told the story in 1924, did not appear in the archives of the Children's Home and Aid Society.

In his later telling, up to then, up to late in 1916, the boys of the BBR had been doing what they did without any adult supervision, beyond the advice he offered. "They took to interference" from the new committee of adults "about like a cat takes to water." They ignored the "advisory board." In response, the advisory board or committee decided to suspend all activities of the boys of the BBR while they reorganized its structure and took control. And they sent a notice to that effect to the BBR's elected council. Ralph Goodman, then the mayor of the BBR, called a meeting (Robbins was conveniently away at the time). Goodman asked the council what should be done with an advisory board that issued such a notice. The boys in the council passed a resolution and sent a copy of the resolution to each member of the adult advisory board. "Until further notice you are suspended as a member of the advisory board to the Boys' Brotherhood Republic."

Adults might help with fundraising and buildings. They might come in to teach classes. But for the rest they had to stay away. "Please get this straight," Robbins concluded in 1924. "The boys run the place themselves. It's *theirs*."[37]

In 1920, Clara Laughlin, an independent journalist whose work we will return to, described what went on in the Boys' Brotherhood Republic, in an article entitled "Where Boys Rule." One evening she sat in, as she apparently often did, as a debate raged within the "council" of the BBR. The particular issue that consumed the boys that evening was what to do about those boys who were too young to join formally but who needed help and care. After describing the issues and the arguments, she finally turned to Jack Robbins, who had apparently been a silent presence throughout all the discussion. Robbins was, she concluded, "a great, animating spirit," an adult but "a boy in feeling," always to be known as "Jack" by everyone. Because he had once been "a friendless boy," who had suffered, he had, she said, resolved "to do *something* . . . to make life easier and better for other boys." He had "no money, no influential friends, hardly anything except the completest understanding of boys that ever was, and a way with them. . . . A silent—even, taciturn—fellow is Jack." Robbins learned by listening. "Meeting after meeting he sits through, usually in a back seat, and never says a word, no matter how hot the discussion waxes." If and when "disorder" arises, the boys remained in charge. "Jack never intervenes, and the boys never appeal to him."[38]

And yet Robbins's values pervaded the institution. The application form for membership or citizenship in the BBR asked a series of core questions: "Are you aware of the fact that the B.B.R. is ruled by boys . . . ?" "Do you approve of it?" Clearly, success depended on writing "yes" to both. "Are you in favor of reform school for 'bad' boys?" No, of course. "If it was proven to you that a boy landed in a reform school because of the fact that he never had a chance, would you serve on a committee to get him released so that we may give him another chance?" Again, "yes" was the only possible answer (see figure 6).[39] When the BBR created a "store" for its citizens, identified as the only store in the world "exclusively owned and managed by Boys for Boys," it was a "cooperative" store, organized as a "profit sharing corporation," chartered under the laws and regulations of the BBR. The boys also handed out leaflets in support of socialist candidates. In November 1916, the BBR "complained" to the US Attorney that shoe-shining parlors on the west side of the city were making boys work over twelve hours a day.[40]

When the BBR produced a pamphlet in late 1916 or early 1917 celebrating its accomplishments, it included quotations from a range of adult authorities. In addition to Judge Ben Lindsey, the celebrated Denver juvenile court judge and sex reformer, and Judge Merrit Pinckney, of Chicago's juvenile court, the pamphlet gathered statements from a number of socialist luminaries, including Jack London ("A Boys Brotherhood Republic in every city shall be your second motto"), Mother Jones ("Real boys with a real purpose"), and Upton Sinclair ("Chicago will be a worthwhile city in twenty years if all its boys become citizens of the Boys' Brotherhood Republic now").[41]

Robbins's conceptualization of a boys' "republic" may have borrowed from the George Junior Republics, from the "Freetowns" and the boys' towns that were a presence across turn-of-the-century America. But just as Robbins's politics were different from the increasingly right-wing commitments of William George, so did the location of Chicago's Boys' Brotherhood Republic differ from that of other "junior republics." As was written (or reproduced) in promotional booklets both in 1923 and in 1938, unlike the George Junior Republics, which depended on what was understood as a temporary removal or separation away from the city, the BBR created a space in the middle of Chicago. The boys remained within the metropolis, where they would have to work and live. And parental authority was not just absent, but irrelevant. According to the

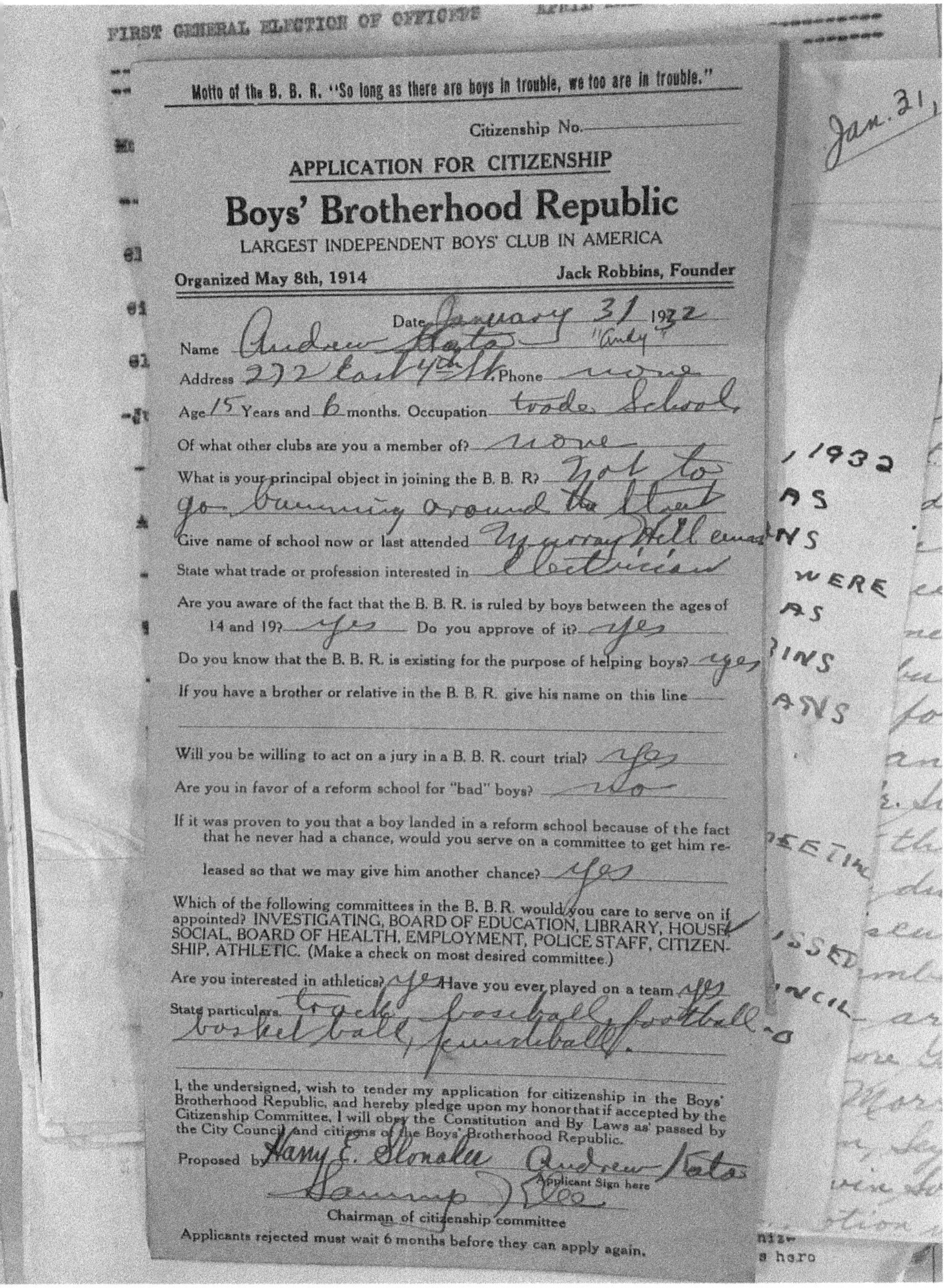

Motto of the B. B. R. "So long as there are boys in trouble, we too are in trouble."

Citizenship No.________

APPLICATION FOR CITIZENSHIP

Boys' Brotherhood Republic

LARGEST INDEPENDENT BOYS' CLUB IN AMERICA

Organized May 8th, 1914   Jack Robbins, Founder

Date _January 31, 1932_

Name _Andrew Kata_ "Andy"

Address _272 East 4th St._ Phone _none_

Age _15_ Years and _6_ months. Occupation _trade School_

Of what other clubs are you a member of? _none_

What is your principal object in joining the B. B. R? _not to go bumming around the street_

Give name of school now or last attended _Murray Hill ema_

State what trade or profession interested in _Electrician_

Are you aware of the fact that the B. B. R. is ruled by boys between the ages of 14 and 19? _yes_ Do you approve of it? _yes_

Do you know that the B. B. R. is existing for the purpose of helping boys? _yes_

If you have a brother or relative in the B. B. R. give his name on this line ________

Will you be willing to act on a jury in a B. B. R. court trial? _yes_

Are you in favor of a reform school for "bad" boys? _no_

If it was proven to you that a boy landed in a reform school because of the fact that he never had a chance, would you serve on a committee to get him released so that we may give him another chance? _yes_

Which of the following committees in the B. B. R. would you care to serve on if appointed? INVESTIGATING, BOARD OF EDUCATION, LIBRARY, HOUSE, SOCIAL, BOARD OF HEALTH, EMPLOYMENT, POLICE STAFF, CITIZENSHIP, ATHLETIC. (Make a check on most desired committee.)

Are you interested in athletics? _yes_ Have you ever played on a team _yes_

State particulars. _track, baseball, football, basketball, punchball._

I, the undersigned, wish to tender my application for citizenship in the Boys' Brotherhood Republic, and hereby pledge upon my honor that if accepted by the Citizenship Committee, I will obey the Constitution and By-Laws as passed by the City Council and citizens of the Boys' Brotherhood Republic.

Proposed by _Harry E. Slonaker_   _Andrew Kata_
           Applicant Sign here

Sammy Lee

Chairman of citizenship committee

Applicants rejected must wait 6 months before they can apply again.

Figure 6: BBR citizenship application, early 1930s, New York Boys' Brotherhood Republic (copied unchanged from the Chicago Boys' Brotherhood Republic, early 1920s). Harry Slonaker Papers, History San Jose, San Jose, CA.

booklets, the BBR internalized "John Dewey's idea of 'preparations for life in the midst of life'—mastery of an environment rather than removal from it."[42]

The motto of the BBR was: "So long as there are boys in trouble, we too are in trouble." And the "we" was crucial. And expansive. As was the focus on "bad boys." Never delinquents; never criminals, and certainly not dependents. Never any of the professionalized labels that littered early twentieth-century social science and social reform. The purpose of the BBR, according to its 1914 constitution, was first, "the helping in any possible way of unfortunate and needy boys, the developing physically, mentally, and morally of the citizens of the Republic," and as well, the passage continued, "the boys of the community." The focus always remained on the boys, the bad boys, whether with or without families, with absent or present parents, in or out of institutions, and on how they suffered because of poverty and because the adult world drove them toward crime and punishment. The recurrent theme, particularly early on, was that state institutions, that is, juvenile courts, reform schools, probation officers, and police, among others, as well as inadequate or absent or incarcerated parents, produced "bad boys" and criminality. But Robbins and the boys of the BBR also emphasized their capacities as citizens-to-be, and as citizens in the present, at least within the space of the BBR.[43]

One might say, although I have not found it asserted explicitly anywhere, that the BBR fundamentally rejected the legal category of "dependence," which was ubiquitous in the social-reform literature and among the new professionals of the early twentieth century, as well as in the statutes that created the juvenile courts and its attendant institutions. The word "dependent" never appears in any of its literature. In place of "dependence," the BBR offered adolescent boys a shared experience of community and governmental authority. The BBR created what might be called a horizontal, or at least a more horizontal structure of power, one in which no one was a dependent, no one ruled. All were equal citizens. More than just a celebration of autonomy and independence, the BBR institutionalized a less hierarchical and plausibly more democratic way of being for those adolescent boys, one that was framed as well by a hostility to "charity."[44]

A small and fairly crude 1916 pamphlet reprinted the "nine aims" the BBR adopted at its first meeting in May 1914. Those aims included preventing boys from getting into trouble and offering "companionship" to boys who were in trouble. Those were the first two. Third was to aid "all boys" in securing the necessities of life (housing, clothing, education), helping them become "self-sustaining." Fourth was to look after boys discharged from institutions. Beyond those, the meeting committed itself to sending flowers and reading matter to sick boys and to helping them get medical attention, to "report[ing] to the supervisor" cases of mistreatment, to doing everything possible "to keep boys from drifting away from Chicago," and to working "for the physical, moral, and mental welfare" of the BBR's citizens. Finally, the last aim listed was to aid in the enforcement of the child labor law and factory legislation and "street trade" ordinance.[45]

The facing page of the 1916 pamphlet offered thoughts on "service," by an unidentified citizen, along with an invitation to join. We, the boy wrote, "have been told that service is the key note of the coming age." The boy citizens of the BBR, were "out for service." They wanted a city with "clean stores, clean streets, clean shows, clean homes, clean places to work, and clean places to play—for everybody." For "other" boys, that is, for those not in the BBR, they wanted to offer friendship: "By just being friends with the latchstring out at our home when you need us most." And for themselves, "it is enough to know that we are growing while the growing is good." Meanwhile, "ALL WE NEED" is a city hall and a "little friendly counsel—mixed with plenty of patience—ALL BOYS NEED THAT." And last, once again, "but best of all, JACK ROBBINS, with all his time, free to guide us. We'll do the rest." They were not, the writer concluded, "philanthropists, charity workers, or reformers." They were just "plain citizens on the job," working to "make our city [the BBR, not Chicago] the finest on the map." And "OUR SERVICE IS FREE."[46]

In a slicker and more professional 1923 pamphlet, produced to promote the organization and to raise funds, a page was devoted to "questions" often asked about the BBR. What were the purposes of this organization? The pamphlet identified six: First, "Self-development and protection—to be truly brothers and friends." Second, "To secure a fair chance for *any* boy who needs it, whether a member of the Republic or not, without regard to race or religion." Third, "to call attention to, remove, or modify" those "conditions" of city life that made it almost impossible for a boy to "work, to play, or to grow in a natural, wholesome way." Fourth, to "bring about a better understanding of boys" by the panoply of adults who dealt with them (including fathers, mothers, and teachers, police officers, or anyone connected with orphan homes, reform schools, and the like.). Fifth, "To protest against institutional care of boys when any other is at all possible." And sixth, "To protest against any form of charity, as a substitute, for opportunities for self-help, friendship, or community co-operation." There followed another slogan or motto: "Something for nothing gets you in bad all along the line." This last had already appeared on the "service" page of the 1916 BBR pamphlet.[47]

Was there anything new about this organization, the 1923 pamphlet continued? No. There was nothing new in the notions of brotherhood or of the republic or of "the methods of psychology" that Jack Robbins used "in directing their energy." But the combination, relying on the "control and metamorphosis of the usual gang activities," produced "a new venture in the field of social adjustment." Unlike the George Junior Republics, to which the BBR compared itself, the idea or aim of the BBR was prevention, while the George Junior Republics became substitutes for the usual reform schools.[48] The BBR also cost less, and it did not require removal from ordinary life. What "ordinary life" meant for those boys was not explained. (It surely included work, but one wonders about family life and schooling and about the pleasures and dangers of life on urban streets.) Unlike most boys' clubs, to make a second comparison, it offered "a more complete outlet for the gang spirit," and it substituted democracy for the "monarchial leadership" of boys' clubs. Citizens became committed to "justice and the welfare and protection of others." That commitment kept them from delinquency. And it also taught them "correct business habits and attitudes through the advice and guidance of Mr. Robbins," along with that of the boys who served on the employment committee.[49]

On a second page, apparently written by Ralph Goodman, the BBR's first mayor, the 1923 pamphlet described both the target constituency for the BBR and what "boy work" meant. On the first, on the target, "We get the boy headed for court before he gets there, and he is welcomed if he has been there, and it makes no difference if he is the kind that would never get there." That is to say, the BBR took in children labeled delinquent as well as those identified as dependent, as well as boys just looking for a boys' club. And on the second, on what boy work meant: Boy work did not "end" once a boy had a job, food, and a place to sleep. It might start by procuring those things, but it went further: The "stimulus" that a boy needed to become "a useful citizen" was only possible "*through the genuine friendship of an understanding friend such as only a boy can be. . . .* THIS IS OUR WORK." Or, to introduce a notion that we will return to often, a boy needed a pal or pals. And ensuring that boys had pals was crucial work. Indeed, it may be that providing "pals" for those who lacked them was the most important purpose that the BBR could achieve. Pals were the concrete instantiation of the horizontal structure of governance that the BBR worked to create.

Jane Whitaker, once again writing in the *Day Book*, agreed, although she wrote in part to convince adult men to be pals to boys. "If you know anything at all about a boy, even the worst boy that ever was, you know one thing—that a boy has got to have a pal." Lucky boys had "dad-pals." Unlucky boys might have pals that might lead them "down to the depths" toward criminality. But still, a boy needed a pal. The rest of Whitaker's article moved in two directions.

On the one hand, the structure of the BBR aimed to help boys be pals to one another and to others who were in trouble. The article sketched the offices and committees and councils and boards within the BBR that did the work of being "pals." But the piece ended by making an appeal to adult readers who wanted to become "pals," who wanted "to help these boys who are trying to help other boys." There was, she thought "nothing in the world that gives you quite the same happiness in the corner of your heart that you keep covered from the world as the knowledge that you've been a pal to a boy."[50]

What was a pal? According to a red typescript or poster, perhaps intended to be placed on the wall above a citizen boy's bed, a pal was someone who "knows all your faults, but likes you anyway . . . the one who can tell you about your faults without making you feel cheap." He will make sacrifices so that you don't have to suffer. He is the one you don't have to lie to. He is happy for your success, and sorry for you in failure. He is the one that can be depended on, always. "Try to get a PAL by being a REAL PAL yourself." (see figure 7).[51]

* * *

The BBR eventually offered much that looked like the offerings of a typical boys' club of the time, including classes and athletics and elections for the government, and even, later on, a "fresh air" summer camp. It had other aspects that made it look more like a boarding school, including dormitories. It also created spaces, courts and stores and committees, and a savings bank and a welfare office and a newspaper. These were spaces where boys could perform or, from an external adult-centered perspective, "play at" adult roles. These were spaces not unlike those of the George Junior Republics and other boys' towns. One might also note that the BBR combined Robbins's early plans for "Last Chance Clubs" and for "Big Brother Clubs," plans which he had rhetorically separated when he had talked to journalists in 1913 and 1914.

The BBR would serve two kinds of boys: both those already identified as potential juvenile delinquents and other boys who needed their own space within a local community. At the same time, Robbins and the BBR constantly challenged the identification of the delinquent as distinct. All boys were vulnerable. All could become delinquent. And all boys needed pals. Distinguishing the delinquent and the dependent from the merely poor or under-cared-for was wrongheaded. All boys shared common needs, most of all the need for support and for the space and the time to be with one another.

The primary goals of the organization, as supposedly articulated in that archetypal first meeting in 1914, were, first, and above all else, to keep children

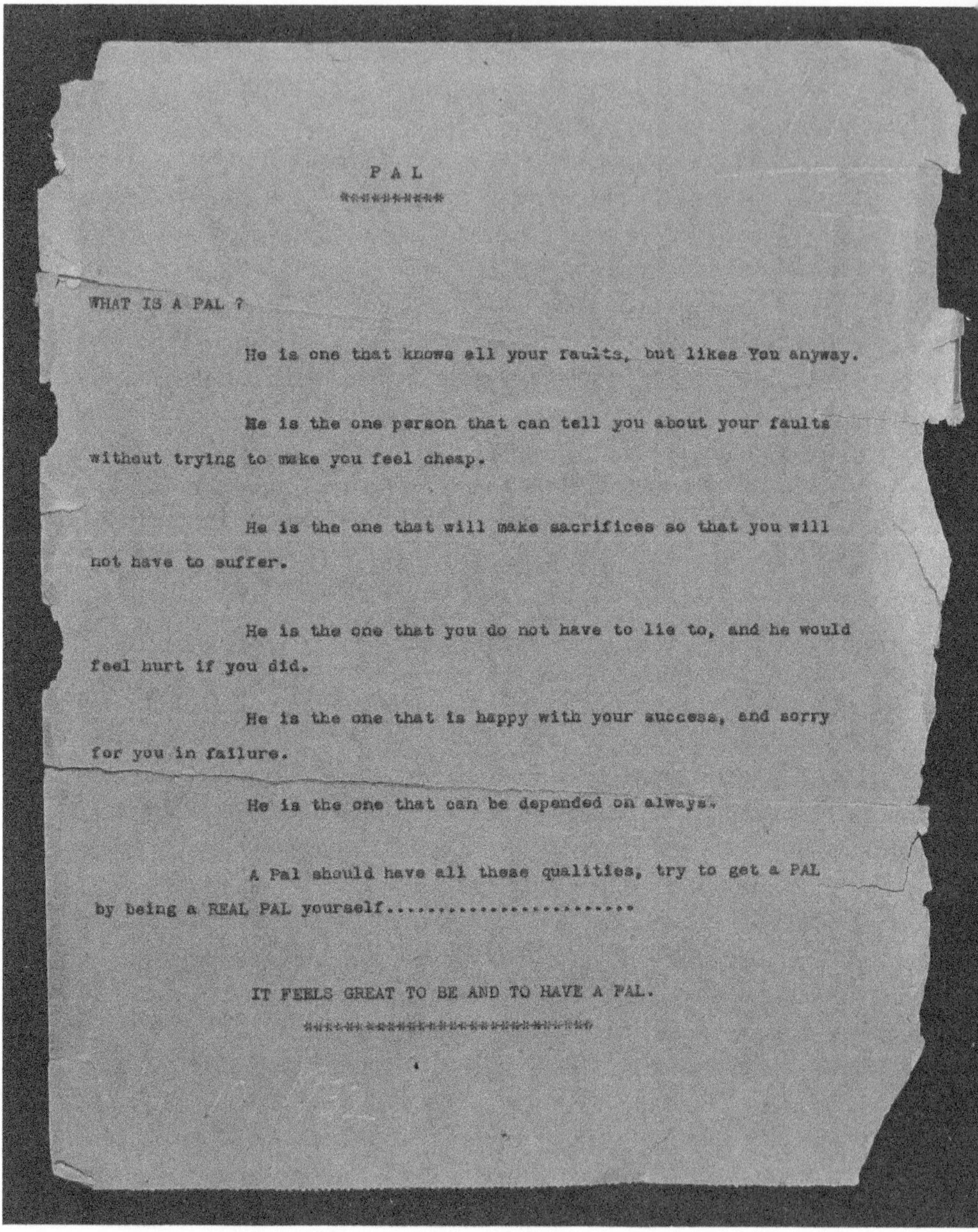

P A L
****

WHAT IS A PAL ?

He is one that knows all your faults, but likes You anyway.

He is the one person that can tell you about your faults without trying to make you feel cheap.

He is the one that will make sacrifices so that you will not have to suffer.

He is the one that you do not have to lie to, and he would feel hurt if you did.

He is the one that is happy with your success, and sorry for you in failure.

He is the one that can be depended on always.

A Pal should have all these qualities, try to get a PAL by being a REAL PAL yourself..........................

IT FEELS GREAT TO BE AND TO HAVE A PAL.
****

Figure 7: "What Is a Pal?" poster, early 1930s. Harry Slonaker Papers, History San Jose, San Jose, CA.

out of the juvenile court and reform schools, and second, to provide a "home" for those released from reform schools and foster care and orphan homes. Those goals required cooperation with the formal institutions of the carceral state. The founders, the boys and Jack Robbins, were not establishing an autarchy, separated or isolated from the adult world. And over time it appears that the Boys' Brotherhood Republic became a more conventional institution, with adults a growing presence, as well as continuing relations with police and courts. Because otherwise those goals could not be achieved.

But early on, not. Or only pragmatically and instrumentally. The goal was to negotiate with the outside adult world, not to integrate into it or accept its terms. The BBR sustained an identity apart, as a "republic." It dealt with and negotiated with adult correctional and coercive institutions—almost as one government negotiating with another—but it did not integrate with them. In that sense as well as others, the BBR differed from the George Republics and other "youth republics." The George Republics were, to use Light's illuminating language, "total environment[s] that removed young people from participation in labor, politics, the military, and other public engagements and substituted an adult-supervised simulation instead." Every part of that definition would have been countered by the "citizens" of the BBR, who did not see themselves as removed, did not understand themselves as under adult supervision, and most of all, did not believe they were simulating adult life.

At least through its first years, Robbins and the citizens of the BBR mostly understood themselves as inhabiting a world apart. They struggled to create an alternative legality that also served boys who were by force of circumstances compelled to accept the brute existence of state power. It would not be simply a boys' club. It was certainly not a substitute reform school. It had gang-like features, but it was not a gang. Nor were those in the BBR playacting or performing adulthood. It was a self-governing republic.[52]

Thus in January and February 1917, the BBR had twice been robbed. The first time thieves had "cleaned" it out, taking furniture and a Victrola and a new suit bought to mark one boy's transition from knickerbockers to long trousers, to adolescence or near-adulthood. They also stole skates and two punching bags. The thieves had apparently locked themselves into the building in the absence of "a negro boy caretaker," while all the other boys were at work. (The story does not explain whether the caretaker was a "citizen" or an "employee.") As a result, the BBR had detailed its own police force to discover who the thieves were. After a second robbery, the *Chicago Tribune* interviewed Ralph Goodman, identified by the paper as the "president" of the BBR, and Jack Robbins, its "advisor." Goodman and Robbins thought the thieves were a "poolroom gang" who stole out of revenge, because the BBR had taken away many of their steady customers, boys who had once had nowhere else to go. What would the BBR do if it caught the thieves? "They will not be turned over to the police." The BBR would handle it themselves.[53]

One year earlier, in January 1916, a speech to the boys by the radical socialist Mother Jones emphasized the "inhumanity" of the law, of state law. At that moment, an adult visitor present at the meeting, a sanitary inspector for the health department, interrupted. He said he "respected her gray hairs," but objected to Mother Jones's message. They went back and forth, and then she was permitted to continue with her speech. Judge Harry Fischer of Chicago's Boys' Court, who was also present, then advised the boys at the meeting not to listen to those who would "inflame their minds against authority." But it is unlikely that they followed his counsel.[54]

Governance of this republic, a structure that, according to Jane Whitaker, once again put to shame "the man-administration of the big city of Chicago," lay both with politically elected officers, notably a mayor and a city clerk, and with many standing committees, eight of which were mentioned in article 11 of the 1914 constitution. Three of those committees were of particular and continuing significance: a Jobs Committee, an Investigative Committee, and a Citizenship Committee. The others were a "Board of Education," a "Board of Health," an "Athletic Committee," a "Social Committee," and a "House Committee."[55]

The adult media paid a great deal of attention to the elections within the BBR. The *Chicago Tribune* regularly covered them. And those who won would continue to identify themselves by their offices in the BBR, sometimes for the rest of their lives. The obituary of Abert Marks, one of the executors and trustees Robbins intended to have appointed in the will he drafted in 1957, and apparently a successful attorney, marked his teenaged mayoralty of the BBR as perhaps his most significant accomplishment. An uncompleted memoir drafted by Herbert K. Abrams, another of the executors and trustees, and later on a distinguished public health doctor, also marked his election to the BBR mayoralty as an early achievement.[56]

But it was three committees—jobs, citizenship, and investigative—that negotiated the relationship of the BBR with an adult outside world. Those committees constituted or produced the "semi-autonomy" of the "republic." The BBR was not a charity organization. It was a republic filled with citizens. And citizens needed to hold jobs in order to pay taxes.[57] The jobs committee existed because the republic depended on the work that the boys did. That is to say, it depended on the jobs that they held in the city, outside the BBR. Theirs was not the "sheltered childhood" imagined by the adult creators of junior republics or by most Progressive reformers. Schooling was not ignored, but it played an apparently secondary role within the lives of the boys. The "Board of Education," to turn momentarily to another of the BBR's constitutional committees, was not, at least according to the constitutional text, concerned with whether boy citizens went to school. Its duty, rather, was to formulate "methods and programs by which the citizens shall be developed mentally and morally." And that development apparently turned more on speakers brought into the BBR, on evening classes, and on enrichment activities, than it did on whether citizens went to school.

The structure of life in the BBR depended on the reality that nearly all of the boys were workers. And solving the precarity of employment for them was crucial to the BBR's long-term success. The 1914 constitution defined the mission of the employment committee as requiring it to deal with three tasks, all of which remained central to life in the BBR. First of all, it was the duty of the committee "to devise such plans by which . . . unemployed citizens may secure positions." Second, the committee was "to find ways and means whereby boys of Chicago who are out of work may secure jobs, and generally look out for their interest." And third, it was the committee's responsibility to "run, finance, and devise, a day each year which shall be known as Boys' Job Day." The second and third tasks were not ones limited to the boys who were already citizens of the BBR. As Robbins said, in addressing a convention in 1918, "When we pick up a boy who has no home or is a runaway we place him in the dormitory. We get him a job and we keep him there till he gets $15 in money and has a suit of clothes. We have 273 boys in the Republic, and each has $100 invested in the home." Boys of the age to become "citizens" of the republic, that is, between fourteen and eighteen, were primarily understood as workers, not as students. The citizenship form that all applicants filled out, at least as of the early 1920s (I haven't found any from earlier), devoted one line asking the applicant to provide the name of school "now or last attended." But it also asked for the boy's "occupation" and "what trade or profession" he was "interested in"[58] (see figure 8).

According to Ralph Goodman, writing in a local Jewish paper, while "sociologists" and "so called boy workers" were arguing about the causes of crime, and in particular about "baby bandits," the BBR was doing something about the problem. How? By finding jobs for boys. An early meeting at the BBR decided that what caused crime was that two thousand boys were competing for the few available jobs. A 1916 resolution adopted by the members of the BBR went in part as follows: "Whereas, a large proportion of boys go wrong while

Figure 8: BBR Job Day business card, 1920s. Sheldon Glueck, Social Ethics course teaching notes, Historical and Special Collections, Harvard Law School Library, Cambridge, MA.

out of work and while seeking positions; and, . . . Whereas, it is the duty of the Boys' Brotherhood Republic to find ways and means to protect these boys and abolish the causes which tempt them to become delinquent . . ." And therefore, the resolution proposed to make April 10th "Boys' Job Day" for the city of Chicago, just as the constitution had called for. The jobs committee then called on Chicago's mayor, who made the day an official one for the city. And the BBR's Job Day became a regular event, always noted in the local papers, often remarked on as a good thing by the national press. As the *Ohio State Journal* wrote: "We cannot imagine a nobler effort. . . . Giving a boy something to do naturally turns him from the path of idleness, which is crowded with so many dangers these days. Whoever has some work that a boy might do, does wrong if he does not find the boy. 'Boys' Job Day' is to help him out." A paper from West Virginia quoted "the manager of a big concern in Chicago," who said, "I think this is the best idea that has been advanced in a long time." And he pledged to give three boys jobs at wages from $7 to $10 a day. An early story in *the Day Book* described three boys, certified by the BBR, who needed jobs. They were "bright" and "intelligent," with "pep and vim" along with "good common sense." But they had trouble finding work because they had spent time in a reform school. On the other hand, securing work might "readily bring out the true manhood within them." By 1917, when a new version of the "Jobs Day" was proclaimed by Chicago's Mayor Thompson, he hoped for a thousand jobs, so that boys would be "at least partly self supporting." That would keep them "off the streets and out of trouble."[59]

Meanwhile, the citizenship committee decided on the eligibility of applicants for BBR citizenship. The BBR was a place for adolescents, those over fourteen, not for the very young. (By the 1920s they created a "junior" form of citizenship for younger boys, particularly for the younger brothers of full members.) Nor was it for those who had become adults. "Citizens" of the "republic" had to leave at eighteen, when they joined the adult world and became alumni. According to Robbins, writing in 1922, alumni identified many of the boys who would end up joining. There was no entitlement, however; and Robbins emphasized that many applicants were turned down. A boy had to "win" his way in, just as he would have had to if he wanted to join a gang. The gang metaphor was a recurrent motif, as were notions of wolf survival that Robbins drew from Jack London's novel *White Fang*: "Our boys are a good deal like White Fang. They grow strong through fighting for what they want."[60]

Not all boys who wanted to could become citizens. Some boys were probably too "bad" to get in, although that did not mean that Jack Robbins had abandoned them. Even after the BBR was established, Jack Robbins continued to try other forms of child "saving," for those who would fail at citizenship or who would be, for one reason or another, ineligible. Thus in the *Day Book*, in late 1915, he wrote a piece directed to readers who were not "prudes." The story was about two boys who needed care. Each of them had become "criminal." One had stolen a suitcase he was supposed to deliver to a hotel. He then spent nine months in St. Charles Reform School. Since then he had been the "victim of police persecution." His "criminal tendencies . . . were developed in his natural fight for existence." His life in institutions had made him "an enemy of the police and of the law. The rest of the badness in him he . . . picked up in the slums." He was now sixteen and homeless. The other boy was admittedly of "criminal tendencies." He had never learned "right from wrong," and he had been "brutalized by ill-treatment and morally stunted by improper environment." He owed "the world no good will." He had spent eight of his nearly seventeen years in institutions. Robbins hoped there was a Good Samaritan or Good Samaritans who would give each boy a chance (he reminded readers of the kindly Mrs. White who had provided a home for the pseudonymous Harold Wray). But he said nothing in the piece about what the BBR might offer them. Robbins, one might imagine, was implicitly distinguishing these actual boy criminals from the possible or potential or inchoate criminals that were the BBR's citizenry. He may have been marking a distinction between those eligible for citizenship and those who were not. Surely there were many deemed ineligible, although, as we will see in the next chapter, there may have been very bad boys who wanted to join the BBR.[61]

The investigating committee, the third of the core committees, negotiated much of what might be called the foreign policy of the BBR: its relationships with an outside world, with the adult world. Its "motto" was that it investigated "all personal difficulties of boys." That meant, according to the constitution, first, "to look into all matters of charity, but not to accept charity for the organization unless accepted by the City Council." Second, it meant to ask for "any or all moneys expended in behalf of needy boys." Third, it meant to "investigate all matters in relation to the delinquency of boys as such matters arise." Fourth, it meant "to collect and distribute books, magazines, clothes, etc., from persons in the community and distribute such to boys who are in need."

Apparently, the third of those four duties quickly became its primary one. And over time that charge turned into a much more expansive—and politically and legally fraught—set of missions. The investigating committee's work included making "an average of three calls a week in homes where there are boys in trouble," meeting "boys who are discharged from orphan homes," and communicating "with boys who are in institutions." It also investigated and reported on cases of mistreatment. Its members went to court to advocate for boys in trouble. It met with the police and with correction officers. A 1938 description of the BBR reported that the investigating committee's motto had changed to "While there is a boy in jail, we too are prisoners." By then, the committee's relationship with the courts and the jails and the police was described as "friendly." Not so much, though, earlier on.[62]

* * *

Consider three episodes in the early history of the Boys' Brotherhood Republic.

In late October 1915, according to *the Day Book*, the "wideawake" boys of the BBR declared war on the introduction of fingerprinting both into the juvenile court and into the Boys' Court, the court for young offenders who had aged out of Chicago's juvenile court. They went to legal aid to "fight this injustice." Ralph Goodman, then the mayor, wrote that mandatory fingerprinting "did not please our boys because we felt it was too hard on a boy and was apt to do more harm than good. It would undoubtedly make a boy feel bad to know that his finger-prints were on file forever in the juvenile court, and in the sensitive young mind of a boy it would probably be the cause of bringing him up before the judge again, and of course we didn't want to see that." They regarded the practice as a "crime inviter" and "absolutely unfair." They won a victory when Judge Merritt Pinckney, of the Juvenile Court, promised that no fingerprints would be taken in his court. Chief Justice Harry Olson, a leading eugenicist and the judge of the Boys' Court, promised that only the fingerprints of "mental defectives" would be taken in his court.[63]

As Goodman told the story, he met with Olson. Olson agreed that for others, for ordinary boys, it was not good to keep such records. But what of the feebleminded? Olson thought they should be kept away from society. Forever? If possible. Goodman and Olson then made a bargain, as Goodman remembered it. Olson promised to stop the practice of fingerprinting boys and to provide the BBR a 360-acre farm where "demented and feeble minded boys could be kept." And to show his enthusiasm, Olson "donated" or promised to donate "a live bull to the colony." Not surprisingly, there had not yet been any work done on purchasing or constructing that colony. Nor would it ever come into existence. (And I find no further mention of the bull.) But the boys of the BBR would not be fingerprinted. And stopping fingerprinting led the "citizens" of the BBR to raise a banner in their "city hall." It said: "In memory of our victory for the boys of Chicago, November 20, 1915."[64]

A second story: In the summer of 1916, William Ulrey, a twelve-year-old boy, still too young to join but on the waiting list to become a citizen of the BBR, was killed on the Michigan lakeshore grounds of the very elite Saddle and Cycle Club. He died of lockjaw or tetanus poisoning, after a gardener, Nicholas Moga, threw pruning shears at him. Ulrey had been trespassing on club property.

What had happened? At Moga's trial, two companions of the boy described how they had left one beach to go to the pier at the Edgewater Hotel, so that they could dive. They had received permission to cross the Saddle and Cycle Club's grounds and its fenced-off beach to get there. When they wanted to go home, the waves were too heavy for them to swim around the grounds. They knew they would be arrested if they walked on the road in their swimsuits. So they decided to recross the club's grounds, near the lake, where they thought they would not bother anyone. When they encountered Moga, the gardener, they asked him for permission. Instead he chased them, and, when it looked like they were getting away, he threw the shears at Ulrey (or Ulrich), wounding him on both sides of his spine.[65]

The BBR turned the story into a critique of elite clubs like the Saddle and Cycle Club. At a general meeting, the citizenry voted first to offer their aid to the state prosecutor. Still, prosecuting Moga was a secondary concern.

They planned to gather fifty thousand signatures in a petition to protest the "silk stocking" directors of the club who insisted that their gardener had the right to hurl heavy shears at a little boy because he was a trespasser. One speech at the meeting questioned whether any property was so "sacred" that a boy could be killed for trespassing on it. Another speech, given by Harry Branovitz, by then the BBR mayor, began, "A boy has been murdered because he had the nerve to trespass on grounds which belong to a club for men who probably never did a lick of work." According to the *Chicago Examiner*, the BBR had undertaken "a finish fight" for "freedom for boys" and for the "immortal boy's right of trespass." This was their "first great fight for boys' rights." The BBR emphasized that it wanted to indict the cold-blooded directors who were using their wealth and influence to suppress the story, rather than the laborer, who was doing their bidding. "Please make clear," said the BBR city clerk, "that it is not our intention to prosecute Moga. It is to protect boys."[66]

Apparently, Ulrey's father was angry that the BBR had abandoned the prosecution of Moga. A citizen of the BBR responded in the *Day Book*: "Would it bring your boy back if this man was sent to prison? Would you derive any benefits if this man was taken away from his family?" Jack Robbins made a statement that continued that theme. The boys of the BBR were "humanitarians," not "prosecutors." Thus they were less interested in sending a poor worker to jail. Moga, he thought had merely intended to scare Ulrey, and it seemed to Robbins that he was not getting "a square deal." Still, "We don't want it understood . . . that we are conceding the property of the Saddle and Cycle Club where Ulrey was injured as private. The grounds, in our estimation, are public, but Moga was employed there." Moga, Robbins concluded, had lost his temper because in his ignorance he did not know "the ways of the American boy."[67]

Soon, the story of Ulrey's death became a negotiating opportunity to open up the beaches of the city. In December, the citizens of the BBR once again insisted that they were not after Moga. They wanted to ensure "that both sides in the trial get fair treatment." What they would continue to fight for, however, was "the right to use the property in front of the Saddle and Cycle club." They believed it was public property, and the club had "no right to hog it and drive boys away." The BBR hired an attorney. They drafted a petition to various state officials asking them to determine exactly what rights boys had to use the various beaches in the city and whether a private club had the right to put up barbed wire to keep nonmembers out from what was, they insisted, public property. Relying on an opinion by a member of the Illinois Rivers and Lakes Commission, that the lakeshore in front of the club was public property ("The riparian rights of the property owner along the shore give him simply access to the lake, but no special privileges"), the BBR circulated petitions to be presented to Chicago's mayor.[68]

At the end of July, the *Day Book* ran a longer article about the Saddle and Cycle Club's beach, about its fences and the guards who kept "common bathers" from "profaning" the sands of the club." Not that the beach was being used. The next beach over was crowded, but the "swells" of the club found lake bathing "too common" for their taste. When the *Day Book*'s reporter walked by the club after taking a swim in the lake, he saw Colin C. Fyffe drive by in his "costly car." Fyffe was the "attorney to millionaires and million dollar corporations," and he was leading the Saddle and Cycle Club's fight to keep boys out. But he never used the beach, either.[69]

By early August, the BBR's attorney had met with Chicago's corporation counsel. According to him, the Saddle and Cycle Club's assertion of ownership of the beach violated federal law, laws governing navigable waters, the state's river and lakes law, and the police powers of the city. He didn't think the club had "a leg to stand on" when it ran a barbed-wire fence into Lake Michigan and claimed that "the boys of the city must not go upon the beach behind that fence." The attorney thought the "proper beginning" would be for the city to condemn the land along the lakefront to become a park or a public beach. But he also noted: "If the corporation [of Chicago] does not act, the Boys' Brotherhood Republic will, . . . and it will start condemnation proceedings." He was preparing a brief that would be used to open up the beaches of Wilmette, further up the North Shore of Lake Michigan.[70]

The Jewish *Sentinel* praised the "remarkable methods" of the BBR, an organization founded, as the paper noted, by a "co-religionist, who was formerly an inmate of a reform school," and "maintained by an unusually aggressive group of young Jews living on the West Side." Instead of devising "gang methods" with the object of "getting even" violently, as a Gentile juvenile group might have done, the case was being handled as if by "the most capable lawyers." All should be surprised and pleased at the legal sense and ability of the boys. Whether they succeeded or not, they had triumphed "in revealing to all how law abiding such boys can be." (The *Sentinel* went on to suggest that the BBR might take their legal skills into other regulatory arenas, including enforcement of the law forbidding boys under fourteen from entering burlesque shows—not something that apparently much interested the boys.)[71]

On the other hand, as if to prove that they had not become entirely moderate and law abiding, on the first anniversary of the boy Ulrey's death, the BBR

MEMORIAL: MEMBERS OF <MARK><SPAN CLASS="HIT">BOYS</SPAN></MARK>' ...
Chicago Daily Tribune (1872-1922); Aug 6, 1917; ProQuest Historical Newspapers: Chicago Tribune
pg. 3

THE CHICAGO DAILY TRIBUNE: MONDAY, AUGUST 6, 1917.

Figure 9: The BBR marches on the Saddle and Cycle Club, 1917. *Chicago Daily Tribune*, August 6, 1917. Image published with permission of ProQuest LLC. Further reproduction is prohibited without permission.

citizenry marched onto the grounds of the Saddle and Cycle Club as a memorial to his death. They marched through once and attempted to do so a second time. But the police were called to stop them. The boys prepared to "storm" a fence put up to keep them out. "A juvenile riot impended," according to the *Chicago Tribune*. But then, in the nick of time, the president of the Saddle and Cycle Club gave the boys permission to swim on the club's beach. The threat of violence had worked. And the boys showed their gifts for civil disobedience along with their legal skills (see figure 9).[72]

The third episode represented a return by the BBR to one of Jack Robbins's earlier passions. By early 1918, in copy that ran in dozens of papers around the country, the BBR announced plans to send two members, accompanied by Jack Robbins, to find "the meanest, the toughest, the most no-account, the most dishonest, the most evil, vicious, wicked—in fact, the worst boy morally that a human being can be." The goal was, once again, experimental. That bad boy would come to live in the BBR, where he would be transformed. No longer to Nevada. Instead, the boy would come to live in Chicago's BBR, the "boy governed institution where the youth of the windy city are trained and moulded into bigger and better boys." The experiment would "prove" that "bad boys" were "the products of society and environment." Or as Jack Robbins wrote to the editor of the Perth Amboy paper: The "idea" was "to prove to the world that good environment and not reform school will reform boys."[73]

According to the newspapers, a committee of boys would leave in February to tour twelve large cities in search of the 100 percent bad boy. One member of the committee thought that they would need no more than six weeks to turn that boy into a 100 percent good boy.[74] The tour was designed to find a boy "so thoroughly evil, dishonest, vicious, wicked; so downright 'tough' that everybody who knows him—even his own mother—is sure that his case is hopeless." When they found this boy, they were going to "transplant him to Chicago, and make him a member of our Republic." That would "give him a human chance and develop the spark of manhood that every boy has in him." While he was in Chicago, he would not be "preached to and scolded and prayed over." He would be "allowed to work out his salvation in a natural way, under the guidance of fellow members of the Boys' Brotherhood, who were once almost as tough as he." The present experiment would be "watched by thousands of big hearted men and women who believe as we do, about the spark of goodness in the worst of boys."[75]

A skeptical column in a Pittsburgh paper, under the headline "Would Grow Wings on Prize Bad Boy," began with praise for the nobility of the enterprise. But it then worried whether the boys would take enough precautions to make sure that the chosen boy was not mentally defective. Would the experiment disprove an organic theory of bad boyness? The author was not supportive of either position. That is, he approved neither of eugenics nor of the BBR's faith that "society and environment" lay at the root of what made a bad boy a bad boy. Allowance ought to be made for "what some call pure cussedness, but which often turns out to be only a desire for fun." But mostly the author wanted to question the existence of a 100 percent bad boy, though the author conceded the "brotherhood" would have no difficulty in finding a boy who will give them much trouble, enough to teach them that there might be "some virtue in the environment of the woodshed."[76]

The Perth Amboy paper provided a more extended response to Jack Robbins's and the boys' renewed efforts to find the worst boy. Robbins was remembered as a "rabid socialist" and as a follower of Upton Sinclair and Jack London. He was also remembered as having been a tobacco salesman before he had assumed a new identity in Chicago. Robbins had written the paper to announce a planned visit to the city (along with Trenton), as he and the boys continued their search for the "worst" boy. This time Robbins thought it likely that "a real bad boy" of the sort they were looking for would be found in Perth Amboy, since the city "never did anything to stop boys from going wrong."[77]

Robbins's last comment about Perth Amboy led the paper to interview various local reformers and officials (those "whose activities bring them in constant touch with boys and their doings"), to discover if it was true that nothing was being done for boys in the town. Predictably, those interviewed rejected the notion that the worst boy would be found there. The local prosecutor said that nothing more than an occasional burglary or petty larceny could be found. And suppressing the "junkman evil" (presumably, junkmen offered a market for fencing or reselling what boys might steal) would reduce what problems there were. The "malicious mischief" that characterized a truly bad boy was almost unknown in the city. Another Perth Amboy official thought that Kaiser Wilhelm was a better candidate for selection as worst boy than anyone in New Jersey. In any event, "why pick on Perth Amboy and Trenton?" The head of the local YMCA admitted that there were some bad boys. "Where is the city that hasn't" got such? But all that most boys needed was guidance, and they were being molded properly by the YMCA into "great specimens." In any event, Robbins wouldn't know what was going on in Perth Amboy, because he long ago "shook the dust of the city he claims to love . . . off his feet," well before the creation of the varieties of institutions that now served boys. What institutions? Those included a YMCA, a YMHA, a recorder's court, and a juvenile court in the county seat in New Brunswick. Robbins knew nothing of the work these institutions were doing. Nor had he any awareness of the public parks newly built. Nor was he aware of the many voluntary organizations that had come into existence. When the journalist interviewed Miss Alice Goddard, the local librarian, she emphasized that many boys found their minds occupied at the library, though she also conceded that they also needed more playgrounds and a better juvenile court system as a "preventative and corrective" measure. She worried that the recent closing of the schools and the playgrounds was a problem. (Was that because of the 1918 flu pandemic?) The city recorder considered the work of Robbins "as so much nonsense."[78]

In May, following visits to Pittsburgh, Philadelphia, Wilmington, and elsewhere, and before moving on to New York and Brooklyn, Robbins, the "one time resident," finally arrived in Perth Amboy. He was accompanied by the mayor and the city clerk of the BBR. The paper labeled them a "queer trio on a queer errand." They were going to spend a day going through the juvenile court records in their search for a 100 percent bad boy. In Pittsburgh they had found an 81 percent bad boy, but no worse than that. They hoped for more from Perth Amboy. They needed an "incorrigible," a boy who associated with "thieves, vicious or immoral persons," who was growing up in "idleness and crime." Or one who frequented "houses of ill-repute" or saloons or places where there was gambling. "He must be a boy who often patronizes pool rooms or bucket shops, . . . who is known to wander about the streets at night without any lawful business or occupation." He should be a boy found in railroad yards and who jumped on moving trains. "He must be a user of vile, obscene, vulgar, profane, or indecent language." He must be a gang leader, and he should have been arrested no fewer than five times. He must be identified as a "hopeless case" by juvenile probation officers.[79]

Robbins and the BBR officers now expected that six months of kindly treatment at the Boys' Brotherhood Republic home in Chicago would be sufficient to produce positive change. "Any boy can be reformed if work on him is started at the right time." That is, if the work began before he was seventeen or so, before he became "hardened." One needed to turn "energy and enthusiasm into the right channels." The citizens of the BBR would set the "right example" for him. The experiment would provide a solution to the "boy problem," including the growing problem of juvenile delinquency that the European war might have exacerbated. After all, 50 percent of the citizens of the BBR had once been "notorious bad boys." If membership in the BBR had worked for them, why not for him?

Apparently, no boy in Perth Amboy qualified for the designation of the worst of the worst. Likewise, a return visit to Pittsburgh once again revealed to the "Chicago hunters of evil" that no one was quite bad enough. The percentages were not high enough. "Mex" stole Robbins's pen, which might have allowed him to win the prize. But then he made the mistake of telling the truth and of showing too much eagerness to go to Chicago. It looked like a Cleveland boy would win in the end, even though he too had some good qualities.[80]

In June, Robbins and the boys of the BBR thought they had found a bad enough Pittsburgh boy. But Walter Black, Pittsburgh's chief probation officer disagreed. And he did so "with wrath and bubbling indignation, and a certain sense of outraged civic pride." The identified bad boy wasn't the worst boy in Pittsburgh. He may have begun his criminal career as "an arson bug" at age seven. But "pooh-pooh," said Probation Officer Black. He had a boy in court who had started stealing horses at six. Second of all, Chicago had more bad boys (worse boys) than Pittsburgh, looking at the juvenile-delinquency statistics. And third, under no circumstances would he release the boy. There was no reason to allow a transfer of parole to the BBR in Chicago. He thought the whole idea of Robbins's project was wrongheaded, since it made a hero of a bad boy, and it created an incentive for the boy to live up to or down to his badness.[81]

What happened next is not clear. Papers around the country announced that the search for the worst boy was over and that the Pittsburgh boy had "won." But whether Black, the probation officer, did in the end release him to go to Chicago was not said. Newspaper attention, fickle as always, disappeared. The story died.[82]

* * *

At about the same time that the search for the worst boy did or did not reach a conclusion, the twelfth annual "Boys' Work Conference" met at the University of Pennsylvania in Philadelphia. The conference was held under the auspices of the Boys' Club Federation and sponsored by the Federation's journal, by then called *Work with Boys: A Magazine of Methods*. Robbins had been invited to speak to the conference, and he came, along with the "boy mayor" and the "boy city clerk" of the Boys' Brotherhood Republic. Their talks on the second day of the conference produced much controversy and discussion. Disagreement with him "caused a flutter on the convention floor." There was worry that he and the boys were being heckled, but Charles C. Keith, writing in the journal, thought Robbins had brought it "down upon his own head." His "spectacular method" of advertising for the worst boy in America, was enough "to invite criticism from all over the land." Keith also noted that, as of the hour of publication, Robbins's "pursuit" of the worst boy still continued.[83]

When Jack Robbins spoke on the second day of the Boys' Work Conference, he looked, according to Keith, "much milder than his advertisements. He appeared to be perfectly docile and harmless." The boys who accompanied him were said to be "capable, frank, withal boyish." And also, "genuine, hearty, unashamed boys." One of them would lead the cheering and singing of the attending club boys at the closing banquet. He had a "particularly pleasing personality." Keith, the editor, hoped the boy "survived the exploiting tour without hurt, and that his head was no larger than his hat when he returned in triumph to humdrum Chicago." It was. he thought, hard "to reconcile the conservatism of this man [Robbins] and his boys with the rash and braggart method of his publicity literature."[84]

Jack Robbins began his speech by acknowledging that there was much opposition to a self-governed club. What was his role as its superintendent? By design it was limited. To take one example, Robbins said he could not "of myself come and tell you the story of our republic." When the invitation came to him, he "turned it over" to the boys, evidently his usual practice. They decided on two delegates to go with him to talk at the conference.[85]

Robbins continued: Most of the boys had once been delinquents. Robbins was not yet ready to say, four years after the founding of the BBR, whether self-government was entirely successful as a cure for delinquency. Still, they got jobs for boys, and they held "boys' job days" (in 1917, they secured boys 713 jobs in one day, and in 1918, they secured 1037 jobs for boys in a day). They had a dormitory for boys without homes or who were runaways. They had little destruction in their facilities. He described the cheap chairs they bought, nearly all of which still survived.

He then turned the dais over to Manford Haskell, the elected clerk of the BBR, who spoke next: "I am not a boy evangelist, . . . But I am a lot better than I used to be." Still, he remained not "particular" what time he got to church, and he could still take care of himself "in a scrap." He was sure he belonged to "the very best club in America"[86] (see figure 10).

Haskell, the BBR clerk, continued: When a fellow quit his job, "we" believe that the fault lay with the employer. And when a fellow left home, there may have been "something wrong with the home." There were no bad boys. They stuck together in the Republic. They helped the fellow that was down. "And if we can't cure him with silk gloves, well, maybe some other gloves are better." (Presumably, boxing gloves.) The club was self-supporting. They all worked, fought hard, and earned what they had. Employers waited for weeks to get a boy from the Republic because they knew such a boy would "give his very best." He "must make good." They did all they could "for the boys of Chicago."[87]

Joe Williams (or Willens), the BBR mayor, then spoke (see figure 11). He told how he had been elected. He emphasized that the club had no gymnasium, no swimming pool, no marble walls. He had joined in order to fight "a fellow whom he had a grouch against. But he found that the club had a better way." He then told how the BBR had started a successful campaign to stop the practice of fingerprinting every boy the first time caught by the police. "No matter what for—even if it was for jumping on the back of wagons."[88]

Figure 10: BBR city clerk Manford Haskell, 1918. Author's collection.

The BBR presentation ended.

Several conference delegates jumped to their feet, wanting to speak. But there was no time left that day. The next day, time was reserved for discussion with and about Jack Robbins and the BBR. One of the delegates began by challenging the claim that there were no bad boys. Mr. Albert, the chair of the

Figure 11: BBR mayor Joe Willens, 1918. Author's collection.

meeting, responded: The statement came from a boy, from Manford Haskell, and he would rather hear a boy say that than a grown man. He himself (Albert) was not sure whether there were boys who were naturally bad. Someone from Chicago spoke: He thought that while placing boys "on their good behavior" produced some results, he thought there "must be good advice and a guiding hand, seen or unseen" (Robbins, presumably) that lay behind the BBR.[89]

Then sharper critiques began. A Mr. Jarvis, from Indiana, thought that Robbins was not being clear about the jobs his boys were offered and took. He also wondered whether Robbins was doing anything to "make true patriotic Americans out of his boys." Mr. Woodhall, from Troy, New York, was opposed to "the entire scheme," though he wished to be "charitable." There was "too much misdirected energy," and he was surprised to hear a superintendent admit that he was "permitted—permitted, mark you—to open his own mail. That a fourteen-year-old lad permits him." The job day, he thought, produced slackers. By contrast, in Troy, a boy had to sign up with the Chamber of Commerce. And "God help the boy who jumps from a job without first serving notice."[90]

Mr. Hughes, from Milwaukee, wanted to know how Robbins determined the goodness or badness of a bad boy in a city while only spending a few hours there. How, in particular, could he know that Milwaukee was the third-worst city in the United States in terms of its "bad boys"? Mr. Lewis of New York noted that employers needed references. Mr. Thompson, from Montreal, thought that Robbins was taken too seriously. His enthusiasm should be acknowledged. "And like a pup with a newspaper, he is going to chew it." From Lynn, Massachusetts, came a defense of the self-governing character of the newsboys' club there.[91]

Many objected to "all this foolish advertising" on Robbins's part. "Yellow gets nowhere." And a Montreal delegate wanted to know why one had to leave Chicago to find the worst boy in America. The boy who agreed to move to Chicago to be reformed was reformed already.[92]

Robbins then came up to answer questions and to try to "satisfy" critics. He gave some numbers. There were 273 members in the BBR; thirty-two were over eighteen; and twenty-three of those were now in the service. (This was, of course, in the midst of World War I.) Jarvis, the master of ceremonies, asked why he had not mentioned that earlier. Robbins responded: "Because we are not stage patriots." That declaration brought down the house. Round after round of applause followed.[93]

"I believe in advertising," Robbins continued, "whether you like it or not." The papers were willing to publish about "our Republic," "if we say it in the right manner. If one paper doesn't use it, another will." He admitted that not all boys stuck with the jobs they got on their job days. But he liked the job days because they were "a good publicity stunt." He did not go to other cities and try to undermine established clubs. That charge was unfounded. The newspapers exaggerated. He gave them facts, and they exaggerated. He "must not be blamed for all that appears."[94]

A Mr. Atkinson then spoke. He thought Robbins made "the blunder of his life" by looking outside Chicago for the worst boy. He also thought Robbins was "too free" in giving opinions to the newspapers. Still, he cautioned, one should not "reject the fruit of a tree because there is a caterpillar on that tree." People were "too hard" on Robbins, who was sincere and doing good work.

But most of those in the audience "frankly disliked his methods."[95]

FOUR

As Clara Laughlin Saw It: War, Energy, and Democracy

Jack Robbins continued to find ways to publicize the Boys' Brotherhood Republic, using the news and public events. And he remained the subject of a curious audience of journalists. But by the time of the 1918 "boy work" conference, it was increasingly the boys of the BBR, particularly its officers, that the public and the papers attended to.

In May 1918, for example, while in the midst of their renewed search for the worst boy, Robbins and the two BBR officers who had come with him to the Philadelphia conference took a side trip to New York City. They went to protest the scheduled execution of a boy, Paul Chapman, convicted of murder. The articles in the *New York Tribune* that covered that trip focused on the boys, leaving Jack Robbins to the side.

According to the articles, the boys met with Chapman's lawyers, and they also tried to organize members of local New York boys' clubs, "to collect a monster petition" to present to the governor. Joe Willens, the BBR mayor, couldn't understand "what's the matter with New York boys, that they need us to wake them up, . . . but, anyway, we fellows out in Chicago couldn't stand . . . to have a boy sent to the electric chair. We just had to get busy and come over here to help him get a new start in life." They had already talked with the New York governor when he visited Chicago in February, and he had said then he would meet them "half way." That probably meant that he intended to commute the sentence to life imprisonment. But now, in May 1918, they wanted more than that from him. They proposed to take Chapman back to Chicago, where he could live in the BBR. They would return him to New York when he was twenty-one, "a good, self-respecting man." There was nothing really wrong with him. "He just got a wrong start, and nobody helped to put him right." It didn't hurt that they had discovered that Chapman was born in Chicago.

While the boys were in New York, Mayor Willens had gone to Brooklyn to see Chapman's mother, to inform her of their plans, but she was not at home.[1]

The *Tribune* then turned the Chapman tale into a story about Chicago boys sightseeing in the city. They had not come to "seek their fortune or even to see the Statue of Liberty. The legends of Broadway, of penniless boys, hungry boys, and clever boys, all destined to be millionaires, took a new turn" with their arrival. The article quoted BBR clerk Manford Haskell talking about how tired he was from walking everywhere. The boys took pictures of "bootblacks" and other boys working in the city, and also of "babies playing on the East Side." They were, the paper reported, mandated to make a "full report" to the BBR citizenry when they got back to Chicago.[2]

The story concluded by describing the "one dissipation" they were allowed during their visit: a dinner at Sherry's, a famous New York restaurant. Jack Robbins, described as the founder of the BBR and their "guardian," had approved the dinner, although he did not attend himself. "Sherry's is nothing in my life, . . . but these boys have heard a lot about it." They were "just aching to sit down to dinner in a roomful of millionaires." The "fellows" in the BBR had chipped in enough money "for a feed at Sherry's." They each got two dollars. Robbins wasn't certain how much one could eat for that amount at the restaurant. The hotel staff warned the boys that "boys in short trousers and purple and white striped sweaters might not be welcomed" at the restaurant. But they were unable to discourage them—and the dinner was a success.[3]

In December 1918, the New York governor commuted Paul Chapman's sentence to life imprisonment. Jack Robbins wrote and published a passionate protest. Chapman should tear up the commutation, Robbins argued. He should demand his liberty, instead. A commutation was not what "we" fought for: "You are innocent and must go free. The boys of America are aroused as never before."[4]

The entry of the United States into World War I offered new opportunities for publicity. An article produced by the Associated Press headlined: "So-Called 'Bad' Boys Now Help Lick Kaiser." The story told about how BBR boys, who once "poured molasses on the cat at the age of 2 years, smashed window panes and chewed tobacco at 4, and stood before the yawning gates of reformatories at 15," now were employed in war industries and in harvesting fields. As many as 1,300 youths were placed in a single day as a result of the BBR's Boys' Job Day. There were plans to extend the organization to "all parts of America," in part to aid "young boys who have been left in stringent circumstances" because older family members had entered military service. Robbins was quoted as emphasizing that salaries were high in munitions plants, and boys were building substantial bank accounts. All the boys engaged in "war work" were getting "splendid results." Many of them were parolees from reform schools and other institutions. The BBR made a special effort to recruit "these lads," who often had difficulty finding jobs. Then, as so often, Robbins slipped into what may have been fantasy. He illustrated "the efficiency" of the BBR by describing the case of the "meanest boy of New York state," from Brooklyn, who had been sentenced to be executed. But after a "committee" of the BBR made a plea to the governor of New York, the boy was pardoned. He was now, according to Robbins, a high officer of the organization. And right now, Robbins concluded, "all our boys have but one big object: Help whip the Kaiser."[5]

But the war also increased anxieties about the "boy problem." An editorial in the *Perth Amboy Evening News*, headlined "Conservation of the Boy Crop." began by acknowledging that the writer had not previously taken the boy problem seriously. "'Boys will be boys,' and most of them turned out all right, good, honest, useful citizens, and for the rest we built prisons." But now, in 1918, the problem needed to be taken seriously, because "we" were "losing man power 'Over There' and we will go on making heavier and heavier sacrifices of life to the end that all the world shall be free from the hand of Hunnish despotism." And yet, the war had led to an increase in delinquency. No one knew the reasons, but it was a "fact," a matter of "court records and police blotters." The editorial then went on to sing the praises of the Boys' Brotherhood Republic in Chicago, as showing that "the way to reform a bad boy" was "to let loose his boyish energy and pent-up enthusiasm in ways wholesome and up-building." And not preaching to or punishing him.[6]

In August 1919, the Chicago Boys' Brotherhood Republic once again managed to gain the attention of newspapers across the country. Ben Lindsey, the Denver juvenile court judge and Progressive author, who had offered an early endorsement of the BBR, was to be fined five hundred dollars for contempt of court, for having refused to reveal to a criminal court what a boy had said to him in confidence in his juvenile court. The case was a complicated murder case involving accusations of sodomy. The BBR began a campaign to raise fifty thousand pennies. "If Colorado needs the money Chicago boys will furnish it." The fund existed, as the *Washington Herald* put it, because they remembered "Boyland's primal law: 'Thou shalt not squeal.'"[7]

Occasionally, conflict within the BBR would leak out, although mostly the BBR presented a unified front to the outside adult world. In October 1919, though, the *Chicago Tribune* "exposed" a scheme concocted by Jack Robbins, identified as a "youthful official," along with the then-mayor of the BBR, Jack Dwork. The goal was to have Judge Victor Arnold removed from Chicago's juvenile court and to have Judge Merritt Pinckney, the former judge, who had retired three years earlier, and who was on record as a supporter of the BBR, installed in his place. Arnold had ruled in a case that a father was free to give his unruly son "a licking." The judge defended himself. He was not opposed to the BBR, he said, as long as it was run for the "good of the boys" and not as a publicity scheme. This case was, he said, only one out of the thirty thousand cases he had decided. And he maintained that he had not been wrong in his decision: The boy needed a "thrashing," and it would do him more good than ten years in the reformatory would. Robbins, though, saw this ruling as an abuse and as an opportunity for free publicity, at least as the *Tribune* presented it. But three former BBR mayors, including one who was by then working as a probation officer, resigned from the BBR in protest.[8]

* * *

By 1920, the BBR had become an established institution, a presence in Chicago's thick landscape of social welfare and child-saving institutions. In that landscape it stood out because it embodied a kind of socialist solidarity, what might be called a horizontal constitution, that distinguished it from the hierarchical structures of most institutions organized for or to save boys in trouble. While Robbins, like other reformers of his day, framed his understanding of what boys needed using the language of masculinity and manliness, still, his version of manliness was always gentler and less focused on power or strength than predominant versions. It emphasized care and community, notions captured both by the language of the "pal" and the structures of self-government.[9]

In April and May 1920, Robbins once again organized a tour, with the goal of "nationalizing" the Chicago model. As before, he traveled with two "officers" of the BBR. Along the way, the two boys, identified by *the Washington Herald* as newsboys, visited the White House, where they asked Joseph Tumulty, President Wilson's secretary, to establish a national commission on boy welfare. The boys were asked if such a commission should be headed by a boy? "Undoubtedly," one boy replied. "If the commission is to prove successful, . . . it should have the benefit of the advice and counsel of boys who have, with our organization, demonstrated their ability to establish self-government." (Articles also devoted space to the boys' use of their savings to stay in the Waldorf-Astoria Hotel in New York, to attend Broadway shows, and to ride in hired automobiles [see figure 12]).[10]

Max Swiren (Elbow on Table) and Maurice Berkson.

"Home ain't nuthin' like this," was the expressed opinion of Max Swiren and Maurice Berkson, Chicago newsboys, each sixteen years old, and stopping at the Waldorf-Astoria Hotel in New York city. Max and Maurice, be it known, are District Attorney and Senator, respectively, of the Boys' Republic, and are in New York on a lecture tour. Before they left their beloved "Loop" they were given enough money to cover their expenses by members of the Rotary Club. Strutting along Peacock Alley with their thumbs in their vest armholes, Max and Maurice gave the swells the "up and down." "Nothin' in it; nothin' at all," said Max. "All these birds do is show off their soup-and-nuts frocks and pose like movie guys. No brains! No brains!" The only thing that perturbs them is that nobody will "take our kale and we want to spend our pack like millionnaires, so we can get the best of it."

Figure 12: BBR boys at the Waldorf-Astoria Hotel, 1920. *Daily Standard* (Kingston, Ontario, Canada), May 17, 1920.

What the BBR did appealed to some wealthy individuals. Edmund Hulbert, a banker who played a leading role in establishing the Federal Reserve Bank and was a close advisor of Woodrow Wilson, had become a strong supporter. He served as the chair of a board of trustees, which was apparently begun under his leadership. As he said in an interview in 1920, he agreed with Jack Robbins and with the premise of the BBR that "responsibility builds character. . . . They *accomplish* things. And it is all done by giving them [the boys] responsibility." Hulbert also quietly agreed to pay Robbins a small monthly salary, so that Robbins would no longer have to work as a tobacco salesman. And he was able to draw in a few other like-minded individuals to serve on the board.[11]

Criticism remained common among reformers and academic observers. The economist James Franklin Page questioned "the wisdom of a scheme of education which holds before young boys the machinery of government to the degree that the Republic does, or that places such large responsibilities on the shoulders of young boys, or that permits the criminal and the dark sides of life to be held before the young boy's vision to such extent as the plan of the Republic permits." Still, he concluded: "The principle of service which lies at the heart of the Republic is wholly commendable. . . . Work for boys is useless; work with boys is rewarding; work by boys is the keynote of future evangelism."[12]

By then, Wilfred S. Reynolds, the head of Chicago's Children's Home and Aid Society, was receiving enough inquiries about the BBR from colleagues running agencies elsewhere, outside Chicago, that he drafted a standard letter of information. The letter began with the understanding that "the fundamental principles" of the BBR were "sound," so long as "their operation" was "carefully guided and safe-guarded." What was "fascinating" was that the boys were doing "what grown-up men do." If one succeeded at "permitting a boy to imitate a man, he will be attracted and will be interested in so doing." The "scheme" drew in boys "who otherwise would engage in non-constructive, and in fact hurtful activities," such as participating in a gang. Without the BBR, their "leisure time" might have become "unguided, un-supervised, and in aimless channels."[13]

On the other hand, Reynolds warned of "certain" dangers: In particular, the model of the BBR risked offering too much democracy. "While this type of organization must be democratic, boys have not mature judgement and will take advantage of the freedom of democracy and through it will oftentimes take advantage of other boys." In that, they were no different from adults, but the results could be "disastrous." Writing in bland bureaucratic terms, he described what happened when a boy got into legal trouble. The "Republic" might then be used by the "boy members" to "express their displeasure that one of their brother acquaintances has been disciplined by court action," even though the discipline was "entirely justifiable and proper." There was then a tendency for the organization to critique or to challenge "well founded action on the part of the community which happens to displease the immature minds or feelings of these youngsters." This sort of thing had to be "guarded against."[14]

He noted that others also criticized the BBR out of a belief that boys were too young to be "imitating" adult responsibilities. The boys in the organization grew "too rapidly toward the mature." Reynolds did not agree with that criticism. Instead, he emphasized that in Chicago "a large number of active, comparatively unprivileged boys have been kept in protective channels through their participation in this type of organization."[15]

He acknowledged that this type of organization worked best with boys of "keen intellect." In Chicago, Jewish boys apparently benefited most, although he noted that there was also a successful branch in a largely Scandinavian section of the city.[16]

Reynolds admitted that his own organization, the Children's Home and Aid Society, had not been successful in its efforts to deal with the "boy problem." Why had the BBR succeeded where other child-saving organizations failed? The answer was, once again, the presence of Jack Robbins, who was "not a so-called Social worker." Robbins had "passed through the experience of [being] the unprivileged boy himself," and he had "a keen appreciation of those elements which interest and displease boy life." By 1920, according to Reynolds, Robbins had managed to attract "quite a group of substantial men and women to the support of this movement."[17]

Reynolds concluded this standardized letter with further praise for the BBR. So long as safeguards were put in place, it could be recommended to others "It is possible," he allowed, "to keep this movement free from the 'charity' idea[,] and it is possible to make it purely democratic," at least for some boys. One ought "to confine its participation to the boys that really need to be occupied by some facility other than they are able to properly find upon their own initiative through the ordinary community facilities." That is to say, it served boys who would not be reached by conventional boys' clubs and social services, those who otherwise would be out on the streets or in trouble with the law. He noted that the organization was cheap to run because the boys did the work.[18]

By 1920, then, the BBR was a recognized presence in Chicago institutional life. The BBR served the larger Chicago community, doing what other organizations failed at. The national newspaper coverage meant that boy workers from around the country wanted to learn about it as a possible model. And it expressed democratic values and practices, perhaps sometimes too much so.

* * *

Around the same time, Clara Laughlin (see figure 13) began to publish articles about the BBR. She had recently spent some portion of her very busy life immersed in the BBR. Laughlin, a prolific author who wrote fiction and movie scripts and many books about travel, as well as about social conditions in Chicago, often with an emphasis on the underappreciated labor of women (she was the only journalist who pointed to the significance of Myrtle Carpenter in producing Jack Robbins's success), had been sitting in on many meetings at the BBR. She wrote at least five articles for national journals about what she had observed.[19]

In October 1919, she published a long article that focused on the democratic character and promise of the BBR. It appeared in the *Ladies' Home Journal* (where else would you expect to find such a piece?), along with a shorter article in the same issue. The *Journal* appended a short editorial at the front of the article that proclaimed that what the Chicago boys were doing was a form of "real red-blooded work that beats any Americanization program in existence." It continued: "Here are boys doing for boys—by boys and with boys—a piece of work that many will say isn't true because it can't be true."[20]

Laughlin's long article began by challenging the common and prevalent notion that the war had made some boys worse because there were fewer adult men around to keep them "in order."[21] The citizens of the BBR disagreed: "There are no bad boys." By which the BBR meant that all boys were basically alike in their needs and in their nature—and nothing had changed because of the war. Both the BBR and Laughlin rejected notions of the deviant or the delinquent as being ontologically different and therefore properly separated from the "normal." All eugenic notions were rejected. Those who looked like "bad kids" were just "boys that never had a chance." To "prove" that all boys were basically alike, that any of them would respond well if treated well, the BBR had initiated the search for the "worst boy."[22]

According to Laughlin, the notoriety of the search for the worst boy came into being not because of the boys' desire for publicity, and not at the initiative of Jack Robbins, who went unmentioned, but because an Associated Press reporter had taken that statement by the boys, that boast that there were "no bad boys" and that all that was needed to change the apparently bad was the care and attention that the BBR offered, and put it onto the wires. News-

Figure 13: Clara Laughlin, 1910. Clara E. Laughlin Papers, Sophia Smith Collection, Smith College, Northampton, MA.

papers all over the country ran with it. And the challenge led "every town and hamlet," and many parents and probation officers, to claim that they had the worst boy. Letters poured into Chicago. The boys of the BBR read all of the letters, some describing boys for whom "everything had been done that the law allows, except hanging," and who might be getting ready for that when they "got old enough." The Chicago boys, she said, might have liked to take in all of them. But instead they sifted and sorted, until they arrived at a list of boys in twenty-seven towns and cities. And then they set out to find the right wrong boy.[23]

Two representatives were chosen to travel the country over, to each of the twenty-seven towns and cities, to "size up" the candidates. (Jack Robbins still went unmentioned.) Before leaving Chicago the two rehearsed what they would say and do, before the whole of the BBR. They had to prove that they could properly articulate what the BBR stood for to the rest of America. "We're going to represent you," they said . . . "so you ought to know what we're going to say. If you don't like it, now's the time to holler—not afterward."[24]

Here is the gist of what the two planned to say as they traveled the country, as Laughlin reported: They were not going out around the country looking merely "for a kid who stays out nights because he ain't got sense enough to go to a good home. We ain't looking for a kid whose father's afraid his boy won't grow up good, or whose mother cries because her baby boy don't tell her where he's going after supper." No. They were "looking for a kid that's never been able to call any man father. We're looking for a kid that's never had any mother to care whether he went straight or not." They were looking for a boy who "stays out nights and sleeps in wagons and under sidewalks because he ain't got no place else to sleep. We're looking for a kid that thinks everybody's agin him and that he's got to steal if he wants to live." And they continued in that vein, at least in Laughlin's rendering.[25]

The audience of boys found that acceptable. And then the two began their journey. Robbins's accompanying presence remained unmentioned.

Did they find such a boy? They did, Laughlin wrote, after conducting tests of their own devising, and without taking anybody's word for who was worst. (She did not identify where and how they found that boy.) Meanwhile, newspapers offered them "big money" for the exclusive story. And a vaudeville manager telegraphed them often, offering one hundred dollars a week for ten weeks, for that worst boy. "The boys were not a bit surprised to find out how foolish some big folks are."[26]

When they returned to Chicago, reporters and photographers were waiting, hoping to catch sight of the boy they had chosen. But the worst boy came later, when no one noticed. And his identity was kept from most of the boys in the BBR. He had a "black record," but that was hidden from the others.

They got him a job, placed him with a decent family, got him involved in "clean sport and good citizenship." And he "made good" almost without trying! "Today that boy is a splendid chap, and simply crazy to give other fellows a chance."[27]

Laughlin continued, mushing together various stories about the BBR. According to her, those same boys went on to Albany where they called on the governor to commute the death sentence of Paul Chapman. New York's governor, she wrote, looked at them "in amazement," and asked "what business" it was of them? Their answer was the BBR mantra: "Wherever there's a boy in trouble, we're in trouble." The story continued as if the governor commuted Chapman's sentence in response. And he so liked "their way of doing things," that he asked them to be sure to create more BBRs, so that when his own son would be big enough to do work like they had done, there would be an organization like it for him to join.[28]

Laughlin's article then took a turn in a different direction. According to her, a "bunch" of Chicago boys, a gang, had heard about what the two representatives had done. This was a different group, this gang, filled with boys who would properly draw the attention of the police. That is, it was a criminal gang, made up of genuinely bad boys, true delinquents. These were boys who knew many ways to make trouble. Some in the gang were missing. Thirty-nine out of one hundred were doing time in prison or awaiting trial in jail. "Boys of school age, mind you—only ten, twelve, fourteen years of age, hardly any of them as old as sixteen years." Yet there were murderers among them, and half were "gun toters." Stealing automobiles was "baby's play" for them, preparation for "pay-off holdups, suburban bank robberies[,] and like crimes." A table attached to the article in the *Ladies' Home Journal* presented, without sources or citations, statistics for two "gangs," before they connected to the BBR. In one, 15 percent were bank robbers, 80 percent were pickpockets, and 50 percent carried guns at all times. In the other, 40 percent were murderers, 50 percent were "automobile bandits," and 20 percent were in jail. The table appended a statement: today 98 percent were "decent," presumably because of the good work of the BBR.[29]

Laughlin editorialized: "Sounds awful—doesn't it?" It was, and the boys in the criminal gang knew it, although they didn't feel they were so terrible. "They just wanted excitement, as every boy does." Yet wherever they looked for excitement, it got them "in bad."

The gang's leader reflected on the bad things that were happening to them, how many of them were in jail or in prison. The police caught them. They couldn't get away. He was "sick" of the "whole business."

But what to do? The adults they interacted with, adults who opposed "gun toting and hold-ups and automobile stealing," offered them nothing ("nothing to get excited about"), except "washing behind your ears and about putting a penny in the plate." Would the BBR offer a better way than the adult reformers, the child savers? Perhaps worth a try, the leader thought. "More fun, a million times more than we ever had—an' more excitement—an' it don't get 'em in bad, either; it . . . leaves 'em [free to] enjoy themselves all at one time." Most importantly, those in the BBR managed it without anyone leading them by the hand. They did it "themselves. . . . It's kids for kids, an' it's *dif'runt!*"[30]

The rest of the gang didn't believe him; it was all too good to be true. But they took a chance, and they sent the leader to talk with the BBR. The leader went and watched, and he asked the citizens of the BBR how to make gang members into something more than "jailbirds." The boy leaders of the BBR promised to help.

According to Laughlin, the BBR then rented a hall over a saloon for one dollar, one with windows "thick with dust, . . . floor foul with dirt, whose atmosphere seemed to embalm all the odors of stale beer and rank tobacco and unclean clothing in the world." (Laughlin liked to give the *Journal's* predictably middle-class female readers a taste of another world.). On a Monday night, all the boys from the criminal gang were there, filling up the place. These were "boys who wanted to learn how to be good citizens," along with boys from the BBR, who were there "to teach them how."

What was said at that meeting was, as she put it, "the real stuff!" None of the talk that made boys "so uncomfortable." Gang members were told how to have fun, how to be part of a good gang, how to follow a leader and how to compete to be the leader, and to do things that no one believed they could do. And they learned how to do those things "without getting in bad." Just practical talk. And the result was that all the gang members joined the BBR.[31]

Laughlin's narrative skipped around. Another time, two BBR boys went to a national convention on housing problems held in Chicago. One of the boys spoke up, after having listened. "I never was in a place before where people, instead of getting up and saying what they think, read these here things you call papers." He had listened to talk about many things, about cubic feet of space and what to do with garbage. But no one mentioned what houses are "princip'ly for—which is [for] boys!" Maybe that was an overstatement. But one might think that planning should include thinking about how boys would be part of households. Yet too many houses were built as if boys had nothing to do but mess them up or break things. The boy continued, in Laughlin's narration: "Maybe you've noticed that a house can be very large and yet not seem to have room enough in it for a hearty, healthy, growing boy. And maybe you've lived in a small house or a small flat where [there] were four or five or six or seven people of all ages, from a baby that wakes easily to a grandma that's nervous, and know how much room there is for a boy in a house like that—which is the kind that most boys live in. Boys get in the way of older folks, and lots of older folks jump on boys for things that are not bad things at all, but just bothersome to other people."[32]

There was, the boy continued, in his lecture to the housing convention, a time in every boy's life when he "naturally hankers" to be an "outlaw." He craves excitement, and he "aches to cut loose." He is tired of doing as he is told. He wants to do things his own way. Meanwhile, the adult world insisted on leading him down a path "that others have tried and found safe, respectable and uninteresting." In the grip of the hankering for excitement, a boy might then try to "beat" the game. And he might end up in a life of crime. If that happened, it was not the boy's fault. It was the fault of older people who had failed to show the boy that "playing the game" could be fun.

Too many of those who tried to show boys how to play the game did it by way of pretense, "playing pretend." Presumably, this language was a somewhat buried critique of the George Junior Republics and similar sites, where, under adult supervision, boys played at adult roles. But, Laughlin continued, channeling the voice of the boy addressing the housing conference, you can't do that with a "real red-blooded boy." He wants the "real thing." And he would rather be an "honest-to-goodness boy bandit" than a "make-believe goody boy" pretending he was "some use in the world." Boys needed real things to do, of the sort that they soon would have to do when they became men. And that was how the Boys' Brotherhood Republic came to be.[33]

At this point in her article, Clara Laughlin turned briefly to Jack Robbins ("a boy still, though grown folks might, looking at him, think him a man") and to his story about the origins of the republic in 1914. He was then, according to her version, living on the west side of Chicago "where boys are sure enough thick. Boys, boys, boys . . . everywhere. . . . And so the Brotherhood started." She passed by the struggles that occurred as it grew. That story was "full of combat against the stubborn prejudices of a world of folks who think of boys as 'problems' to be 'solved.'" Her overarching point, once again, was that the only real solution was to make boys responsible for their own fates and situations—and to give them a structure of republican self-government by which they could serve one another.

The structure of the BBR, using forms drawn from city governments, depended on an active citizenry and on a restricted citizenry. Any boy in Chicago could draw on the services of the BBR, particularly its job-seeking services. "But only the right kind of boy" could be "admitted into what is called 'the citizenry' and be given that sacred thing—a vote." And there had to be space available for that boy. In 1919, according to Laughlin, there was a long waiting list of applicants. The BBR could only accept so many boys as could be kept busy and active working on civic activities and for "the common good." Others had to wait.[34]

She described what she called the "institutional" committee, elsewhere known as the "investigating" committee: how it took the names, addresses, and records of all boys to be released from correctional institutions. The committee's members visited each of those boys. These committee members were "young citizens who have worked hard all day." Most of them were also "doing [some] sort of night study." And yet they went "on miles-long street-car rides during their evenings off . . . [to] locate the boys who have to 'begin over.'" They learned about home conditions. They worked to win the boy's confidence, which was not an easy task after a boy had completed a stint in a reform school or a jail. And the boy would be released into their care.

Then she retailed the narrative of how the boys of the BBR challenged mandatory fingerprinting. In her version, the boys who confronted the eugenicist Chief Judge Olson listened respectfully when he explained that it was important for the safety of citizens that some classes of boy offenders be fingerprinted. Olson agreed that "boys arrested for throwing a snowball or otherwise getting in people's way should not be treated like young criminals." A compromise was reached. Those merely "letting off steam" would not be fingerprinted. And the boys reached an understanding of the ways fingerprinting protected society. All this progress was achieved, she wrote, for the cost of car fare. Adult crime commissions could learn from their success.[35]

She turned to the recent problem of boys spending nights in all-night movie houses. The situation occurred when, in the midst of World War I and a labor shortage, city boys had left school and city work to do farm labor. "They set off, amid great hurrahs, to save the nation." Unfortunately, not many stayed long on the farms. They were not good at farming, and the farmers were not good to them. So, they drifted back to Chicago. But they didn't want to go home. And so, out of embarrassment, many of them were sleeping in all-night movie theaters. They "would rather sit, hungry, in a nickel show than tell their folks they hadn't saved the nation." But these theaters were not safe places for them to be, for reasons she did not feel the need to detail. And the boys of the

BBR, according to Laughlin, were "on the job." They "trudged around at night looking for boys who needed them." They rescued the boys from the theaters. They did work that should have been done by "adult citizens of the 'We should worry' class." According to her, had those adult citizens done their work there would be no Bolshevist leaders in the "old world," who had lived in the United States and left "full of fury" against American law and order.

The story about the boys in the all-night movie houses then shifted to attend to one boy found in a theater, who wore what looked like what had once been fancier clothes. The BBR boys took him back to their headquarters, gave him food and a place to sleep. The next day he got new clothes, and they took him downtown and got him a job.[36]

Who was he? The spoiled child of wealthy parents who lived in another city. He had wasted his "too big" allowance. He gambled and "got in wrong," and he ran away. Even after he joined the BBR, he continued to spend more than he had, borrowing from boys who had nothing, and he didn't pay back what he owed those poor boys. The suggestion was made that his parents should be called, to pick him up and to pay back his debts. But the members were "aghast" at that suggestion. One did not "snitch" just to get back a little money. Instead, they let him stay, "and he made good." And eventually his parents moved to Chicago, after he told them his story. Laughlin's conclusion: "Nor are these the only parents who have come to Chicago in the same way and gladly taken up a new life with a young son happy in a new manliness."

Laughlin next described the BBR's employment office, focusing on the ways the boys who ran the office worked to find out what they could about the employer and the conditions of employment. She noted the BBR's yearly "Boys' Job Days," which were now proclaimed by Chicago's adult mayor and which, she said, yearly found places for eight hundred to a thousand boys. She emphasized that employers would rather have a boy's BBR citizenship card than any other recommendation.

There were those, in its early days, who predicted that the structure of the republic (or perhaps its connections with socialists) would "ruin" boys for business, would make them "smarty" and "insubordinate." But exactly the opposite was the truth. BBR citizens had learned the "boss" side of the "game." They had training in cooperation, along with initiative and loyalty. "There is the same difference between them and the type of boy who used to be considered ideal, as there is between the soldiers of democracy and the soldiers of autocracy." She added that fifty-one members of the BBR had served in the late war, two of whom gave their lives "for world democracy." All were volunteers.[37]

In the last part of the article, Laughlin noted that the boys were also devoted to athletics, dancing, summer camps, indoor games. They were regular boys. An anecdote about a wrestling tournament seemed to end with the champion telling the boys to cut out booze and tobacco and go to bed early. But then Laughlin learned that this "champion" was just out of the hospital having been treated for extreme delirium tremens. She thought that knowledge would disappoint the boys. She worried that they would be disillusioned at discovering his alcoholism. "But, foolish me!" The boys knew all about the matter. "But that's all right. He knows what's the right thing to do, even if he ain't strong enough to do it. We know. He wants to see us go straight, even if he can't."

At a Chicago City Council meeting devoted to a bill to fund and support backyard gardens, one of the BBR citizens asked to speak. The mayor agreed. "I just want to remind this council," the boy said, "that the most important crop Chicago raises is boys, and mighty little is spent weeding it."

Laughlin turned back to the BBR itself. Citizens paid taxes. They gave their services without pay. All they wanted in compensation was "a place to function and some aid of the supervisor"—that is, of Jack Robbins. The demography of the BBR, at this moment in 1919, included 275 active citizens, about eighty "juniors" or prospective citizens, and about sixty-odd alumni, boys over eighteen.

What was great about the BBR, she concluded, lay in all the ways it prepared citizens for "life in the struggling human mass: learning to climb and to yield, to govern and to be governed, to find themselves through seeking others, and to do a great many other things which go to make up life as it is lived in its fullness to-day." They made their own rules. "In everything," it was "their own understanding on which they act, the will of their own majority that prevails." Their debates were not on abstract or pretend questions (is it better to be right than to be president?), but on immediate problems of republican self-government.[38]

In the same issue of the *Ladies' Home Journal*, she also published a smaller second piece, ostensibly directed to the boys of America living outside of Chicago. This article was framed as a how-to guide to creating a local Boys' Brotherhood Republic. It followed Robbins in its emphasis on the need for advertising and on avoiding adult spaces and leadership. One may wonder why the *Journal* offered space and a venue for articles advocating an autonomous boys' republic. Who was the target audience? Readers of the *Journal*? Their sons? Perhaps it is not surprising that we don't see many or any groups that followed the model.[39] (Laughlin, it should be noted was herself an early creator of how-to guides, particularly travel guides. So, perhaps she was simply practicing her craft in this smaller article.)

And then, in December 1919, she published one more article about the BBR, in a different popular magazine. Here she reflected back on what she had learned from writing the long article in the *Ladies' Home Journal*. Laughlin restated the democratic promise of the boys of the BBR:

As I see it, the tomorrows of our democracy are very largely in the hands of these multitudinous youths. The attitude they take toward work, wages, government, social responsibility, human progress will be the determining factor in all those things . . . We shall all dance as they pipe. That is democracy. If I could hope to live my old age in a world dominated by men whose boyhood was moulded by the Boys' Brotherhood Republic, I'd beckon that old age and bid it hasten. But I get terribly afraid, sometimes . . .

She shifted the argument slightly. What the boys did, she argued, was "of value not only in training them for future citizenship." It was also "of very real value NOW, to themselves, to their community, and especially to other boys." They could do things, using "their superabundant energy," which had been withdrawn from "pursuits which annoy or scandalize adults." Instead, they helped "the old world swing along at a livelier pace, to a heartier tune, toward a better destiny." She knew of "no other organization now working for human betterment . . . more deeply rooted in right principles and fuller of vigor for extending its branches."[40]

* * *

Why were there so many boys in reform schools and before the juvenile court? For Harry Branovitz, an early boy officer of the Boys' Brotherhood Republic, the answer was not that different from that of Clara Laughlin. Or, for that matter, of Jane Addams. It had much to do with the "superabundant" or "accumulated" energy that marked adolescent boys. "If the city doesn't furnish" a boy "a place where he can dispose of his accumulated energy in the way of athletics, congenial surroundings, etc., this will usually break out of his system, create certain impulses, which will make him commit foolish and mischievous deeds which are considered in the eyes of the law as a crime." He continued with advice for Progressive reformers. Instead of using "our money" to take trips to Europe to investigate subways and other "foolish and grafting" expenditures, reformers should build places where boys can go, have fun, use the gym, swim, and secure "proper guidance and training." The BBR, he continued, was fighting for "this fact." If Chicago's judges and officials didn't do what needed doing, "the boys of Chicago through the BBR. must undertake it themselves." He warned the mayor and other city officials to "keep" their "eyes on us and watch us."[41]

The BBR's starting point had been a faith that boys' energy could be a force for good. Robbins and the boys resisted imagining the Boys' Brotherhood Republic as a form of parental or substitute parental control. Rather, the goal was to acknowledge boys as actors and agents in their own lives.

The BBR was, in its nature, a space where boys of a certain age lived mostly apart from parental authority, a space they could imagine was their own creation. The goal was to keep boys away from the carceral state, away from the oppressive and intensely hierarchical institutions and agents that reformers imagined substituted for parents. Robbins and the boys really didn't care about parents, present or absent. Parents were close to irrelevant. Nor did they care about institutional surrogates for parenthood. He and they took boys where they were, on the streets and in gangs, as citizens in process of becoming. Not at school and not at home, where many reformers imagined that they ought to be, under control. Implicitly, they took account of the "discovery" of adolescence—thus the BBR's constitutional insistence that citizenship be limited to those between the ages of fourteen and eighteen. It replicated, safely, what gangs offered as well. And as we have seen, Robbins and the officers of the BBR continually identified the BBR as a better kind of gang.

The "boy problem," which, properly understood, included the institutions adults created to solve the boy problem, brought the BBR into being. And Robbins was perfectly capable of mobilizing some of the rhetoric of the "savers" and early social scientists when doing so served his and the boys' purposes. Yet what the BBR and Robbins offered was different because they had so little interest in the recreation of an imagined privatistic and familial past. In particular, he and they had no interest in finding or recreating parental authority. The goal was to redirect the autonomy and freedom that were the lived experience of many boys on the streets into the self-governance of a republic of citizens.

One might imagine that he and they regarded "parens patriae" as articulating a false consciousness. Reform schools and the like were not recreating an idealized home for the boys who found themselves on the streets. And they were not preparing their charges for responsible adult lives away from the streets. Indeed, the manual training schools and orphanages to which many boys were committed released boys back on to the streets when they were done with them, abandoning them when they graduated, without skills and without resources. With luck, some of them found a safe haven in the BBR.

Although Jack Robbins had innumerable opinions about the legal system and about the institutions of American life, neither he as supervisor nor the boy citizens were engaged in a program of law reform. He and they took the coercive legal institutions that were intended to disarm and to regulate and shape the boys as detestable, but also as ever-present. Those institutions constituted the conditions, the grounds, on which he and they would have to build lives, a settled and inescapable feature of boy life in Chicago. To the extent possible, the BBR would "save" homeless boys from reform schools and from the farm labor that was masked as foster care. But the existence of those institutions and practices also made the BBR possible.

The boys of the BBR worked to challenge particular rules or laws—as with their effort to oppose mandatory fingerprinting, their efforts to ease restrictions on public access to the beaches of Lake Michigan, and their protests against long incarcerations for boy criminals. But they took carceral and bureaucratic institutions as a given, as being more or less inescapable. Or, rather, as being escapable in particular circumstances but inescapable as a context or a frame for living lives. The BBR offered a way out but not a legal challenge.[42] Nor were the boys of the BBR apparently much interested in child labor laws or in compulsory education laws. They wanted to avoid or to exit from whatever went on in the courts and in reform schools and foster care. They wanted protection from intrusive policing. They wanted jobs for boys. They wanted to be left alone. They wanted their own space.

Or to put it slightly differently, the boy problem, understood as a disruptive challenge both to adult authority and to the institutions adults created to solve the problem, produced the conditions for the distinctive freedoms, the democratic self-government, of the BBR.[43]

Robbins and the BBR boys for the most part avoided the scientistic or bureaucratic language that pervaded the adult institutions. As child saving became social work, became professionalized and medicalized, he and they continued to talk about "bad boys." They mostly avoided labels and social and psychological categories. They entirely avoided the notions of an emerging "positive" criminology that talked in terms of identifying those who were or were becoming "criminals." There were, of necessity, distinctions made between boys who came to the BBR because of probation or parole, as opposed to other reasons. But the environmentalism of the BBR was thoroughgoing. It was legal happenstance, contingency, that made some boys delinquent and others dependent and others merely looking for companionship. Boys, dependent or delinquent or whatever, needed to be together in a safe environment. They needed to be protected from the coercive state, which might constitute them as criminals.

Boys needed other boys; they needed freedom. They needed the opportunity to be together and to work together. They needed to escape labels of "incorrigibility" and "dependency" and "delinquency." And they needed each other.

What Robbins and the boys who made and managed the BBR cared about was freedom, both in the obvious sense of getting boys out and away from the violence of state power, the institutions that robbed them of their freedom, but also in the somewhat different sense of leaving boys free to construct their own institutions, to live free lives as democratic citizens, away from the constraints of parental and bureaucratic pseudo-parental control (parens patriae). But this second notion of freedom also implied leaving boys "free" to care for one another within the space of an institution like the BBR. The notion and the reality that they were capable of governing themselves countered "the terrifying abyss of insignificance" that recent social psychology identifies as a central precondition for the production of violent youths or delinquents.[44]

To understand Robbins's and the boys' stance, in the conditioning context of the institutional and penological developments of the 1910s, one has to imagine him and the Boys' Brotherhood Republic both as drawing on the various streams of "reform" and control that predominated in the legal culture and, at the same time, as—in many ways—resisting and fighting against those streams. From one perspective, Robbins was just another reformer in his time, rhetorically to the left of other Progressives who dealt with the "boy problem," but reliant on the same categories and understandings. Like several others, including Jane Addams and Randolph Bourne, he celebrated the energy and "ardor" of the young, their promise as future American citizens. From another perspective, though, he and the BBR insisted on the immediate citizenship of his boys in the present, on their right to self-government in the present. The boys, in their view, were not seen as children, or as no more than potential adults or adults-to-be who needed to be guided and molded by kindly adults if there were any hope for them becoming responsible individuals.

From the perspective of many mainstream reformers, what Robbins meant to do was something close to turning over the asylum to the inmates. A kind of institutional insanity. But from his perspective, he and they meant to recognize American citizens as citizens. Like Randolph Bourne, he drew from various strands an insistence on living democratically in the present, even for the young, as well as a resistance to the repressive powers of the old. To use Bourne's words: "Democracy means a belief that people are worthy; it means trust in the good faith and the dignity of the average man. The chief reason why the average man is not now worthy of more trust, the democrat believes, is simply that he has not been trusted enough in the past." Except Jack Robbins would have substituted "boy" for "man."[45]

It is important to add that the public face of the BBR paid relatively little attention to the violent crime that must have been part of the "juvenile delinquency" that had brought many of those who would end up in the BBR to the attention of the police and other public authorities. What the relationship was between the "jackrollers" that Chicago sociologists studied in the 1920s and the boys in the BBR remains unclear. (One wonders what happened when the violent gang that Laughlin described as asking to join the BBR actually joined.) Robbins was always honest that the BBR did not succeed with everyone. And it may be that the "citizenship committee" filtered out the more "criminal" or violent young people.

To understand Robbins's perspective, as well as that instantiated in the BBR, one might borrow from Saidiya Hartman's recent work on troubled young African American women in Harlem and Philadelphia in the 1920s. The bad boys were not precisely the same as the "wayward girls" Hartman focused on. The BBR's citizens remained tied to the structures of the law. The boys were subjects of as well as subjected to legal institutions—and over time they only became more so, as we will see. For the most part, they possessed the privileges of whiteness. And there is no moment when the boys who joined or found their way into the BBR seemed to enter an entirely separate space, as Hartman imagines her girls might have found. The BBR had to serve boys already caught in the law's grip. What the BBR offered was more an alternative form of socialization, not the radical rejection of authority that Hartman imagined her girls might momentarily have embodied.

Still, the similarities are manifest. Like "waywardness," the categories used to label "bad boys," including "delinquency" and "dependency" and "incorrigibility," were all at bottom efforts by child savers and juvenile authorities to control what could not really be controlled: boyhood. And the BBR internalized some of the same "fugitive gestures" that Hartman explored. It too was a "cramped creation." The law accompanied everything that the BBR did. But it did not define what the BBR and Jack Robbins were about, which was to offer "help for the chanceless," for those boys who confronted violent and inhumane circumstances. For "bad boys," like "wayward girls," the greatest challenge was how to continue to live a free life.[46]

The committees and the politics of the BBR were reactive and resistant. "Wherever a boy is in trouble, we are in trouble" was the mantra. But they did not allow the juvenile court and the other institutions that put a boy into trouble to constitute who they were—at least, not fully and not in the most important ways. The boys in the BBR were among those who were understood to be "ungovernable." They were, to use Alexandra Cox's language, those deemed "to be incapable of change and incapable of being changed." And yet the BBR gave them, or allowed them to give themselves, nothing less than democratic government.[47]

But government was something more than the formalities of offices and elections and a simulacrum of bureaucracy and administration. It was more than the pretense of being a "republic." What was most important, to return to a theme explored earlier, what made the BBR work in its early days, was the presence and involvement of pals. Pals who could be relied on and who would care for you. Such pals were crucial. And it was the presence of pals that marked the success of the BBR. Love, one might say, took priority—a love that was not to be found elsewhere, neither in homes nor in the policing and penological institutions of Chicago, nor in the gangs or other sites where children "swarmed." But such love required leaving the boys in control of a space that was theirs, allowing them to live free lives as citizens. It required leaving them free to be pals to one another.[48]

FIVE

Who Was Jack Robbins? Or, Things Unsaid, 1920–1958

In October 1920, the *Chicago Daily Tribune* ran a story about Jack Robbins under the headline, "Boys' Republic Chief Gives Up Wife for 'Pals.'" It came with the subhead, "Sacrifices Own Happiness to Befriend Lads."[1]

Apparently, Robbins had met Clara Hofkin, daughter of a wealthy Philadelphian, at a convention, perhaps the same 1918 "boys work" convention where he and the boy representatives from the BBR had become its "liveliest feature." At the time they met, she had been "diverting herself" doing "welfare work." Their honeymoon took the form of a tour of several of the boys' clubs he had supposedly founded in various cities. When they got off the train in Chicago, they were met by a delegation of boys who presented them with a loving cup paid for with the "nickels and dimes" of "lads" he had "picked off of the prison trail." The boys admonished the bride: "You mustn't take Jack away from us—we can't get along without him." She denied any such intention. She had married him, she said, to help him in his work.

The story next described a dance held at the BBR several months later, where several couples announced engagements. Robbins told them not to forget the BBR: "Come see us once in a while," he enjoined. Marriage had not changed him, the boys responded. He had not abandoned them or the work. So, neither would it change them. Robbins flinched.

All was not well in the Robbinses' home. Jack's wife had tired of the "club." She told him, "You can't fool your whole life away with boys." She wanted him to go into "business." And soon she made him choose: "Me or the boys."

The boys won.

She went back to Philadelphia. Her lawyers called him. Divorce proceedings began. And for the rest of his life, Jack Robbins would be identified as "divorced" or "single."

At least, that is the story that the *Chicago Tribune* told. The vital statistics found by way of Ancestry.com suggest another mystery. The dates are obscure and contradictory. In 1920, a Mrs. Cora Robbins (spelled Robins) appears with a Jack "Robins" in the census records. They were living together as married boarders on South Marshfield Avenue in Chicago. Jack was identified as working for a "boys institute." Cora was identified as being from Pennsylvania. Was the Cora Robins in the census records the former Clara Hofkin? According to the Philadelphia newspaper records, Clara Hofkin had married a doctor, Alexander Maysels, in Philadelphia in March 1919. She was twenty-eight or twenty-nine at that time. Later records describe her 1919 marriage to Maysels as her first and only marriage. So, what was her marriage to Jack Robbins? Or to put it differently, was there ever a marriage between Clara Hofkin and Jack Robbins?[2]

In the third decade of the twenty-first century, more than a century after the establishment of the Boys' Brotherhood Republic, in the wake of child sex-abuse scandals often involving men who claimed to care for boys, it is impossible to read the hundreds of journalistic accounts of Jack Robbins's early twentieth-century relationships and not wonder what was going on. What meaning should one ascribe to the statements by boys about how much they loved and needed him? What did it mean that he chose, as his wife said, "to fool" his life away with boys? How did he travel around the country with the boys he took with him as they went to conventions and searched for the worst of the worst boys?

And yet, one would be hard pressed to read even an innuendo of sexual impropriety in any of the journalistic accounts, or in reports by investigators hired by potential funders and agencies. There is nothing, even by those most hostile to him and to his institution.[3]

We might imagine that Jack Robbins had a closeted gay identity. There was certainly a homoerotic quality to the intense interactions many noticed between big brother and little brothers. And the available evidence suggests that he had a great need for the adoration and attention he received from the boys. His life, so far as we know it, was fundamentally shaped by his intense and continuing relations with adolescent boys. But more than that one cannot say.

In the manuscript version of her autobiography, Clara Laughlin described Jack Robbins's gifts as follows: "He has a way of being a pal with boys, that no one has ever to my knowledge—been able to copy. Perhaps it isn't necessary to be born that 'way'; but I'm sure it isn't possible to do it like a garment. Either you feel about boys the way Jack does; or they know that you don't." Then she turned to her version of the origins of the BBR: "The beginning of it was when Jack used to invite one or two of the boys he knew, to his small room, evenings, to talk things over with them; or go for walks with them. They then rented a room for one night a week, at a dollar a week or some such sum, so they could ask more fellows than Jack's room could accommodate, and they could have 'meetings.'" Passages like these could be read in several ways, allowing us to read her as coming close to outing Jack Robbins. Such readings are profoundly anachronistic. At the same time, I don't mean to suggest that Laughlin was not a sexually knowing observer, because my reading of her draft autobiography as well as of many of her newspaper columns in 1917 and 1918, suggest that she was well aware of the varieties of human sexual experience. (Her novels, on the other hand, carefully remained within late Victorian conventions.) It is possible that Clara Laughlin was trying to suggest what she could not say or write explicitly. But beyond the evident reality that Jack Robbins felt passionately about the boys he worked with, and that some of them at least reciprocated those feelings, there is not much more to be said or written. One might say that he had needs that his involvement with the boys of the BBR satisfied, but that is to say no more than that he found some kind of happiness in the work he did and in the relationships he formed and sustained. Being the big brother was, after all, his calling.[4]

It is also surprising that there was so little talk of sex or sexuality or dating or pregnancies in any articles about the BBR. There is a relentless focus on criminality, that is, on theft and violence, though little I can find on sexual violence or improprieties. For Robbins, as well as for those who wrote about the BBR, the burdens of boyhood were defined by a repressive adult world, and yet seemingly not by the sexual life and norms of the adult (or adolescent) world. There were dances and social gatherings at the BBR, and, as in the *Tribune*'s story about Robbins's short-lived marriage, engagements were announced. But few ever wrote anxiously or otherwise about boys getting girls pregnant. Or about venereal disease. It was all apparently sexless.

And yet, of course that wasn't the case, could not have been true, although I have only found one late moment, during World War II, when a buried reality appeared momentarily in the remaining records. Ben Reitman, a sex reformer and radical doctor, once Emma Goldman's lover, was Jack Robbins's friend. He hosted a regular "International Night" at the BBR, where various speakers of multiple "races and creeds" spoke to the boys. After he died in late 1942, Reitman's memorial service was held in the clubhouse of the BBR.[5] A few months earlier, Reitman treated a high school girl, Betty Martin, for syphilis. She had "admitted to sexual contacts with 210 boys, 86 of whom were in the BBR." Reitman wrote to Robbins after having examined about thirty boys in the BBR, having done a blood test on eighteen of them. Fortunately, none of those he had tested showed evidence of syphilis. "So far so good. But, of course, it's too early to make any statement that none of the boys are infected." He needed to see all the boys who had "active contact with the young lady" every two weeks for the next three months.[6]

But then Reitman turned to what was really bothering him. "In talking to the boys that I've examined I did not find a single boy who exhibited . . . remorse, shame[,] or regret. If I did not know you so well and love you so much and appreciate your deep interest in your boys, I should say that you 'reared a generation of vipers.'" Reitman continued: "Their stupidity, asinine contempt for womanhood, their indifference to being a party to a young girl's shame, disease[,] and motherhood is one of the most pathetic experiences I've had in my life." In talking with the boys, he noticed that they

```
dreamed of sinking a Japanese warship or of leading commando
raids in Italy or Germany. They fantasized doing heroic deeds as
soldiers. . . . [B]ut not one of those boys had the decency or
the guts or the courage to stop that gang attack on a mere child.
Any one of those 200 boys who contacted her would have made
himself a hero if he would have prevented that terrible massacre.
But—that's too late. I don't know whether you understand how
brutal, inhumane[,] and vicious most of those boys were. They
were absolutely vulgar and stupid. But what's the use of telling
you that . . . [?][7]
```

Reitman was also bothered that not one of the boys offered to pay him for their examinations, and he asked Robbins to send him a little money for the work he had done. He was evidently short of funds, and he had to borrow to pay his rent and his bills.

Then in a final paragraph he returned to his anger with the young for their heedlessness. He had heard that Robbins was thinking of giving up the BBR. (In fact, Robbins would leave the organization two years later.) Reitman urged him to do so. He wanted to close all boys' clubs. He thought, at least at this point in his life, that "the money and the love and the effort that the public have given to afford recreation, clean amusement, health-building athletics and spiritual development to our youth," girls as well as boys, was "wasted." He didn't need to tell Robbins "how many young girls have a sexual contact with a soldier and then go see their girl friends and encourage them to do likewise." He continued, free-associating somewhat: "You didn't like the way I talked to your boys. You thought I was too frank when I told them if they ever had a contact to use a rubber and wash it with soap and water. You thought I talked too freely to those innocent boys—innocent boys? It's to laugh."[8]

What of girls? Throughout the hundreds of columns in America's newspapers devoted to Jack Robbins and his creation, there is remarkably little attention given to the significance for girls of an institution like the Boys' Brotherhood Republic. Girls played only a small role in the stories of the BBR boys, both while running wild or uncontrolled (swarming) and after they had become citizens. And it is, to twenty-first-century eyes, remarkable how inattentive journalists and child savers and reformers were about girls, particularly in the years before 1920. Frederick Thrasher, who wrote a sociology of Chicago's gangs in the 1920s, wondered inconclusively why there were not more girl gangs and he devoted a few pages to the few girls who joined boy gangs. To read the pages of a Progressive journal like the *Day Book* reveals intermittent attention to "fallen" girls and how they would fall (what it meant if they went to dance halls and elsewhere). Jane Whitaker wrote many articles about the working lives of young women, as did Clara Laughlin (though Laughlin was still more concerned with the oppressions that wives confronted). Girls could be a problem as well. But they were a different problem and, one might add, to journalists a lesser problem. The wealthy reformer Caroline Bayard Dod Colgate, who served as a member of the board of directors of the New York City BBR in the 1930s, thought that "fastidiousness" about girls was inculcated by the tenets of the BBR. The result, she thought, meant that a girl became "good" because that would be the only way for her to "get her man." But I suspect that she wrote with little direct engagement with the boys of the BBR.[9]

And who were the boys of the BBR, racially and ethnically? Race and ethnicity were never talked about in any of the articles written about the republic in its early years. Certainly they were not discussed by Jack Robbins. And religion played no part in the practices of the BBR. But as we have seen, early on the Boys' Brotherhood Republic was understood to be composed primarily, though not exclusively, of Jewish youths. In the first third of the twentieth century, the west side of Chicago, Lawndale, where the BBR was located, was understood to be an impoverished but Jewish part of Chicago. Lawndale had a larger and more concentrated Jewish population than any American community outside of New York City. The area would change dramatically by World War II, and it would eventually become largely African American, as would the Boys' Brotherhood Republic. But not in the years around and after World War

I.[10] Writing around 1920, Clara Laughlin, after insisting that "neither race nor creed nor color nor party politics" had anything to do with brotherhood as the boys practiced it, acknowledged that "most of the boys" were "children of the foreign-born and, in large part, of the East European races." Many of them were "on the eve of United States citizenship." A 1927 letter to the Rosenwald Fund described the BBR as 95 percent Jewish and complained that funding responsibility properly should rest with the Jewish community. There were, the writer wrote, "thousands of Jewish boys in the Lawndale district needing care and supervision. . . . The big thing that the Boy's Brotherhood Republic does is to keep the boys off the streets, which is a big thing. The practice of self-government is also of great value, but the boys surely are entitled to a great deal more than what they are getting."[11]

Chicago's Boys' Brotherhood Republic remained for many years a predominantly white and a predominantly Jewish organization. In the photographs in a book published in 1938, *Life of the Boys' Brotherhood Republic*, discussed later in this chapter, a few African American faces appeared—but only a very few. In the late teens and early 1920s, Robbins and the BBR opened branch boys' clubs in several locations of Chicago, areas with varying ethnic identities, including one in Hyde Park, near the boundaries of the African American community. None of these branches survived for long.[12] A 1921 article on the "Problems of the Colored Child" noted that the Boys' Brotherhood Republic was one of several social service organizations that only "indifferently" touched the lives of Chicago's African American children. The indifference was so great that at about the same time, the Chicago *Defender*, the leading Black newspaper, headlined an article proposing that a BBR branch be built in an African American Chicago neighborhood on the south side of the city with, "Do Chicago Boys Want a Boys' Republic?" And it would be the better part of two decades before the first "Negro" Boys' Brotherhood Republic would come into existence in Chicago.[13]

* * *

Who was Jack Robbins? The question was a matter of some concern for at least a few charitably inclined wealthy Chicagoans, who worried about the "boy problem" in their city.

As mentioned earlier, Edmund D. Hulbert, for one, admired Jack Robbins. Hulbert was one of the leading bankers in Chicago, a Democrat and a close advisor of Woodrow Wilson, someone who played an important role in establishing the Federal Reserve Bank. He died unexpectedly in 1923, as he was completing a merger of three of the largest banks in Chicago. He had contributed to the BBR from early on in its history. Apparently he saw himself as someone who had also started as an impoverished boy. Hulbert led the board of trustees of the BBR, and he quietly helped make it possible for Jack Robbins to devote himself full time to the organization, by paying the supervisor 150 dollars a month so that he could quit working as a tobacco salesman.[14]

A few months after Hulbert's death, there was a memorial event for him, with speeches and music performed by the BBR's own band. Six hundred members of the BBR, past and present, attended the City Club. There Hulbert's adult friends agreed to build a new clubhouse for the BBR, as a monument to the banker.[15] James P. Soper, who owned a lumber company, took the lead. He had succeeded Hulbert as the head of the board of the BBR. He committed $10,000 to the project, as did Mrs. Mary B. Blair, who was listed as the "treasurer of the Board of Trustees." Other prominent and wealthy individuals, including Charles Seabury, the vice president of the insurance giant Marsh and McLennan and a director of the BBR, also subscribed for a project that would end up costing around $60,000.[16]

Eventually, when it was completed in the late 1920s, this building would become Hulbert Hall, with a picture of Edmund D. Hulbert prominently displayed inside.

But in October 1925, Soper wrote to Julius Rosenwald, the liberal Jewish financier and foundation founder, and the largest shareholder in Sears Roebuck and Company. Apparently, the financial situation of the BBR was unsettled. The commitments from other board members had fallen short. According to a note found in the Rosenwald papers, someone thought the board was composed of too many women, which may have also meant too few board members with immediate access to large sums of money. The BBR was going to have to get a mortgage, although if Rosenwald would gift them with $10,000, perhaps not.

The Rosenwald Fund devoted most of its resources to the support of African American institutions, but it also contributed to some Jewish charities. Rosenwald's advisors suggested a solution to the BBR's financial problems. Ownership of the new building would be transferred to the Community Trust of Chicago to hold it in trust for the benefit of the Boys' Brotherhood Republic. How much this solution would interfere with the practices of the BBR was left unclear. Another note in the Rosenwald files suggested that the Community Trust would have "complete jurisdiction over club affairs," although there is no evidence I have found of much interference ever by the Community Trust into the daily life of the Republic.[17]

In any event, that transfer occurred late in 1927. And around then, Julius Rosenwald would make a gift of $10,000 toward the completion of Hulbert Hall (at first he had only committed to making a $5,000 gift).[18]

But before he made that gift or grant, Rosenwald, or his associates, solicited what information they could about the BBR, as a part of doing due diligence. They drew on an earlier inquiry conducted by the National Information Bureau, a new organization created during World War I by the great foundations to investigate potential charitable recipients.[19] It is not clear who had asked for that earlier inquiry. Around the same time, around 1920, the Chicago Association of Commerce had been asked to endorse the BBR, and its leaders had apparently written to several people for reviews. Rosenwald's associates drew on those reviews as well. Rosenwald's staff asked William J. Parker, the head of Chicago's YMCA, to interview a variety of "boy workers" about the status of the BBR. In December 1925, Parker completed the task, having talked to a number of people in and around Jack Robbins's world. Alfred Stern, Rosenwald's son-in-law at that time, then made inquiries as well.

The leavings of those inquiries include a copy of a long letter written earlier, dated March 1921, by Philip Seman, perhaps drafted in response to inquiries from the Rotary Clubs and the Chicago Association of Commerce; a summary letter by Spencer Williams, the acting director of the National Information Bureau (also written in 1921 but copied to Rosenwald in 1926); William J. Parker's own letter of evaluation, drafted in 1925; and Alfred Stern's own letter from 1927, describing his visit to the BBR and his conversations with Jack Robbins.[20]

Seman, the head of the Hebrew Institute, we have already met in chapter 3 as a man with an intense dislike of Robbins. In 1921, about the same time Seman wrote the report that eventually found its way to the Rosenwald Foundation, Jack Robbins had written to W. S. Reynolds, the head of the Chicago Home and Aid Society, to complain about Seman. Seman had, he thought, "misrepresented and falsified" things to the Rotary Club, which had promised to help Robbins start a Central City branch. As a result, the Rotarians had stopped responding to Robbins. A week earlier a group of the BBR boys had dropped in at Seman's Institute. One of them, a boy who knew Seman, was called in to Seman's office. According to Robbins, Seman told the boy:

> We needn't expect any help from the Rotary Club or anybody else,
> the best we can do is disband, there is no use for you fellows to
> do anything because the B.B.R. work is all a fake, Mr Hulbert
> found it out and dropped it, . . . the Association of Commerce
> will not indorse it, Mr Reynolds who at one time was a strong

supporter of the B.B.R. finally discovered that there was nothing
to it and he took away your office and dropped out of it, the only
people who still hang on are a few foolish old women.

Soon, Seman would establish a rival to the BBR in Lawndale, called the American Boys' Commonwealth.[21]

Seman's 1921 report, which was passed on to the Rosenwald Foundation, began with his first encounter with Robbins, in 1914, at a time when the BBR consisted of Robbins and seven boys. They had asked permission to meet at the Hebrew Institute, which Seman ran. Seman had agreed. It mattered that Robbins had managed to get the cooperation and support of some respectable Jewish professionals, including M. J. Karpf, who by the 1920s would be superintendent of the Jewish Social Service Bureau of Chicago, and Luba Robin Goldsmith, a pioneering woman doctor.[22] It also probably did not hurt that most of the original group of boys were of Jewish origin.

The early BBR met at the Institute for about a year and a half. During that time, according to Seman, all the professionals became "thoroughly disgusted with Jack." And they soon abandoned the BBR. Jack Robbins was, he thought, a failure as a "boy leader." A "boy leader" should be "physically attractive, with broad shoulders and head erect, clear eyes that are intelligent and that sparkle, a mind that is alert and is possessed of a constructive imagination," and so on. His training and experience ought to "bring out the best that is in the boy." The boy will think, "When I grow up this is the kind of a man, I'd like to be." But Jack had none of those "qualifications or qualities." (Seman wrote in a register common to more elite German Jews writing about Yiddish-speaking, working-class Russian and Eastern European immigrants.)[23]

A crisis then occurred in late 1915, while Seman was conveniently away from the city. A group of "anarchists" arranged to have the famous radical Alexander Berkman come speak at the Institute. He was fundraising to assist in what Seman remembered as the trial of the Los Angeles bomb throwers, the McNamara brothers.[24] When the leaders of the Institute denied the anarchists permission to hold the meeting, they became "very furious and threatened the institute with boycott." Seman refused to allow his space to be used for anti-government purposes. He would not, he wrote, "tolerate anyone to occupy the platform of the Institute when his subject matter would incite a normal people towards [against?] the principles upon which American democracy has been based and otherwise preach violence and destruction." Robbins, not surprisingly, charged that the Institute suppressed free speech. He encouraged the boys to leave. Which they did.[25]

Since then Seman had continued to follow the "progress" of the BBR, "rather carefully," though mostly from a distance. What he observed sustained "his conviction," first, that the boys had "very poor leadership, most undesirable from a constructive viewpoint." And second, "that their teaching, so far as real citizenship is concerned," was bad. He disliked everything that was distinctive about the BBR, including its politics and the boys' activism. For example, when Ellen Gates Starr, a close associate and companion of Jane Addams, ran on the Socialist ticket for alderman, "youngsters" in the BBR were permitted to stand on corners and act as "soapbox orators." They also distributed handbills throughout the 19th Ward. The BBR's mayor went to the "real City Hall," and he was allowed to sit in the "real" mayor's chair. Likewise, in the Maxwell Street police station and in the juvenile court: "These youngsters were seated with the judge and would take on parole boys who would come before the court. . . . There they sat, these youngsters—untrained—with no experiences behind them." They were themselves "mere boys . . . who should be urged and encouraged to prepare themselves for the responsibilities of manhood and good citizenship." They had no business acting as "as arbiters, wise as judges, ready to be the saviours of the boys who sinned." He also hated what he called "Boy Job Finding Day." It was absurd that such a task was put into the hands of boys. This ought to be seen as work requiring the "keenest knowledge of vocational guidance." He hated the notion of electing boys "to travel throughout the United States to discover the worst boy in America in order to make a good boy out of him. A spectacular bit of advertising which never should have been allowed." He also mentioned the effort to return the retired Judge Pinckney to service in the juvenile court and displace the present judge.

All this illustrated a "gross injustice done the boy in the guise of service and preparation for good citizenship." (And, one might add, his language also illustrated his dismay at the success of the boys of the BBR in working with and within Chicago's political and legal institutions.)[26]

Seman was "opposed to this spectacular method of conducting boys' work." He was "opposed to the man-boy" (presumably Robbins). He pontificated:

> Those of us who have reached our fortieth year and look back upon
> the twenty or more years of responsibility that has weighed
> heavily upon our shoulders, and then look forward probably to
> another twenty or thirty years of responsibility, . . . must be
> determined in the sound fundamental truth that boys should be
> permitted to be boys and nothing else during the short period
> that nature allots, and that during that period the boy should be

put in touch with every refining influence for good in the personality of those whom he comes in contact with as teachers and leaders, who would guide and direct them to see the beauties of nature through the field, the skies and other wonderful nature's gifts to man as well as to the cultural opportunities offered our citizenry by a local community in the parks, the playgrounds, the libraries, the museums, the opportunities and facilities offered educationally, etc.[27]

Seman claimed to "believe in self-government." He believed in what he called a boys' brotherhood, but he believed in it only if it had "the proper, intelligent, well trained direction, and further the assurance that in the guise of self-government license may not be taken for liberty." Because of his "love" for the "boy," and his desire to lead the boy to become a good citizen, he hoped that those who had "shown an inclination to encourage both Jack Robbins and the activities of the Boys' Brotherhood Republic even to the extent of crying out that Jack Robbins has been inspired by God, will not further run away with their emotions alight." He hoped for "a saner and more constructive method of lending influence in making for a boy-power in our community, which will bear fruit when the boy becomes a man."[28]

Spencer Williams's letter on behalf of the National Information Bureau, dated June 13, 1921, but based on "a very thorough investigation" conducted a year earlier, was equally critical of Robbins and the BBR, although less histrionic. He began descriptively. The BBR at the time, 1920–21, maintained four boys' clubs or "cities," all in Chicago. Costs were met by taxes paid by the seven hundred "citizens." The BBR was also receiving funds from the Chicago Women's Club, the Boys' Shelter, and prominent businessmen. The Chicago Rotary Club had once given support but had withdrawn assistance "as the result of an investigation."[29]

Williams had interviewed sixteen businessmen and social workers "of standing" in Chicago. The consensus was that "there was some value in the fundamental idea . . . of a self-governing club for boys." But the club (or clubs) offered "little discipline or training, either self-imposed or otherwise, and . . . no educational facilities, vocational training[,] or anything of that kind. There seemed to be a minimum of direction of effort." The effect of the "system" of the BBR encouraged the boys to "exaggerate the importance of their own judgments and estimates and that this tendency was increased by the considerable publicity secured by the Republic." He conceded that much of the publicity was "unsought," the result of the newspapers' need for copy.

For Williams it was critical and damning that the board of directors of the BBR exercised no direct supervision. Jack Robbins was in entire charge, and Robbins was "formerly a cigar salesman, and a man without training in work for boys except to such degree as he had been able to teach himself." Robbins was "inclined" to hostility to organized social work, and he influenced the boy leaders to share in that hostility. Those in charge of other organizations disliked Robbins's methods. And, according to Williams, there was also a "faction" of the boys who had turned against Robbins, including one boy who had succeeded in obtaining "an official position" in Chicago. That said, Hulbert, he noted, believed "thoroughly" in the BBR's methods, and continued to pay Robbins's salary (this was written before Hulbert's death), as did "Miss Carpenter," identified by Williams as of "Community Service, Incorporated."[30]

What support the organization had secured rested "on the basis of sympathy rather than scientific knowledge of boys' work." And it also rested on the "spectacular" ways the boys had been able to attract attention. Its business management did not come close to what was needed. Only the most "rudimentary accounts" were kept. There was nothing like a "satisfactory audit of accounts" available. As a result, the Boys' Brotherhood Republic could not be recommended for support by the National Information Bureau. And yet, Williams concluded by noting that Marshall Field, the department store magnate, had become interested in the BBR, and Hulbert was still "enthusiastic."

William Parker's 1925 report was more measured.[31] He began by noting that the branches Williams had mentioned had all closed. What remained in 1925 was the original boys' club on the west side of Chicago, in Lawndale, which would eventually move to the new building on Hamlin Avenue, to what would become Hulbert Hall.

What he called "The Club" was the product of Jack Robbins's "peculiar genius." It was the "embodiment" of his ideas. He was its "center," and he was "the only social, professional worker. . . . The institution" remained "largely a one-man affair."[32]

Who was Jack Robbins? Parker went back to beginnings. Robbins was "of Russian-Jewish ancestry." He first appeared as "Jacob Robinovitch," as a "dependent" committed by the juvenile court to the Glenwood Manual Training School. (Actually, Robbins was too old for the juvenile court commitment story to be true. Robbins was born in 1882, and the Chicago juvenile court did not come into existence until 1899—by which point Robbins would have aged out of Glenwood. The commitment, if it had occurred, had to have come from some other agency, not from the juvenile court.) At Glenwood, according to Parker's sources, Robbins had been "a trouble maker and a fomenter of discord." When he should have been doing his "assigned work," he instead found boys with "grievances." And then he "appeared as a critic of the management and a champion of the boys." After two years, he left the school under murky circumstances.[33]

According to Parker, Robbins then went to New York, where he spent years of "great hardship, probably suffering actual hunger and exposure," until he found success as a tobacco salesman. He represented a Louisville business. His "keen sympathy" for the "underdog," for those "having an unfavorable chance in life," was already apparent. Parker acknowledged that "there can be no doubt about the genuineness or the strength of this sympathetic interest."

Parker then retold the story of the BBR's sojourn at the Hebrew Institute, much as Seman had. "Mr. Robbins ardently championed the cause of the anarchist group." And when the Institute refused to allow a "benefit performance" to raise money for the defense of the accused bombers, he and the boys left and found other quarters.

According to Parker, Robbins met Hulbert early on, as he was first organizing what became the Boys' Brotherhood Republic, relying on the "plan" of the George Junior Republic. Hulbert offered to pay him $150 a month if he would devote his full time to the "Boys Club." And this scheme had continued, now paid by Hulbert's widow. He also succeeded in gaining the support of many members of the Chicago Women's Club, some of whom had contributed "liberally." Mrs. Marshall Field III, gave $5,000 a year, and someone else contributed $2,000 a year. Mrs. Frederick de Coningh was especially active. And Hulbert drew in James Soper, who was now chair of the board of trustees.[34]

There were in 1925 eight women and three men on the board. One of the men was very dissatisfied with the financial records and management. Another man on the board had withdrawn from service because he was uncertain about the organization's future. The board had no representation from the neighborhood where it was located, which is not surprising, given how impoverished Lawndale was at the time.

Efforts to open new branches around the city had all ended "disastrously." In the Hyde Park branch there had been "extremely serious misconduct" by the boys there. Parker did not blame Robbins for that. He could only be held responsible in the sense that he had "general management." (In Alfred Stern's report on his interview with Oscar Wander, who had worked with Robbins in Hyde Park, the blame was placed on ethnicity. Most of the Hyde Park boys were of Irish descent, in contrast to the Lawndale boys who were mostly Jewish. "Irish boys did not subject themselves to self-government as well as the Jewish." But beyond that, many of the boys in Hyde Park had police records for "minor delinquencies.") Parker, the head of the citywide YMCA, added that the YMCA had just opened a boys' club in Hyde Park, which had better facilities. "It would seem" that "Mr. Robbins' method of management," that is, "complete self-government by the boys," worked only when Robbins was "present!" And when Parker asked Robbins about his policy now regarding opening new branches, Robbins replied that he would no longer try to open any more, saying. "I have all I can do to run this one."[35]

Parker was not bothered by the "extravagant statements" made by Robbins and the boys. In his opinion, Robbins was "uneducated"; he was "not a student." He did not understand the theory or practice of social work. Parker thought Robbins "of very limited intelligence; . . . unprepossessing in appearance and rather uncouth in manner." Such a man was "liable to make unwarrantable statements, not because of a deliberate intention to deceive anyone, but because of his mental and spiritual limitations." Robbins was "very unpopular" among nearly all social workers, especially among those doing "boys work." Parker, though, thought that they took Robbins "too seriously." They hated his "craving for publicity." Parker did not see why that should annoy them. He regarded it "as a foible which may amuse us rather than a reprehensible trait of character."

Parker's summary: Robbins was a "lone worker" who found it difficult to adjust to other people—that is, to adults. He had not trained others. He was regarded by some as a "dangerous radical." Parker, though, thought the critics did Robbins an "injustice." Robbins had a "genuine permanent interest in boys," and he made "great personal sacrifices in order to help them." The work of the "club" was not as good as its literature claimed, but still, it impressed him as having "genuine merit." It had a wholesome influence on large numbers of boys who needed what it offered. Presumably, he meant boys who were not served by the existing YMCAs.[36]

The last letter, presumably the one that led to a favorable outcome for the application of the BBR, came from Alfred Stern.[37] In 1927, Alfred K. Stern was still Julius Rosenwald's son-in-law and a core member of the board of the Rosenwald Fund. He came from a wealthy North Dakota banking family. In the 1930s he would serve as a housing commissioner in Chicago. After Rosenwald's death in 1932, he would divorce Rosenwald's daughter (who would take over direction of the Fund), and then he married Martha Davis, the daughter of the American ambassador to Nazi Germany. Martha Davis was a committed Communist. Eventually, Alfred Stern and his second wife would flee to Czechoslovakia, after the two of them were accused of spying for the Soviet Union. He died in Czechoslovakia in 1986.[38]

But in January 1927, he wrote to "Mother and Dad," that is, to Julius Rosenwald and his wife, to report on a meeting with Jack Robbins. According to Robbins, there were then 712 members of the BBR, though the building they were in could only house five hundred. Of the 712, 511 were Jewish boys. He and Robbins had decided who was Jewish by looking at names. And yet, "practically their entire support" came from non-Jews. About three hundred boys attended every night. There were six or seven "Negro boys," and the rest were a mixture of Italians, Polish, and other ethnicities. Each boy was taxed twenty-five cents a month. But those who could not pay, who were likely to become good citizens, could still be "accepted," without an obligation to pay.

Stern described the BBR's constitutional structure. In addition to the boys, there was the "guidance and supervision" of Robbins, and by then he had an assistant, and there was a paid athletic manager. Sixty of the boys had some office or membership on a committee. Those officers took their responsibilities "very seriously."

Robbins and Stern went to dinner, after which they hailed a cab to go to the BBR clubhouse. The driver, "a Jew," was a former member, and he praised the club. The driver noted that he had a brother and a cousin who were members now.[39]

That evening Stern wandered around the club and was "very much impressed by the whirl of activities." Lots of athletics, plus a game room where pool and checkers were being played. He did notice that the books in the library were little used. Those they had were "not good to read[,] having been donated by various individuals who very likely sent their over supply of books without any thought as to their appropriateness for boys."

He "could not help but feel, after having been there a short time," that the club served a good purpose, "even though it may have some objectionable features[,] such as the fact that it revolves around one man." It kept about three hundred boys off the streets, many of whom had police records and who had come to the club from the juvenile court or from the Glenwood Manual Training School or from "similar sources." Along with an "outlet for their energy in the gym," their committee work developed "a sense of responsibility and self control which they would not otherwise get."

He then described a meeting of the council of the BBR. Other adults sitting in on the meeting included Mrs. Mary B. Blair and Mr. and Mrs. Charles Seabury. He found it "very interesting and unique" to watch "boys trying to act like grown-ups in conducting their own affairs," always with Robbins "on hand for guidance." In looking around he saw "a number of Jewish faces." But what most impressed him was that the boys had "clean faces" and looked as though they watched their appearance. He had expected to see "a bunch of rowdies and vagabonds."

He concluded by marking his disagreement with Seman's critique. He "heartily" agreed with Parker's conclusion that the BBR was serving a good purpose. If the directors affiliated the BBS with a "permanent organization" like the Community Trust, it might overcome its "weakness, which was its dependence on Jack Robbins' individuality." He and Parker were going to meet with Seabury, in order to get a better sense of the financial situation of the club. The two of them would then draw up a "possible offer" for Rosenwald to consider.[40]

And the result apparently was the transfer of ten thousand dollars.

* * *

Over the two decades after the end of World War I, Chicago—and the nation within which the Boys' Brotherhood Republic operated—changed dramatically. Most immigration came to a halt after 1924. With the first Great Migration, Chicago's African American population, which as of 1910 numbered forty thousand, grew to 278,000 by 1940. Public anxiety over crime shifted from the "boy problem" to fears of organized crime and of bootlegging. The adult criminal gang replaced the boy gang as a repository of anxieties in the public imagination. Heterodox socialists like Jack Robbins were no longer understood as participants in an inclusive social-reform movement. The familiar markers of the interwar period, including new understandings of criminality, different class and racial politics, a great Depression, and the looming presence of Fascism and Naziism, all shaped the lives of those involved with the Boys' Brotherhood Republic. Boy work declined, and compulsory public schooling gradually became an ordinary expectation for adolescents, even for poor adolescents. Where around 6 percent of the population finished high school nationally in 1900, over 50 percent did so by the time the United States entered World War II.[41]

During those years, Jack Robbins's capacity to attract public attention waned. He continued to move around the country, often at the invitation of women's groups and clubs, who asked him to lecture. But newspaper coverage declined dramatically.

In March 1924, Robbins spoke at Chicago's Traffic Club. One report on the event emphasized that the BBR made "good citizens out of boys whose environment, lack of home life, lack of opportunity and encouragement handicapped them in the battle of life. With the hand of society against them for their peccadillos, and the street corners and the poolrooms for their educational training quarters, it is not to be wondered at that they viewed decency as 'sissyism,' and considered it to be tough to be manly." Robbins's speech emphasized the boys' independence. It was followed by a talk by Ralph Goodman and another member/citizen. And then Captain Wesley Westbrook, the warden of the county jail, gave a "warm endorsement" of the organization's success "in saving the wild, homeless youngsters of the street corners from a life of uselessness and perhaps crime." An attorney then added to the chorus of praise. A second report on the event noted that two boys were introduced as exhibits A and B. One, Harold Krowech, whom we will meet again, had run for the BBR's office of city judge in order to reform judicial procedures in the BBR. According to him, the BBR used to let the prosecuting attorney ask too many irrelevant questions, and juries were selected without sufficient care. But things got better, he thought, with his election. Exhibit B, Nathan Schwartz, told of how "otherwise normal boys" were "rescued" from the Chicago courts.[42]

In 1932, a New York City version of the Boys' Brotherhood Republic came into being. As in the case of the Chicago BBR, there were several competing origin stories. Sometime in 1930 or 1931, a group of New York reformers asked Jack Robbins to survey the resources that served the "boy in trouble or the potentially delinquent" on the Lower East Side. Not surprisingly, he found that there was nothing that met the need, "in spite of the fact that there are more social agencies in this general neighborhood than perhaps in any other section of the city." Robbins's report also revealed that he was already meeting with a group of over one hundred young men (average age twenty-three), who belonged to the Avenue C Boys' Club. The members were, he thought, committed to serving as the nucleus of a New York BBR. They would become "Big Brothers" to a BBR citizenry. That meant they would staff a supreme court to which boys convicted in a BBR court could appeal, and the members of the Avenue C Boys' Club would, in exchange, be able to make occasional use of the gymnasium and other spaces of the BBR. Apparently, there were also wealthy New Yorkers already committed to providing the necessary real estate, and Robbins was working with Spencer Miller Jr., a former assistant warden at the Sing Sing penitentiary and the director of a labor education bureau. There were at least preliminary conversations about acquiring a building on East Third Street, near Avenue C.[43]

Around then, Robbins convinced Harry Slonaker, who had once been an early citizen of the Chicago BBR, to become the founding "supervisor" of a New York BBR. Slonaker was working as a salesman in the fur business, which brought him frequently to New York City. How should he begin? Slonaker followed the Robbins Chicago model. As he remembered it a half century later, he "pounded the pavements" of the Lower East Side, "searching for likely candidates" to work with him to found a New York BBR. Eventually, he found eight boys shooting craps on a street. He relied on "subtle persuasion" to convince the boys to join him. They became, as he modestly put it, "the nucleus of an organization and program which has served and enriched the lives of thousands of boys" (see figure 14).

Slonaker and the eight boys began by renting a small store, twelve feet by eighteen feet in size, as headquarters. They furnished it with benches "purloined by the boys from 3d street tenants." They quickly outgrew that space, and then they rented a storefront on Houston Street near Avenue B, which they also soon outgrew. And at that point they came back to the building on Avenue C that Robbins had earlier identified. The owner had died, but those managing his estate were willing to give it to the new organization.[44]

Two Chicago "citizens" were sent to help Slonaker set things up on the Lower East Side. A third Chicago boy citizen hitchhiked his way to New York as well. Jack Robbins appeared, and he spoke at several early meetings.[45]

At first, the New York City version hewed close to the Chicago model, to the point that the New York office borrowed unchanged citizenship forms and other records from the Chicago Republic. The mantra "Where Boys Rule" was emblazoned on its walls. Quickly, though, the New York BBR became somewhat more conventional, with more adult presence, and with far more resources than the Chicago BBR. While Robbins still insisted that the chief virtue of such an organization should be its "freedom from adult control," yet apparently, that was much less the case in the structure and organization that came to characterize the New York Republic.[46]

At least one early article about the success of the New York Republic focused on the contrast between a boy who joined up and his friend who chose a life of crime. Of the friend who chose crime: he "went to prison last week; he'll come out again in a couple of years a full fledged outcast. His life has ended before it began." But, in contrast, "there are hundreds of boys who started out as he did who will never go to prison. Why not? Because, 'We are citizens of the Boys' Brotherhood Republic.'" That contrast was exactly what Jack Robbins and the early Chicago BBR had earlier denied and struggled against. Apparently, the mantra no longer held: "So long as there are boys in trouble, we too are in trouble."[47]

Perhaps the sense of differentiation between boys who could be saved by joining the Republic and those juvenile delinquents who would become criminals began to affect the Chicago BBR and Jack Robbins as well. Certainly, a

Figure 14: Harry Slonaker, photographed by Alfred Eisenstaedt, circa 1932. Harry Slonaker Papers, History San Jose, San Jose, CA.

new rhetoric and a new set of analytic tools came to define child welfare in the decades after World War I. The discipline of criminology, which received its canonical form in the writings of the University of Chicago Sociology Department, was devoted to describing young criminal lives, understood as separated and distinguishable from the broad run of boys. For the most part, the modal works in the discipline fought over how to identify what was distinctive in the lives of those who would become criminally delinquent, what made them different from other boys. And that presumption of difference (and of the task of the discipline as being to discover and explain that difference) also loosened any sense of children being constituted as criminals by carceral institutions and state power.[48] There was less talk of the "boy problem" and more of a focus on how to prevent criminality, which often became a focus on how to isolate the criminal or the criminally inclined from others. There was a continued emphasis on "prevention," and observers of the BBR now praised it as offering "delinquency prevention." There was less emphasis on care and shared responsibility or on a general "boy problem."[49]

As for Jack Robbins, he appears by the 1920s to have found a more settled identity as the "supervisor" of the Boys' Brotherhood Republic. He no longer penned articles that declared war on conventional child-saving institutions. He still appeared occasionally in local papers around the country, where he advocated for the need for local boys' clubs and similar institutions. He traveled several times to Europe.[50]

It is in any event hard to read too much into the much spottier coverage of Robbins and the BBR in the 1920s and 1930s and 1940s. On February 28, 1921, after a seventeen-year-old committed a bank robbery, Robbins managed to get himself quoted, along with other professionals and experts, about the explosion in youth crime. He was, Robbins said, of the view that youth crime came from a growing "contempt for law, political alliances between crooked politicians, police and dive-keepers' pull in the administration of justice, unemployment[,] and a general 'soreness' felt by youth against 'everything in the world.'"[51]

In 1936, Jack Robbins, recently returned from a trip to Europe, announced an appeal to Chicago's Jewish community to help him "personally" supervise "the emigration, rehabilitation, education and American assimilation" of a dozen German Jewish boys between the ages of twelve and fourteen. The boys were in a "pitiful" condition, and they had not been able to attend school because of Nazi edicts. But they were "intelligent, clean, honest, ambitious lads," who could be molded into good American citizens. He intended to place the boys in "modest" American homes, not the homes of the wealthy, which would do them an "injustice." He would find them jobs, and he expected them to become self-supporting "almost as soon as they arrive[d]." But he needed help from the Jewish community to speed that transition.[52]

Robbins had mostly made his peace with institutional authority and with bourgeois society. His later efforts to create new BBRs around the country were initiated with the support and involvement of adult professionals. In 1925, he directed a sixteen-year-old, Harold Krowech, who the year before had become the elected judge of the BBR, to set up a branch in Los Angeles. But Dr. Miriam Van Waters, a local juvenile court referee and a feminist, was said to be managing the research and the financing for a Los Angeles "republic."[53] It needs to be added that, except for the New York BBR, most of the efforts to establish BBRs in other cities failed.

In 1937, Robbins was back in Los Angeles for the purpose of forming a "club." Evidently nothing had come into being over the previous dozen years. During that same tour, he visited Berkeley, where he spoke about a club being formed in Seattle. He also noted that there was no need for one in San Francisco: "Agencies of all kinds are doing a splendid piece of work there with youths who run afoul of the law." In Berkeley, he was introduced by Mrs. Elizabeth Lossing, the head of the local police department's "crime prevention bureau," and by the chief of police. A few days later, identified as a "nationally known figure in boys' social service work," he spoke before the Exchange Club of Stockton, California, in the Central Valley. There was apparently interest in creating a local BBR "city" there: "The overprivileged boy has more than he needs, and the underprivileged, troublesome youth has nothing." Underprivileged boys did not join "adult-supervised" boys' clubs, because they had been "shaped and built in a different world." They did not feel they "belong[ed]." A small BBR that was understood to prepare "problem boys" for eventual entry into the Boy Scouts or the YMCA then began in Stockton, and it was still in existence in 1943, funded by the Community Chest. And in Modesto, thirty miles away, in the "Okie" community of "Little Oklahoma," a young man was evidently inspired to establish a version of the Boys' Brotherhood Republic, which had a momentary existence.[54]

In May 1937, the *Christian Science Monitor* ran an article about the "Bangor Brotherhood Republic," said to be a flourishing institution in Chicago and in New York, which was becoming a "national institution." The movement to nationalize it reportedly came out of a *Reader's Digest* article which had generated more than five hundred letters from all over the country. Former mayors of the BBR would take over new branches. Other boys who were at present members would be sent to college on free scholarships, where they would study sociology, psychology, social work, and related subjects. According to the article, Robbins thought that growth ought to proceed slowly, since all branches had to "live up to the original principles."[55]

A 1937 memoir by Caroline Colgate, the wife of the heir to the Colgate fortune and a backer of the New York BBR, praised Robbins for allowing boys to "perform" self-government. At the same time, she also emphasized that the BBR effectively combated "subversive propaganda." Its success, she thought, meant that "neither socialism nor communism" would be able to "arouse interest in these boys."[56]

To observe that his radicalism may have been muted is not to say that Jack Robbins was accepted into Chicago's power structure. His name never appeared on any of the innumerable boards or advisory committees that supported juvenile justice or the amelioration of poverty in Chicago. He apparently gained the support of a few wealthy Chicagoans, but not to the extent that he became part of their world.

On the other hand, he would be sent, along with a lawyer who had once been a member of the BBR, to represent the state of Illinois at the 1934 Attorney General's Conference on Crime in Washington, DC.[57] And in 1930, a list of recommended book titles he compiled for the boys of the BBR, with the aid of Sinclair Lewis and "several university professors," would be highlighted in the "Turns with a Bookworm" column of the *New York Herald Tribune*. The list included Berkman's *Prison Memories of an Anarchist*, Dostoyevsky's *Crime and Punishment*, Dreiser's *Sister Carrie*, Tolstoy's *Resurrection*, Twain's *Connecticut Yankee*, Wells's *War of the Worlds*, and Zangwill's *Children of the Ghetto*, among other titles. That list was soon critiqued by a librarian for overemphasizing fiction and for the absence of portraits of heroic men.[58]

The BBR also presented a less radical face to the city of Chicago. A 1923 notice mentioned that a police detective had spoken to the boys at the BBR. He praised them and their organization, noting that "good boys will never tolerate bad boys. . . . Just as a bad apple will spoil the entire barrel, so will one bad boy spoil the kids of his neighborhood." Another notice that year mentioned that the warden of the county jail, along with a recently paroled young man, gave a lecture at the BBR. The recently paroled young man advised the boys to "obey the parents." In 1924, the BBR participated in a "Boys' Loyalty Parade" (see figure 15).

Much of the news of the BBR now appeared as items in the "womens' club" pages of the *Chicago Tribune*. Many other stories focused on sports events held at or by the BBR, particularly boxing contests and basketball games. Notices in the papers attended to the stamp club within the BBR. The BBR also held a

Figure 15: The BBR in 1939 (cartoon). Source unknown, in the Edmund D. Hulbert scrapbook, Chicago History Museum.

successful summer camp in Wisconsin, run much like other "fresh air" camps, though with fewer rules and amenities.[59] The Chicago BBR continued to hold Job Days, reframed as a "free employment service." By 1940 the "day" had an adult director, presumably paid. The headline of a *Tribune* story that year announced that there were thirteen "youths" applying for every job. There was, of course, still a Depression going on.[60]

On the other hand, in 1930, the BBR had made the explorer Dr. Frederick A. Cook, whose claims to have reached the North Pole were generally debunked and who had spent five years in prison for fraud, its "permanent physical director." Cook was also given a life membership, previously only awarded to Mrs. Marshall Field, an early benefactor, and to Teddy Roosevelt. The boys felt the doctor had not received "a square deal." Cook planned to establish a health center at the BBR, and he also may have worked as a chemistry teacher.[61]

In August 1938, representatives from the Boys' Brotherhood Republic participated as invited speakers at the International Police Congress in Toronto. A question debated at the meeting was whether swing music had a "demoralizing influence" on youth. Most of the police chiefs interviewed were not opposed to such music, although Sanford Bates, the director of the Boys' Clubs of America, who had previously been the first director of the Federal Bureau of Prisons, did. "A boy or girl could not be in full possession of his faculties," he felt, "when jittering to the driving rhythms of a swing band." By contrast, Mayor Sheldon Millman of the BBR described a recent "jam session" in Chicago attended by one hundred thousand young people. "Youth has to have an outlet for its exuberance. Swing provides it by furnishing an emotional relief. It is definitely not demoralizing. Would you prefer to have the youth of the country hang around streets shooting dice?"[62]

* * *

Who was Jack Robbins? For most of the 1920s and 1930s, the letterhead of the BBR, indeed, most every piece of paper I have seen that was produced by the organization, was emblazoned with "Jack Robbins, Founder and Supervisor." And yet, what did those titles really mean? He insisted on his relative marginality to the life of the organization. The boys ran the place. He denied that he served as an authority, even as he asserted his presence. He hid behind the ambiguity of being a "big brother." Nothing more. He wanted credit and he didn't. Who he was remained a mystery, as did his relationship with the boys and with their organization.

In 1938, the Chicago BBR produced a celebratory pamphlet, a small book entitled *Life of the Boys' Brotherhood Republic*, surely intended as a fundraising device.[63] The book is a compilation, combining several journalists' accounts, many photographs of the boys and their activities, fulsome descriptions of several donors, and a listing at the back of the men and women who constituted the boards of directors of both the New York and the Chicago BBRs (see figure 16).

What it was as well was an effort to describe the "life" of the BBR without the presence of Jack Robbins. He was almost entirely removed from its history.

WHERE BOYS RULE

Figure 16: Dedication page and selected pages from Life of the Boys' Brotherhood Republic (Chicago: Boys' Brotherhood Republic, 1938). Author's collection.

A Typical Court Trial. Trials are held every Sunday night. A B.B.R. jury consists of six selected citizens. Any citizen is eligible to serve on a jury. (The boy in chair on the right was on trial when this picture was taken.)

Awaiting the Verdict. This interested group of citizens is anxiously awaiting the verdict of the six-man jury, which is deliberating the fate of a citizen on trial for a minor offense. They have heard the judge instruct the jury as to the seriousness of the occasion, and are wondering what effect the evidence brought out by the witnesses will have upon the jury's decision.

A Court Trial at the B.B.R. in New York. The prosecuting attorney is making his final speech to the jury.

Figure 16: (Continued)

Editorial Room For "Boys' World." In this room the B.B.R. news staff publishes its twelve page mimeographed news-paper. The boys do all the work of editing, planning, and mimeographing the paper, which is distributed among all the citizens and friends of the B.B.R. "Boys' World" operates under a free press rule, and there are no restrictions to keep the editors from expressing their opinions freely on any subject.

WHILE THERE IS A BOY IN JAIL, WE TOO ARE PRISONERS. *(Motto of the Investigating Committee).*

Charles G. Dawes, when *Vice-President* of the United States, entertained a delegation of B.B.R. citizens. The boys were his guests at his residence. He conversed several hours with them. In this picture he is shown playing a game of baseball with them after lunch. The picture was taken on the Vice-President's front lawn. In the background is his residence in Evanston, Ill.

General Harry C. Hale entertaining a group of citizens by giving them a feed and some sound advice.

Figure 16: (Continued)

THERE ARE NO BAD BOYS

Folks say we do a lot of things
We hadn't ought-a had
We never mean a bit of harm
Nor do them to be bad
But when a chance just comes
  along
With fun a-peekin' through
We take it mostly just because
We've nothing else to do.

Boys are an awful problem
All the grownup people say
But honest all we really want
Is just a chance to play
And all us boys from country
  towns
And from the cities too
Will quit what you call mischief
If you showed us what to do.

The First Unpedigreed Dog Show *ever held in this country was originated by the Boys' Brotherhood Republic. It was held at the B.B.R. headquarters with 106 entries. The above picture shows four B.B.R. citizens entering their dogs. Later, the plan was taken up by the "Herald and Examiner" which continued working in conjunction with the B.B.R. for four years. The last show was held at Dreamland, one of the largest halls in Chicago.*

"Accepted" citizens are told of the ideals of the B.B.R. by a member of the citizenship committee.

This Play *is typical of the dramatic productions which are presented every so often by our drama group. The above play was presented by citizens of the Republic at the Studebaker Theatre. It is a two-act comedy translated from the Spanish of Miguel Ramos Carrion by Clarence Stratton. All roles from the portly Don Indalecio to the chic Marija were taken by citizens of the B.B.R. A good crowd filled the theatre.*

Figure 16: (*Continued*)

Thematically, the book was a mass of contradictions, combining the communitarian and anti-capitalist themes that had long shaped the BBR with more sentimental and conventional, pro-capitalist, adult-centered understandings of what a boys' club should be. On its front, the title, *Life of the Boys' Brotherhood Republic*, stood with a photograph of a neatly coiffed blond boy. On the back of that front cover, one found a page of drawings of many boys, made by a "boy citizen." The boys portrayed were white, but of diverse ethnicities and with messier hair. These were placed below the mantra, "Where Boys Rule," and above a sentimental dedication: "To all those who understand that boys are at heart adventurers, romancers, and brave little crusaders; who help them find the paths of true adventure and shield them from the tragic mistakes that beset the boy alone." Who it was who understood what boys were at heart and who shielded them from mistakes was not explained. The next page, labeled a "forward," began with the creation of the BBR "by a group of boys," alone, with the 1914 motto, "So long as there are boys in trouble, we too are in trouble." In 1938, twenty-four years later, this "boys' club" still served "at the shrine of 'the other fellow.'" On the other hand, the paragraph continued, the members of this club, by now "about 10,000" in number, had "never acknowledged that boys needed reforming." And the second motto of the "club" remained "There are no bad boys."

The foreword continued with a paragraph devoted to the work of the BBR in interceding on behalf of boys: gaining them parole and freedom, taking them from the police, from the juvenile court, and from reformatories. Boys accepted into membership would find "wholesome companions and a natural outlet for their interests and energies." Soon they too would serve under the "motto." The result, the foreword continued, was that "society," meaning the adult world, might "feel relieved of any concern regarding" these boys' "usefulness."[64]

The next page characterized "the Republic" as a distinctively "modern method of treating juvenile delinquency problems." The page is dominated by a poster-like modernist drawing of a boy looking up from tenement streets at a very white and clean building, over the title "The House of the Modern Age."

For the next several pages, the pamphlet reproduced photographs, haphazardly taken from the previous twenty-four years, with descriptions of the meetings and committees and councils of the organization. A little box on page 4 noted that the BBR was "indorsed" by the Chicago Association of Commerce and was a member of the Council of Social Agencies of Chicago. On pages 7 and 8, the cooperative store and the savings bank were described.

Page 9 might be seen as a distillation of the multiple and contradictory streams that produced this 1938 portrait. One photograph shows a large group of boys entering the "city hall" over a posted sign with the quotation: "Because we have known the torment of thirst, we are digging a well where other boys may drink." This was a slight modification of a quotation found at the front of Ernest Thompson Seton's popular children's book *Two Little Savages* (1903). Seton was a writer of nature books and books about Indians. He was also one of the founders of the Boy Scouts, an organization Robbins had once denounced.[65] To the right of the first photograph was a second photograph of four serious-looking boys, members of the "investigating" committee, "out on a case." They were on their way to meet a boy just released from reform school. The committee was described as the "most important" in the Republic because it gave "a fellow, who is down another chance." At the bottom of the page was a photograph of a "welfare" meeting of various committee chairmen with the BBR's mayor, a meeting that occurred monthly. And on the center right of the page, under the photograph of the investigating committee, was a little box devoted to the slogan "THINK OF YOUR MOTHER." This slogan had been voted the best of many submitted by BBR citizens in a contest. The creator of this slogan was said to be a boy who "has no mother and does not know where his father is."

The next page was devoted to praise of Edmund Hulbert, the banker whose friends had donated the funds to build a "clubhouse," Hulbert Hall, for the organization. The page also included an ambiguous paragraph about financial support of the organization. The "inner work" of the BBR was said to be "self-supporting," reliant on the taxes each "citizen" paid. "But the building, equipment, and upkeep" were "furnished by friends who wish to share in the fine work this organization is doing for boys." The impetus for that support was given by "older boys" from the "pioneering" days of the organization, who convinced charitably inclined individuals to offer financial support. Nothing was said about the Community Trust, which owned the building.[66]

The next pages continued with photographs of the boys in meetings, and portraits of prominent alumni and distinguished visitors and supporters. A few of the photographs were of the new New York City branch and its adult founders. Page 15 offered a list of books and magazines that had described the work of the BBR, including a Dutch journal. Page 17 included a photograph of the boys who participated in the "first unpedigreed dog show" and a photograph of the actors in a drama club production of a comedy translated from the Spanish, including several boys in women's clothing. In a box was a poem, a riff on the notion that "there are no bad boys," one that contrasted sharply with the original impulse of the BBR. According to the author, what seems like "mischief" was just a desire "to play." And boys would quit "what you call mischief," if only adults would show the boys "what to do."

There followed descriptions of sporting events and contests and the summer camp, Camp Freedom, recently established in Burlington, Wisconsin. The motto of the camp was: (1) Be fair and (2) Be gentle. These were "the only two existing rules."

On page 29, a photograph showed a large number of boys staring at a new motto: "Charity is the killer of a boy's best trait: initiative." One imagines that in 1938 this critique had a different meaning than the critique of charity that Robbins had articulated in 1914 and 1915 in *the Day Book*. Page 35 reproduced the "nine aims" the BBR had adopted at its first meeting in May 1914. The first two were, once again, "to prevent boys from getting into trouble," and "to offer companionship to boys who are in trouble." At the bottom of the page, in a box, was a new "aim": "A Boys' Brotherhood Republic citizen, gets what he goes after, but he only goes after what he has a right to get."[67]

The next page offered a bullet pointed list of the "highlights" of BBR history—without any mention of Jack Robbins. And in the next ten pages, the pamphlet reproduced excerpts from articles and testimonials devoted to the BBR. Pages 44 and 45 reprinted two *Reader's Digest* articles, one about the founding of the Chicago BBR and one about the founding of the New York branch. Both of these articles did mention Jack Robbins in passing. But it is striking that no other mention of him occurred anywhere else in the pamphlet. Indeed, several of the reprinted articles were edited, apparently to remove any mention of him.

The last two pages described how to establish a BBR. While the authors of those pages insisted that success depended on starting "from the bottom," and on the initiative of boy "charter citizens," still this section was written to adults and for adults, to the "social worker" and the adult "thinking citizen." Not to boys. And the back page of the pamphlet included lists of the "board of directors" of the Chicago BBR and of the New York one. Jack Robbins, "supervisor," was listed as a member of the Chicago BBR's board. The New York board of directors was double the size of the Chicago one, and it included several more prominent and wealthy backers. The bottom of the back page solicited support: "Your investment will go a long way towards making the boy of today into a dependable man of tomorrow."[68]

My point, to conclude this examination of the 1938 book, is not that Jack Robbins's themes and values had disappeared. They had not, although an overlay of more conservative goals and values jostled with his. The need to draw in charitably inclined rich people, as well as the need to draw on the support of social workers and court personnel, were manifest. Yet there also remained a defiant or resistant insistence on the BBR's long-standing goals and its continuing identity. It was all there, sometimes on the same page. The point, rather, is that Jack Robbins himself had practically disappeared. No photographs. Only two glancing mentions in fifty pages of text. What that absence means, whether he was removed from sight because of concerns about his politics or his sexuality or because of irritation with his manner or personality, is impossible to say. The point is that he was mostly gone, written out of the history of the organization he created, at a time when he was still the titular "supervisor."

* * *

In 1940, as the possibility of American entry into the war loomed, the elected council of the BBR voted to make military training compulsory for all citizens of the republic between the ages of sixteen and nineteen. At the meeting, one "citizen" protested, arguing that no part of the BBR had ever been compulsory. But "this is an emergency," was the response. The boys had "heard their mothers and fathers talk about the suffering and oppression in the countries they came from, Poland, Russia, and Hungary. . . . 'We voted to have training camp, so we can be prepared to fight for our freedom,'" said one boy, "and we know what that word means." They had named their summer camp "Camp Freedom." As the *Tribune* noted, it lived up to its name. No rules, but also no modern conveniences.

On the other hand, the boy who had protested conscription was soon elected to the highest office in the Republic, the mayoralty, ousting those who had tried to impose compulsory military training. He won in a landslide, on a platform opposed to "military conscription" at the BBR. Compulsory military training was, he said "against every ideal our republic stands for." It was something that belonged to the outside world, to the adult world. The *Tribune* article about the election added that a number of older boys in the BBR had voluntarily enlisted in the armed forces.[69]

Also, in 1940, several BBR citizens established a corporation modeled on the Junior Achievement Clubs associated with the adult Lions Clubs. The goal, it was said, was to put city boys through the "paces of business enterprise." The corporation planned to produce metal address signs. And in 1943, in two of his last official acts as the "supervisor" of the BBR, Jack Robbins initiated a $25,000 fundraising drive, which would be sufficient to maintain the program and the summer camp, and then, in a return to past hopes and aspirations, he launched "a campaign" to collect three million pennies from American boys. The pennies would be used to purchase a ranch in memory of Judge Ben Lindsey, the Denver juvenile court judge, who had once been the intended beneficiary of an earlier BBR campaign. The ranch, which would be located either in the Midwest or in California, would be "a vacationland for underprivileged boys." It would be governed, as all BBRs were, "by the boys." And it would become "a fitting, living memorial" to Lindsey's "unselfish career."[70]

In 1942, when Jack Robbins was issued a draft card, he still listed 1530 South Hamlin Avenue, the home of the BBR, as both his place of employment and as his mailing address. He also identified Sheldon Millman, by then a former mayor but apparently also still living at that location, as the one person who would always know where he was.[71]

In the late 1940s, the Boys' Brotherhood Republic was identified as one of several clubs sponsored by the Young Men's Jewish Council. At about the same time, Solomon Frankel, who had replaced Jack Robbins as the adult in charge, was identified as the "director" of the BBR, no longer merely a "supervisor." In 1954, as the racial citizenship of Lawndale and of the republic changed, William M. Simmons from Cleveland, an African American and a former professor of "social administration" at Tennessee State University, was appointed to replace Frankel as director. In 1956, the predominantly African American South Side Boys' Club (with track star Jesse Owens as executive director) merged with the Boys' Brotherhood Republic and another youth center to create the Chicago Youth Centers. By 1959, *Jet* Magazine identified the BBR as 90 percent African American.[72]

* * *

Jack Robbins retired from the BBR in the mid-1940s and moved to Los Angeles. He lived in a cheap hotel, but at some point he bought property in the San Fernando Valley. He was in his sixties. In October 1943, the *Los Angeles Daily News* reported that the BBR had long been preparing to establish a Los Angeles branch. This new initiative was energized by the "recent zoot suit disturbances." Jack Robbins emphasized that he "did not want to step on toes or cause ill favor with any social service agencies." The plan was to create an organization that would "appeal to the type of boy who gets a thrill from being on the street, enjoying independence," the sort of boy who had "to steal to live." He restated the BBR's long-standing focus on self-government, allowing "the boys to work problems out for themselves." Still he also planned to work with the district attorney, the sheriff, a US district court judge, and Superior Court Judge Georgia Bullock. He also worked with the comedians Bud Abbott and Lou Costello to set up a youth foundation in their names. Ralph Goodman, who had been the first mayor of Chicago's Boys' Brotherhood Republic and had become an advertising executive, visited Los Angeles to offer his "moral and physical assistance" to the new organization; Robbins was named the "governor." According to Irvine Robbins, Jack's grandnephew and eventually the administrator of his estate, Jack Robbins also became interested in the conditions confronting poor African American boys in Watts.[73]

At some point, Jack Robbins connected to the film business.[74] The early television series the *Loretta Young Show* devoted three episodes to stories about boys in the early days of the Chicago Boys' Brotherhood Republic. Robbins received coauthorship credit for two of the stories, and he appeared in one of them (see figure 17).

The storylines of the three episodes concerned relations between absent parents and boys reformed or in process of reformation by the BBR. The themes in these episodes all drew on familiar terrain. Jack Robbins's insistence on the failures of parents is a constant presence. Yet they also moved into the bathetic and conventional wisdoms of 1950s child saving and psychology, focusing on the psychodynamics of the parent-child relationships. In one, "Big Jim" (1954), a citizen of the BBR meets his mother, played by Loretta Young, who has been away for many years. He discovers she is still a pickpocket, but he convinces her to live with him and to reform. In a second, "Nobody's Boy" (1954), borrowing a phrase that Robbins had often mobilized in the early years of the BBR, the story begins with an angry boy in reform school. A kindly social worker, played by Loretta Young, puts him in touch with the BBR, and the BBR's citizenship committee admits him into the organization. He discovers that his father, who is serving a prison term, has no knowledge of his existence. They begin to correspond, and then the father is paroled. For a short while father and son live together, while the boy wrestles with the question whether to stay with the BBR. The story ends when the father rejoins the criminal world and the boy commits himself to stay with the BBR.[75]

The plot of the third teleplay, "Reunion" (1955), was somewhat more complex and deserves more space. The script (unfortunately, there is no surviving video of it that I have found, unlike the first two, which are available and can be watched on YouTube) captured the complex relationship to law that characterized the BBR, even as it also absorbed, as all three teleplays did, 1950s understandings of motherhood and parenting. It began with a preface, delivered by the actor Joseph Cotton, who stood in that day for Loretta Young as the show's host. The preface described the earlier two BBR plays as "based on the work" started by "a thoughtful, selfless gentleman" named Jack Robbins. After reciting the motto of the BBR, Cotton described the warm public welcome

Figure 17: Jack Robbins and Loretta Young, 1954 (publicity photograph). Author's collection.

for the first play and the public's demand for a second. "We" happily obliged. And so "Nobody's Boy" appeared. But then letters "demanded a third." But the production company couldn't do it, at least not right away, because they had run out of weeks in the year. But now, in a new year, 1955, there was space to meet the demand and to bring to the small screen another story about the Boys' Brotherhood Republic.

The plot of "Reunion," written by Gene Levitt, a prolific writer for early television, from a story for which Jack Robbins received credit, took place entirely in juvenile court. Jack Robbins is present, as played by Chick Chandler, as are three boy members of the BBR. In addition, on stage (or in court) there are a kindly probation officer, a more bureaucratic representative from the Manual Training School, and a judge. A latecomer to the court is a nervous and anxious woman, Mrs. Graff, played by the well-known actress Nina Foch. According to Levitt's script's point-of-view shot, Mrs. Graff is "about 35, but her age is a matter of conjecture." The script continues: "Her eyes reflect neither youth nor maturity, nor does the shape of her mouth, nor her carriage, nor anything else tell us more. There is the shell of a woman. This is something of blood and flesh and bone and muscle, but it is nothing of spirit. Her hair-do is neat and uninspired. Her dress is cheap and new and an alien thing to her body."[76]

The court is hearing a petition for custody of a boy. The petition has been brought by the BBR on behalf of the boy's mother (I am skeptical that would ever have been possible, legally, even given the looser procedural standards of the juvenile court—but it worked as a theatrical device). The boy, Paul, is not present on stage or in court. He will remain offstage. He is waiting in the judge's chambers. Paul had first been in court six months earlier, following the death of his father, at a time when no one knew that his mother was still alive. (To reduce the tension the reader must be feeling, the nervous woman in the courtroom, Mrs. Graff, is his mother.) The court had placed the boy in the training school. The boy had escaped from the school after one month. But he was captured three days later. He had escaped again, with the aid of some of the boys in the BBR. The investigator for the training school testified that the boy, Paul, "intelligent but uncooperative, unstable, potentially mischievous and rebellious," had "a complete disregard for authority." He was also "sullen and unfriendly." There was hope that these defects would "alter" once a "period of shock" had passed.

Why did Paul behave so badly? He was disillusioned because he had discovered that the father he idolized was nothing but a criminal who had been shot to death while resisting arrest. The kindly and more sympathetic probation officer next testified that Paul's "uncooperative conduct" resulted from the constraints of being in the training school, which made it impossible for him to search for his mother. Once his father was revealed to have been dishonest and criminal, he no longer believed what his father had told him, which was that his mother was not alive. And he was determined to find her. The response of the cooler and less sympathetic investigator for the training school was that the mother was not competent to take custody of the child, and the investigator urged the court to "recommit" the boy to the training school.

The judge next turned to the boys of the BBR in the courtroom. Eugene was sworn in. A boy of seventeen. He had been in the BBR for seven years, ever since his parents were burned to death in a fire. (This would not have been possible early on in the history of the BBR. No one could join at the age of ten.) When had he first met Paul? Eugene answered: The man who ran the corner newsstand near the BBR clubhouse had told him about Paul. Paul had been stealing money (pennies) from the newsstand and food from the grocery store. The grocer wanted the BBR to get to the boy before the police did. Had Eugene succeeded in doing so, the judge asked? No, Eugene answered ("guilt shows"). The police already had arrested Paul.[77]

But Eugene helped Paul escape from the police. "I whispered to him to run when the policeman went for me . . . then I kicked over the edge of a vegetable stand and ran." Eugene added: "Mr. Robbins doesn't know about this." Nor did anyone else in the BBR. The judge: "Why are you telling this now?" Eugene: "Because I'm under oath." Eugene's testimony continued. He brought Paul to Hulbert Hall, got him clean clothes and a meal and pocket money. Then he took Paul to see "the boss." That is, he took him to Jack Robbins. The judge: "You wanted to get Paul to join the BBR?" No, that wasn't it. Eugene wanted "to get the BBR to join Paul, in looking for his mother." The judge lectured the boy: he approved of the goal of helping Paul find his mother, though "the court could not—and does not—approve of any individual taking the law into his own hands, for any reason whatsoever . . . Obstructing an officer of the law in the performance of his duty is a crime against all of society."

The judge turned to Jack Robbins. "When Eugene . . . brought Paul to you, did he tell you that Paul had escaped from the Training School?" Yes, Robbins answered. Did Robbins then notify the training school? No, he had not. Why not? "I would have been violating a confidence, Your Honor. I could advise Paul to go back . . . but I could not tell the Training School where he was." (As a "big brother," Robbins was as bound by boyhood's resistance to being a snitch as any of the BBR's citizens would be.) What did he advise the boy? He advised him to stay with "us, while the BBR boys looked for his mother." What did the boy say? Nothing. But he was "confident" his mother would be found. The BBR mayor then appointed an "investigating committee," led by another boy in the courtroom, Fred. Fred testified that it took them three days to find the mother.

The plot now shifted to Fred and the mother, Mrs. Graff. She was found in the drunk tank in a local jail in Gary, Indiana. When this was said in court, the mother fainted, and the judge ordered a recess (which allowed time for a commercial break). When she had recovered, Fred tried to give her a glass of water. Jack Robbins helped. "This is a test," he told her. Still, she wanted to leave. "Without Paul?" She didn't think the judge would ever give her Paul, since she was a drunk. Robbins: "You *were* a drunk." Mrs. Graff: "And maybe I still am!" After more time passed, she did drink the water. Fred managed a "grin."

The judge questioned Fred: Did Mrs. Graff have a house, a place to live? No. Did she have a job? No. Did she have any money? No. "She didn't have any of the things a grown-up is supposed to have. . . . But then I told her that I had come because of her son, Paul, and everything suddenly became different! Then she had a million dollars! That was the reason she was so bad off, Judge! She didn't have Paul! She didn't have anything to live for!" Did she tell him that? "No, sir, not in so many words. But I could figure it out." Her husband had just up and left one day without a word, taking Paul. He vanished into thin air. The husband was a confidence man who took Paul because it made him look respectable when he met people. He said he was a widower to play on their sympathy.[78]

Fred then telephoned the BBR. He knew that Paul would be happy to hear he was right, that his mother was alive. But he called too late. Paul had heard that a probation officer was coming to the BBR home. And once again, he ran. Did the boy run away from the BBR? No, one of the BBR boys ran away with him so that he would not be alone. Why, asked the judge? Once again to obstruct the law? Fred didn't answer. The judge: "Does the BBR think that their own boys' government is the only one to respect? Is that the BBR attitude?"

A third boy got up in the court. Lou was "short, Cagney-cocky, and crew-cut." He was the one who hid Paul away, ran with him, not Fred. Fred sat down. Lou now testified. He lived at Hulbert Hall. He was between foster homes right now. He was an orphan, and he was an alumnus of the training school. He had been a habitual thief. "And I might still be there—and still stealing—if I didn't happen to meet up with Mr. Robbins by accident one day, while he was visiting . . . our place." But, said the judge, obstructing an official from doing his duty was also breaking the law. Lou: "That's not news to me, Judge." Yet you helped Paul to hide from the probation officer. Why? Because he (Lou) knew what it was like on the inside of the training school. And he knew that Paul would suffer there. "We had to hold out a while, Judge—for his sake. I'm sure it was the right thing to do, your Honor." Why? "Because I was the one who got to tell Paul that we had found his mother." And what did Paul say then? He said: "She won't have to worry about being poor any more. I'll take care of her." Lou: "How about that, Judge? Rocks in his head, huh?—a kid like that couldn't support a sparrow, let alone a drunk—!" He stopped short, "realizing too late the tyranny of his careless words" (that those words might hurt Mrs. Graff).

Mrs. Graff took the stand. The court spent time on her lack of a permanent residence, on the fact that she had not been able to hold a job for any length of time. "The questioning is becoming bombardment. Her defenses are poor." The judge concluded his questioning by asking her: is she fit to be awarded custody of a ten-year-old boy? She answered: Of course not. "She isn't even a woman. A woman is human. . . . And how could she be human? How could she be something living? How could she when her heart was torn out six years, five months . . . and four days ago. . . . How could she be anything except a drunk? And a charity case." She then turned to the BBR boys—and she was transformed. She thanked them for their charity. And she told them that "the fight has just started." That boy in there (pointing to the judge's chambers), "that boy is mine." She tried to walk out of the courtroom, to leave. But the judge stopped her, threatening to jail her for contempt of court.

The ruling: The judge denied her custody of her child. But he gave her "temporary custody," based on the "courage" she displayed "when purposefully put to the test by the court." So, she got actual custody, which would become full custody, depending on her future conduct. She went into the judge's chambers to get Paul. Fade out. The end.[79]

It is, of course, not easy to read such a script and reach any kind of conclusion about what it means. In true 1950s fashion, the psychodynamics of the parent-child relationship took priority, as they did in all three of the teledramas drawn from the BBR. The judge is a stock good judge. And the boys are, to some extent, classic stereotypes of charming rough boys, not-so-little rascals. And yet, Robbins and Levitt managed to slip in what we might call the alternative legality, or higher-law disobedience, that marked the Boys' Brotherhood Republic from its inception. The judge was treated respectfully. And yet his rule and his rules were violated repeatedly, with impunity. The boys were, in their way, governing themselves. It was clear that they understood there were more important things to do to lead an honorable life than to be obedient.

Apparently, these episodes were successes, as marked by the demand to have repeated showings. And, at least according to Robbins, there were plans for thirty-nine more half-hour episodes about the BBR, though as far as I know no more were made.[80]

* * *

During the 1950s, Jack Robbins came back to Chicago often, particularly for events that celebrated the success of "his" republic. In 1951, some of the "first" citizens, those who had been there in 1914–1916, held a reunion. Forty-eight alumni attended, including physicians, lawyers, engineers, and businessmen.

A second event to honor Jack Robbins was held in 1953, with over one hundred alumni present. At that time, the *Tribune* noted that there were over thirty thousand alumni (presumably one more exaggeration that the newspapers reproduced). In 1955, twenty-one former mayors of the BBR organized a celebratory dinner in his honor. At that dinner, attorney Abert Marks, who would become one of the named trustees and executors of Robbins's will, spoke. "How can we tell the world that there is no such thing as a juvenile delinquent?" He answered by identifying the varieties of successful career paths that those who joined the republic followed. In 1956, there was once again a dinner, attended this time by four hundred former club members. And in December 1957, one more dinner occurred for the man whom the attendees identified as their "boss."[81]

Harry Slonaker, who had been sent by Jack Robbins in the early 1930s to found the New York BBR, had left New York by the early 1950s (after some upheaval there). He moved with his wife to San Jose, California, where he worked to create a boys' club. Evidently, in 1956, he was having difficulties with the work, and he wrote to Jack Robbins for advice. Robbins replied, happy that Slonaker was willing to express his worries, happy to offer advice. He cautioned Slonaker not to join the national organization of the "Boys Clubs of America." The Chicago BBR had belonged to it for fifteen years, and Robbins thought that there had been no benefits. The national organization never stopped pointing out to the world that he, Jack Robbins, was not a college graduate. "They never really gave us any money or friends. All we got from them was literature and instructions. . . . You will see!" The leader of the national organization (by then, a Mr. Armstrong) did not like "self-governing boys clubs." Robbins warned Slonaker that they would try to force Slonaker to change his methods and program and that membership in the Boys' Clubs of America would not help him "gain entry" to "the big corporations." Slonaker should not tie himself to "rules and regulations . . . made by men who never had any experience with boys." The goal, Robbins advised, ought to be to make the San Jose boys feel that the "Boys' City is theirs and that you are only helping them. It is not too late to train them to make them feel that way."

He commiserated with Slonaker, who had apparently just been appointed as a member of a San Jose grand jury investigating juvenile delinquency. (The mid-1950s was a moment when juvenile delinquency, sometimes framed as "alienated youth," had once again become a matter of great cultural worry. See films like *Rebel without a Cause*.) "That Grand Jury Job you needed like Bull-Dog Feldman needs another wife." There were, he thought, four thousand grand juries meeting across the US. All were "solving the Juvenile Delinquency problem." And yet the problem kept growing. It seemed as if cities were "building more juvenile detention homes because the old ones are too small." He had recently passed by the Hollywood Boys' Club and gone inside. It was a big building, with nine workers and (only) thirty-two boys playing pool and ping-pong. And yet there was already a drive for a bigger building, one that would cost $250,000. With it, were they finally "going to solve Juvenile Delinquency?"[82]

Robbins concluded by reflecting on his own situation. He planned to put his "little property" (2138 Vine Street, in Hollywood) on the market. If he sold it, he would "probably" move back east. One of his "boys" lived in South Bend, Indiana, with his wife and no kids, and he had asked Robbins to share his home. The boy was a doctor, "and it sounds like a good set up." He was also considering becoming "a guest at the Kings Home for Old Men." (The James C. King Home for Old Men was a "refined" home in Evanston.) But he worried that the management required him to turn over all his belongings to them in exchange for their care. He was, predictably, scared when he read their rules and regulations. Those read "as if their 'guests' were Juvenile Delinquents."[83]

Two years later, when he died, he was still living in Los Angeles. His property remained unsold. The one published obituary, in the *Chicago Tribune*, did not list a cause of death. He was, according to the *Tribune*, survived by one sister.[84]

SIX

Jack Robbins's Will

Jack Robbins's will, dated December 2, 1957, was written and witnessed in Chicago, the week before what would be the last event held in his honor. It had some of the formalities and features of a professionally drafted will, but it raised enough legal issues that one imagines that Gerald Resnick, the attorney whose name and address can be found at the bottom of the will, and who may have drafted the text, was either incompetent or was overborne by a willful client. Perhaps it would be best to regard Resnick as no more than Jack Robbins's scrivener.[1]

The will began by directing that there be no religious ceremony after Jack Robbins's death. "It is my desire to die and be interred as I have lived." He wanted an "immediate cremation," without ritual.

He then divided his estate into two parts. One part, worth around $10,000, went as gifts to his sister and her son (both of whom lived in Canada) and to Chicago's Multiple Sclerosis Foundation. This part raised no issues. The second part, the part that produced a case, consisted of two parcels of real estate in Los Angeles, in California. Those lands, or the proceeds of their sale, worth a bit more than $20,000, were given in trust to three trustees, all from Chicago, all with connections to or former membership in the Boys' Brotherhood Republic.[2] Robbins gave those trustees full discretionary power to support the purpose articulated in the trust. That purpose was "to provide for the care, comfort, support, medical attention, education, sustenance, maintenance or custody" of a "Negro child or children" whose father or mother "or both" had been convicted and imprisoned for having committed "a crime or misdemeanor of a political nature."

Robbins next gave four examples of what he meant by a crime of "a political nature":

1. Convictions and incarcerations for violating laws that "proscribe, limit, abolish, enjoin[,] or regulate the teaching, advising, adopting, advocating [,] or implementing any political, geopolitical [,] or social-political doctrine, thesis, theory [,] or philosophy, or speaking or writing in support thereof." He never mentioned Marxism or socialism or communism. But anyone living in postwar America would have understood what he was identifying. He noted violations of the Smith Act of the Federal Government, the 1940 law that made it a criminal offense to advocate the violent overthrow of the government or to organize or be a member of any group or society devoted to such advocacy, as an example of what he had in mind.

2. Convictions and incarcerations for contempt for refusing to answer questions about "religious, social, economic[,] or political opinions, beliefs, persuasions[,] or affiliations past and present." Robbins identified "appearances" before the House Un-American Activities Committee (commonly known as HUAC) or the Internal Securities Committee of Congress, along with the prosecutions that resulted from refusing to answer their intrusive questions (e.g., Have you ever been a member of the Communist Party? Do you know if x or y was ever a member of the Communist Party?), as examples of the kinds of convictions he had in mind.

3. The varieties of ways dissidents were arrested and convicted for having made "false" statements with regard to political "affiliations, beliefs, or associations." In particular, he marked refusals to sign the loyalty oaths that were ubiquitous at the time. He mentioned the anti-communist provisions of the Taft-Hartley Act and prosecutions under the McCarren Walters Immigration Act and prosecutions under Illinois's Broyles Bill (a state loyalty-oath law that had harmed the career of Albert Soglin, one of the named executors and trustees of Robbins's will) and the various state or local versions of HUAC as examples of the kinds of provisions that concerned him.

4. Convictions or incarcerations for involvement in the trade union movement or for exercises of the right to bargain collectively or to go out on strike.[3]

All of these examples, which together constituted a relatively complete compilation of the characteristic repressive acts identified with McCarthyism and the postwar anti-communist crusade, were mentioned only as illustrative. They exemplified the kinds of crimes for which parents of the "Negro child or children" beneficiaries might have been convicted. Robbins meant to guide the trustees in their deliberations, not to restrict them.

He knew, he continued, that "law" was an "ambulatory institution," contingent and changing. He expected that after his death, new repressive laws would be adopted, once again "calculated to limit, abolish, or circumscribe the field of activity in unorthodox or unpopular political or economic causes or philosophies." People would "be arrested, convicted, and imprisoned as a result." He did not believe the age of repressive laws had come to an end. So, he left decisions about the distribution of the trust proceeds to the trustees' discretion, with the sole constraint that the beneficiaries had to be "minor Negro children of such defendants." But it was up to the trustees to decide what "in the future" might constitute a "crime or misdemeanor of a political nature" that would be used to punish the parents of those Negro children.

He trusted his chosen trustees: Herbert K. Abrams, by then already becoming an internationally prominent public health doctor, who worked in occupational health both in the United States and in China; Albert Soglin, a mathematics teacher who had unsuccessfully challenged the Broyles (loyalty-oath) law in Illinois and would eventually become a much-loved teacher at Chicago's Loop College (which later became Harold Washington College); and Abert Marks, a Chicago lawyer whose obituary gave priority to his early achievement of having been elected the mayor in the Boys' Brotherhood Republic. Abrams had also once served as the mayor of the BBR, after a term as the BBR's city clerk. All three of them grew up in the Lawndale neighborhood, where the original BBR was located, and all went to the same high school, Marshall High School. I can't find direct evidence that Albert Soglin was ever part of the BBR. But his younger brother, Seymour, had been a member of the BBR city council in 1940, at the time that the BBR reversed its previous decision to make military training mandatory. So, it is altogether likely that he as well had once been in the BBR. In any case, Robbins had selected them to make decisions that gave effect to his wishes. But he also deferred to them and to their discretionary judgment, only insisting that the trust proceeds support a "Negro child or children."[4]

In a final section of the will, Jack Robbins looked back on his life in relation to this bequest. He was "aware" of the will's "unusual and unorthodox" character. Perhaps unnecessarily, he added: "Unorthodoxy or lack of conformity have never been a deterrent or governing factor . . . in my life."

There followed a kind of credo:

First, he had always believed in "full, complete, and unabridged freedom of expression in a democratic society." To restrict such freedom to those who expressed "orthodox or popular" values was a contradiction in terms. The majority, "the orthodox and conformists," had no need for legal immunity or protection. It was the advocate for the unpopular who needed "the unabridged and inalienable right to differ and be heard." Second, in his lifetime he had been "associated and affiliated with causes, campaigns, beliefs[,] and organizations" that advocated or espoused "unorthodox or unpopular causes." And he had lived to see that many of those "concepts and philosophies" became "heralded and accepted" as part of the "progress of our society." They had become parts of everyday life, "natural and respectable concomitants of the democratic processes." Yet, he continued, earlier, those who advocated for those concepts and philosophies "were persecuted, ostracized, and sometimes jailed, and their families were left destitute and devoid of all means of support and maintenance." He had learned from "a long line of such experiences" about the ways people put themselves in jeopardy as a result of exercising their right to dissent. But he had also learned that "irrespective of this jeopardy" there were "brave and intrepid men and women" who would continue to insist on their right to be heard, "personal security notwithstanding." Third, he wished to preserve the right to dissent, "the right to be different." That is why he created the trust in the form it took. He regarded the trust as his final "contribution to a more democratic way of life." And finally, he reiterated that the "right to disagree, the right to dissent, the right to be different"—these were "the warp and woof of the fabric of democracy, . . . fertilizers that feed and nurture the tree of liberty and freedom."[5]

The second of those four paragraphs in his credo looked back, I expect, to his work as the supervisor of the Boys' Brotherhood Republic, and before then to the days when he was first known as the "big brother to chanceless waifs." It looked back to a time when it must have felt risky and dangerous to defend troubled boys who were members of the "dangerous classes." Back to a time when he identified himself with those dangerous classes. It also may have looked back even further to a past identity (imagined or real) as a traveling socialist agitator.

But that second paragraph may also have looked forward, or so his lawyers would later argue, toward an African American liberation movement that was struggling to undo the structures of racial segregation. The identification of "Negro child or children" as his intended beneficiary looked to the world he was living in, to postwar America and to the increasing significance of race in defining constitutional rights and freedoms. Jack Robbins had avoided talking about race or ethnicity earlier in his life. Others noted that his BBR was in a heavily Jewish community and that many of the boys were Jews. He did not.

But if he wanted his will to "speak" to the moment, to what was happening in the late 1950s, it would have to engage with the distinctive presence of African Americans as those most harmed by oppressive public power. As we will see, that engagement created contradictions and ambiguities in the will that made its interpretation uncertain, but also shaped lawyers' strategies.

To read the will in light of the narrative of Jack Robbins's life makes it clear that what mattered to him was freedom: freedom of expression, freedom from a repressive state, as well as freedom to create institutions that would allow for the care of those who most needed it. Freedom for those who wanted to live a less hierarchically shaped life. The trust he drafted was an awkward and prolix last effort to do something: to offer care and protection to those left behind, uncared for and unprotected, in the face of the cruelties and repressions visited on the victims of state power and violence. And it was written as an act of freedom. It was itself a form of civil disobedience.

SEVEN

Enter the Lawyers

What happened after Jack Robbins died? Unexplained mysteries appear as they have so often in this story.

I don't know how Jack Robbins died. And although he died in Los Angeles, nothing was ever said about who was with him when he died or who managed the cremation he had asked for. The will named the three Chicago trustees, Soglin, Abrams, and Marks, to serve as executors of the will. Presumably Robbins thought the will would be probated in Illinois, where they all then lived.

However, because the property was located in California, and he died in California, it would be California courts that would rule on the legality and enforceability of the will and trust. And the Chicago trustees/executors were not appointed to serve as executors in California. Why not? As with so much in our story, there is no clear answer. According to the 1949 California Probate Code, a nonresident could serve as executor if he or she came within the state and submitted to the jurisdiction of California courts. Did that mean that the three named executors chose not to come to California, or were they not informed of the case? Or did the judge in the case exercise his discretion and reject them? We don't know, though it is important to add that no one objected when Irvine Robbins, Jack Robbins's nephew, was appointed as administrator of the estate, cta (cum testamento annexo), by the California Superior Court. That is to say, Irvine Robbins substituted for or replaced the named executors for the purposes of probating the will in California. And all the attorneys involved apparently agreed to that substitution.[1]

Irvine Robbins was Jack Robbins's closest living relative other than his sister in Canada, certainly the closest living in Southern California. He was not mentioned in the will. Irvine had moved to the San Fernando Valley by the mid-1940s, after having grown up in Canada and the state of Washington in the household of Jack's brother, Aaron Robbins (born Rabinovitz), who owned an ice cream store. Although Jack Robbins did not choose to give him any role in the administration of his estate, Irvine Robbins likely had contact with his uncle during the later 1940s and 1950s, when both were living in Southern California.[2]

I have no idea how Hugh R. Manes, a young Chicago-raised lawyer practicing in Los Angeles, was brought in to serve as attorney for the estate. It is possible that one of the named executors/trustees contacted him or the Southern California branch of the American Civil Liberties Union (ACLU) once it became clear that the California courts had jurisdiction and that probate would not occur in Illinois. The appointment of Irvine Robbins as administrator of the estate, cta, may have happened through a petition drafted by Manes, though it is as likely that Manes was hired by Irvine Robbins, a businessman who could certainly pay Manes's legal fees.[3]

More importantly, one would like to know how and why Lee Mishkin appeared to contest the will. Why did he care enough to litigate? I wonder how he even became aware of his great-uncle's death and of the provisions in the will.[4] I find no evidence that he or his immediate family ever had contact with Jack Robbins as Irvine Robbins did. Lee Mishkin was Robbins's grandnephew. According to Hugh Manes, he was "one of three children of a deceased child of a deceased sister of testator."[5] Mishkin was born in 1927, which meant he was about a decade younger than Irvine Robbins. Mishkin spent his childhood mostly in Oakland, though later his family moved to Los Angeles. He had gone to UCLA. By the 1950s, he was establishing a successful career as a cartoon animator. In the early 1950s, he served as an animator for the early television cartoon series "Crusader Rabbit." By 1960, he was the layout artist for "Calvin and the Colonel," a television cartoon series based on the notorious radio and television show "Amos and Andy," although the cartoon version hid the racist blackface roots of the earlier show. And he was also then working on "King Leonardo and his Short Subjects," another network cartoon which went through 106 episodes. Soon thereafter he would begin work on the wildly successful cartoon "Mr. Magoo." Later he would direct his own shorter and more experimental cartoons. Those more personal works were marked by liberal political values (for the time) and an embrace of countercultural images. Nothing I have found suggests that he would have been hostile to the sentiments or values in his great-uncle's will—at least, not enough to challenge the terms of the will.[6]

Nor could he have expected a financial return if he had won his case. If that portion of the Robbins estate that was in litigation were distributed by intestacy, which is what would happen if Mishkin succeeded in his challenge to the will, Mishkin would be one of at least ten collateral heirs who would share something less than $22,000 dollars under California's intestacy laws (Irvine Robbins was also a collateral heir, and with an interest superior to that of Mishkin). After subtracting the lawyers' costs and the other costs of the litigation, significantly less than $1,000 dollars would remain for each grandnephew or grandniece—and almost certainly much less than that—*if* he won, and *if* he were determined by a probate court really to be a collateral heir.[7] It hardly seems worth the effort, unless Mishkin were passionate about preventing the Negro child or children of an incarcerated radical from receiving an award. Which, once again, seems unlikely.

So, once more, why was he suing, challenging the trust that Jack Robbins had tried to create? Even if he disliked his great-uncle, assuming that he knew him at all, what were his goals?

I also wish I knew how and why Clore Warne became the attorney who represented Lee Mishkin. Warne was a relatively high-powered lawyer, and he was presumably not inexpensive, if he took on the litigation as a private case. What was in it for him?

It is easy to imagine likely scenarios that explain how Hugh R. Manes came to represent the estate. Manes had grown up in Chicago, but on the South Side of the city. He spent his adolescence at a military academy in Wisconsin. So, he was probably more middle-class than most boys in the BBR. It thus seems unlikely that he was involved with the BBR. But it is altogether possible that he would have known one or more of the trustees. After graduating from Northwestern Law School, Manes moved to Los Angeles, where he worked closely with A. L. (Al) Wirin, the leading civil liberties attorney in the city. At first he may have worked full time for the Southern California ACLU, which was also what Wirin was most identified with. By 1960, Manes was becoming the Southern California ACLU's point person on police-misconduct matters. He was a man of the moderate left, but he remained identified with the Democratic Party, for which he ran for office unsuccessfully. If the Chicago connections don't explain how he was found to represent the estate, one might imagine that he could well have been a referral, if someone involved in the estate had called the local ACLU office. He was after all a young lawyer building a career.[8]

But Warne on the other side? Why was he representing Lee Mishkin and challenging Robbins's will? Warne was also, like Manes, a civil liberties lawyer, also deeply involved with the Southern California ACLU. He was also more senior and more successful, with several appearances before the US Supreme Court. He probably did not need the work.

By the time of the case he was in his late seventies. As of the late 1950s, his left-wing credentials were stronger than Manes's. Both Warne and Manes had appeared a few years earlier before the board of governors of the state bar to challenge the effort to exclude or disbar "reds." He also remained a member of the Lawyer's Guild, as did Manes. His practice in the 1940s and 1950s included civil rights work, alien land-law cases, racially restrictive covenant cases, and representation of radicals in Cold War anti-communist cases. Both he and Manes were core members of the Southern California ACLU. The case challenging the Robbins will is the only instance I can find where he opposed a radical in court.[9]

Warne had a deep but complex past as a radical lawyer, beginning in St. Louis prior to World War I.[10] His close friend and neighbor Carey McWilliams, a lawyer and soon to be the editor of the *Nation* magazine, described Warne as someone whose commitment to civil liberties was always combined with a residual "political commitment." Eason Monroe, the head of the Southern California ACLU, had misgivings about Warne, although they remained friends. (Warne had voted against Monroe as the director of the local branch because Monroe had been fired from a teaching position in San Francisco for refusing to sign a loyalty oath. At least that is what Monroe believed.) Monroe described Warne as "a very successful lawyer, . . . a kind of field marshal of . . . [his] firm, a very outspoken, sharp-tongued, quick-minded man who, I think, had been very close to the Wobblies in his younger years—a kind of anarchist, an interesting anticommunist, but on sectarian and factional grounds rather than on philosophic grounds. I've never quite been able to figure out where Clore stands philosophically on general political questions."[11]

Throughout the 1930s and 1940s, Warne's political work continued, even as he built a profitable legal practice in Southern California. He served on the Sleepy Lagoon Defense Committee that defended those accused of the "Zoot Suit Murders," and, earlier, on the Tom Mooney Defense Committee, working to free the imprisoned radical. He served a term or two as the chair of the executive board of the local branch of the National Lawyers' Guild. He represented the Communist Party presidential candidate, William Z. Foster, when Foster was stopped in 1932 from speaking in Los Angeles, under California's criminal syndicalization law. He also represented a suspected Soviet spy in 1938–1940. In 1943 he authored a resolution to the State Bar, asking it to work to eradicate discrimination. The resolution was understood as preparatory to an offer to represent Japanese Americans in the internment camps. Throughout he was known, according to the prominent radical Los Angeles lawyer Ben Margolis, as "a very active, hardworking, and able guy."[12]

In many ways, Warne seems more likely to have served as Robbins's lawyer, or as the lawyer representing Robbins's estate, or as the drafter of the ACLU's amicus brief in support of the enforcement of Robbins's trust, than as the lawyer hired to challenge the Robbins will. So, what was he doing challenging Robbins's will? It remains mysterious why Clore Warne here represented a side that worked to prevent those already punished for taking dissident radical positions from receiving the small award to support care for their children.

Meanwhile, the Southern California ACLU, generally recognized as the most left-wing of local ACLU offices, often quarreling with the more conservative national office in New York, was everywhere in the case. The legal staff produced an amicus brief drafted by John T. McTernan, another Los Angeles lawyer well known for representing radicals and ex-communists. McTernan was himself an ex–Communist Party member and the law partner of Ben Margolis.[13] But more importantly, the ACLU board was evidently strategizing internally about how to present the case.[14] And since all the attorneys involved with the litigation were core members of the Southern California branch, including Warne—who was at the time on the ACLU's executive committee—it is unimaginable that the discussions going on in that office did not include him as well as Hugh Manes and John T. McTernan.[15]

It seems hard to avoid the speculation that the whole suit was a setup, perhaps an improvisation produced from within the ACLU. The lawyers involved wanted a test case. Can we imagine that Manes or Wirin asked Warne to take the other side so that the legality of the will could be tested? And that he or they then found Mishkin to contest the will as a potential beneficiary, if that part of the will (the trust) went by intestacy, after the failure of the trust?

What did the lawyers of the Southern California ACLU want from the California courts, if this speculation is correct? They wanted validation of a will that celebrated radical political speech. That is obvious. But still, why choose to spend time on this small case, which was distinctive mostly for its oddity?

Retrospectively, looking backward from the conclusion to the case, one might imagine that the Southern California ACLU lawyers wanted an opportunity to join civil liberties to civil rights and anti-discrimination law. All these lawyers had fought, and mostly lost, many cases involving the speech rights of ex-communists and other radicals, in the movie business and elsewhere around Los Angeles (and around the country). All of them had spent much of the previous decade trying to keep radicals and those with radical pasts employed and out of jail—mostly unsuccessfully. And as of the end of the 1950s, most of the Cold War laws and practices that Robbins referenced in his will had to be understood as constitutionally settled, or at least as not worth relitigating in the short term.

But here was an opportunity to change the subject in a productive way and to make clear to courts the intertwined relationship between left-wing political speech and the speech that was becoming identified with civil rights.[16]

That is to say, or to imagine or to speculate, that at the end of the 1950s the ACLU of Southern California wanted to use the growing public support for civil rights protest following the Montgomery Bus Boycott to build support for other forms of protest that had been branded as illegal and communist. The Robbins estate case, with its odd attempt to make a gift to a "Negro child or children" of someone convicted of "political crimes," offered an opportunity to do exactly that.

To frame the case in such a way may be to give the speculation more strategic intentionality than it can bear. Perhaps it was just that the lawyers, like others, worked to situate this case within the surround, the news of the day, which in 1960 was all about racial discrimination and civil rights. They took what lawyers sometimes call "judicial notice" of a relevant context. What is clear, though, is that the lawyers involved with the Southern California ACLU worked to ensure that race relations would be central to the narrative, to the ways Jack Robbins's case would be understood.[17]

The core mystery remains: Why did Clore Warne take the case? Why did he agree to represent Lee Mishkin? And implicitly, why was Mishkin challenging the will at all? And for those mysteries, I have no answer beyond what I have already suggested. All one knows is that Clore Warne took the task of representing Lee Mishkin seriously, as a good lawyer would. He wrote serious briefs that argued in support of the holding in the Los Angeles Superior Court. In effect he offered the justifications that neither lower court judge bothered with.

* * *

Robbins had identified a "Negro child or Negro children" as his intended beneficiary or beneficiaries—but for the rest, neither race nor civil rights appeared in his will.

And yet, to track the briefs as written in the case between 1960 and 1962, as the case worked its way through the California courts, is to watch a shift, in the historical moment of the early 1960s, in the understanding and representation of what Robbins intended to create. The core question—about the nature of illegal activity that might or might not be encouraged by the Robbins trust—

changed. The will as interpreted became something new. Or, at minimum, the lawyers who were defending Jack Robbins's trust worked to make something new out of this small and inconsequential case. And along the way, doing that work meant arguing that the will ought to be interpreted in light of conditions and circumstances that Jack Robbins could not have known about when he was still alive.

The underlying message of the lawyers' arguments was that Jack Robbins died too soon. If he had lived longer, he would have used language in the ways that the lawyers wanted him to.[18] In effect, they pointed to the historical moment that they were living in. That is, they pointed to a moment at the end of, perhaps "after," the anti-communist crusade that had shaped their lives as lawyers for the previous decade and more, but also to a moment when "civil rights" suddenly dominated the news and presumably became central to how civil liberties should be understood. The law jobs of the Southern California ACLU were changing. Or better, the lawyers were working to change the work they did.

It is important to add that the ordinary, routine, and brutal criminalization of African Americans, young and not-so-young, in Los Angeles and elsewhere, was not, at that moment, part of their arguments, nor, one suspects, of their consciousness. Nor did they attend to the conditions of imprisonment of radicals or of others. What did concern them were the occasions for what was coming to be known as civil disobedience. Was it a valid purpose for a trust to encourage resistance to unjust laws? And if so, which laws were so unjust that a court might recognize their enforcement as a legitimate occasion for civil disobedience? In a sense the case, *In Re Robbins' Estate*, became one about what respect for the rule of law, or (dis)obedience to (unjust) laws meant. And it also became a case about a moment when respect for the rule of law came to be framed as circling around and through the injustices of Jim Crow segregation in the South.[19]

Here is the sequence of briefs and arguments as they were submitted between 1960 and 1962.[20]

1. The case began formally in April 1960, when Irvine Robbins, through his attorney Hugh R. Manes, filed a "Petition to Determine Heirship and Instructions" in the Los Angeles Superior Court. The goal of the petition was a ruling that under California law, Jack Robbins's creation of a trust fund for the "Negro child or children" was tax-exempt as a charitable trust. With no evidence submitted other than the text of the will itself, Harold Schweitzer, the superior court judge assigned the case, ruled that the trust could not be enforced. The trust was "invalid both as a charitable and as a private trust." Therefore the

property passed as intestate property to the heirs at law, including (possibly) Lee Mishkin.

Judge Harold Schweitzer was the author of several prominent anti-communist decisions, and he was the subject of regular good press from the conservative *Los Angeles Times*. (Notoriously, he was the judge in the case of Jean Field, whose children were taken from her after she was discovered to have criticized the Korean War and to have advocated for racial equality in letters to her children.) In *In Re Robbins*, Schweitzer gave four grounds or "findings" for his decision: (1) that the trust was not limited to objects of a charitable nature; (2) that it was established for political purposes; (3) that it tended to induce or encourage the commission of illegal acts; and (4) that its objects were too vague, indefinite, and uncertain. No justifications or explanations were provided for those findings.[21]

2. Manes's brief on appeal to the District Court focused on the question whether Jack Robbins had created a valid charitable trust, though there were also subsidiary questions, particularly about whether, if it were not a valid charitable trust, it could be reconstituted as one by way of the *cy pres* doctrine.[22]

To answer the core question required defining what was a valid "charitable purpose." Manes's somewhat carelessly copyedited brief ranged widely. He took language from the post–Civil War Massachusetts case of *Jackson v. Phillips*. There, the Massachusetts Supreme Judicial Court had held that funds given to support abolitionist activity, from a trust drafted at a time when slavery was still constitutional and national (after the *Dred Scott* decision and before the beginning of the Civil War), constituted a valid charitable purpose. The court in *Jackson* ruled that a charitable purpose was one "to be applied consistently with existing laws, for the benefit of an indefinite number of persons— either by bringing their hearts under the influence of education, by relieving their bodies of disease, suffering[,] or constraint, by assisting them to established [*sic*] themselves in life, or by erecting or maintaining public buildings or works, or otherwise lessening the burdens of government." Stirring up "sentiments against slavery and to aid future slaves" exemplified a valid purpose in *Jackson v. Phillips*, even though slavery was still legal at the time the trust in the case had been drafted. (On the other hand, in a part of the opinion in *Jackson v. Phillips* not referenced by Manes or anyone else, the court also held that a second trust in the same will, to support votes for women and other forms of women's rights, did not articulate a valid charitable purpose because doing so would encourage illegality.)[23] Manes also cited other cases that recognized and enforced trusts that worked to destroy discrimination against "the colored races." Even trusts that supported a "communistic community" as a "social experiment" had passed muster under the liberal interpretive principles that he argued properly governed court tests of charitable trusts.

Whether or not "the reasoning or purpose" of a radical outsider like Jack Robbins gained "popular approval" was immaterial, so long as the trust could be understood as being "rational, and not contrary to the law and mores of the community." Quoting an Irish case, Manes noted that trusts had been "upheld" as charities "for the benefit of insignificant sects and of peculiar people." All that was required was that the gift giver believed he was providing a "public advantage," and that his belief must appear to be "at least rational," and not contrary to the "law of the land" or to principles of "morality." Not, to use the recurrent phrase, "contra bono mores"—that is, against good morals, or against the conventional morality of the times.

What the testator, Jack Robbins, wanted done was not "contra bono mores." Who were the beneficiaries in this case? Clearly the beneficiaries were the children of Negro parents convicted of crimes, and their need for care was clearly "charitable" in character. Robbins also wanted to promote the First Amendment. And that too was a valid charitable purpose, not contra bono mores, although Manes emphasized that that intent (which certainly would have been more controversial in Cold War America) was "subsidiary" to the goal of providing for the health and welfare of a class of children. It did not really matter what was the "reasoning or the rationale" of the testator, given that the "objective" of the trust was to "keep children of imprisoned parents off of the relief rolls," an undeniably "valid charitable purpose."

Nor did it matter, as the lower court's "findings" seemed to suggest, that the trust might be understood to encourage unlawful activity. That suggestion was "remote, speculative, unreasonable[,] and irrelevant." By the same logic, one might understand "the First Amendment as promoting the overthrow of the government, the Fifth Amendment encouraging the guilty to invoke it as a shield against prosecution, and the Nineteenth Amendment [*sic*] encouraging drunkenness" [Manes meant the Twenty-First Amendment]. Even if there were persons who were willing to go to jail because they were "secure" in the knowledge that their children might benefit "from the provisions of this meager trust," even so, children should not suffer for the "sins" of their parents.

At that point in the brief, Manes stopped to note that Robbins had not lived long enough "to see the prosecution of the Negro," as "he" struggled "to emerge from his ghetto." Implicitly, Manes was noting how much the "news" or the context had changed between late 1958, when Robbins died, and May 1961, when Manes submitted his brief. And he was asking the court to take "judicial notice" of that new context. He followed with a citation to *NAACP v. Alabama*, the 1958 US Supreme Court case that recognized that the NAACP could rely on the First Amendment to protect its membership rolls from the prying eyes of the state of Alabama. Manes insisted that the appeals court should take "judicial notice of the political, social[,] and economic unrest in the South arising out of the clamor of the Negro for equality of treatment." He continued: the arrest and jailing of sit-ins and other methods of "lawfully resisting segregations laws" were "political activities of the nature contemplated by testator." But again, as he concluded this section, the beneficiaries were not African American adults involved in the civil rights movement, but their children, who would "benefit from testator's humane and provident thoughtfulness." Thus, by curious logic, Robbins's will contained a valid charitable purpose, which was to benefit the children of men and women whose actions were not within the expressed contemplation of the testator at the time that he wrote the will.

NAACP v. Alabama became a recurrent reference in all the briefs submitted. In that case, a unanimous Supreme Court had worked to stop the continuing efforts of officers of the state of Alabama to bankrupt and destroy the civil rights organization (the US Supreme Court's decision reversed an Alabama Supreme Court's decision that approved a $100,000 fine, imposed on the NAACP for not revealing its membership lists). Justice Harlan's opinion for the Court validated the NAACP's right to privacy and anonymity, its right not to reveal its political membership, and also a newly articulated constitutional freedom of association. It is unimaginable, though Manes never made the connection explicit in this or in later briefs, that he and the other lawyers litigating *In Re Robbins* did not recognize that the rights that Harlan's opinion articulated were structurally indistinguishable from rights not validated for members of the Communist Party or other radical organizations. And they were, of course, also exactly the rights for the exercise of which the parents of the "Negro child or children" had been convicted, under the examples that Jack Robbins's will had specified.[24]

Indeed, to carry the story in directions that Manes and the ACLU brief writers would have avoided, in *Beilan v. Board of Public Education*, decided on the very same day as *NAACP v. Alabama*, the Supreme Court in a 5–4 decision held that schools were within their rights to demand that schoolteachers reveal long-past membership in a Communist organization. By refusing to answer, a teacher showed himself to be "insubordinate" and "lacking in frankness," and that meant the school board had grounds to fire him. And in *Communist Party of the United States v. Subversive Activities Control Board*, decided three years later, at about the same time as Manes was submitting this first brief in Robbins, a similarly divided court confirmed the legality of the McCarran Internal Security Act, which required the Communist Party to register and to expose its members—exactly what was not required of the NAACP in *NAACP v. Alabama*. In his opinion for the court, again decided by a 5–4 vote, Frankfurter held that the right to freedom of association may be revoked when in conflict with national security.[25]

Manes's brief went on to challenge the lower court's findings that the trust failed because its beneficiaries were "vague and indefinite." To the contrary, the brief argued, that lack of precise definition was exactly what made the trust valid, since a charitable trust cannot have ascertained beneficiaries. Likewise, Manes's brief turned to the question of cy pres, to the "in the alternative" position that if the appellate court were to rule that the charitable intent could not be carried out as written, then the doctrine of cy pres should be invoked. Cy pres is a discretionary power given to courts, by which a trust that has become unenforceable can be redrafted to come as close to the original goals of the trust as would be consistent with the relevant law. Cy pres meant that Jack Robbins's goals could be realized, or they could come close to being realized. There were, Manes concluded, organizations, conveniently the NAACP and the ACLU, whose "activities and purposes" were in alignment with that of the testator. If the funds were given to them, as a result of an invocation of cy pres, those organizations could help ensure that Robbins's broader intent of benefiting "Negro children" could be realized.

3. Warne's reply brief on behalf of Mishkin labeled Manes's notion that Robbins had created a valid charitable trust "simply absurd."[26] He returned the focus to the Cold War politics that underlay the text of the trust. The trust tended "to encourage the commission of serious crimes." What crimes? Or, rather, what criminals? "The class of criminals thus favored—whom the testator refers to as 'political criminals,'" included those convicted under the Smith Act and those who committed criminal contempt ("of Congress and of the federal and state courts"). Those were the testator's own examples, but the intent could as easily have included "political assassins, spies[,] and traitors." Those kinds of transgressions too fell logically within Robbins's notion of "political crimes."

Nor did the trust qualify as "charitable." Need was not mentioned in the trust document, only that the "Negro children" had to be the offspring of those convicted of political crimes. The parents could be wealthy, so long as "their crime was of sufficient [political] importance to merit the testator's bounty." Nor did it fall into any of the other recognized charitable categories. Beyond that, its objects were "too vague, indefinite, and uncertain"—just as Schweitzer, the lower court judge, had concluded. It could not stand as a private trust, since it was framed in a way that violated the rule against perpetuities. And since it failed *in toto*, it was not salvageable through cy pres.

Warne noted that Manes's brief focused "at some length" about "the need to assist the Negro in the South in the realization of civil rights." But those comments were nothing but a non sequitur: they expressed a wholly different trust purpose than that which Robbins had contemplated when he drafted his will. Warne distinguished arrests and convictions for exercising "civil rights" from "political crimes." A "Negro" who "merely" sought to exercise "constitutional rights" would not be convicted of any crime, and "most certainly could not be deemed a 'political criminal.'" Robbins's concern had not been with those involved in the lunch counter sit-ins, referring to the civil rights demonstrations occurring right as Warne wrote, but rather "<u>with the Negro who ran afoul of legislation of a far different sort</u>" (underlined by Warne)—that is, of legislation that all were bound to obey and to abide by. Indeed, he then returned to his favorite hyperbolic example: the child of a convicted murderer might qualify for the largesse so long as the victim was of "high office," so that the murderer could be understood as a "political assassin."

Manes's brief, in Warne's reading, also produced another "straw man" in its invocation of the First Amendment. The trust was not aimed at "<u>mere education or even political advocacy</u>"(again underlined by Warne). Rather, it encouraged those who committed "<u>overt criminal acts . . .</u> by assuring them that their minor children will be cared for should the parent be apprehended." Nor did it promote the well-being of the children. To read the will's provisions revealed that its primary objective was to aid the parents. And again, he reiterated that it could even be used to benefit the child or children of a wealthy individual, so long as the crime was sufficiently important to "merit" the "testator's bounty," in the opinion of the trustees.

The will, "it must be emphasized," Warne wrote, was not about "mere possible eccentricity." Rather it was one that furthered criminal activity.

The rest of the brief mobilized a variety of sources and texts, and it reinterpreted the cases that Manes had mobilized to show that they, unlike those found in Robbins's will, dealt with "highly commendable moral objectives, with at most some incidental political overtones." Warne took apart the definition of a "charitable purpose" that Manes had drawn from the early cases, including *Jackson v. Phillips*. The Robbins trust had nothing to do with keeping children of imprisoned parents off of the relief rolls. Nor did it achieve some "moral reform," since its only purpose was to "aid and assist a selected class of criminals."

4. Manes then filed a reply brief" that doubled down on the arguments he had made. It added more references to Southern civil rights cases.[27] It defied "common sense," he wrote, to imagine that a parent was going to allow "himself" to be convicted and imprisoned in the hope of a benefit for his children. The bequest was therefore "collateral to, rather than the cause" of criminality. And he challenged Warne's speculation or presumption that the will was founded on an "unlawful intent." In the absence of "clear and convincing evidence" to the contrary, such a trust should be sustained. For this he pointed once again to *Jackson v. Phillips*, which had upheld a trust expressly devoted to encouragement of the violation of then-legal slave laws.

It was, Manes continued, "abundantly clear" that the intent was not crime, but the right to dissent. In this reply brief, he moved the value of free speech to the front, as an expression of Robbins's charitable intent. And he referenced a list of California cases that upheld "the advancement and preservation of ideas, discussion[,] and speech . . . as a valid charitable—albeit political—use." He quoted at length from the final pages of Robbins's will about the need to support the expression of "unorthodox or unpopular concepts."

And then he moved on to what he really wanted to write about: Jack Robbins's "observation" in the last part of his will that new fields of oppression would undoubtedly appear was, Manes asserted, "confirmed by the persecution in the South of advocates and supporters of integration." That statement was footnoted with an "appendix" containing a few recent cases and law review articles about the sit-ins and African American protests then continuing in the South, concluding with a "note": "The foregoing is not intended as a complete bibliography on the subject, and by no means is." According to Manes, Robbins had, "not by accident," limited his "bounty" to "Negro children." He knew "the close nexus between the Negroes' struggle for equality of treatment and justice and the not infrequent abridgment by some states of his basic liberties." There followed a footnote to a second appendix that included references to the cases that followed *NAACP v. Alabama*, where Southern courts interpreted the new mandate that allowed the NAACP not to reveal its membership lists. That list apparently countered Warne's claim that "the mere exercise of constitutional rights" did not result in a "valid conviction."

He quoted the late Justice Robert Jackson on political repression. In a time of "fear, ignorance[,] and mistrust," advocates of ideas might be harassed and persecuted, convicted of crimes. Otherwise-valid laws might be "perverted into instruments of oppression against unpopular minorities." Convictions might be "eventually . . . invalidated." But "an unjust conviction [might] be upheld," at least in the short term, "deferring vindication to a day when popular passions have given way to rational judgment—and at times even posthumous absolution." There followed citations to a variety of notorious political trials that ended in (presumptively unjust) convictions, including those of the anarchists Sacco and Vanzetti, the socialist congressman Victor L. Berger, and John Thomas Scopes of the infamous Scopes monkey trial. He referenced an appendix providing short descriptions of each of those accused radicals and their convictions. He avoided putting any recent post–World War II Cold War–era trials in his list. He stayed away from the examples that Jack Robbins had carefully mobilized in his will.

The trust, he acknowledged, did not distinguish between those rightfully and those wrongfully convicted of crimes. The children of the imprisoned were "rendered no less destitute in either case." And therefore, the bequest did not encourage crime. The "crime" had already been committed, and the offender had been jailed before the benefits could be "bestowed." Nor was the trust "invalid" because the testator "intended to aid the children of heretics and minorities."[28]

5. On appeal, a three-judge District Court of Appeal panel, headed by Justice John Joseph Ford, affirmed the lower court's refusal to enforce the trust.[29] The intermediate court's opinion drew a distinction between a valid charitable trust, which might well involve advocacy for a change to existing laws, and an invalid trust, whose purpose was illegal. This purported charitable trust was, Ford believed, on the wrong side of that line. Ford entirely avoided the question of civil rights. He focused attention on the examples of convictions that Robbins had mobilized in his will. And then, relying on statements drawn from standard doctrinal treatises, he concluded that "a trust cannot be recognized as valid where its purpose is illegal." This trust did not mean to achieve "a change in the law by lawful and orderly means." (Clearly Ford was avoiding or not thinking about civil disobedience.) Instead, it rewarded "members of a defined class of convicted persons" by supporting their children. And since there was no valid "general charitable purpose" to be found, the trust could not be rescued by cy pres.[30]

Manes petitioned for a rehearing. Warne answered the petition. The petition failed.[31]

6. Manes's brief to the California Supreme Court, more carefully written and proofed than what he had drafted earlier, expanded on themes already raised.[32] It began with the claim that this was "the first reported case in California—and possibly in the United States" where a charitable trust was invalidated on the "unprecedented ground" that a trust to benefit Negro children of parents who had exercised their rights promoted crime. He saw the

case as presenting four questions: first, whether a trust that offered aid to children of imprisoned law violators encouraged the commission of illegal acts, which thereby made the trust an "invalid charitable use"; Second, whether a trust that meant to promote "freedom of speech and to safeguard the right to dissent," expressed a "valid charitable intent; third, whether a trust may validly confer benefits solely on the Negro children of parents imprisoned for violation of laws that abridged First Amendment freedoms; and finally, if the answer to the third were in the negative, whether, if the trust were otherwise valid, it could be redrawn using the cy pres doctrine.

The trust, he argued, did not benefit those who committed crimes, "unless peace of mind be deemed a benefit," but only their children. It offered no inducement to the criminally inclined. "Put still another way, the sins of the parent should not be visited upon the child." And, somewhat further on in the brief, he wrote that it defied common sense to contend that a parent would allow herself or himself to be convicted and imprisoned in the hope that children might benefit from the trust. Far from conflicting with public policy, such a bequest eased the financial burden on the community which might otherwise have to provide for the minor's support and welfare. He quickly surveyed the California court's long-standing liberal stance on charitable trusts. Then he moved on to claim that promotion of First Amendment freedoms was itself a valid charitable intent. The principal purpose of the trust was to promote freedom of speech, and the "objects" of its bounty were Negro children of those jailed for holding unpopular opinions and ideas. "Thus," in a transition toward what Manes most wanted to argue, Jack Robbins, when he drafted his will in December 1957, "recognized" what the Supreme Court would only come to understand one year later: "the close nexus between the exercise of First Amendment freedoms and the civil rights struggle of the Negro—especially in the South." Robbins's death preceded "the eruption of state prosecutions of Negroes under trespass statutes and other criminal laws for demonstrating against the ignominy of their status." But "presumably," if and when such demonstrators were convicted and imprisoned, their children would qualify as beneficiaries. "Yet, how can it be argued that this trust" induced the "crimes"?[33]

The District Court of Appeal had objected to the "class of crimes" that justified the bequest, and it placed weight on how Robbins had described the "political crimes" that concerned him. But that objection misconceived his basic concern, which was "to preserve the right to dissent, the right to differ and to be different." (It may be that Manes was trying to divert attention away from one part of what Robbins had written, the description of the political crimes, by focusing on another passage in the will, the credo.) Manes acknowledged the lawfulness of prosecutions and convictions under the Smith Act and the Taft-Hartley Act's non-communist test oath. These were Cold War examples that Robbins had himself provided. But they were, Manes continued, instruments "for the suppression of lawful, albeit unpopular ideas." (Here he cited, one might think somewhat irrelevantly, *NAACP v. Alabama*. Once again, though, it may be that Manes was making connections to associational rights that he hoped judges would make as well.) But Manes went on to challenge "the harassment and persecution of ideas hostile to the status quo." Such conditions were "perverted into instruments of oppression against unpopular minorities." Again, all the citations were to civil rights cases from the South.

The District Court of Appeal had also held that the doctrine of cy pres was inapplicable because there was no general charitable purpose articulated in the will to aid Negro persons or to help Negro children. The encouragement of freedom of expression, which was, he insisted, the clear purpose of the trust and a valid charitable purpose, had been disregarded in that court's decision. The appellate decision had overlooked "the regrettable fact that in some regions of the country, integration and civil rights are not only hated ideas, but espousal of, or adherence to, such doctrines is equated with subversion."[34] And, he continued, the lower court also ignored "the close nexus between freedom of speech and the Negroes' resistance to segregation and other forms of discrimination." Thus there was a general charitable purpose: to benefit "Negro persons" or their children. And there was no good reason not to apply *cy pres*.

7. Meanwhile, in December 1961 and January 1962, immediately after the petition for rehearing failed before the District Court of Appeal, John T. McTernan and Fred Okrand, the Southern California ACLU's general counsel, wrote several letters in preparation for filing an amicus brief. McTernan wrote to Constance Baker Motley, the lead attorney for the NAACP in *Bailey v. Patterson. Bailey* was a long-standing federal case about bus and train segregation in Mississippi, that would in early 1962 be decided per curiam by the Supreme Court. The Court would rule that any claim that a state statute requiring racial segregation was constitutional had become frivolous, thus disposing of efforts in several southern courts to weaken the decision in *Brown* (and the reversal of *Plessy v. Ferguson*). But at that moment in late 1961, the case was still moving through the lower federal courts. McTernan hoped Motley and the NAACP would send him the appendix she had drafted to a stay application and to the Court of Appeals decision. The appendix provided a listing of all (or an extensive selection of) Mississippi's racist laws. And Okrand wrote to Archibald Cox,

then the solicitor general in the new Kennedy administration, asking for the brief submitted by the Justice Department to the Court of Appeals.[35]

McTernan, who would draft the amicus brief for the ACLU, also wrote to the Congress of Racial Equality (CORE) and to Robert Carter at the NAACP.[36] The letters, which were identical, began by sketching the trust that Robbins had created. He explained that the brief the Southern California ACLU would be submitting as amicus would argue there were two "key words" in Robbins's "testamentary language": "Negro" and "political." For McTernan, writing in late 1961, the word "Negro" was at least as important as the word "political," although Robbins might not have agreed in 1957 or 1958. Indeed, what Robbins might have meant by "political," and what McTernan meant, both in his letters and in his brief, could not have been more different. McTernan's notion of "political" was defined not by political radicalism or the repressive legislation and inquisitorial practices of the anti-communist postwar era, but by civil rights.

"Today," he wrote in these letters, "the American Negro expresses his dissent and his determination to be 'different' . . . by resisting discrimination and segregation." The brief the ACLU was readying pointed out the jurisdictions in the Deep South with laws on the books that were "explicitly racist in nature" and others that were used in a racist manner against "Negroes struggling for equality." These laws were mobilized to criminalize sit-ins and the Freedom Rides. Under the Fourteenth Amendment, convictions for violations of those laws "could not be a crime in the conventional sense because such laws were unconstitutional." Therefore, there were "significant" arenas where the trust "could operate not only without encouraging violation of or disrespect for the law[,] but actually in support of the noblest objectives of our constitutional guarantees."[37]

The position that McTernan was developing, to be expanded in the brief he drafted for the ACLU, was the notion that the convictions of the parents were not evidence of disrespect for law. To the contrary, those convictions involved resistance to unconstitutional laws, and they were, therefore, motivated by respect for the rule of law. (This position was close to the position that Martin Luther King Junior would soon express, more powerfully, in his "Letter from a Birmingham Jail.")

McTernan requested assistance from CORE and from the NAACP. He wanted them to provide "the most complete information" possible of all legal proceedings involving "the enforcement of statutes, rules, or decisional policy against Negroes by State authorities where the Negroes involved were seeking to achieve either (a) equality of treatment or (b) the exercise of freedoms that should be available to all irrespective of race." Please, he asked, provide all possible details about the parties and the proceedings. The purpose of his request was to be able to present to the California Supreme Court "a general survey of the use of criminal and other laws against Negro and other dissenters from the American version of apartheid." The California court was a liberal one jurisprudentially. He was confident that it would rule in a helpful manner. And he hoped that the opinion produced would have a use beyond the particulars of *In Re Robbins.*

He realized that he was making a "heavy" demand on his correspondents who were, of course, very busy people in late 1961, at that crucial moment in the history of civil rights litigation. Indeed, Melvin Wulf, the assistant legal director of the national ACLU, soon wrote to Okrand criticizing McTernan for asking so much of the NAACP and CORE. Wulf suggested that the Southern California ACLU rely on Jack Greenberg's recently published and quite comprehensive book, *Race Relations and the Law.* That tome wouldn't include the most recent sit-in cases, but everything else would be there. And they could leave off bothering the NAACP and CORE.[38]

Obviously, McTernan meant to overwhelm the California Supreme Court with descriptions of Southern racism. And he meant to "depoliticize" Robbins's will, at least in the sense that politicization referred to anti-communist Cold War repression.

The amicus brief McTernan soon submitted began with a preliminary paragraph: At a time when "conformity" provided "both the individual's sesame to success and his shield from 'trouble,'" Robbins's will made a "special call" on the ACLU. Jack Robbins had intended to leave his "worldly substance" to encourage "free expression for the unorthodox and the unpopular." He advocated for thought "at the frontiers of politico-social inquiry." And he sought to encourage such expression "by softening the blows of unpopularity" on the "families, the children, of those who differ[ed] from the existing order." He must have been "doubtless mindful" of the "massive efforts of the Negro people to achieve a new dignity in this country by securing in law as well as in practice a belated performance of the promise of the Civil War amendments." And therefore, he directed his "beneficence to the protection of the children of those who placed racial equality ahead of personal security."[39]

The brief then quickly surveyed the California cases that established that testator's intent controlled the proper construction of a will. Robbins's intent, the brief continued, was clear: to reward the children of those convicted of crimes of a "political nature." The meaning of "political" was crucial. And the error of the lower courts was in their failure to focus on "his" meaning of that key word.

As McTernan reinterpreted the will, when Robbins had written about convictions of a "crime or misdemeanor of a political nature," he had not meant "crime" at all, "in the conventional sense." What he meant were exercises of First Amendment rights, "the most profoundly political guarantees in the entire Bill of Rights." The purpose of the trust was then to "encourage the use by dissenters and the unorthodox of these rights <u>even when such exercise results</u> in the conviction of crime" (underlined in brief). In that sense, those who dissented and differed did not foster "disrespect for the law" or encourage "the violation thereof," as the District Court of Appeal had ruled.

The "principal area" where "the Negro differs and dissents today" was "against the American form of apartheid." McTernan moved into a discussion of the "many places in this land" where segregation was enforced. The citations were all to parts of the Mississippi Code. The text described the "hundreds of prosecutions and convictions of Negroes (and whites)" who had "disobeyed those laws" or who had "resisted discriminatory community practices by demonstrative actions only to be convicted under the more general statutes which purportedly protect the peace but in this instance buttress segregation and racial superiority." When Robbins used the words "crimes of a political nature," McTernan continued, he was "aiming his bounty" at "Negroes" who were "subjected to the reprisal of law enforcement devoted to defense of repellent racial theories."[40]

And then McTernan rehearsed the familiar line of cases (*Shelley, Brown, Yick Wo*, and more) that established that state action that imposed "differential treatment based on race" was void under the Fourteenth Amendment. Those temporarily convicted under such laws "in the highest sense" promoted "respect for the law, the constitution[,] and human dignity." They had only been "convicted" of crime "in form."[41]

The trust purpose, reframed in McTernan's view, was "fully consistent" with California public policy, which "condemned" racial discrimination. (In this context, he entirely ignored the long and intense history of discrimination and segregation, using private covenants and discriminatory and violent policing practices, that marked African American life in Southern California, a history that would soon lead to the explosions of the 1960s, including the Watts rebellion. Both Warne and McTernan, it should be added, had long played significant roles in challenging discriminatory housing segregation.[42]) The trust "can be read" (creatively) "as benefitting only the children of Negroes who seek a non-discriminatory policy in other states," not California. When such "persons" would be convicted of crimes, their convictions were ones that offended both the national Constitution and California's policies. As a result, "to hold that such a trust must fail as fostering 'disrespect for the law' or encouraging 'the violation thereof' renders this State's policy a hollow mockery." On the other hand, to enforce the trust would reenforce California's anti-racist policy by giving "aid and comfort to those who, at the risk of conviction under contrary and invalid laws, seek change" elsewhere. This reading was, he concluded this section of his brief, an entirely "natural" interpretation of what Robbins meant by "political." It was, as a result, an interpretation "not only favored" but "mandatory." Again, one has to wonder if anyone noticed that the clear implication of this argument would be that the only plausible beneficiary would be the child of someone arrested and convicted in the American South, not in California.

In the last section of the amicus brief, McTernan worked to explain away Robbins's own examples of what he had meant by "political crimes." He emphasized that Robbins had insisted on the freedom of the trustees to make different choices. But then he tried, in a somewhat cryptic survey of the recent cases, to suggest that many of Robbins's examples remained open to constitutional challenge, which would mean that convictions might be reversed. None of the four examples Robbins had provided in his will were of "clear-cut" crimes, such as burglary or rape, "whose content is well established by centuries of law enforcement." Whether the First Amendment barred "inquiry" into individual opinion was "far from settled." And even "inquiry" into Communist Party membership had been approved only by narrow 5–4 majorities of the Supreme Court. Other inquiries into membership had not been upheld. Here he once again cited *NAACP v. Alabama*. Challenges to the powers of legislative committees (challenges to HUAC, for example) would continue. "The scope of valid inquiry, and thus of permissible challenge," therefore, had not been "delineated with finality." There was room for future "attack." Even if the trustees chose to be guided by Robbins's illustrations, the trustees could give those illustrations a construction that would not have rendered the parents' conduct "a condonation of illegality."[43]

8. Warne responded both to Manes's brief and to that of the ACLU.[44] The decision of the District Court of Appeal was, he began, nothing more than "a routine application of well-established judicial doctrine." Both of the briefs advocating for the enforcement of the trust described it in terms "unsupported by the record." It was not a trust that promoted freedom of speech; it was a trust "expressly established to reward those convicted of certain crimes." The "questions presented" by Manes were not those presented by the case. It was not about freedom of speech or First Amendment rights or of aid to "Negroes" or to the children of those presently in prison. The only relevant questions were

whether a trust whose object was to encourage those who violate and defy existing law, by freeing them of parental responsibility, could be understood as a valid charitable trust. And whether the court could apply the cy pres doctrine. Both questions needed to be answered with an emphatic "no."

Warne rehearsed phrases from the leading treatise on trusts and from the California civil code. He noted that the code held that the validity of a trust was to be interpreted by the same standards as the lawfulness of contracts. So, he quoted the California civil code on contracts: on the illegality and unenforceability of contracts for illegal purposes. A valid charitable trust, like a valid contract, could incorporate purposes involving a change in existing law, but only when the means used were "lawful and orderly." Here, though, the purpose was to reward someone for having been convicted of "a political crime." Allowing such a trust to exist was not in the best interests of society. And it differed from trusts the courts had approved that were "concerned with highly commendable moral objectives, with at most some incidental political overtones."

He "comment[ed] briefly" on several of Manes's arguments. The trust did not "assist the Negro in the South in the realization of his civil rights." Indeed, according to Warne, a "Negro" seeking to exercise constitutional rights could not be "deemed a 'political criminal.'" Manes's brief's focus on freedom of speech was a "straw man. . . . The testator's preoccupation with criminal conduct cannot be equated with concern for constitutional rights." The will was not aimed at education or political advocacy, but, instead, it encouraged the commission of overt criminal acts. It did not promote "the well-being of the Negro children involved." Its object was to aid the parents, with the children as "incidental beneficiaries. And it rewarded those "to be convicted," not those already serving time in prison. It encouraged a particular kind of conduct, and the reward was made dependent on judicially established guilt. It did not distinguish between valid and invalid convictions.

As for the amicus brief by the ACLU of Southern California, according to Warne it amounted to an awkward effort to rewrite the charitable purposes in Robbins's will—and to hide an inconvenient truth. Warne reemphasized that "truth": In spite of his "lengthy exposition" of his motives, Jack Robbins never indicated any concern for civil rights.[45]

* * *

And yet, those defending the trust won. The California Supreme Court, in a 4–3 decision with an opinion by Roger Traynor, ruled in favor of enforcing the trust. It did so, though, without once mentioning civil rights. And the race of the beneficiaries, that they had to be "Negro children," was nowhere in the opinion, after Traynor's opening quotation from the text of the trust.[46] One wonders what Manes and McTernan thought about their "victory."

Traynor's opinion dismissed the notion that the funds in the trust might induce a parent to commit a crime he or she might otherwise not commit. That worry was "far outweighed" by the benefit to society and to the interests of the "innocent children" involved. One should not "visit" on children the "sins of fathers."

Traynor noted that Manes and McTernan had emphasized the vague boundary that divided constitutionally protected speech from illegal activities. They had claimed that one could "save" the will by interpreting it as referring "only to parents who have been unlawfully convicted for engaging in constitutionally protected activity." But Traynor rejected the invitation to limit the trust in that way. One might imagine that he regarded such a move as dishonest, since Jack Robbins had not drafted his will thusly. Traynor went further, although without mentioning civil rights. He refused to "search" for "any such limitation." He assumed that Robbins intended to benefit the children of those convicted "of even valid laws of which he disapproved." Robbins, in Traynor's reading, meant to encourage challenges to such laws by violations of them, regardless of whether such challenges succeeded in the short or the medium term. It was, rather, the purposes for which the property was to be used, not the "motives" of the testator, that were determinative. For Traynor, assistance to those children was a valid charitable purpose. Robbins's motives for doing so "died with him."[47]

Traynor ignored what Manes and McTernan had foregrounded. He bracketed off questions about the relative wrongfulness of the charitable purpose, so long as a child was the ultimate beneficiary, the recipient of the material reward. And he said nothing about the African American civil rights struggle or about the rights of privacy and association that the lawyers for the trust had drawn from *NAACP v. Alabama*. A child, or children, should not be blamed for parental wrongdoing (a claim that would have resonated with Robbins's lifework). Perhaps in ironic affirmation of that position and of his rejection of what Manes and McTernan had argued (a buried judicial joke), the first case Traynor cited as authority for the proposition that a child should not be blamed for the sins of her or his father was an obscure 1889 Mississippi opinion. In the case, a four-year-old child, race unspecified, was permitted to pursue compensation from a railroad company after he was struck and injured by one of the company's trains. The Mississippi court dismissed the apparent contributory negligence of the father for allowing his son to cross the tracks and failing to protect him.[48] "Infants have legal rights, distinct from their parents," Traynor held. He continued: "It seems repulsive to our sense of justice that, because the parent is negligent of his child, others may with impunity be equally negligent of its helplessness and equally indifferent to its necessities."[49]

In effect, Traynor approached a position that allowed a testator—or at least this testator, Jack Robbins—to use his money for purposes that were illegal, so long as there was a rational and politically coherent reason for doing so, and so long.as there were children who would be the material beneficiaries. Testator's freedom foreclosed further inquiry into motives. For the most part, courts should not try to determine the legality or illegality of a testator's purposes.

One might take Traynor's opinion as an indirect and implicit validation of the use of a private trust as a tool of innovation and challenge, in situations of risk, political and otherwise. His opinion offered a kind of judicial approval—or at least acceptance—of a way to protect children from the consequences of the risks parents and other adults took, of the use of a trust as a kind of insurance policy. In this opinion, as well as elsewhere in the corpus of his writings, Traynor refused to moralize about lawbreaking. Indeed, he came close to articulating a position that understood political lawbreaking as a source of innovation and as a necessary institutional challenge. This position was not far from the one that Jack Robbins had tried to articulate in his will.[50]

Throughout his opinion in *In Re Robbins' Estate*, Traynor avoided mention of the "murderer or assassin" that Warne had imagined. It is easy, though, to construct similar hypotheticals that might have complicated or challenged Traynor's stance.

EIGHT

And Then What Happened?

On April 23, 1962, the Associated Negro Press described a "special hearing" of the California Supreme Court in a "hotly contested case." The news service characterized the case as about a trust fund left by a "white Chicago philanthropist" for "Negro children" of parents "convicted of crimes involving civil rights and politics." Jack Robbins, the "benefactor," had grown interested "in the plight of Negroes in the Watts area." He had left $27,250 to those children. He had had "success as a shoe salesman." And the "deadline release" quoted his will as his "last contribution to a more democratic way of life." As executor, "Irving" Robbins had, according to the news service, hired Hugh R. Manes and John McTernan to argue before the state supreme court. "Irving" Robbins was described as Jack's brother, "and the head of the Baskin and Robbins Ice Cream Co. of Los Angeles."

After the decision was announced a few days later, Manes told the *New York Times* that Jack Robbins had given up his work at thirty to do "social work." He had become, according to Manes, "interested" early on "in the fight of Negroes for civil rights." He had been "clairvoyant" in knowing "that in some sections of the country some Negro parents would try to overthrow some discriminatory laws set up politically to deprive Negroes of their due Constitutional rights." He knew what would happen, that parents would be jailed in Alabama, Louisiana, Mississippi, and Georgia. And he recognized that their children would suffer as a result. According to Manes, Jack Robbins knew "what he wanted his trust fund to do. It was no more an encouragement to break the law than for the NAACP to encourage Negroes to exercise their civil rights as a birthright."[1]

After the California Supreme Court published its decision, the Associated

Negro Press (ANP) provided a second release for its member newspapers. This one celebrated the court's reversal. Jack Robbins was identified in the news release as a "white social worker," and, more accurately, as "a former Chicagoan and founder of the Boys Brotherhood Republic on the west side." He had, the ANP reported, set up the trust fund to go to the children of "victims of racial problems."[2]

Jet Magazine had first noticed Jack Robbins's estate in January 1959, soon after he died. At the time, it identified the estate as a $40,000 trust fund dedicated to the care of Negro children left homeless after parents were killed or imprisoned because of racial segregation. The paragraph notice identified Robbins as the founder of the Boys' Brotherhood Republic, once all Jewish, now 90 percent Negro. In May 1962, in a second short article, it headlined the still-undecided case as being about an "heir" [Mishkin] who was contesting the $22,250 will meant to support "bias victims."

A few mainstream papers covered the decision as well (but not the *Los Angeles Times*).[3]

None of those articles told me what I most wanted to find out—that is, who got, and how they got, and what they did with what they got. Which "Negro child or children" was or were awarded the benefits of the trust, and how was the decision made by those given managerial authority over the trust?

I still don't know the answers to those questions. I have not found a single document that tells or suggests what was done with the property. Nothing has been found, neither in court nor in governmental records, nor in personal papers. The Los Angeles Superior Court has apparently lost the probate records. I am relatively sure that the named trustees did nothing about making an award to a Negro child or children. And the case, of course, disappeared from the newspapers.[4]

Did anyone ever benefit from the trust? Again, I don't know. But it is at least possible that the trust was distributed by someone else, though not by the trustees named in Jack Robbins's will. It is possible that such distribution was made in ways that were close, or close enough, to what Jack Robbins had intended when he wrote his will.

How so? Here is an informed speculation.

We start with who the trustees were. Or rather, we start with who became the trustee for the gift to a "Negro child or children" after the California Supreme Court reversed the lower court holding that the trust was unenforceable and illegal. The will had identified Abrams, Soglin, and Marks, all living in Chicago, as the trustees. But it is likely that when the case was sent back to the trial court, to the Los Angeles Superior Court, to Harold Schweitzer, that the judge then made a different discretionary appointment of a trustee. The three named trustees had already been removed or excluded from serving as executors. Perhaps he regarded them as excluded from serving as trustees as well. It is easy to imagine a variety of reasons why Schweitzer would not have appointed them as trustees. Or, once again, perhaps the three chose not to come to California and "submit to the jurisdiction of the court," which would have been obligatory if they were to serve as trustees.[5] So, what would Schweitzer have done? Plausibly, he then awarded the trust proceeds directly to Irvine Robbins, the administrator cta ("cum testamento annexo," that is, as a substitute for an executor) of the estate. Robbins was a California resident; he was not tarred with a "political" identity. One wonders if Hugh Manes or the lawyers for the ACLU much cared who served as trustee (or what a trustee might do with the trust proceeds) now that the case was won, once the doctrinal principle was established.

Or, to put it more positively, perhaps Irvine Robbins volunteered to become the trustee for the estate. And perhaps Schweitzer then gave him the fiduciary responsibility of disposing of the trust proceeds. So, to continue the speculation: the money from the sale of Jack Robbins's two properties then became Irvine's, to be held in trust and to use in accordance with the text of the will.

And then what happened?

Irvine Robbins, who was in the middle stages of building an ice cream and franchising empire, was a registered Republican and a civic-minded southern Californian. He was not at all involved in left-wing causes, and he had never had any connection with the Boys' Brotherhood Republic. Indeed, he had no connection to Chicago at all that I know of, other than the happenstance that his uncle had long lived there. He and his wife were much involved in the Southern California public schools and in the League of Women Voters in Southern California. He lived at the time in Encino in the San Fernando Valley. He was also a charter member of the Honor Lodge of the Encino B'nai B'rith, a Jewish charitable organization.[6]

What did Irvine Robbins do with the funds from his uncle's trust? The answer is, once again, that I don't know. He never made any public statement about how he would give effect to the trust. And so far as I have discovered, he made no report about the trust to any public agency. But, in the mid-1960s, he convinced the Encino B'nai B'rith to fund and to build a boys' club in Pacoima, in the San Fernando Valley.[7]

Pacoima was a relatively impoverished and isolated, largely African American community in the San Fernando Valley. Pacoima also held a growing Mexican American population (including, famously, Richie Valens, the singer). The African American community in Pacoima had come into being during World War II, because the community bordered on a large Lockheed factory in Burbank. It remained, at least until the 1980s, the only part of the San Fernando Valley where African Americans could live, given the presence throughout the Valley of redlining and restrictive racial covenants and other discriminatory real estate practices. After World War II ended, a development of small houses, the "Joe Louis Homes," designed by the prominent developer Joseph Eichler, were built there. The homes were designed for African Americans leaving worse circumstances and conditions. The name both signaled to whites to avoid it and was intended to make it attractive for African American families.

Postwar Pacoima was a diverse community, including some homeowners and a few professionals. But it lacked many of the services and features that characterized postwar suburban life in the rest of the San Fernando Valley. In 1955, a column in the *Los Angeles Times* described Pacoima in terms redolent of how northerners typically imagined poor southern Black communities. It was, so the article said, a "smear of sagging, leaning shacks and backhouses framed by disintegrating fences and clutter of tin cans, old lumber, stripped automobiles, bottles, rusted water heaters and other bric-a-brac of the back alleys." Pacoima lacked curbs, paved sidewalks, and paved streets. Pacoima had what the columnist described as "dusty footpaths and rutted dirt roads that in hard rains become beds for angry streams."[8] Public investment in Pacoima was mostly limited to using it for urban landfills.

At one time, there was talk of building a state college in Pacoima. Instead, it was built in Northridge, at the other end of the San Fernando Valley. That meant that an African American student from Pacoima confronted a fifty-mile round trip daily. The dormitories and other housing in Northridge were apparently not open to African American students. As late as the mid-1960s, the campus of Valley State College, as it was then known, had only sixty African American students in a population of eighteen thousand students.[9]

In 1967 and 1968, at the instigation of Irvine Robbins, the Honor Lodge of the Encino B'nai B'rith built a boys' club at 13479 Van Nuys Boulevard, in Pacoima. Apparently Irvine Robbins provided a large proportion of the funds used to build the boys' club's first clubhouse. And Irvine Robbins remained for many years a member of the Pacoima Boys Club's board of directors.[10] In 1967, the local Congressman, James Corman, put into the Congressional Record a celebration of the new club, calling it "one of the most successful projects in behalf of the youth of the San Fernando Valley." The Congressman's notice singled out Irvine Robbins for his work and his contribution. In 1973, then-

California governor Ronald Reagan appointed Irvine Robbins to a state committee. In describing the qualifications that justified Robbins's appointment, he identified Irvine Robbins as a "founder" of the Pacoima Boys Club.[11]

Irvine Robbins never suggested that his contributions to the club, his gifts, came from the estate of Jack Robbins. As far as anyone knew, they were his gifts, made through the Honor Lodge of the Encino B'nai B'rith, not ones made from Jack Robbins's estate. And perhaps my speculation is wrong. Perhaps his work for the Pacoima Boys Club was just his gift, alone. And yet, it all fits, doesn't it? Jack Robbins did insist that the trust proceeds support a Negro child or children. Prior to the years when he became the administrator cta of his uncle's estate, Irvine Robbins betrayed no interest in race relations or in the lives of impoverished Black children in the San Fernando Valley. But then, after having become the administrator of his uncle's estate, he did.[12] One can well imagine that Irvine would have thought that a boys' club in what was then still a predominately Black community, one located not far from the house in San Fernando his uncle once owned, would be a worthy and fitting recipient for the proceeds of his uncle's trust. Doing so would give effect to what his uncle would have wanted, given his uncle's history as the big brother to chanceless waifs and the founder of the Boys' Brotherhood Republic, and his directive that the trust proceeds go to a "Negro child or children." (Irvine probably did not know or did not care that Robbins disliked and felt alienated from conventional boys' clubs.)

Irvine Robbins, no radical, and building an extraordinarily successful career as a businessman, would surely not have wanted to trumpet his uncle's left-wing and radical past. And he certainly would not have wanted to identify himself with the Communists and fellow travelers that Robbins identified in his will as likely beneficiaries. But, on the other hand, he might well have thought that supporting a boys' club in a Black neighborhood was fulfilling his uncle's wishes. He could quietly do what he was obligated as a trustee to do.

And to go further, by the mid- to late 1960s, Pacoima, a relatively isolated community, a near-ghetto, was exactly where protest and dissent were happening. Much of the 1960s student protest at the local college, then called Valley State College (now California State University—Northridge) was identified with students from Pacoima, who had started an Afro-Pac [Pacoima] organization that soon merged with a Black student union. A four-hour occupation of the college's administration building on November 4, 1968, driven in part by the demand for admission of more students from Pacoima, as well as for fair employment on campus, as well as by the racist practices of athletic coaches, led to the arrests and felony convictions of the "Valley State 19." The leaders were sentenced to one to twenty-one years in the California prison system, apparently the longest sentences ever imposed on any student protestors anywhere in the United States. Valley State College protests also led to the establishment of a Black Studies program and a Mexican American Studies program at the college. In the late 1960s, the Pacoima community contained Black nationalist associations, Black Panther Party members, and more mainstream African American political actors.[13]

Jack Robbins had made clear in his will that he wanted his trustees to direct his funds where social and political conflicts happened, and he left the location to the trustees' discretion. As he had written, he had expected new repressive laws would be adopted, once again "calculated to limit, abolish, or circumscribe the field of activity in unorthodox or unpopular political or economic causes or philosophies." People would "be arrested, convicted, and imprisoned as a result." That was why Jack Robbins had made it clear that the trustee or the trustees had full discretion to decide what to do with the funds, so long as those funds went to a "Negro child or children" of those engaged in whatever political protest occurred.

So, Irvine Robbins could quietly make his uncle's trust into his own contribution to a worthy institution. He would exercise his discretion in making a gift to the Pacoima Boys Club, while working with the men's group of the Encino B'nai B'rith. He could choose a location that in its way was emerging as emblematic of 1960s protest. That Jack Robbins had other trustees in mind when he wrote his will was irrelevant. Irvine Robbins was, in the end, the trustee of the part of the estate intended to benefit a "Negro child or children." And there would be no challenge to his decision.

Or so it seems might possibly have been the case.[14]

* * *

As for the ACLU of Southern California: according to its official history, it "heartily endorsed the across-the-board demand for civil rights," as the "turbulent sixties" began. It would be involved in the long struggle to desegregate the Los Angeles schools, and it "enlisted a vast cadre of volunteer attorneys" after the 1965 Watts Riot.[15] By the 1960s it would also become a leading voice for challenges to the death penalty and to other forms of state-sanctioned violence.

Meanwhile John McTernan continued to practice law. He remained a lawyer of choice for Communists and ex-Communists. In the late 1960s, he represented Angela Davis in her struggle not to be fired from the University of California. In the 1970s he represented farmworkers. And in 1984, belatedly, he was awarded the Loren Miller Legal Services Award of the State Bar of California. In the 1940s both he and Clore Warne had worked with African American lawyer Loren Miller, challenging racially restrictive covenants in property deeds, in the struggle to desegregate Los Angeles.[16]

In 1963, soon after the conclusion of the Robbins case, Clore Warne published a short essay, written as a book review, on the right of association. The piece was really a reflection on *NAACP v. Alabama*, the 1958 decision where the Supreme Court had unanimously held that the NAACP did not have to reveal its membership lists. One wonders if Warne took this piece as an opportunity to explain himself, and to qualify (maybe counter or reconsider) his earlier argument that Robbins's trust was illegal.

In the essay, he connected the implicit freedom of association possessed by the NAACP, which he understood as a newly articulated freedom, to the criminal convictions of those who refused to answer questions or to reveal memberships in proscribed political organizations. Such convictions were, of course, exactly the kinds of convictions that Jack Robbins had focused on in his will. Once again *NAACP v. Alabama* offered the key. Warne surveyed the field of "associations" that should be protected, including political parties. And soon and predictably he landed on the Communist Party.

What of the prosecutions of Party members and other radicals under the various statutes that were mobilized during the 1940s and 1950s? According to Warne, the numerous opinions by members of the Supreme Court reflected "an ambivalence" about "defining and protecting the right of free political association," particularly around Communist Party membership. That is to say, the US Supreme Court had never arrived at a unified position. He quoted from Hugo Black's dissents in those cases. He looked forward to the presence of Justices Byron White and Arthur Goldberg, newly appointed to the court by the Kennedy administration, and to the retirement of Felix Frankfurter, who had written many of the majority opinions that justified repression. Those appointments, combined with that retirement, presented the prospect of a widening of the freedom of association to such groups and situations. Someday soon, he implied, the court would rule that speech protections extended to men and women accused of political crimes, even Communists. And that assertion suggested Warne's underlying agreement with the arguments that McTernan and Manes had made in *In Re Robbins*.[17]

Sometime during the later 1960s, Clore Warne suffered a disabling stroke. According to Eason Monroe, "in ironic fashion," it affected "more his speech than his general physical well-being. Of course, Clore had made his living and made his mark in the world with his tongue, and to have that immobilized was for him very tragic."[18] He died in 1973.

And Hugh R. Manes set out on a very successful career as the lawyer to go to in police misconduct cases. When he died in 2009, he had become wealthy suing the Los Angeles Police Department. He also trained lawyers how to handle cases about "excessive force" or other allegations against the police. "He offered free monthly seminars" on how to do it, and he established "the Police Misconduct Lawyers Referral Service" that matched attorneys with clients.[19]

* * *

As for the two named litigants, Irvine Robbins and Lee Mishkin: How might we imagine that each of them interpreted Jack Robbins's legacy?

We have already met Irvine Robbins, the dutiful administrator of the estate and, perhaps, the successful trustee of the contested portion of the will. During the rest of his life he moved in directions that one can imagine might have surprised, or even shocked Jack Robbins, the one-time socialist. And it is worth remembering that Jack Robbins had never asked him to play any role in settling his estate. Meanwhile, Lee Mishkin's trajectory, after having challenged Jack Robbins's will because of its deviations from mainstream understandings of who could be the beneficiary of a trust, might, with a little creative license, be understood as offering a paradoxical critique of exactly that mainstream understanding.

Irvine Robbins became famous in ways that typified new understandings of freedom in late twentieth-century America. He had opened an ice cream store in Southern California in 1945, following in the footsteps of his father, Jack Robbins's brother. Irvine's brother-in-law, Burton Baskin, also had an ice cream store. In 1947, each of them had been cited in Pasadena for short-weighting two quarts of ice cream. Two years later the two, the brothers-in-law, joined forces. According to family and company legend, they flipped a coin to decide whose name went first. Thus was born Baskin-Robbins, which modeled choice as a value above all else. Having many choices, many flavors to choose from, was becoming the meaning of freedom. Freedom from the restrictive tyranny of vanilla, chocolate, and strawberry. By 1955, probably sooner, Baskin and Robbins identified their stores with the logo of thirty-one flavors. "To make a trademark . . . of their big flavor list was the suggestion of . . . their advertising agency. Then the agency worked this design into every form of company stationery, into truck panel design, store fronts, product packaging and every type of display material." Thirty-one flavors, though Irvine Robbins's 2008 obituary mentioned that they had created more than a thousand flavors. And Baskin and Robbins also pioneered in franchising, placing responsibility (the burdens of freedom) on those local proprietors who managed stores, freeing the company from direct oversight and responsibility.[20]

Eventually, Irvine Robbins lived in a house with a pool shaped like an ice cream cone and with a soda fountain inside the house. His son, John Robbins, rebelled. John Robbins became an advocate for a vegan, plant-based diet, for the need for more and different food choices. And he became a different but also a successful entrepreneur and a very successful author. He emphasized the need to make the right choices, rather than the wrong choices. And Irvine's grandson, Ocean Robbins, continues today with blogs and books that advocate for still more healthy choices (see figure 18).[21]

Meanwhile, Lee Mishkin, Irvine's opponent in the will litigation and a more distant relative, continued in his career as a cartoonist, working both in television and in the movies. After the success of the *Mr. Magoo* series, he went on

Figure 18: Irvine Robbins of Baskin-Robbins Ice Cream, 1976 (publicity photograph). Photo by Tony Korody/Sygma/Sygma via Getty Images.

to draw and sometimes direct some of the iconic cartoons of the 1960s, 1970s, and 1980s, perhaps most famously the *Jackson 5* cartoon and the cartoon images used in the television version of *Batman* (POW!). Later on he established a school for cartooning in Vancouver, Canada, and he became much loved as a teacher in the world of cartooning.[22]

Around 1970 he also directed and drew a series of more experimental short films, with questioning titles: *How the First Letter Was Written, How the Elephant Got His Trunk, Why People Have Laws, or Shiver, Gobble and Snore, Why We Have Taxes, or the Town That Had No Policeman*, and *Is It Always Right to Be Right?* The last of these, with narration by Orson Welles, based on a parable by Warren H. Schmidt, first published in the opinion section of the *Los Angeles Times*, won the Academy Award for best animated short in 1971. Drawn using the archetypes of countercultural imagery, as if it came off of murals on the walls of Haight-Ashbury or the Lower East Side, the short subject cartoon *Is It Always Right to Be Right?* offered an apparently happy parable about how to overcome the generation gap and the racial gap. Each—both the generation gap and the racial gap—was portrayed, at least in the script, as being founded simply on the foolish insistence of each side on being right. The solution was easy. Once those on one side learned to listen to those on the other side, to admit that they might be wrong, and to agree to a "Declaration of Interdependence," all would be well. In the fashion of Hollywood, the film had constructed a happy ending in which communication across racial and generational divides came easily and would soon solve all problems. The overt narrative was that "mainstream" and "underground," dominant culture and counterculture, could get along, could live together, if everyone just learned to listen a little, if everyone stopped misunderstanding those on the other side.

But that conclusion was a thin one. And the interdependence the film offered was nothing more than a piece of paper, hardly enough, given the harsh images that pervaded the film. If one ignores the sappy ending, what remains from watching *Is It Always Right to Be Right?* are those images and the violence portrayed. The drawings were strikingly at war with that happy narrative, the script. Resolutions—solutions, peace—could not occur so easily. And that difficulty in resolution seems particularly the case in the section of the film devoted to African American demands. That part of the short film is filled with images of the Vietnam War and of police violence, of dirty streets and fat cats oblivious to suffering, policing, and violent repression. It is filled, too, with images of riots and rebellion. What remains in one's consciousness after viewing Mishkin's film were all the ways underground and alternative communities were under attack (see figure 19).

Figure 19: Still from Lee Mishkin's *Is It Always Right to be Right?* (Santa Monica, CA: Stephen Bosustow Productions, 1970). ULMIA (Indiana University Libraries Moving Image Archive), Bloomington, Indiana.

The film is better seen as an articulation of conflicted understandings of freedom and about what it meant to insist on being "right." And it suggested the absence of anything like a serious response to the breakdown of a common culture. The film highlighted the continuing presence of giant generational and racial gaps. One was left with violence and confusion.[23]

How that state of affairs connected to the worldview of Lee Mishkin's uncle, to Jack Robbins, to the man whose will Mishkin had challenged and tried to overturn, I leave to the reader's imagination.

Conclusion

Remember Harold Krowech, the sixteen-year-old boy sent by Jack Robbins in 1925 to start a Boys' Brotherhood Republic in Los Angeles? He was, according to the *Los Angeles Evening Post-Record*, a "handsome, personable, youth, tremendously in earnest." His goals for the Los Angeles outpost had a familiar ring: "We don't want to point [out] the error of their ways" to the boys of Los Angeles. Nor did he want to "jam religion down their throats—or make them feel like remorseful criminals." Rather, the goal of a Los Angeles BBR was to bring boys "into contact with fellows who want to make prosperous, intelligent and honest citizens of themselves. This environment will do ten times the work of any reformer's preaching."[1]

In Chicago, where he was born, Krowech had been elected the prosecuting attorney and then the judge of the Chicago BBR. He was the youngest of six children of William and Alice Krowech, both of whom had been born in Russia. Yiddish was their native tongue. The father worked as a "bushelman," a tailor's assistant, in a tailor shop. Apparently Harold had come to Los Angeles because his parents had decided to move there, not just because he had been sent on a mission by Jack Robbins. By the 1930 census, when he was twenty-one, he still lived with his parents, along with two siblings. His father worked as a tailor. But the family was now able to own a home. He went to college at UCLA and then to USC Law School. By 1933, he was admitted to the California bar, and, for at least a year or two, he worked as a deputy public defender for Los Angeles County.[2]

By the mid-1930s he began to craft an identity as an expert on the "youth" problem. One might imagine that he had learned something from Jack Robbins about self-promotion, and perhaps his early years as a citizen in the Boys' Brotherhood Republic had given him a sense of mission. On the other hand, his framing of the "youth" problem and of how to solve it was dramatically different from what Robbins had offered for the "boy problem" twenty years earlier. And we might see him as something of an embodiment of what juvenile justice was becoming, in at least two different ways.

In February 1936, he appeared on the *American School of the Air* radio show to speak on the subject, "Youth Flings Its Challenge." A year later he became the chairman of the Juvenile Crime Prevention Committee of the Junior Barristers of the Los Angeles Bar Association. In that role he spoke at a public forum on the "Juvenile Crime Prevention Problem." By June 1939, he headed an effort to send attorneys to speak to public school audiences to explain "the pitfalls of crime." In interviews and in articles published in bar journals, he explained how this program would solve the crime problem. Young people needed to know the law, he said—by which he meant that they needed to know the consequences of committing crimes. They needed to know how they would be punished. Parens patriae, the notion of a caring and equity-oriented juvenile justice that treated the young instead of punishing them, disappeared. Instead, young men, who typically had "little or no conception of the penalties for their offenses," who had "distorted and even fantastic ideas" about the law, needed to learn that our "penal code prescribes one to ten years in the penitentiary for grand theft." That knowledge might dampen a boy's desire to steal cars.

The goal of Krowech's program, to which the FBI's J. Edgar Hoover offered his support, was to educate and to warn youth "regarding the importance of observing and enforcing laws." To bring the law to the child instead of the child to the law. And, according to young lawyer Krowech, no one could "relate the dangers of a life of crime to youth with more telling effect than the lawyer." Along the way, he continued, the program was "revolutionizing" two core legal concepts. First, it abandoned the idea that "ignorance of the law is no excuse." Instead, it posited that "to know the law is to respect it." (I'm not really sure how that new legal concept abandoned the old legal concept.) But second, the program challenged the notion that the attorney's primary duty was to defend the criminal. Instead, the job was "to prevent crime in the first place." Just as it was the doctor's duty to "correct disease of the body," it was the lawyers' duty to prevent crime.[3]

Prevention was everything. The lawyers who participated in his program would not "preach" to students. Instead, they appealed for cooperation. They expected to "convince youth of the eternal truth that an offender against society's laws always pays the penalty." And they imagined that their meetings with public school students offered a "course" of "legal therapy" that would prevent students from becoming criminals. The therapy was "a rational one . . . designed to become a part of the child's consciousness and as such to be reflected in his social attitude." It was a "group therapy" that removed "the obstacle of individual differences among children," and it was also an "experience therapy" in which "none of the emotional disturbances which confront a child in the ordinary criminal process" were "present." And the attorney "by indirection" brought to the child "the experience of the law." The fact that an attorney was "an arm of the court" was of "good psychological effect." It was also "a common interest therapy," predicated on "the common background and interest of the attorney and child." This common interest was established by using young lawyers and by selecting attorneys who were graduates of the schools at which they spoke. It was as well a "realistic therapy," based on real case histories of boys confronting juvenile justice. And finally, it was a "participation and self-expression therapy," where the child had the opportunity to ask questions that mattered to him. "Often the question period" disclosed "anti-social attitudes—misconceptions of the law and purely imaginary beliefs resting in the minds of the young people."[4]

By the early 1940s, Krowech was identified as "a distinguished member of the Los Angeles bar and a nationally known figure." He would continue to chair the state bar's committee on youth crime, and he continued to advocate for "clearer thinking" on the problem. In 1945 he spoke as a "noted authority on all juvenile problems." And he was a member of the board of the city's child-guidance clinic.[5]

But in the later 1940s he disappeared from the newspapers. One suspects that his legal practice moved away from youth crime. The only organizational work he was identified with after the mid-1940s was as a member of the Board of Guardians of the local Jewish Home for the Aged.[6]

That said, he apparently continued to serve, how often I don't know, as a "referee as needed," a temporary judge, in cases before the Los Angeles juvenile court. And in 1965, he privately published a volume, a sort of a chapbook, of poems. These were "based upon the writer's experiences and feelings of children," stimulated by his work as a referee. They were "dedicated to children everywhere."

His artless poems, written without punctuation and with lowercase titles, obsessed about the presence and absence of mothers and fathers in children's lives. The first poem in the volume, "attachment," began: "mother dear / the one so near / who will not separate / to leave him clear / to seek and find / his values dear." A second, called "child in juvenile court," worried that without an X-ray he could not know a boy's "hidden fears and pains" and terrors. Other poems reflected on the inequality that mothers showed to some children over others. One, entitled "in juvenile court detention," imagined a child turning "a hundred times / at night / waiting for / mothers sight." Others focused on "mothers tears" and "mother works." And others attended to the coldness of fathers.[7]

I know little else about the life of Harold Krowech. But what I do know is that he twice limned core features of what juvenile justice was becoming: first as crime prevention and second as an occasion for psychodynamic diagnosis. And each time what he expressed represented a rejection of what the Boys' Brotherhood Republic had once stood for: which was to trust the young to govern themselves and to reject adult power, both in its punitive and in its caring guises. In his early days as a young lawyer, Krowech had articulated the punitive recognition that juvenile delinquents were on the road to becoming criminals and that they were basically indistinguishable from adult criminals. The job of the caring adult, the lawyer, was to stop them from becoming that. Prevention was all. And when prevention failed, fear and coercion and the violence of state power were all that remained. In his later work as a referee, at least in the poems he wrote, he articulated the therapeutic and psychodynamic focus that dominated postwar social work and child welfare. The child in court ought to have been cared for and protected by parents. He was there, in court, because his parents had failed. He needed therapy. Probably his parents did, as well.

In neither stage of his career did Krowech ever mention race or poverty. Indeed, there were no signs of community at all in Krowech's work. No pals, no gangs, no community, only private individuals who might choose to do wrong but who might be scared straight. And then there were private families that failed in their tasks of care and prevention.

One can only wonder what Jack Robbins thought of Krowech's work. Even more, one wonders how consciously Krowech worked to distance himself from Jack Robbins's legacy. In Robbins's several efforts to start clubs or organizations in Los Angeles after 1925, well covered in the Los Angeles papers, Krowech never appeared, although several other former BBR citizens, alumni who had moved to the West Coast, did. Nor was Krowech ever, best I can tell, involved with the Southern California ACLU. Had Harold Krowech run away from his past? Or is it just that the times had changed, and Harold Krowech was at one with those changes?

* * *

A story is implicit in these pages: one about how the legal and public cultures, which once obsessed about "bad boys" or boys in trouble or the "boy problem," changed over the course of Jack Robbins's life and beyond. In the years after the early 1920s, professionals and policymakers rethought or reimagined that "boy problem." Boys in trouble became "troubled boys" and scary criminals. For the most part such boys needed to be controlled and dealt with using the coercive tools of a violent state. The movement from Jack Robbins, the "big brother," to Harold Krowech, the lawyer, may be imagined as marking that change.

Looking backwards from where we are today, in the third decade of the twenty-first century, what is striking about the understandings and the practices of those adults who in early twentieth-century America dealt with "the boy problem" was that nearly all then recognized that the boundaries were porous between dependent boys, mistreated boys, violent and even dangerous boys, the delinquent, and "merely" poor boys. All were still boys. All were still children, to be distinguished from adults.

The achievement of the juvenile court, a now mostly discredited innovation of the turn of the twentieth century, was to mark or to reinforce the sharp divide between adult criminals and boy criminals. But that divide left those in charge needing to confront the uncertainties and the problem of the relationship between boy criminals, delinquents, and a world of other troubled youths who needed care. How to deal with the blur of categories, the diversity of boys, they confronted? How to know who the boys before them were and what they were becoming? How to deal with hunger and abandonment and racial discrimination and ethnic segregation and an absence of meaningful work and homes without rooms for adolescent boys and absent parents and schools that seemed little more than warehouses for the young, as well as the viciousness of some of the young? The boys they dealt with were part of a "swarm" of children, who often seemed to be dominating and controlling American urban streets. The "swarm" annoyed and often endangered adults—passersby, employers, store owners, occasional schoolteachers, relatives, and more—who had to deal with them. They also threatened other children, young people. But nearly all those who worked with "bad boys" of whatever ilk still wanted to ensure that those in the swarm were not treated as adult criminals.

Boys (and girls) were to be cared for by kindly state actors, especially if they were not being cared for properly by parents. Or, as a California juvenile court judge put it in a 1953 speech that offers an odd and late echo both of phrases from the Boys' Brotherhood Republic and of the general goals of Progressive Era reform: in a criminal trial when the wrongdoer was an adult, "the people," all eleven million Californians, "proceeded against the wrongdoer." On the other hand, in juvenile court, where the wrongdoer was a child, all eleven million Californians were reconstituted to work for, not against, the boy. "That's a lot of people to be working for you—but it's not too many when a 'fellow needs a friend.'" Children, including adolescents, were not adults. And they should be treated (not punished) as not-adults. They should be cared for and befriended.[8]

Jack Robbins and the committees of the Boys' Brotherhood Republic had no faith that any part of the adult world, and certainly not the juvenile court, was constituted to be a boy's friend. But he shared with mainstream reformers an insistence on distinguishing or separating, on maintaining, the boundaries between the young and the not-so-young. He and the boys were no different in this regard than the Progressive Era child savers and reformers they critiqued and challenged. All began with a commitment to separate all those children, including so-called juvenile delinquents, adolescents, from adult criminals, as subjects of study and as subjects to be reformed (or in the case of the BBR, to govern themselves). All saw a commonality shared by categories of children that we might today understand as distinguishable, one from the other.

That Progressive Era understanding, that insistence that the child in trouble differed from the adult criminal, did not disappear, but it would soon be countered and complicated by a second separation, one between the boy criminal and other boys. In the 1920s, emergent criminology, shaped both by psychology and by sociology, came to focus on the longitudinal study of criminal lives. Its core question: How is it that this individual, this child, became "a criminal"? One result of asking that question was the construction of what Myers calls "a new youthful subjectivity: the incipient or pre-delinquent."[9] The academic and clinical study of delinquency—as well as of policing—produced (or reproduced, since it was surely already present in the wider public culture) a desire to understand what it was (nature, nurture, culture) that led some to acquire a compulsion or desire or need to break the law. What became positive criminology contained what an early critic identified as the implicit assumption that "the delinquent was fundamentally different from the law-abiding."[10]

Thus, the separation between child and adult was complicated by a second separation, one between the criminal or delinquent child and the law-abiding or "normal" child. That second separation began with the factual or empirical realization that, as Krowech's "Juvenile Crime Prevention Committee" put it, "a tremendous proportion of adult criminality has its inception in conviction of crime before the age of twenty-three."[11] This second separation was ratified, or reified, or reinforced, given a kind of determinative force, by racialization, which often allowed social scientists and policymakers to reinterpret the surround, "the community," as having distinctively criminalizing features. Race or racialization was the handmaiden of this second separation. The criminal child—usually Black or Brown or Red—was the subject of study, not the noncriminal child, usually white, even though social scientists like the Gluecks knew and acknowledged that the juvenile delinquent began, and sometimes remained, enmeshed in a community composed for the most part of noncriminals, or, at least, of those not identified by the police and the criminal processes as criminals. Still, the road was an easy one to notions like the now discredited figure of the "superpredator," to an understanding that there existed some in the society, some few, one hoped, who, for whatever reasons (biology, psychology, culture), were hardwired for violence and crime.[12]

Today, more than a century since Jack Robbins became the "big brother to chanceless waifs" and then founded the Boys' Brotherhood Republic, our "boy problem" is, I suspect, both similar and different than it once was. The boundary between adult crime and juvenile crime is hazy at best. The young are understood to be as scary as the old. Maybe scarier. Studies of child soldiers from around the world are said to epitomize a violence to be feared in the young, a violence without judgment or rational calculation. There is no accepted theoretical perspective on the psychodynamics or the genealogy or even the trajectory of a criminal life, though the distinctiveness of a criminal identity, whether a juvenile or an adult, is mostly taken for granted.[13] The separation of the criminal from the noncriminal child remains constitutive of public policy and of the legal or carceral culture, even though everyone knows how contingent and haphazard it is that some choose or are moved in one direction and others in another. Racialization remains at the core of how delinquents and criminals are perceived, both in public discourse and in the academy.[14]

Today, jailed and imprisoned juveniles confront a harsh and bureaucratic set of institutions with thin and inconsistent remedial goals. Those institutions are hard to distinguish from those that deal with adult criminals. Delinquent identities and behaviors are said to justify the mobilization of state violence, which will immobilize them. Their rights, or more precisely, their lack of rights, are hard to distinguish from those claimed or asserted by or denied to adult criminals. The goal of much, maybe most, public policy, is to separate the criminal (young or not young) from the rest of us, from the law abiding. And what happens to them once separated is a matter of relatively little interest, one not thought to be worthy of significant public funds. So, except when occasional scandals force momentary public attention, juvenile institutions are understood as just one part of the apparatus of a carceral state, a part whose goals are immobilization and incarceration and separation from the rest of us. And punishment. Care is often forgotten, certainly minimized, as the criminal law and penology are made harsher and more unforgiving. Like the young Harold Krowech, we focus on prevention, not care. Like the later Harold Krowech as well, we imagine that all would be well if parents only did their jobs better.[15]

That story is one I have not told, although some dimensions of it are implicit in the narrative. It is a story about how one understanding of the "boy problem" was replaced by another, and about the continuing failures of efforts to prepare young Americans for citizenship across the twentieth century and beyond, and about the continuing and increasing mobilization of the violence of state power to isolate those who can be identified as the rightsless and dangerous young. And it is also a story about the public's continuing discomfort with exercises of freedom by the young.

I have not written a history of juvenile justice and of the collection of racialized and class-based institutions that produced "juvenile justice" and that may or may not have had shared purposes and that may or may not have been and remained part of a larger structure of carceral institutions. I have not written a history of the ways juvenile justice worked to justify itself by way of notions of protection of childhood or care. Jack Robbins and the Boys' Brotherhood Republic lived in the shadow of those looming and growing and not yet well understood structures of knowledge and of power. Those institutions and practices were a context, an environment, within which Jack Robbins and the BBR worked through what they meant by freedom and citizenship. Those structures shaped who they were. But Jack Robbins and the BBR were more than just an expression or an articulation of those structures.

* * *

Jack Robbins, both in life and in death, as well as his creation, Chicago's Boys' Brotherhood Republic, embodied an underground but not inconsequential stream in American constitutional life.

In exploring that stream as he and they expressed it, in allowing myself to be seduced by the words and the practices and schemes and projects that Jack Robbins talked about and sometimes created, and that American newspapers and journalists momentarily publicized, I have sometimes wondered what it is that I am learning. Is there anything "useful" or valuable for us today about Jack Robbins's odd efforts to be recognized as an adult caring for and empowering younger people, and in the several ways that his contemporaries responded to him?

Today, few people, as best I can tell, ever imagine that a goal of reform could possibly be to turn over power and authority to children in trouble, children now often understood as "troubled" or dangerous. Debate continues about what we as adults should do for them or to them and what the right policies and practices are that we would impose on them. We debate what children need, but do not ever consider withdrawing, granting them autonomy and respect and community to shape their own lives. We do not think to leave them to true self-government and to their capacities to make communities, as Jack Robbins once tried to do. Robbins's understanding borders on the ridiculous, is truly lost to us (as it already seemed, one has to acknowledge, for many of his contemporaries).

Jack Robbins and the BBR as it was in its first decade, during the 1910s, may be the merest of historical oddities, the detritus or leavings of the past. Just as the small case that concludes his story in 1962 was only an occasion for a few lawyers to try to work through how they would understand and use civil disobedience, in the early days of the civil rights movement. The conditions of freedom that Jack Robbins imagined for his boys, not to mention the conditions under which he led a caring and free life, not to mention the work of his lawyers after his death to make his will an enforceable one, are all just parts of a noisy and messy past.[16]

So, what did I learn from this journey through and beyond his life? My answer carries back to Clara Laughlin and her exploration of the energetic and democratic life of the BBR. Her reflections on what she learned from the time she spent in 1917–1920 with Jack Robbins and the BBR are worth restating.

It would be silly to draw a coherent understanding of freedom out of the statements Jack Robbins made and the slogans that survive of the early years of the Chicago Boys' Brotherhood Republic. He was a magpie, and he was derivative. He and they took selective bits and pieces from what was all around them: from Progressive social reform, from John Dewey, from novels and children's literature, from the social gospel and from socialists. Images of wolf packs and gangs but also notions of the dignity of work and a deep hostility to coercion. I suspect, though it was never highlighted, that there were also traces of Jewish ethical discourse and of laborite solidarity. There was much too about being thrust into city life, of making a life on the streets of Chicago. Of the pleasures and compulsions of living an urban life in twentieth-century America.

Ideologically, Jack Robbins was a repository of positions and stances and occasional claimed identities that changed with the zeitgeist. His "socialism" was never placed in opposition to business, and eventually, as expressed in his will, it morphed into a commitment to racial equality and to a focus on the needs of "Negro children." Earlier, he said nothing about race at all. But we can imagine that in the postwar world, race and the need to undo the harms of discrimination took the place in his consciousness of all the multitude of industrial and urban conditions and circumstances, once perhaps identified with the wrongs of capitalism, that left boys uncared for and on the streets of American cities.

There were a few notions that stood out, particularly in his early days. These probably continued to define him and the values of the boys he worked with. They included distrust of adult authority figures, including parents and parent substitutes, and an intuition that charity harmed beneficiaries, combined with a belief in voluntarism and a more-than-occasional celebration of business and athletic success. There was fury that society—that is, the adult world—did not care, did not make caring space for boys, did not really love them as they ought to be loved. There was attention paid to masculinity—to the need to understand boys as becoming men and as living lives as citizens. At the same time, the BBR's understanding of masculinity seems gentler than how early twentieth-century manliness is often portrayed, in the historical literature and elsewhere. It is not focused on a fear of femininity or emasculation. And unlike many other educational reformers, Jack Robbins and the BBR denied that living a life in rights-bearing and democratic citizenship was playacting. It was, at least within the boundaries of the BBR, what boy life or adolescence should be.

Was the investigating committee of the BBR, the committee that did most of the work negotiating the release of boys from coercive state institutions into the BBR and its citizenship, a "child-saving" institution? In some ways, perhaps. Obviously so, literally. But that is not how it understood itself, nor how it was understood within the constitution of the BBR. It was, rather, a central feature of the notion of a shared identity that defined the boys' collective responsibility.

So: We are all boys. (Whether Robbins and the boys meant to include girls remains unclear.) Happenstance means that some boys will be caught by the police and then become, at least for a while, inmates of penal institutions. But they are us. And we are them. And it is our responsibility to do what we can to bring us all together within the self-governing republic that is the BBR.

Two concerns, two notions of freedom, stood out over all else: Care or collective responsibility, on the one hand, and the possibility of democratic citizenship, on the other hand. Both, particularly the second, drew on the sources already mentioned. Notions of citizenship, of a republic marked by self-governance, located in the city, one that built on the actual lives—including the work lives—of boy citizens, were what sympathetic adults noticed about the BBR. It was most of what American newspapers reported about Jack Robbins and the BBR. Adult commentators loved to imagine that the BBR's institutions—perhaps especially its regular elections for offices—served as preparation for what lay ahead. Useful pedagogically, but not "real" yet, not until the boys had grown up. Little different, perhaps, than elections for class president in the public schools.

But the first concern, signaled by the mantra "Where any boy is in trouble, we too are in trouble," was what most marked the early BBR. The mantra challenged efforts to divide good from bad, law abiding from criminal. Indeed, the mantra could be translated to mean: "We are all bad boys." It did not only mean that "there are no bad boys," a recurrent trope found elsewhere (and one that Jack Robbins often mobilized in his early days). Instead, it implied that boys would care for boys, regardless of the labels that would be attached by others to individual identities and behaviors, and regardless of the situations they might find themselves in. Boys had a shared and collective and ongoing responsibility in the face of the harsh and unforgiving world of reform schools, courts, and prisons. And in the face of the labels of delinquency and criminality, and the experience of dependency and abandonment.

We all care for each other. We are pals. And it is as pals who work together that we exercise our freedom.

One might imagine, to connect the latter part of this book to the first, that Jack Robbins was trying to articulate something similar in his will. To create a trust for the care of the African American children of those convicted of Cold War crimes was his way of showing a certain kind of solidarity, of being a pal. Once again, we are all bad boys. Or, in this case, we all might be subjected to the consequences of having been labeled "Communists" or "dangerous radicals," or of having been convicted as political lawbreakers. No one should be abandoned. And we can do what we can within the constraints and the conditions within which we live. We can and should use the resources we find ourselves in possession of, in ways that mark and manifest our commonality.

As Clara Laughlin wrote in 1920, that understanding of freedom might serve as a model for the highest aspirations of American citizenship and democracy. But whether or not it is or was used thusly, whether such a model remains a plausible aspiration, it is that understanding that animated Jack Robbins and the Boys' Brotherhood Republic. At least, that understanding was the animating force during the BBR's early days. And perhaps it still remained so when Robbins wrote his will.

Acknowledgments

The summer after my first year of law school, my wife moved temporarily to Ithaca, New York, to train to become a Montessori teacher. I followed her there, and when I realized I had nothing to do during the day, other than develop immense skill at the pinball machines in the local bars, I signed up for two summer school courses at NYU Law School, including one on "juvenile delinquency." So, once a week I took the bus back to the city, where I had enrolled in a small and boring class that combined law and social work. I availed myself of everything that the class offered, including the chance to sit in on proceedings in the juvenile court, and my wife and I talked a good deal about incorrigible children, of how boys and girls became "persons in need of supervision." But I was already a history nerd. So, separately, I read a bit into the history of the juvenile court. I read Anthony Platt's recently published critical history of the origins of the Chicago court, and I used the Cornell Law Library to find more historical writings. And then I followed closely (in the more indirect ways one followed events in those pre-Google days) the controversy at the University of California at Berkeley about Platt's tenure denial and, soon thereafter, about the closing of the criminology program that he was a part of.

Reading about juvenile justice was a nice distraction during that summer, the summer of 1971, the last "free" summer I experienced before retirement. But I never thought much about doing more. I might have momentarily contemplated becoming some kind of law worker in a juvenile court. But that was at most a fleeting impulse. And I quickly went on to other things.

Until one day, nearly a half century later, while recovering from chemotherapy, in the midst of a global pandemic, while under doctor's orders to remain entirely isolated, I decided to find out what I could about an individual who had left a weird will in a Cold War–era case in California. Like others, I turned to online services, which was all I could do at a time when libraries were closed. I put in the name "Jack Robbins" into the search engine at Newspapers.com. I had to eliminate many "Jack Robbinses" who didn't fit the little I knew. And then, surprisingly, there were many hundreds of hits. Suddenly, as I moved from one middle-size city newspaper to another, I found myself immersed in the "boy problem" and juvenile delinquency in Progressive Era America.

The initial research depended entirely on the availability of online resources. That I could conduct such research at all was thanks to the resources and the generosity of Princeton University and of Firestone Library, and to the immense availability today of online archives. Without Newspapers.com and other online newspaper archives, as well as Ancestry.com, I would never have discovered the right (but very left) Jack Robbins, who, for a time, made news in an era when newspapers "made" much of the news. I would certainly not have been able to follow him on his travels.

I also benefited from the help of kind and competent librarians and archivists in libraries and collections around the country who, when they were able to do so, located and sent me books and PDF files and JPG images of crucial documents. In pursuing those sources, in accumulating what became my own archive about Jack Robbins and the Boys' Brotherhood Republic, I received crucial and invaluable financial support from the William Nelson Cromwell Foundation, as shepherded by John Gordan and Sarah Barringer Gordon.

I leave it to readers to consider the ways that those resources and that modality of work either distorted or revealed what would not have been knowable through earlier ways of doing historical work. Because Jack Robbins doesn't appear in other histories of Progressive reform or of juvenile justice, I have never been able to shake the fear that much of what I think I have discovered is nothing but an artifact or a fiction produced by a flawed method. And yet, I know he lived. And I know there was a Chicago Boys' Brotherhood Republic. And I certainly know that the "boy problem" in Progressive Era Chicago was experienced as a real problem. There was and is more historical work to be written, using several different methods and modalities of work, about that reality in the American past.

Still, challenges and uncertainties are intrinsic to the kind of historical project that this book came to be. Ways of doing history are changing. Those changes are deep and far-reaching, and they go beyond the contingencies and fragilities of life in 2020 and 2021. And they raise difficult epistemological issues. I don't, however, think those epistemological issues are entirely new.

There is no escape from the mysteries that studies of the past produce. And exploring those mysteries, using the tools that our present moment offers to us to tell stories that are true, or as true as we can make them be, remains central to the joys of the work.

So, to conclude: I was lucky to fall into a subject that absorbed me and allowed me to tell a different kind of history than I had previously written. I was blessed to live in a time and a place and in a situation where I could pursue that passion, in the face of novel and difficult challenges. I was particularly blessed that Nancy Hartog tolerated this new passion as I recovered from illness (and later on that she read my early drafts with her characteristically brutal critical intelligence). And then I had the immense good fortune that numbers of friends were willing to read more, and to talk with me about what I had done, at first using remote forms of communication. I was and am fortunate indeed.

* * *

More particularly:

Throughout my research I relied on a number of online services. I was particularly dependent on Newspapers.com, on ProQuest (for access to the *Chicago Tribune* and the *Los Angeles Times*), on the Library of Congress's *Chronicling America: Historical American Newspapers* database, on the University of California, Riverside, California Newspaper Project, and on the Illinois Newspaper Project of the Illinois Library. I also relied heavily on Ancestry.com.

I am also grateful to several archives and repositories:

To the Los Angeles County Law Library, to the archives of the Los Angeles Superior Court, and to the California State Library, all of whom worked to find me necessary legal materials.

To the University of California Los Angeles Research Library, Special Collections, for the American Civil Liberties Union, Southern California Branch Papers.

To Cate Mills, curator of Library, Archives, and Multimedia, at the History San Jose Research Library, for access to the Harry E. Slonaker Papers.

To Marian J. Matyn, archivist at the Clarke Historical Library, Central Michigan University, Mount Pleasant, MI, for access to the Van Lieu Minor Papers.

To the Sophia Smith Collection at Smith College, Northampton, MA, for access to the Clara Laughlin Papers.

To the University of Chicago Library, for access to the Julius Rosenwald Papers.

To the University of Illinois Chicago Library, Special Collections, for access to and permission to quote from the institutional files of the Chicago Home and Aid Society of Illinois Records.

To the Chicago History Museum, for access to the scrapbook of Edmund D. Hulbert.

To Mary Elizabeth Brown, Tappan Rare Book Librarian, at the American Heritage Center, University of Wyoming, for access to Gene Levitt's script "Reunion," from the *Loretta Young Show*.

I am grateful for the research assistance of Ben Postone, Marla McMackin, and Haris Durrani, who helped me find crucial materials.

Nicole Chase, the executive director of the Boys and Girls Club of the San Fernando Valley, and Crystal Jackson, head of the Pacoima Historical Society, both helped me explore my speculations about the place of Pacoima in the story of Jack Robbins's will.

Howard Erlanger, John Langbein, and Bill LaPiana helped me find speculative answers to some mysteries of trusts and estates law.

Geneva Smith cite-checked the manuscript, saving me from several errors.

* * *

I twice had the privilege of readings of early versions of the work at Bill Nelson's online legal history group (the successor to the NYU legal history workshop). Thanks to Kim Scheppele, I had a reading of chapter 3 before the online remnant of the Law and Public Affairs Program at Princeton University in March 2022. I also presented an early version of chapter 2 to a criminal law and legal history workshop at Columbia Law School in July 2022.

Dov Weinryb Grohsgal, Farah Peterson, Risa Goluboff, Bill Nelson, Judith Resnik, Craig Green, Margot Canaday, Laura Weinrib, Catherine Fisk, Michael Grossberg, Barbara Welke, Geneva Smith, and of course Nancy Hartog, read the manuscript in various iterations. Each challenged some of my interpretations and saved me from errors. None of them is responsible for what remains.

Early and late, I also gained and learned from conversations (by email, by Zoom, and in person) with Martha Minow, Dan Rodgers, Anne Cheng, Kim Scheppele, John Demos, Sarah Yerima, Yaacob Dweck, Carolyn Yerkes, Amy Dru Stanley, Maeve Glass, Bill Gleason, Naama Maor, Doris Rueda, Laura Edwards, Michael Willrich, and David Tanenhaus. Robert Mennel was kind enough to suggest several sources and references that I had missed.

Conversations with Maddie Pollack, Sarah Yerima, Mitra Sharafi, Dov Weinryb Grohsgal, Emily Sung, and Ling Ritter were life-affirming and invigorating.

And I was grateful that Maddie and Matt Miller volunteered to look for the Nevada "ranch."

Through the happenstance of conversations with Judith Resnik, I came to the University of Chicago Press. There, I was lucky to be assigned to Timothy Mennel, whose reading of an early draft was spot-on, who found perceptive readers for the manuscript at a somewhat later stage, and who has been a great support. Andrea Blatz guided me through the mysteries of "Permissions," Jessica Wilson provided rigorous and helpful copyediting, and Adriana Smith worked with me through the later production stages.

I dedicate this book to the students, graduate and undergraduate, who taught me and worked with me and—fortunate me—often befriended me. In the years I worked at Princeton University and thereafter, they brought joy into my life, and they made legal history exciting and often thrilling and fun. They took me to places I never imagined going. And they brought me intimations of better worlds. I'm immeasurably grateful to them.

Notes

INTRODUCTION

1. The availability of these articles in searchable form opens up possibilities that are new for historians. For a short moment, 1913–1920, newspaper and magazine editors across America produced and reproduced stories about Jack Robbins, and they worked to gain his presence and that of "his" boys in their newsrooms and elsewhere for interviews. That fact is now knowable through the magic of twenty-first-century online databases. These databases are flat and positivist sources, to use Emma Rothschild's apt characterization. They are true for what they are. Each reveals solely that a newspaper editor chose to ask a reporter to write an article or to conduct an interview, or that the editor took from one of the news services a story about Jack Robbins or about the boys of the BBR. And the conditions for their production, as well as the truth value of the content contained in the "stories," varied enormously. See Emma Rothschild, *An Infinite History: The Story of a French Family over Three Centuries* (Princeton, NJ: Princeton University Press, 2021). See also Steven Schlossman, *Transforming Juvenile Justice: Reform Ideals and Institutional Realities, 1825–1920* (DeKalb: Northern Illinois University Press, 2005), xiii–xiv, for a description of the labor necessary to conduct similar historical work a generation ago, at a time when there existed no online index for newspapers.

2. On the actors' need to fit their stories to the news values of journalists, see Edwin Amenta and Neal Caren, *Rough Draft of History: A Century of US Social Movements in the News* (Princeton, NJ: Princeton University Press, 2022), xi. See, for a focus on readers' responses to Chicago's newspapers (mostly the *Chicago Tribune*) between 1912 and 1917, David Paul Nord, *Communities of Journalism: A History of American Journalism and Their Readers* (Urbana and Chicago: University of Illinois Press, 2001), 246–77. For a labor and spatial history of American newsrooms, in a slightly later period, see Will Mari, *The American Newsroom: A History, 1920–1960* (Columbia: University of Missouri Press, 2021).

3. The references are to J. Willard Hurst, *Law and the Conditions of Freedom in the Nineteenth Century United States* (Madison: University of Wisconsin Press, 1956), and to Morton Horwitz, *The Transformation of American Law, 1780–1860* (Cambridge, MA: Harvard University Press, 1977). I draw the notion of an "underground stream" from Clancy Sigal's memoir about growing up in Jewish Lawndale. See Clancy Sigal, *A Woman of Uncertain Character: The Amorous and Radical Adventures of My Mother Jennie (Who Always Wanted to Be a Respectable Jewish Mom* (New York: Carroll and Graf, 2006), 29. See also Jacqueline Jones, *Goddess of Anarchy: The Life and Times of Lucy Parsons, American Radical* (New York: Basic Books, 2017). For reflections on the "mainstream," see Hendrik Hartog, "Four Fragments on Doing Legal History, or Thinking with and against Willard Hurst," *Law and History Review* 39, no. 4 (November 2021): 835–66. And for early thoughts about the relationships between underground streams and American constitutionalism, see Hendrik Hartog, "The Constitution of Aspiration and 'The Rights That Belong to Us All,'" *Journal of American History* 74, no. 3 (December 1987): 1013–34.

CHAPTER ONE

1. Luther L. McDougal III and Myres S. McDougal, *Property, Wealth, Land: Allocation, Planning and Development*, 2nd ed. (Indianapolis: Michie Company; Bobbs-Merrill Company, 1981). *In the Matter of Estate of Robbins*, 57 Cal. 2d 718, 371 P. 2d 573 (1962). The senior casebook author, Myres McDougal, was a prominent liberal Cold Warrior. The first edition of that casebook, published in the late 1940s, was a controversial effort to reframe property law in ways that integrated and took account of the transformations of the New Deal; see Myres Smith McDougal and David Haber, *Property, Wealth, Land: Allocation, Planning, and Development; Selected Cases and Other Materials on the Law of Real Property* (Charlottesville, VA: Michie Casebook Corp., 1948). In the 1950s and 1960s, McDougal coauthored, with the political scientist Harold Lasswell, books that produced a "New Haven school" of international law and policy science.

2. Other cases in that section of that casebook included one that dealt with the ability of American testators to make gifts to Soviet citizens and a series of cases that explored the Rule against Perpetuities—the rule that, to be overly simple, held invalid any transaction, conveyance, or gift that had the effect of removing property out of the market, thereby making it into a "perpetuity." A note followed the Robbins case that discussed the legality of gifts that encouraged divorce or separation. See McDougal and McDougal, *Property, Wealth, Land*, 238–74.

3. Traynor's willingness to interpret statutes in ways that promoted care of children can be seen in *Estate of Garcia*, 34 Cal.2d 419, 210 P.2d 841 (Cal. 1949). For more on Traynor's opinion, see chapter 7.

4. "Attack Will Fund for Negro Children of 'Political Victims,'" *City Daily Law Journal-Record*, April 21, 1962, 1; "California Supreme Court Upholds Trust Fund for

Negro Children," June 28, 1962, 1; "Negro Child Fund Upheld by Court," *New York Times*, May 27, 1962, 67.

5. Jack Robbins was the stage name of one possibility. Born Irving Wheeler in southern California, he sometimes went by Irving Decker. In the 1930s, this Jack Robbins had married a young woman, soon to be a movie star, eventually called Carole Landis, a marriage that was annulled because she was under the age of consent. He had become a stand-in for Bob Hope in several movies, was arrested for possession of drugs in the early 1950s, and was once removed from a train for refusing to buy a ticket. He owned land in the San Fernando valley. He refused to identify a political party he belonged to, and at least once he was refused entry into Canada, perhaps for political reasons. But he did not die at the right time. And he was too young to have a grandnephew. Then there was an older man who did die at the right time. This Jack Robbins was the founder of Robbins Music Corporation, which marketed sheet music and whose music was much used in early talkies. While this second Jack Robbins died at about the right time, and he apparently spent much time in southern California, he died in the wrong place, in New York City, where his estate lay. So, not he. There was also a football-playing Jack Robbins who quarterbacked for the University of Arkansas. And a southern California veterinarian who was both prominent and controversial. And in Chicago there was a Jack Robbins who owned a well-known clothing store called Jack Robbins Clothes. In New York City, a Jack Robbins translated Yiddish. There was an undertaker named Jack Robbins in Nevada. And there were others.

6. All of the named trustees lived in Chicago at the time the will was drafted. And at least one of the California lawyers had Chicago origins as well. Some of the trustees can be identified as having been active with Chicago left-wing causes and institutions. One of the trustees, Albert Soglin, the father of Paul Soglin, a longtime mayor of Madison, Wisconsin, signed several petitions in support of the Rosenbergs before their execution, and he was fired from Chicago-area teaching positions for refusing to sign a loyalty oath, although he eventually gave in and signed. He became a much-loved teacher at a local community college. Another trustee, Herbert Abrams, was on his way to becoming an internationally prominent public health doctor, later teaching at Arizona State University, but he was then teaching at the University of Chicago. The third, Abert Marks, was a Chicago lawyer.

7. Irvine Robbins, who was appointed the administrator of the estate, was born Rabinovitch in western Canada. Lee Mishkin, who challenged the will, had been born in Oakland in California. But Mishkin's father was born in Montreal in 1900, and his mother's birth name was Rabinovitch. See chapter 8 for more on both of them. Jack Robbins's sister, Anna Wigdor, who would inherit from him in the noncontroversial part of his will, was born in Russia in 1885, but she lived most of her life in Montreal. Twice she crossed the border to visit her brother, Irvine's father, in Tacoma, Washington. See Ancestry.com. Note that there are many Rabinovitzes and Rabinovitches identified with Deretchin/ Derechin/ Derechyn/ Dzjarecyn, many of whom perished in the

Holocaust. See "Deretchin," Eilat Gordon Levitan, accessed August 10, 2023, http://www.eilatgordinlevitan.com/deretchin/deretchin.html; and "The Dereczyn Memorial Book," JewishGen, updated August 1, 2017, https://www.jewishgen.org/Yizkor/Derechin/Derechin.html. There were several Jacob or Yaacob Rabinovitches, with several spellings, living in Chicago in the early twentieth century. One or another is probably "my" Jack Robbins. The most likely candidate is Jacob Robbins (name change from Rabinovitch), born on August 2, 1882, who was naturalized in 1916, according to US naturalization records indexes. The trouble with that identification is that it lists his year of arrival in the US as 1910, which might be when my Jack Robbins arrived in Chicago, but he had surely been in the United States for several years before that. The naturalization record lists two other Rabinovitches, Benjamin (who lived with that Jack Robbins at 1138 South Ashland) and Solomon, who lived elsewhere, as witnesses to Jacob Rabinovitch's naturalization. Neither Benjamin nor Solomon appears elsewhere as a relative of the Jack Robbins I am studying. And I know nothing about either man. The South Ashland address, on the other hand, appears on the letterhead of a letter that Jack Robbins mailed to Jack London in 1915 (discussed in chapter 2). In any event, Jack Robbins appears in the 1920 census as a boarder in Chicago, with a wife, as Jack Robins. He is probably also in the 1930 census, living temporarily as a lodger in the Times Square Hotel in Manhattan. At least there was a Jack Robbins there, born in Poland, originally speaking Yiddish, working as an executive in "social services." Jack Robbins may have been in New York then prior to taking a trip to London. Or at work establishing what would become the New York Boys' Brotherhood Republic on the Lower East Side. A Jack Robbins also appeared that year on the passenger lists of the ship *Bremen*, traveling a bit later in the year from England to New York City. And three years later, Jack Robbins, of Chicago, returned to the US from another trip, from Italy. Ancestry.com.

8. The narrative of his biography can be found in many articles. For an archetypal version, see the opening of Neil M. Clark, "'When a Feller Needs a Friend,'" *American Magazine* 98 (December 1924): 52–53, 138–42. On the Glenwood Manual Training School, see "Who We Are," Glenwood Academy, accessed August 10, 2023, https://www.glenwoodacademy.org/pages/content-migration/about-us. For another version of Jack Robbins's time at the Glenwood Manual Training School, see the letter/report sent to the Rosenwald Foundation by William J. Parker, general secretary of the Young Men's Christian Association of Chicago, on December 19, 1925 (housed in the Julius Rosenwald Papers at the University of Chicago Library). Discussed in chapter 5, the Glenwood Manual Training School was founded by Oscar Dudley, the head of Chicago's Humane Society, with the aid of Robert Todd Lincoln. Most of the early boys sent there had no parents. Boys were cared for while receiving training in farm work. Many were placed with farm families, as apprentices. By the early twentieth century the school was identified as serving predominantly Protestant boys. See Judge Pinckney's testimony, in Sophonisba P. Breckenridge and Edith Abbott, *The Delinquent Child and the Home: A Study of the Delinquent Wards of the Juvenile Court of Chicago*

(New York: Survey Associates, Inc., 1916); see also discussion in chapter 2. Since Jack Robbins identified Yiddish as his first language, one imagines that he was easily recognizable at the young age when he would have attended the Glenwood School as a Jew from central or eastern Europe. He probably spoke with an accent.

His parents can, in theory, be identified by following the genealogical tracks of Irvine Robbins and Lee Mishkin. Isaac Rabinowitz (1853–1889) and Faigle Mishkovsky (1858) were the grandparents of Irvine Robbins and the great grandparents of Lee Mishkin, according to Ancestry.com records. Presumably, they were also the parents of Jack Robbins. But none of the Ancestry.com records for either Mishkin or Irvine Robbins, or for any of their parents, recognizes the presence of a son of Isaac and Faigle named Jack Robbins or Jacob or Yaacob Rabinowitz. Did that mean that he was sent off to an orphanage? Possibly. (See Ancestrylibrary.com.) Nor do those records mark an arrival by either Isaac or Faigle into the United States or Canada. On the other hand, there are several Isaac Rabinowitzes in the records with birth dates around 1853 who lived in New York City or New Jersey.

9. "Tells Lives of Reformed Boys," *New Orleans Times-Democrat*, August 28, 1913, 10; "All Sculptors Do Not Work with Senseless Clay and Cold Marble," *Bismarck Tribune*, March 10, 1919, 4; "The Human Sculptor," *Washington Herald*, March 21, 1919, 6; "Soul Sculpture," *Baraboo Weekly News*, July 24, 1919, 2.

10. "Socialists Make Plans," *Perth Amboy Evening News*, July 5, 1906, 2; "Tenants Organizing to Fight High Rents; Mass Meeting Is Planned to Voice Opinion," January 4, 1908, 1 (misprinted on front as December); "Lower Rent Strike Grows," January 10, 1908, 8. He was installed as the vice president of the local Raritan Club. *Perth Amboy Evening News*, January 9, 1908, 1.

11. "W.D. Haywood May Speak in This City," *Perth Amboy Evening News*, January 14, 1908, 1; "City Briefs," January 16, 1908, 7; "Try to Bring Haywood Here," January 17, 1908, 1; "To Confer with Haywood," January 18, 1908, 1.

12. "Many Heard the Lecture," *Perth Amboy Evening News*, February 8, 1908, 1; "Rent Strike Abandoned," February 8, 1908, 7.

13. *Perth Amboy Evening News*, March 13, 1908, 1; March 21, 1908, 7; April 8, 1908, 5; April 11, 1908, 5: "Yesterday I insured eight. . . . Today I will insure more in Woodbridge. Everybody who owns horses wants to see me. Eleven letters this morning from horse owners. I don't feel the panic." As we will see, Robbins's socialism was never framed as standing in opposition to business success.

14. See Daniel S. Voorhees, *Report of the Joint Committee on Treasurer's Accounts, and of the State Treasurer, to the Legislature of New Jersey, with the Treasurer's Report to the Governor on the Finances of the State, for the Fiscal Year Ending October 31, 1908* (Trenton, NJ: State Gazette Publishing Company 1908), 411, https://dspace.njstatelib .org/handle/10929/47018, reporting a payment of $1.79 to S. Reeves Glover for having served and filed papers in Jack Robbins's case. See also Jack Robbins, "Anamosa, Iowa, Oct. 14," *Perth Amboy Evening News*, October 19, 1908, 6. On the Anamosa Penitentiary, see "Historic Stories and Photos from the Anamosa State Penitentiary Prison History

Website," Anamosa State Penitentiary, accessed August 10, 2023, http://www.asphistory .com/. A list of employees and inmates of the penitentiary between the 1870s and 1915 does not show his name. See "Anamosa State Penitentiary," Jones County Iowa, accessed September 14, 2023, http://iowajones.org/institutions/prison.htm.

15. He was mentioned in a few articles in the *Perth Amboy Evening News* during those years, 1908–1913. Apparently, he did return to Perth Amboy for at least a short while. He was part of a committee of socialists who took up the question of child labor in local factories. In one factory they found girls between ten and fourteen, working twelve-hour days. But the investigation went nowhere. There may have been conflict within the party about whether child labor should be a focus of attention, and in any case, factory owners were usually tipped off. Underage employees were "spirited off" out a rear door when state officials entered at the front, and the children lied and gave fictitious ages. See "Supt Shull Talks about Child Labor," *Perth Amboy Evening News*, April 13, 1910, 3, "Socialists Compliment Milwaukee Branch," April 23, 1910, 3. And in October 1911, having moved to Chicago, Robbins worked to establish "an institution of learning for homeless waifs." He did so, with prosperous businessmen, all of whom had once, been like Robbins, "inmates" at the Glenwood Manual Training School. The goal would be a school where education in trades and crafts could be given without tuition fee. See "Jack Robbins Has Society in Chicago," *Perth Amboy Evening News*, October 9, 1911, 2. A month later the organization, now identified as a Socialist Club ("A few years ago this club was afraid to even speak of such as terrible thing as Socialism, now they are keeping Socialist literature in their library"), was meeting in Cleveland and was said to have a membership of six thousand. See "Jack Robbins in Cleveland," *Perth Amboy Evening News*, November 22, 1911, 4.

16. "Jack Robbins Secures Fame," *Perth Amboy Evening News*, February 19, 1913, 3. Tobacco, and particularly cigarette advertising, was, of course, a pioneer of modern advertising. On the news services, see Jonathan Silberstein-Loeb, *The International Distribution of News: The Associated Press, Press Association, and Reuters, 1848–1947* (New York: Cambridge University Press, 2014).

17. "Ex-Waif Brother to Lonely Boys," *La Crosse Tribune*, February 18, 1913, 4. The *Keokuk Daily Gate City* ("Hungry Boys' Friend is Big Hearted Jack," February 17, 1913, 1) identified the United Press Leased Wire Service as the source for the story. As did the *Oklahoma News* of February 19, 1913 ("Salesman Is Big Brother to the Boys," 3). The *Omaha Daily News* (February 17, 1913, 1) headlined: "Former Waif Feeds Hungry Chicago Boys." See also "Salesman Aids Hungry Youngsters as Sideline," *Washington Times*, February 18, 1913, 5; "Only a Drummer, but He Is the Big Brother to Homeless Boys," *Stockton Daily Evening Record*, February 24, 1913, 1; "Traveling Man Offers Advice and Eats Free," *Grass Valley Morning Union*, March 6, 1913, 7; "Once a Waif Himself Will Help Other Boys to Look Out for Themselves," *Knoxville Sentinel*, February 20, 1913, 8; "A Good Friend of Homeless Boys," *Larimer County Independent*, February 21, 1913, 4; "Homeless Boys Find Benefactor," *Evening Times-Star* and *Alameda Daily Argus*, February 25, 1913, 6.

18. "Big Brother Will Build Boys' Home," *Detroit Times*, July 14, 1913, 2; "Jack Robbins Wanted in Copper Country," August 6, 1913, 10. Mother Jones (Mary G. Harris Jones) was a famous union organizer and activist. She was one of the cofounders of the Industrial Workers of the World (IWW).

19. "Jack Robbins Makes Survey of Street Boys," *Detroit Times*, August 11, 1913, 5.

20. "Tells Lives of 'Reformed' Boys," *Times-Democrat*, August 28, 1913, 10. It is not true that Upton Sinclair ever attended the Glenwood Manual Training School. At least, none of Sinclair's biographies mention him spending time there. See Kevin Mattson, *Upton Sinclair and the Other American Century* (New York: Wiley, 2006); Anthony Arthur, *Radical Innocent: Upton Sinclair* (New York: Random House, 2006).

21. He worked for the H. Rippen tobacco company, located in Perth Amboy (advertisements in both Hungarian and in English). See "Former Resident a 'Brother of the Boys,'" *Perth Amboy Evening News*, November 6, 1913, 3. Michael Grossberg, in a personal conversation on December 28, 2022, identified Robbins's calling as that of a "social policy entrepreneur." See Francis Fukuyama, "The Latin American Experience," *Journal of Democracy* 19, no. 4 (2008): 69–79.

22. Oenone Kubie, "The Swarm: Children in Chicago, 1890–1933" (PhD diss., Brasenose College, University of Oxford, 2018), http://ora.ox.ac.uk/objects/uuid: faa166c5-612f-4de4-b5ff-ec3f62f68745. For more on the boy problem, see chapter 2. One should add that the newspapers that covered Robbins did not share a common political identity or orientation, although, as we will see, he wrote a great deal for the reform-oriented *Day Book* in Chicago, and that paper covered him closely. Still, his appeal extended far beyond the radical and reform-oriented press. He was, at least for a time, "news."

23. "Worst Boys in U.S. Found in Toledo, Erie and Milwaukee," *Atlanta Georgian*, October 24, 1913, 1; "Milwaukee Boys Are Third Worst," *La Crosse Tribune*, October 24, 1913, 4.

24. "Plan to Cure Boys' Morals by Kindness," *Detroit Evening Times*, November 5, 1913, 5; "Former Resident a 'Brother of the Boys,'" *Perth Amboy Evening News*, November 6, 1913, 3. The *Keokuk Daily Gate City*, November 21, 1913, 5, took from the news service that Robbins was in Detroit to find one of the worst boys. See also "Jack Robbins Hunts for the 'Toughest' Boy—Will Help Him to Make Good," *Eugene Daily Guard*, November 21, 1913, 1. On Hunter, see "Hunter, Robert," VCU Libraries Social Welfare History Project, accessed August 10, 2023, https://socialwelfare.library.vcu .edu/people/hunter-robert/. Hunter had been a resident of Hull House. Later he became a designer of golf courses.

25. "Searching for City's Most Worthless Boy," *Pittsburgh Daily Post*, November 21, 1913, 1; "What Happened outside Chicago," *Day Book*, November 21, 1913, 27; *Detroit Times*, November 21, 1913; "Hunt for Worst Boy in Pittsburg; Others Are Found," *Newark Star-Eagle*, November 21, 1913, 2; "Toughest Boy in Town Is in Demand Right Now," *Anaconda Standard*, November 21, 1913, 11; "Toughest Boy to Have Ranch Home, *Grass Valley Morning Union*, November 22, 1913, 1; and many more.

26. "Not One Really Truly Bad Boy in Pittsburgh, Says Jack Robbins," *Newark Star-Eagle*, November 22, 1913, 3. The *Detroit Evening Times* (November 24, 1913, 10) added to the report of the failure that it was "getting along towards Christmas." See also "Pittsburgh Boys Not Bad Enough," *Inter Ocean*, November 23, 1913, 5; *Day Book*, November 22, 1913, 29. Versions of the story were also printed in papers across the Great Plains and Mountain West, from Lakeland, Florida, to Valdez, Alaska.

27. "Robbins Plans Boys Club Here," *Perth Amboy Evening News*, November 24, 1913, 8; "Boys in Smoky City Good," *Harrisburg Daily Independent*, November 22, 1913, 9.

28. "Harrisburg Youth Tells 31 Lies in Just 12 Minutes," *Harrisburg Telegraph*, November 29, 1913, 1, 11; "Harrisburg's Boys Are Best in the State," *Harrisburg Courier*, November 30, 1913, 1, 4.

29. "Is Big Brother for Many Boys," *Perth Amboy Evening News*, December 2, 1913, 9; "Jack Robbins Will Arrive in Perth Amboy Tomorrow," December 5, 1913, 1; "Jack Robbins Arrives," December 6, 1913, 4.

30. "Is Big Brother for Many Boys," *Perth Amboy Evening News*, December 2, 1913, 4.

31. *News-Herald*, December 2, 1913, 9.

32. "Jack Robbins Disgusted with Philadelphia 'Kids,'" *New Castle Herald*, December 4, 1913, 2.

33. "Buffalo's Worst Boy Not as Bad as Brooklyn Lad," *Buffalo Courier*, December 19, 1913, 7; "Brooklyn Has the 'Baddest Boy,'" *Buffalo Enquirer*, December 19, 1913, 2; "We Aren'e [*sic*] Eligible," *Buffalo Times*, December 19, 1913, 5. In a later story, Robbins was reported as saying that "Buffalo has the wrong idea in correcting our young boys." The city, he thought, "needs a rejuvenation of its systems and a complete reconstruction of the basic principles and ideas upon which it is laboring at the present time." See "Wrong Ideas in Correctnig [*sic*] Boys," *Buffalo Enquirer*, December 22, 1913, 5.

34. "Declares Worst Boy in Michigan Lives Here," *Detroit Evening Times*, January 8, 1914, 7.

35. "Last Chance Club," *Dayton Herald*, January 16, 1914, 4. The paper noted other such efforts, including creating "republics" established to give a bad boy "strength of character with self-government." See also, among many others, "Twelve Worst Boys to Establish Last Chance Boys' Club," *Bakersfield Morning Echo*, January 11, 1914, 1; "Bad Boys Get New Chance in Life," *Daily Missoulian*, January 12, 1914, 1; "12 Worst Boys on Nine Acres," *Fairmont West Virginian*, January 13, 1914, 2; "12 'Worst Boys' Get Last Chance," *Bridgeton Pioneer*, January 15, 1914, 1; "'Worst Boys' Go West," *Ashland Tidings*, January 22, 1914, 6.

36. "Sinclair, Tires of Utopia," *St. Joseph Daily Press*, February 17, 1914, 4; "Sinclair Tires of Utopia," *Waukegan News-Sun*, February 19, 1914, 3; *Stockton Evening Mail*, March 10, 1914, 4; "Jolt for the Bad Boy Colony," *Monrovia Daily News*, March 13, 1914, 2.

37. Harriette N. Dunn, "Letter, . . . Protests against Some Child-Saving Work," *Day Book*, June 3, 1914, 7; S. R., "Letter . . . the Bad Boy Problem," *Day Book*, June 17, 1914,

10–11. Dunn, who held the office of the secretary of the Illinois Home Protective Association, was, with her younger brother, a persistent critic of the early Chicago juvenile court, in part because of its procedural irregularity but more because it challenged and undercut parental power and autonomy. See David S. Tanenhaus, *Juvenile Justice in the Making* (New York: Oxford University Press, 2004), 86–98.

38. "What Happened in Chicago," *Day Book*, March 18, 1914, 3; "Seeks to Free Boy Slayer," *Odanah Star*, March 20, 1914, 5; "Seeks to Free Boy Slayer," *Portage Daily Register*, March 18, 1914, 1; "Seeks to Free Boy Slayer," *Urbana Courier-Herald*, March 18, 1914, 2. Upton Sinclair also worked for Coppes's release. See "Upton Sinclair Here to Save Elgin Boy Murderer," *Joliet Evening News*, March 17, 1914, 1.

39. *Joliet Herald News*, October 9, 1914, 12; "Goes to Aid of Boy Slayer," *St. Joseph Daily Press*, October 9, 1914, 3; "Boys Will Plead for Another Boy," *Champaign Daily Gazette*, October 10, 1914, 9.

40. "'Big Brother' Club Planned Here by Robbins," *Detroit Evening Times*, April 6, 1914, 1.

41. "Big Brother Club Planned Here by Robbins," *Detroit Evening Times*, April 6, 1914, 1,7, 8; "Best Friend of Bad Boys Is Here," *Lima Morning Star and Republican-Gazette*, April 8, 1914, 5; "Scours Lima for Bad Boys' Records," April 9, 1914, 5; "Ullery Eager for Trip Is Taken to Jackson," *St. Joseph Daily Press*, April 6, 1914, 1.

42. "News of the Day Concerning Chicago," *Day Book*, May 18, 1914, 7, 31; "Big Brother Wearies," *Erie Sentinel*, May 19, 1914, 3. Many other papers used the same title. "Testimony of Mr. Jacob Robbins," in *Final Report and Testimony of Industrial Relations Commission*, 11 vols. (Washington, DC: Government Printing Office, 1916) (S. Doc. No. 415, at 9470–71).

43. Whitaker used one column in 1913 to tell the Dickensian story of her own life as a working girl, including her near starvation while fighting to get a minimally adequate wage. See Jane Whitaker, "Why Jane Whitaker Is Fighting for Living Wages for Chicago Working Girls: Being the Story of the Furnace through Which She Herself Came, Told by Herself," *Day Book*, March 13, 1913, 21–23. She deserves a dissertation or a senior thesis: See—for just one example of her many columns—"Working Girl Shuns Marriage—Won't Bear Children to Work for Low Wages," *Day Book*, March 24, 1913, 21–22. And the subhead: "She works in a candy factory and hates candy—She knows how it's made . . ." See also Duane C. S. Stolzius, *Freedom from Advertising: E. W. Scripps's Chicago Experiment* (New Brunswick, NJ: Rutgers University Press, 2007), 87–88. I have not been able to find where Jane Whitaker went after *the Day Book* closed in 1917. I did find a prose poem of hers in the April 1917 issue of *the Masses*, 37.

44. Jane Whitaker, "The 'Bad' Boy Is Only the Boy Who Hasn't Had a Chance, Declares Jack Robbins," *Day Book*, May 25, 1914, 7–8.

45. Whitaker, "'Bad' Boy Is Only the Boy Who Hasn't Had a Chance."

46. Whitaker, "'Bad' Boy Is Only the Boy Who Hasn't Had a Chance."

47. Whitaker, "'Bad' Boy Is Only the Boy Who Hasn't Had a Chance."

48. Whitaker, "'Bad' Boy Is Only the Boy Who Hasn't Had a Chance."

49. Whitaker, "'Bad' Boy Is Only the Boy Who Hasn't Had a Chance." He made the same claim, about what he did as a hobby while continuing to work as a tobacco salesman, in his testimony before the Industrial Commission.

50. Jack Robbins, "Letter . . . Advice to All Sorts of Boys," *Day Book*, May 25, 1914, 9. He continued: "We want institutions that gives [*sic*] happiness."

51. See "Robbins Leads Boy Mourners," *Perth Amboy Evening News*, June 4, 1914, 1. On June 14, Robbins wrote that he intended to visit Stockton, California, to help men and women there set up a Big Brother club. See "Will Fight for The Erring Boys," *Stockton Evening and Sunday Record*, June 15, 1914, 9; "'Big Brother' Coming Here," *Evening Mail*, June 16, 1914, 1. The letter and article by Upton Sinclair is in *Appeal to Reason* (Gitlow, KS), June 13, 1914, 2. On Ludlow, see Thomas G. Andrews, *Killing for Coal* (Cambridge, MA: Harvard University Press, 2010). Ludlow may have been, in Howard Zinn's words, "the most violent struggle between corporate power and laboring men in American history" (*The Politics of History* [Boston, MA: Beacon Press, 1970], 79).

52. Jack Robbins "Advice to 'Last Chance Boys,'" *Day Book*, June 20, 1914, 10.

53. Robbins "Advice to 'Last Chance Boys,'" *Day Book*, June 20, 1914; Jack Robbins, "Advice to the Parents of 'Last Chance' Boys," *Day Book*, June 25, 1914, 9; Herman Harris, "Strong for Jack Robbins," July 3, 1914, 10–11.

54. Jack Robbins, "Letter to Editor," *Day Book*, July 24, 1914, 9–10.

55. Robbins, "Letter to Editor," *Day Book*, July 24, 1914. /On Hickson, see Michael Willrich, *City of Courts: Socializing Justice in Progressive Era Chicago* (New York: Cambridge University Press, 2003), 241–97; Grace Argo, "Survived and Punished: Incest Victims' Treatment in Progressive-Era Chicago," *Journal of the History of Childhood and Youth* 16, no. 1 (Winter 2023): 28–49; William J. Hickson, "The Defective Delinquent," *Journal of Criminal Law and Criminology* 5, no. 3 (September 1914): 397–403. See a letter by Robbins in the *Day Book*, April 28, 1915, 27, that the public would eventually get wise to Hickson's "fake way" of passing on the sanity of young criminals. In the meantime, though, he would cause the "downfall of many young lads."

56. Jack Robbins, "Letter to Editor: A Problem to Solve," *Day Book*, July 27, 1914, 9–10.

57. Robbins, "Letter to Editor: A Problem to Solve," *Day Book*, July 27, 1914.

58. Robbins, "Letter to Editor: A Problem to Solve," *Day Book*, July 27, 1914.

59. Robbins, "Letter to Editor: A Problem to Solve," *Day Book*, July 27, 1914.

60. Robbins, "Letter to Editor: A Problem to Solve," *Day Book*, July 27, 1914.

61. O. J. S., "Letter . . . Harold Wray," *Day Book*, July 29, 1914, 10 (Negley D. Cochran, the publisher of the *Day Book*, voiced his agreement below the letter from O. J. S., saying "You bet I do"); Louis I. Perlman, "About Harold Wray," July 30, 1914, 6–7.

62. Barry Rabin, "Going to Help Wray," *Day Book*, August 3, 1914, 9.

63. "Upton Sinclair Here to Found Club for Boys," *Fort Wayne Journal-Gazette*, August 18, 1914, 1, 10; "Big Brother Movement: Jack Robbins Is Meeting with Oposition [*sic*]," *Fort Wayne Daily News*, August 20, 1914, 8; *Richmond Palladium and Sun-Telegram*, October 2, 1914, on a meeting in Indianapolis to organize a Last Chance Boys' Club there, mentions that there is one in Fort Wayne.

64. "Chicagoan Here to Found Club for Boys of Street," *St. Louis Globe-Democrat,* October 10, 1914, 10; "Boys Club Opposed by Judge Hennings," October 11, 1914, 9.

65. Charles Edward Russell was a "muckracker" and a socialist. In 1909, he became one of the founders of the NAACP, in the aftermath of a race riot in Springfield, Illinois.

66. "War against Jail for Juveniles Is Started Here," *Oklahoma News,* October 24, 1914, 1.

67. "War against Jail for Juveniles Is Started Here," *Oklahoma News,* October 24, 1914.

68. "War against Jail for Juveniles Is Started Here," *Oklahoma News,* October 24, 1914; Harvey Ferguson, "'Mother' Jones Arrives in City with Co-Workers," *Oklahoma News,* October 24, 1914, 8; "Rescue Boy Prisoner is Robbins' Plan, *Oklahoma News,* October 26, 1914, 1.

69. "Where Oh Where Is Mother Jones? Is She in City?" *Lincoln Journal Star,* November 5, 1914, 10.

70. "Boy Has 1 Day to Make Good," *Day Book,* December 3, 1914, 3.

71. Jane Whitaker, "What Do We Want Our Chanceless Boys to Be—Men or Muckers—Answer Is Ours," *Day Book,* December 5, 1914, 11–12; a mucker is someone described as "coarse or low." See also William Osborne Dapping, *The Muckers: A Narrative of the Crapshooters Club,* ed. Woody Register (Syracuse, NY: Syracuse University Press, 2016). Allendale was founded in 1897 as a private home for homeless children. It still exists, serving children with serious "mental, emotional, and behavioral health challenges" ("Mission and Values," Allendale Association, accessed August 11, 2023, https://allendale4kids.org/about/mission-values/). The Deborah Boys' Club was run from 1908 on by the Young Men's Jewish Council (Frances Archer, "This Was Deborah, Part 2," *Me and My Shadow* (blog), February 17, 2012, https://francesarcher.com/2012/02/this-was-deborah-part-2/).

72. Note that Robbins also used the categories of psychological science when they proved useful.

73. Whitaker, *Day Book,* December 5, 1914, 11–12.

74. "Robbins in Attack on St. Charles Home," *Joliet Herald News,* December 10, 1914, 11.

75. Jane Whitaker, "Jack Robbins Wants Youngest Lifer at Joliet Given Another Chance," *Day Book,* May 21, 1915, 30–31.

76. Whitaker, "Jack Robbins Wants Youngest Lifer at Joliet Given Another Chance," *Day Book,* May 21, 1915. Mr. Sleep quickly remarried. "Family Murdered; Weds Year After," *True Republican,* March 18, 1914, 1; "Celebrity Here; Few Knew of It; Manny Sleep of 'Death Farm' Came to Freeport to Wed," *Freeport Journal-Standard,* March 23, 1914, 6.

77. "Rockefeller Money May Help Murderer," *Day Book,* February 10, 1916, 2. For a few examples of the coverage, see "John D., Jr Said to Be in Plan to Reclaim Convict," *St. Louis Post Dispatch,* February 5, 1916, 1; "J.D. Jr. Tries to Free Boy Lifer," *San Francisco Examiner,* February 6, 1916, 3; "John D. Jr. to Assist 'Lifer,'" *Washington* (DC) *Herald,* February 6, 1916, 1.

78. And to skip ahead still further: In 1924, while working on an "honor" prison farm, Herman Coppes escaped from Joliet. Twenty years later, in 1944, he was discovered living under another name. He was then returned to Joliet. He was part of an unsuccessful prison break later that year, one that led to the death of others. In 1946, he was transferred to the psychiatric division of the prison. He was paroled into the care of his nephew in 1960. He died in Colorado in 1978. See Amy Steidinger, *Joliet Prison Blues: A Century of Stories* (Arcadia, SC: Arcadia Publishing, 2021), 121–23.

79. "Youngster Called 'Impossible Case' Will Jump at 'a Chance,'" *Day Book*, December 24, 1914, 28–29; Jane Whitaker, "Who Will Give a Fair Chance to 'Nobody's Boy'?—He Is Waiting for Your Answer," *Day Book*, December 26, 1914, 24–25. Whitaker also referred back to the story of Harold Wray, who had been in the end helped by "a humanitarian reader of the Day Book" and who had paid back the money spent on him. About this time, Robbins's travels also began to be covered in the foreign-language press. See *Decorah Posten*, January 29, 1915, 2; *Glos Polek* (Chicago), March 4, 1915, 1.

80. "A New Socialist Club," *Appeal to Reason*, January 9, 1915, 2; "Jack Robbins Here, Looking for the Worst Boy?" *Journal Times*, January 13, 1915, 5. For more on Wisconsin outrage, see chapter 3.

81. "'Big Brother' Man Finds Mere Boys Play Pool," *Coshocton Morning Tribune*, March 9, 1915, 1. Nancy Hartog reminds me of the resonance of Professor Harold Hill's song in Meredith Willson's 1957 musical *The Music Man* about the evils of "the pool hall," "Trouble . . . Right Here in River City":

> Now friends, let me tell you what I mean / You got one, two, three, four, five, six pockets in a table / Pockets that mark the difference between a gentleman and a bum / With a capital "B" and that rhymes with "P" and that stands for pool / And all week long your River City youth'll be fritterin' away / I say, your young men will be fritterin' / Fritterin' away their noontime, suppertime, choretime too / Get the ball in the pocket, never mind gettin' dandelions pulled / Or the screen door patched or the beef steak pounded / Never mind pumpin' any water / 'Til your parents are caught with the cistern empty / On a Saturday night and that's trouble / Yes you got lots and lots of trouble / I'm thinkin' of the kids in the knickerbockers / Shirt-tail young ones, peekin' in the pool hall window after school / You got trouble, folks / Right here in River City, trouble with a capital "T" / And that rhymes with "P" and that stands for pool.

Perhaps the song was less silly than it seemed to those of us who heard it in the 1950s and 1960s. There was a recurrent anxiety about the seductions of the commercial pool hall. The 1907 modification of Illinois's 1899 Juvenile Court law defined as delinquent any boy or girl who was incorrigible, and evidence of incorrigibility included patronizing "a pool room or bucket shop." See Kubie, "The Swarm," 90, 248–49 (Hine photograph of boys playing pool); and Frederic M. Thrasher, *The Gang: A Study of 1,313 Gangs in Chicago* (Chicago: University of Chicago Press, 1927), 95–98 (on the significance of pool). See, as examples of the effort to regulate the presence of youth in pool halls, solely from the Iowa newspapers (there were enormous numbers of such articles from any state one would choose), "No Pool or No Mayor," *Marshalltown Evening Times-Republican*, September 25, 1913, 4; "Boys Surrender to Police Here," *Keokuk Daily Gate City and Constitution-Democrat*, August 9, 1920, 7. A column in the *Muscatine News-Tribune* (October 10, 1915, 6) opined:

> Of course, I don't claim that pool halls and shows are directly to
> blame for all the evil and weakness of the youth of the city. . . .
> But . . . nothing else contributes so much to the delinquency of our
> boys and girls.

See also "Muscatine Mayor Orders Pool Hall Owners to Be 'Good,'" *Muscatine News-Tribune*, October 8, 1915, 5; "Council Votes to Close Every Pool Hall in City, *Muscatine News-Tribune*, October 22, 1915, 8. And see the *Mason City Globe-Gazette* (Mason City being the town where Meredith Willson grew up) in which a judge declared illegal the city's ordinance forbidding boys to enter the pool halls (January 8, 1931, 1).

82. "Investigator Fails to Study Messengers," *Pittsburgh Daily Post*, March 21, 1915, 4.

83. "He Would Test the Sanity of Billy," *Greenwood Daily Journal*, April 1, 1915, 1.

84. James S. McQuade, "Chicago. Letter," Moving Picture World 19, no. 5 (January 1914): 550, https://archive.org/details/movingpicturewor19newy.

85. Robert Barton, "Citizens, Present and Future," *Advance* 68 (March 1916): 773–77; same, in *Standard* 63 (March 25, 1916): 933–36.

86. Barton, "Citizens, Present and Future."

87. Barton, "Citizens, Present and Future."

88. Barton, "Citizens, Present and Future." The St. Charles Reform School, or the Illinois School for Boys, opened in 1904, relying on a dormitory-style cottage system. It is still in existence. Today known as the Illinois Youth Center—St. Charles, it is a "medium security facility" for boys and holds up to 318 inmates. See "Our History," St. Charles, accessed September 14, 2023, https://stcharlesinc.org/about-us/our-history/. The John Worthy School, otherwise known as the Chicago House of Corrections, Juvenile Department, opened in 1896. It would be closed in 1916 because of complaints about its prison-like atmosphere. See "John Worthy School," Jane Addams Papers Project Digital Edition, accessed August 15, 2023, https://digital.janeaddams.ramapo.edu/items/show/308. On the complexities of gang identities, for a slightly later period, see Thrasher, *Gang*.

89. Jane Whitaker, "'And a Bunch of Boys Shall Lead Us'—Or at Least We Can Get Some Pointers." *Day Book*, November 8, 1915, 30; "Past-Day Gang Members Meet, *Los Angeles Times*, February 21, 1927, 11; "Alumni Honor Founder of Club for Tough

Boys," *Los Angeles Times*, February 3, 1935, 9; "Boys' Republic Pushes $25,000 Fund Campaign," *Chicago Tribune*, April 17, 1943, 16. According to Clara Laughlin, writing in 1919, Robbins, while lodging on the West Side of Chicago, had found boys in need of a friend. Seven youngsters "gathered round him . . . and [he] talked with them of a Boys' Republic. Sometimes they had a basement room to meet in; often they walked the streets and discussed their dream." See Clara E. Laughlin, "The 'Boy Problem' and How It Has Been Solved—by Boys!" *Chamberlin's* (December 1919): 14–16. Thrasher's 1920s study of Chicago's gangs studied the "boundary line gang" at a different time (*Gang*, 12, 282, 285). Ralph Lee Goodman became the head of a Chicago advertising agency and the president of the BBR's alumni association. He served on the Illinois Crime Commission. He ran for clerk of the criminal court of Chicago in 1942, identifying himself as part of the BBR (campaign advertisement, *Chicago Daily Herald*, October 30, 1942, 10; see also "Youth's Own Cure for Delinquency; Boys Republic Governs Self in Chicago West Side," *Evansville Courier and Press*, January 23, 1944, 6). And in 1954, he ran for Congress as a Republican, losing to Sidney Yates. See *Illinois Blue Book, 1953–54* (Springfield: Illinois Secretary of State, 1953), 794. He died in 1969.

90. "Their Spirit," *Day Book*, August 19, 1915, 11.

91. "Withdraw from Hebrew Institute," *Day Book*, September 20, 1915, 26. See Letter from Philip Seman re: Robbins in the Julius Rosenwald Papers, box 4, folder 10, University of Chicago Library. See chapter 5 infra. On the general context of free speech fights of the era, see David M. Rabban, *Free Speech in Its Forgotten Years, 1870–1920* (Cambridge: Cambridge University Press, 1997); John William Wertheimer, "Free-Speech Fights: The Roots of Modern Free-Expression Litigation in the United States" (PhD diss., Princeton University, 1992), https://www.google.com/books/edition/Free_speech_Fights/uU-fAAAAMAAJ?hl=en. On the Loeb Rule, see Justin Law, "The Courts vs. Teacher Unionism," LAWCHA, May 23, 2014, https://www.lawcha.org/2014/05/23/courts-vs-teacher-unionism-justin-law/#:~:text=Loeb%2C%20the%20Chicago%20Board%20of,in%20the%20schools%20of%20Chicago.

92. "Just Boys: But They Are Worth Saving, So Boy Brothers Take Them in Tow," *Chicago Tribune*, December 21, 1915, 7; "Telling It to Them," *Chicago Tribune*, December 20, 1915, 17. On Hulbert, including his admiration for the Boys' Brotherhood Republic, see Sumner Keene, "Get to the Point," *American Magazine* 89 (1920): 62–63, 266. See chapter 5 for more on how they got to Hamlin Street.

93. See, for example, "Why Chicago Boys Are Bad," *Richmond Palladium and Sun-Telegram*, December 23, 1915, 4. The same list can be found in the Van Lieu Minor Papers, folder 24, box 2, Clarke Historical Library, Central Michigan University, Mt. Pleasant, MI. See also the *Sentinel*, the Jewish-themed Chicago newspaper, of December 24, 1915, at 8, where the same statistics are reproduced: "This and similar information which the Boys' Republic claims to have at first hand is full of interest and importance. It is sociology in the best sense of that misused word."

94. "Boys," *Day Book*, January 22, 1916, 28.

CHAPTER TWO

1. My understanding of the "boy problem" is shaped by Edelman's chapter on "the construction and uses of social problems"; see Murray Edelman, *Constructing the Political Spectacle* (Chicago: University of Chicago Press, 1988), 12–26. See also Michael Grossberg, "Legal Rights for Children? A Historical Look at a Continuing Legal Paradox," in *Children at Risk in America, ed. Roberta Wollens* (Albany: State University of New York Press, 1992), 112. I shall not try to resolve the historiographical debates about the extent to which the juvenile court and its related institutions were Progressive-Era novelties. Nor will I resolve the question of the distinctiveness of Chicago as a site for reform. For a survey of the contemporary literature, see Ronald Tuttle Veal, J. T. Bowne, and G. E. Carr, *Classified Bibliography of Boy Life and Organized Work with Boys* (New York: Association Press, 1919). It should be added that many newspaper editors also saw the "boy problem" as an occasion for what might be called human interest stories.

2. Oenone Kubie, "The Swarm: Children in Chicago, 1890–1933" (PhD diss., Brasenose College, University of Oxford, 2018), http://ora.ox.ac.uk/objects/uuid:faa166c5 -612f-4de4-b5ff-ec3f62f68745. Thrasher uses the image of boys swarming in his study of Chicago's gangs; see Frederic M. Thrasher, *The Gang: A Study of 1,313 Gangs in Chicago* (Chicago: University of Chicago Press, 1927).

3. Robert Ezra Park and Herbert Adolphus Miller, *Old World Traits Transplanted* (New York: Harper, 1921), 68–70, 71–72. For the protean character of the identity or label of "boy" (and I'm not dealing here with its uses as a racial epithet in the Jim Crow South), see Sarah E. Chinn, *Inventing Modern Adolescence: The Children of Immigrants in Turn-of-the-Century America* (New Brunswick, NJ: Rutgers University Press, 2009), 7–8. Chinn brilliantly redefines adolescence, both male and female, around the discordant presence of "fun." See Pamela Riney-Kehrberg, *The Nature of Childhood: An Environmental History of Growing Up in America since 1865* (Lawrence: University Press of Kansas, 2014), 41–72; and Paul S. Boyer, *Urban Masses and Moral Order in America, 1820–1920* (Cambridge, MA: Harvard University Press, 1978). On girls, see Michael A. Rembis, *Defining Deviance: Sex, Science, and Delinquent Girls, 1890–1960* (Urbana: University of Illinois Press, 2011). When Helen Jeter in 1922 tried to explain why the number of boys in trouble with the law so exceeded the number of girls, she moved in two directions. On the one hand, the greater number of boys resulted from the "methods of investigation," since boys were repeat offenders. On the other hand, the "character of offense" also differed. Boys were caught because of "childish pranks" or "gang depradations [*sic*]." Girls were brought into the courts because of "serious immorality," which necessitated "immediate and vigorous action." See Helen Rankin Jeter, "The Chicago Juvenile Court" (Washington, DC: US Department of Labor, Children's Bureau, 1922), reprinted in *The Juvenile Court*, ed. and comp. Robert M. Mennel, 18–19 (New York: Arno Press, 1974).

4. See, for a musical paradigm of carefree childhood, Robert Schumann's 1838 set of thirteen piano pieces collectively entitled *"Scenes from Childhood" ("Kinderszenen,"* *op. 15)*. That notion of a carefree childhood was, needless to say, only available for the children of the bourgeoisie, if then, and also an adult construct (though manifested in innumerable books for children). Bernstein's brilliant exploration of the performance of childhood innocence quotes William Wordsworth's canonical 1804 poem "Ode: Intimations of Immortality from Recollections of Early Childhood." There the poet confronts the fact that "Shades of the prison-house begin to close / Upon the growing Boy." See Robin Bernstein, *Racial Innocence: Performing American Childhood from Slavery to Civil Rights* (New York: New York University Press, 2011), 23. See also Carolyn Steedman, *Strange Dislocations: Childhood and the Idea of Human Interiority, 1780–1930* (London: Virago Press, 1995). For an exploration of Du Bois's efforts to create space for African American childhood, see Crystal Lynn Webster, "'Transfiguring the Soul of Childhood': Du Bois's Private Vision and Public Activism for Black Children," *Journal of the History of Childhood and Youth* 14, no. 3 (Fall 2021): 347–66. For a summary of the "girl problem" as it was understood in the early twentieth century, with a focus on its racial dimensions, see Tera Agyepong, "Who Gets a Girlhood? Constructing Race and Gendered Delinquency in the Juvenile Justice System," prepared for a workshop on Children and the Law at the American Society for Legal History conference in November 2022 in Chicago, IL.

5. E. C. Wines, The State of Prisons and of Child-Saving Institutions in the Civilized World (Cambridge, MA: John Silson and Sons, 1880), 73, 132.

6. Judith Resnik notes the ways Wines grouped together schooling and imprisonment; see *Impermissible Punishments: The Problem Prison Poses in Democracies* (Chicago: University of Chicago Press, forthcoming 2025). See also Boyer, *Urban Masses*; Linda Gordon, *Heroes of Their Own Lives* (New York: Vintage, 1988); Michael Grossberg, "A Protected Childhood: The Emergence of Child Protection in America," in *American Public Life and the Historical Imagination*, eds. Wendy Gamber, Michael Grossberg, and Hendrik Hartog (Notre Dame, IN: University of Notre Dame Press, 2003), 213–39. Famously, New York's Society for the Prevention of Cruelty to Children emerged out of the ASPCA, the society for the prevention of cruelty to animals.

7. Steven Mintz, *Huck's Raft: A History of American Childhood* (Cambridge, MA: Belknap Press of Harvard University Press, 2004). On the long political history of child labor, see Betsy Wood, *Upon the Altar of Work: Child Labor and the Rise of a New American Sectionalism* (Champaign: University of Illinois Press, 2020). See also Michael Schuman, "History of Child Labor in the United States—Part One: Little Children Working," *Monthly Labor Review* (January 2017), https://www.bls.gov/opub/mlr/2017/article/history-of-child-labor-in-the-united-states-part-1.htm; Michael Schuman, "History of Child Labor in the United States—Part Two: The Reform Movement," *Monthly Labor Review* (January 2017), https://www.bls.gov/opub/mlr/2017/article/history-of-child-labor-in-the-united-states-part-2-the-reform-movement.htm. Chinn offers a perceptive and revealing reconsideration of the portrayal of child labor, as it became adolescent work; see *Inventing Modern Adolescence*, 38–76. The extent to which parents retained the capacity to control adolescent boys, and the question of how to do so, were topics productive of an extensive literature of advice. See, for two examples, William Byron Forbush, *The Boy Problem in the Home* (Boston, MA: Pilgrim Press, 1915); and James S. Kirtley, *That Boy of Yours: Sympathetic Studies of Boyhood* (New York: Hodder and Stoughton, 1912). Both Forbush and Kirtley paid much attention to questions of sexual control, which, as we will see, was not an issue attended to much by Robbins and the Boys' Brotherhood Republic. For a discussion of the availability of African American children as the "property" of the formerly enslaved parents, see Dylan C. Penningroth, *The Claims of Kinfolk: African American Property and Community in the Nineteenth-Century South* (Chapel Hill: University of North Carolina Press, 2003).

8. Michael Willrich, *City of Courts: Socializing Justice in Progressive Era Chicago* (New York: Cambridge University Press, 2003); David S. Tanenhaus, *Juvenile Justice in the Making* (New York: Oxford University Press, 2004). My own understanding is shaped by the work of Linda Gordon; see *Heroes of Their Own Lives*, as well as her books *Pitied but Not Entitled: Single Mothers and the History of Welfare* (New York: Free Press, 1994) and *The Great Arizona Orphan Abduction* (Cambridge, MA: Harvard University Press, 1999).

9. It is important not to overstate the contrast between late nineteenth-century "child saving" and the work by settlement-house reformers and others to deal with the early twentieth-century "boy problem." The boundaries were fluid, and "child savers" would transmute into "boy workers" and Progressive reformers. And institutions and practices that historians sometimes identify as creations of the early twentieth century had longer histories, reaching back often to the early nineteenth century. See Sanford J. Fox, "Juvenile Justice Reform: An Historical Perspective," *Stanford Law Review* 22, no. 6 (June 1970): 1187–239. Still, without giving too much significance to Google Ngrams, it is striking that uses of the term "child saving" rise and fall between 1880 and 1905. The invocation of the "boy problem" rises just as that of "child saving" declines—and then falls after 1920.

10. See Helen R. Wright, "Dependency," in *Encyclopaedia of the Social Sciences*, vol. 7, edited by Edwin Robert Anderson Seligman (New York: Macmillan, 1932), 94–95. On the constitutional history of notions of dependency and paternalism, see Aviam Soifer, "The Paradox of Paternalism and Laissez-Faire Constitutionalism: United States Supreme Court, 1888–1921," *Law and History Review* 5, no. 1 (Spring 1987): 249–79; Barbara Welke, *Law and the Borders of Belonging* (New York: Cambridge University Press, 2010). See also Martha Minow, *Making All the Difference: Inclusion, Exclusion, and American Law* (Ithaca, NY: Cornell University Press, 1990), 250–51; Nancy Fraser and Linda Gordon, "A Genealogy of Dependency: Tracing a Keyword of the U.S. Welfare State," *Signs* 19, no. 2 (Winter 1994): 309–36.

11. Sophonisba P. Breckenridge and Edith Abbott, *The Delinquent Child and the Home: A Study of the Delinquent Wards of the Juvenile Court of Chicago* (New York: Survey Associates, Inc., 1916), 210–11 (Pinckney's testimony). On the history of criminology, particularly as developed at the University of Chicago, see James Bennett, *Oral*

History and Delinquency: The Rhetoric of Criminology (Chicago: University of Chicago Press, 1981); Roger A. Salerno, *Boyhood and Delinquency in 1920s Chicago: A Sociological Study of Juvenile Jack-Rollers and Gender* (Jefferson, NC: McFarland, 2017). Fox emphasizes that nineteenth-century reformers always grouped together all of the miscreant young, those identified with vagrancy and misdemeanors, while separating and treating as criminal those who committed felonies ("Juvenile Justice Reform"). On Breckenridge, see Anya Jabour, "Duty and Destiny: A Progressive Reformer's Coming of Age in the Gilded Age," in *Children and Youth during the Gilded Age and Progressive Era*, ed. James Marten (New York: New York University Press, 2014), 230–51.

12. Breckenridge and Abbott, *Delinquent Child and the Home*, 27–35, 48–52, 210–11. For a less social-scientific presentation of the same blurring of lines, see chapter 3 of Jane Addams, *The Spirit of Youth and the City Streets* (New York: Macmillan, 1909), https://www.gutenberg.org/files/16221/16221-h/16221-h.htm.

13. Laws of the State of Illinois (1905), 152–56, at 153, https://archive.org/details/lawsofstateofill1905illi/page/152/mode/2up. See Kubie, "The Swarm," at 90 (Kubie drew the definition from T. D. Hurley, *Origin of the Juvenile Court Law*, 3rd edition [Chicago: Visitation and Aid Society, 1907]).

14. Kubie, "The Swarm," 90. See "Bad Boy Reclamation Not a Bad Work, by Any Means," *Grass Valley Morning Union*, January 15, 1914, 4. In recent years, the term "incorrigible" has mostly been applied to girls—and a good deal of political work by advocates for young women has achieved the removal of the "incorrigible" label. See the transmedia project *Incorrigibles*, accessed August 15, 2023, at https://incorrigibles .org/. In April 2021, the term "incorrigible" was eliminated as a subcategory of PINS (persons in need of supervision) as a part of New York's family code. By then, it was understood as implicitly identifying girls of color as not meeting expectations of stereotypically feminine behavior. See "'Incorrigible' bill passed!" *Incorrigibles*, April 7, 2021, https://incorrigibles.org/incorrigible-bill-passed/.

15. *Report of the City Council Committee on Crime of the City of Chicago* (Chicago: H. G. Adair, 1915), 139. For the best study of boys (and girls) working on city streets across a long period of American history, see Vincent DiGirolamo, *Crying the News: A History of America's Newsboys* (New York: Oxford University Press, 2019). Child workers on city streets offered what DiGirolamo calls the "illusion of the near," quoting the child-labor investigator Edward N. Clopper in 1912. Child work was so proximate and inevitable that it disappeared from view (*Crying the News*, 3).

16. See the portrayals of poor Jewish boys hanging around in Lawndale in the mid-1920s in Clancy Sigal, *A Woman of Uncertain Character: The Amorous and Radical Adventures of My Mother Jennie (Who Always Wanted to Be a Respectable Jewish Mom* (New York: Carroll and Graf, 2006).

17. See Woody Register, "Introduction: The Charm That Truth Never Lacks: A Brief History of William Osborne Dapping and his Crapshooters Club," in William Osborne Dapping, *The Muckers: A Narrative of the Crapshooters Club*, ed. Woody Register (Syracuse, NY: Syracuse University Press, 2016), 3–48, at 12 (quoting Jacob A. Riis, *Children* *of the Poor* [New York: Scribner, 1908], 7–8, https://www.gutenberg.org/files/32609/ 32609-h/32609-h.htm#:~:text=If%20the%20question%20were%20put,society%20and %20the%20%E2%80%9CSunday%2Dschool). On fun, see Chinn, *Inventing Modern Adolescence.*

18. Gordon, *Heroes of Their Own Lives.* For a critique of the continuing presumption on the part of historians that child labor belongs to a more or less benighted past, see Sarah Maza, "AHR Exchange: The Kids Aren't All Right: Historians and the Problem of Childhood," *American Historical Review* 125, no. 4 (December 2020): 1261–85.

19. Historical statistics of the United States (see Hsus.cambridge.org); United States Bureau of the Census, *Fourteenth Census of the United States: State Compendium, Illinois* (Washington, DC: Government Printing Office, 1924), 55. According to Kubie, it was only after World War II that the city of Chicago began to enforce school attendance laws ("The Swarm," 38). On the contested history of compulsory education, see Julia Grant, *The Boy Problem: Educating Boys in Urban America, 1870–1970* (Baltimore, MD: Johns Hopkins University Press, 2014). The literature on compulsory education does not attend sufficiently to the occasional suggestion that a compulsory education, that is, one that would be imposed on recalcitrant parents, meant one that the state mandated through commitments to semi-penal institutions like reform schools. See Judge Isaac Redfield's commentary on *People v. Turner* in *American Law Register (N.S.)* 10 (June 1871): 366–73. On child-labor laws and the resistance to compulsory education, see Stephen Lassonde, *Learning to Forget: Schooling and Family Life in New Haven's Working Class, 1870–1940* (New Haven, CT: Yale University Press, 2005); James D. Schmidt, "'Restless Movements Characteristic of Childhood': The Legal Construction of Child Labor in Nineteenth-Century Massachusetts," *Law and History Review* 23, no. 2 (Summer 2006): 315–50.

20. *Report of the City Council Committee on Crime of the City of Chicago*, 139; Viviana A. Zelizer, *Pricing the Priceless Child* (Princeton, NJ: Princeton University Press, 1994). Parents' need for their children as workers explains much of their engagement with the juvenile courts, which they understood as taking the children away from them; see Naama Maor, "Delinquent Parents: Punitive Welfare and the Creation of Juvenile Justice, 1899–1927" (PhD diss., University of Chicago, 2020), ProQuest dissertation no. 28026706. Truant boys ages seven to fourteen, along with boys of that age identified as "incorrigible," might be committed to the aptly named Chicago Parental School, which was run as a boarding school with cottages housing the boys. See "History of the Chicago Parental School (Northeastern Illinois University)," CARLI Digital Collections, accessed August 15, 2023, https://collections.carli.illinois.edu/digital/collection/carli _colls/id/201/rec/1. See in particular the text and pictures in "The Parental Picture," Chicago Parental School program outline, 1937, available online at CARLI Digital Collection, https://collections.carli.illinois.edu/digital/collection/nei_cps/id/25/rec/16. Parental schools were evidently started in cities around the country. See James S. Hiatt, *The Truant Problem and the Parental School*, US Bureau of Education Bulletin 1915, no. 29 (Washington, DC: Government Printing Office, 1915). Commitments to the Chicago school did not require the consent of parents. How that intersected with the precedent of *State v. Turner* is an interesting question that deserves study. See below for more on reform-school commitments and *State v. Turner*.

21. "Editorial Comment," *Work with Boys: A Magazine of Methods* 15, no. 10 (1915–16): 365.

22. Greg Dimitriadis, "The Situation Complex: Revisiting Frederic Thrasher's *The Gang: A Study of 1,313 Gangs in Chicago*," *Cultural Studies, Critical Methodologies* 6, no. 3 (August 2006): 335–53, at 338. See also *Report of the City Council Committee on Crime of the City of Chicago*, 138–44; Zelizer, *Pricing the Priceless Child*; Grant, *Boy Problem*, 68. On school attendance and the inadequacies of the truant officer, see Kubie, "The Swarm," 38, 152–53. See Register, "Introduction," 12 (quoting Riis, *Children of the Poor*, 7–8). Jane Addams offered a sympathetic portrait of the situation of many boys who "drop learning as a childish thing and look upon school as a tiresome task that is finished. They demand pleasure as the right of one who earns his own living. . . . Many of them begin to pay board to their mothers, and make the best bargain they can, that more money may be left to spend in the evening" (*Spirit of Youth and the City Streets*). One story about the BBR that was picked up in newspapers around the country concerned nine-year-old Arthur Shafter, who was spirited out of the city by the BBR so that he would not be sent to the reformatory for being a truant. Eventually he was returned to what the article called his "parental school." On Arthur Shafter, see "Get the Rattan," *Helena Montana Independent Record*, August 10, 1920, 3; and "Pals Spirit Lad from City to Dodge Term as Truant," *East Oregonian*, August 10, 1920, 1, among others.

23. William Byron Forbush, "A New Apostle's Creed," *How to Help Boys* 2, no. 4 (October 1902): 173.

24. See, for example, *Work with Boys: A Magazine of Methods* 18, no. 1 (1918), before table of contents.

25. "Editorial Comment," *Work with Boys: A Magazine of Methods* 17, no. 1 (1917): 1–3; *Boys' Workers Round Table* (October 1920): 14. *Boys' Workers Round Table*, also sponsored by the Boys' Club Federation, began in 1918. This second journal had a somewhat less "professional" focus, with more poetry and more discussions of "boyology." It soon replaced *Work with Boys*, which ceased publication. An early letterhead of the BBR included—without an author—the quotation "Boys Work for the Benefit of Boys" (January 8, 1920, box 47, folder 533, Children's Home and Aid Society Archives, University of Illinois Chicago Library). There was a continuum between the literature of boyology, mostly directed at parents and religious training, and the social work orientation of "boy workers" and the "boy problem." The subjects of both boyology and the "boy problem" were imagined as white, but the class differences were stark. On boyology, see Kenneth B. Kidd, *Making American Boys: Boyology and the Feral Tale* (Minneapolis: University of Minnesota Press, 2004). Kidd dates the term to 1914, exactly when Jack Robbins became a presence in American newspapers.

26. "Methods of Discipline in a Boys Club," *Boys' Workers Round Table* 1, no. 4 (October 1920): 14. How to read the photographs of child laborers by Lewis Hine? Expressions of pride, independence, oppression? See Oenone Kubie, "Reading Lewis Hine's Photography of Child Street Labour, 1906–1918," *Journal of American Studies* 50, no. 4 (2016): 873–97.

27. On the YMCAs Employed Boys' Brotherhoods: These lacked the self-governing features of the BBR. I see no evidence that those who created them took the notion of a brotherhood from the BBR, though the name similarity is curious. See Harold Lew Webb, "A Program for Employed Boys' Clubs and Its Use," (Bachelor of Associated Science thesis, Young Men's Christian Association College, 1923), https://openlibrary.org/books/OL25487900M/A_program_for_employed_boys'_clubs_and_its_use. If coverage in the newspapers is any indication, Perth Amboy apparently had one of the most active organizations, along with New Britain, Connecticut, and San Pedro, California, on into the mid-1920s. One might suspect that this activity level was so high because of the amount of boy labor that continued to be necessary in such dockside towns. On delinquency and schooling, see Clifford R. Shaw and Frederick M. Zorbaugh, with the collaboration of Henry D. McKay and Leonard S. Cottrell, *Delinquency Areas: A Study of the Geographic Distribution of School Truants, Juvenile Delinquents, and Adult Offenders in Chicago* (Chicago: University of Chicago Press, 1929), 33–53. See also Salerno, *Boyhood and Delinquency*; Bennett, *Oral History*. By the later 1920s and 1930s, the completed citizenship application forms I have read, nearly all from the new New York BBR, emphasized that they were boys "in" school. Indeed, most of them expressed college ambitions. See the Harry E. Slonaker Papers, History San Jose Research Library, San Jose, CA. Holl's study of the George Junior Republics interprets the increasing problems in maintaining meaningful self-government after 1910 as resulting from the fact that more public schooling meant that "more 'normal' citizens" were being removed from the "Republic," leaving only delinquents and commitments and referrals from the juvenile courts. See Jack M. Holl, *Juvenile Reform in the Progressive Era: William R. George and the Junior Republic Movement* (Ithaca, NY: Cornell University Press, 1971), 160–61. On the struggles of Progressive-Era reformers to get children in "street trades" into schools, see DiGirolamo, *Crying the News*, 365–401.

28. Breckenridge and Abbott, *Delinquent Child and the Home*, 6–7. It is important to add that in the next paragraphs Lathrop traced the many instances where, following a period of "wilful adventure," boys and girls returned to orderly living, marked in the boys' case by a willingness to bring home a pay envelope "unopened" and for girls a "return to hard, thankless toil under the parental roof." She continued to believe in an innate tendency to "steadiness" and the emergence of "invincible goodness" (*Delinquent Child and the Home*, 8). See likewise, Wines, *State of Prisons and of Child-Saving Institution in the Civilized World*, 132. Another conception of the "boy problem" placed much of the blame on the failures of the churches to draw the affection of young men; see William Byron Forbush, *The Boy Problem: A Study in Social Pedagogy; with an Introduction by G. Stanley Hall* (Cambridge, MA: Pilgrim Press, 1901).

29. Marilyn Irvin Holt, *Orphan Trains: Placing Out in America* (Lincoln: University

of Nebraska Press, 1992); Boyer, *Urban Masses and Moral Order in America*; Gordon, *Great Arizona Orphan Abduction.*

30. Jane Adams, *The Transformation of Rural Life: Southern Illinois, 1890–1990* (Chapel Hill: University of North Carolina Press, 1994).

31. Breckenridge and Abbott, *Delinquent Child and the Home*, 212–13. On the ubiquity of "escape" from places that adults tried to hold children in, see Kubie, "The Swarm," 153–61. See also Naama Maor, "'We Cannot Be Hoodwinked into Making Paroles': Delinquent Children, State Institutions, and the Boundaries of Juvenile Justice," prepared for Children and the Law: A Conference in Honor of Michael Grossberg, American Society for Legal History Pre-Conference, November 10, 2022, Chicago, IL (exploring the manual training school in Golden, Colorado). Agyepong argues that "escape" from reform schools, which was once understood as not much to worry about and as being inevitable for some significant fraction of the boys committed, became a matter of great anxiety in the 1930s when the escapees were identified as African American. See Tera Eva Agyepong, *The Criminalization of Black Children: Race, Gender, and Delinquency in Chicago's Juvenile Justice System, 1899–1945* (Chapel Hill: University of North Carolina Press, 2018), 112–19. The "sentences" or commitments that forced many urban children to farms were indistinguishable from the "transportations" that characterized many criminal sentences around the late nineteenth- and early twentieth-century world—from the British Isles to Australia and from Eastern Russia to Siberia, to take two obvious examples. See Linda Colley, "Part of the Punishment: Convict Flows," *London Review of Books* 45, no. 1 (January 5, 2023), https://www.lrb.co.uk/the-paper/v45/n01/linda-colley/part-of-the-punishment.

32. Anthony M. Platt, *The Child Savers: The Invention of Delinquency*, introduction by Miroslava Chavez-Garcia (New Brunswick, NJ: Rutgers University Press, 2009), 61–65. On the management of manual training schools, see Maor, "'We Cannot Be Hoodwinked into Making Paroles.'" See, for a canonical version of the dark story of reform school as breeding ground for criminality, Clifford R. Shaw, *The Jack-Roller: A Delinquent Boy's Own Story* (Mansfield Centre, CT: Martino Publishing, 2013), 65–78, 202. According to Mennel, one explanation for Chicago's role as the pioneer in the creation of the juvenile court was the fact that Illinois, unlike other northern states, imprisoned delinquents and lacked alternative public institutions. See Robert M. Mennel, *Thorns and Thistles: Juvenile Delinquents in the United States, 1825–1940* (Hanover: University of New Hampshire by the University Press of New England, 1973). See likewise, Wines, *State of Prisons and of Child-Saving Institution in the Civilized World*, 373. Mennel may be overemphasizing the absence of "public" institutions. Almost all Illinois institutions—orphanages, reform schools, and manual training schools—had denominational religious and usually ethnic or racial identities, which reflected the segregation of ethnic and religious and racial life in Chicago. For a compelling legal portrait of the Chicago Reform School, see Fox, "Juvenile Justice Reform"; and T. H. McQueary, "Schools for Dependent, Delinquent, and Truant Children in Illinois," *American Journal of Sociology* 9, no. 1 (July 1903): 1–23. For life in Jewish institutions, see Daniel

Friedman, *The King of Chicago: The Incredible True Story of a Jewish Orphan's Rise from Despair to Triumph in 1920s Chicago* (New York: Carrel Books, 2017); "Marks Nathan Jewish Orphans Home Information Page," Marks Nathan Chicago Jewish Orphans Home, accessed August 16, 2023, https://jgs.jgsi.org/cmn/cmn-info.html; Aaron Gruenberg, project coordinator, Marks Nathan Oral History Project, *Home Kids Memories of the Marks Nathan Jewish Orphan Home* (Chicago: Jewish Children's Bureau of Chicago: n.d.), https://jgs.jgsi.org/cmn/documents/MN-Oral-History-Memories .pdf. See Agyepong, *Criminalization of Black Children*, for the absence of institutions that served African American children. One needs to add that parents bore complex relations to those institutions. Sometimes they worked to place their uncontrollable children there. More often they worked to get the children out, so that they could be useful to the family (Maor, "Delinquent Parents"). Gilded Age reformers also created other institutions and public spaces, including settlement houses, clubs, and public parks, meant to save not yet "bad boys and girls" from that fate. On parks as public spaces distinctively meant to serve or to manage and control children, see Kubie, "The Swarm."

33. Leo A. Philips, "The Institutional Care of the Normal Dependent Child," *Institution Quarterly* 5, no. 1 (March 1914): 78–83. In 1921 he was president of the Illinois Conference on Public Welfare; see *Institution Quarterly* 5, no. 1: 11–13. He was still the superintendent in 1927 when the *Rotarian* ran an article about Glenwood, describing it as Chicago's largest charity. By then, according to the article, Glenwood had taken nearly eight thousand boys from "broken, neglected homes—many of them from sordid, debauching surroundings," and turned them into "upright citizens." See Seymour Yates, "A City of Boys: Where Leadership and Obedience Are Taught," *Rotarian* (October 1927): 25–26, 45. Not surprisingly, Philips was himself a Rotarian, as the article noted. See also Arthur W. Newcomb, "Making the Man of Tomorrow out of the Glenwood Boy," *Business Philosopher* 6, no. 8 (August 1910): 456–65.

34. Philips, "Institutional Care of the Normal Dependent Child," 78–83.

35. Philips, "Institutional Care of the Normal Dependent Child," 78–83.

36. Philips, "Institutional Care of the Normal Dependent Child," 78–83. For a recent study of the labelling of Progressive-Era girls who were incest victims as "sex delinquents" and "morons," see Grace Argo, "Survived and Punished: Incest Victims' Treatment in Progressive-Era Chicago," *Journal of the History of Childhood and Youth* 16, no. 1 (Winter 2023): 28–49. See Resnik, *Impermissible Punishments*, for an extended discussion of how two centuries of prison reformers danced around the continuing presence of physical coercions, including whippings and beatings.

37. How to explain Illinois's creation of the juvenile court remains a historical conundrum. A predominant scholarly stream identifies it as part of a Progressive reform movement centered in Chicago, with Jane Addams and the settlement-house movement as primary actors. There then remains much debate about how to characterize that movement. On the other hand, Mennel argues that Illinois was actually laggard in the late nineteenth century, that it lacked institutions designed to serve dependent and needy youths (*Thorns and Thistles*, 127). That absence resulted from the power of the precedent of *State v. Turner*. The juvenile court filled a gap, an absence, institutionally and legally. It created a noncriminal institution in a place, Illinois, where the "reform school" was in effect a prison, and where commitments depended on proof of criminality. See Wines as well. Recent scholarship agrees that there was more continuity, less discontinuity in the history of child protection. What the juvenile court and its attendant institutions offered was less novel than older histories contended and mostly continuous with reform measures and child protective measures that reached back into the early nineteenth century. See Fox, "Juvenile Justice Reform" and citations in the introduction to second edition, Platt, *Child Savers*. On the parallel development of the indeterminate sentence in criminal law, see Michele Pifferi, *Reinventing Punishment: A Comparative History of Criminology and Penology in the Nineteenth and Twentieth Centuries* (Oxford: Oxford University Press, 2016), chapters 4 and 5.

38. Julian W. Mack, "The Juvenile Court," *Harvard Law Review* 23, no. 2 (December 1909): 104–22; Ellen Ryerson, *The Best Laid Plans: America's Juvenile Court Experiment* (New York: Hill and Wang, 1978) quoting Bernard Flexner; Miriam Van Waters, "Juvenile Delinquency and Juvenile Courts," in *Encyclopaedia of the Social Sciences*, vol. 7, edited by Edwin Robert Anderson Seligman (New York: Macmillan, 1932), 528–33; Grossberg, "Protected Childhood"; Tanenhaus, *Juvenile Justice in the Making*. On the longer history of the use of equity and parens patriae, see Michael Grossberg, *Governing the Hearth: Law and the Family in Nineteenth-Century America* (Chapel Hill: University of North Carolina, 1985); Fox, "Juvenile Justice Reform." See Lawrence J. Friedman, *Crime and Punishment in American History: The Price of Freedom in the History of American Criminal Justice* (New York: Basic Books, 1993), 416: "What the children thought of it is something we hardly know at all."

39. The juvenile court and its related institutions embodied those novel understandings, though inconsistently and haphazardly, as historians like Michael Willrich have explored. See Thomas A. Green, *Freedom and Responsibility in American Legal Thought* (New York: Cambridge University Press, 2015); Willrich, *City of Courts*.

40. Questions of the capacity of children to form "criminal intent," of how and whether children reasoned morally, and of whether parents and other adults were responsible for children's behavior and misbehavior, were central problems in political philosophy and in the philosophy of education going back to Locke and Rousseau. See Melissa J. Ganz, "'A Kind of Insanity in My Spirits': *Frankenstein*, Childhood, *and* Criminal Intent," *Eighteenth Century Studies* 56, no. 1 (Fall 2022): 53–74; Jay Fliegelman, *Prodigals and Pilgrims* (Cambridge, MA: Harvard University Press, 1984); Holly Brewer and Omohundro Institute of Early American History and Culture, *By Birth or Consent: Children, Law, and the Anglo-American Revolution in Authority* (Chapel Hill: Published for the Omohundro Institute of Early American History and Culture, Williamsburg, Virginia, by the University of North Carolina Press, 2005). It is important to add that the multiple fin-de-siècle challenges to conceiving of free will and moral responsibility as the foundation for criminal punishment and incarceration (who or what is a criminal?) could lead as easily to eugenics—to the assumption that those who committed crimes were hardwired to do so because of a genetic defect—as they could lead to the thoroughgoing environmentalism that characterized someone like Jack Robbins. But everyone involved in the juvenile court, eugenicist and environmentalist alike, rejected a received legal understanding that the child, as a fallen sinner, was responsible for his actions. And nearly all of them believed that public policy, correctly instantiated, ought to provide the solution to the boy problem.

41. Apparently, many of the early judges and advocates for the juvenile court already worried that what they were creating might not pass constitutional or legal muster. The very plasticity they ascribed to the moral sense of the child, his capacity to be molded into something better than his parents or his environment, raised issues of free will and responsibility. Those issues carried the juvenile court right back into the dilemmas that had long shaped criminal law jurisprudence, questions about holding individuals responsible for their actions. And it also raised questions about what ought to be the ends of reform. See Willrich, *City of Courts*; Tanenhaus, *Juvenile Justice in the Making*.

42. See Maor, "'We Cannot Be Hoodwinked into Making Paroles,'" for an exploration of the fuzzy boundary between "punishment" and education, in a jurisdiction that was understood to be a leader in modern juvenile justice. The 1915 Crime Survey's chapter on juvenile delinquency focused on distinguishing the "normal" delinquent from the "subnormal." It recommended creating new institutions for the "feeble-minded" delinquent, and it strongly urged the passage of new laws that would take away from parents the right to interfere with commitments. See *Report of the City Council Committee on Crime of the City of Chicago*, 127–28; Green, *Freedom and Responsibility in American Legal Thought*, conclusion.

43. People ex rel. O'Connel v. Turner, 55 Ill. 280 (1870); *American Law Register* (*N.S.*) 10 (June 1871): 366–73.

44. *American Law Register* (*N.S.*) 10 (June 1871): 366–73. Barbara Welke notes that Thornton might have written less forcefully in defense of the freedom of the child if the child had been a girl (personal communication, March 10, 2023). A third theme in the opinion, one emphasized by Judge Isaac Redfield, the editor of the *American Law Register*, argued that the exercise of discretionary power by state agents was in effect an exercise by a Protestant hegemony over a recalcitrant, mostly Catholic minority, dedicated to forcing those children into Protestant schools. Behind this argument lurked a disquiet about compulsory education laws. See David S. Tanenhaus, "Creating the Child, Constructing the State: *People v. Turner*, 1870," in *Children as Equals: Exploring the Rights of the Child*, eds. Kathleen Alaimo and Brian Klug (Lanham, MD: University Press of America, 2002); Martha Minow, "We, the Family: Constitutional Rights and American Families," *Journal of American History* 74, no. 3 (December 1987): 959–83. On Thornton, see "Anthony Thornton 1870–1873, Illinois Supreme Court Historic Preservation Commission, accessed August 16, 2023, https://www.illinoiscourthistory.org/resources/af1c2dbf-2467-4587-a68d-3825fc66ea81/bio_thornton.pdf. On the eighteenth-century creation of father's rights, see Brewer and Omohundro Institute of Early American History and Culture, *By Birth or Consent*; Danaya C. Wright, *From Feudalism to Family Law: Inter-Spousal Custody Disputes and Repudiation of Mother's Rights* (PhD diss., Johns Hopkins University, 1998), ProQuest dissertation no. 9920805. *State v. Turner* was an early instance of a more general constitutional disquiet with the unfettered discretion identified with indeterminate sentences. See Pifferi, *Reinventing Punishment*, chapter 4.

45. *In the Matter of Ferrier*, 103 Ill. 367 (1882); for examples of discussions of *Turner* in other jurisdictions, see *Milwaukee Industrial School v. the Supervisors of Milwaukee County*, 40 Wis. 328 (1876); and *S*** S*** and L*** B*** v. State*, 2999 A. 2d 560 (Maine, 1973). Mennel argued that the Turner precedent offered one explanation for the absence of reform schools and orphanages in Illinois. He pointed to the 1888 decision in *County of Cook v. the Chicago Industrial School for Girls*, 125 Ill. 540 (1888). This decision was one of many that confronted the question whether public funds could go to support a religious institution, in this instance one run by Catholic nuns. Later decisions allowed such support, on the premise that the religious denominational commitments were saving public funds; see *St. Hedwig's Industrial School for Girls v. County of Cook*, 289 Ill. 432 (1919). Tanenhaus describes how William Dunn and his sister Harriette Dunn, prominent critics of the juvenile court and of child protection efforts in general, mobilized Turner. See Mennel, *Thorns and Thistles*; Tanenhaus, *Juvenile Justice in the Making*, 84–87 When the Glenwood Manual Training School was established in 1883, its charter mandated that before a child could be committed to the school as a dependent by county officers, there had to be a judgment by a jury of six, and the parents had to be notified and offered the chance to challenge the commitment. Presumably those rules were responsive to the *Turner* precedent. See McQueary, "Schools for Dependent, Delinquent, and Truant Children in Illinois."

46. Sheldon Glueck, Social Ethics course lecture notes, 8–9 (undated) (quoting Hartwell and Thompson), 22–24, in the Sheldon Glueck Papers, Historical and Special Collections, Harvard Law School Library, Cambridge, MA, https://hollisarchives.lib .harvard.edu/repositories/5/archival_objects/1200979; Maor, "Delinquent Parents."

47. Platt, *Child Savers*, 4, 99. Naama Maor explores the ways parents learned to use the juvenile courts and reform schools ("Delinquent Parents"). Recent work on "juvenile justice" suggests that little has changed. See the conclusion., infra.

48. Jonathan Simon, "Visions of Self-Control: Fashioning a Liberal Approach to Crime and Punishment in the Twentieth Century," in *Looking Back at Law's Century*, eds. Bryant Garth and Austin Sarat (Ithaca, NY: Cornell University Press, 2002), 109–59 (quoting Roscoe Pound about Star Chamber); Fox, "Juvenile Justice Reform." Van Waters, in her 1932 encyclopedia article, acknowledged that the United States was already falling behind European equivalents to the juvenile courts. Still, she finished optimistically:

> The juvenile court . . . is midway between two goals. It may develop
> into an agency of protection of the rights of childhood . . . On the

other hand, the juvenile court may become a criminal tribunal, hearing only serious cases which public and private social agencies have failed to prevent. In either case the outcome will be similar. By introducing the scientific study of cases, by individualization of treatment, by use of probation and by quickening the sense of collective responsibility for the neglected and forsaken child the juvenile court method has permeated the criminal court and has put yeast into the entire system of justice. ("Juvenile Delinquency and Juvenile Courts")

See also Breckenridge and Abbott, *Delinquent Child and the Home*, 194 (Julian Mack on legal issues). In 1922, Jeter concluded that the "conditions" under which the Chicago court operated had never been "entirely satisfactory." It suffered from "open political attack, from legislative caution and legislative blundering, . . . and from public indifference" ("The Chicago Juvenile Court, 10,*)*; see also *Illinois Crime Survey*, in association with the Chicago Crime Commission Illinois Association for Criminal Justice (Chicago: Illinois Association for Criminal Justice, 1929), 645–737. At the Chicago Home for Girls, the girls got less good food than the staff. Why? the sociologists asked. The head of the school answered that the girls needed to realize that "age and experience do not qualify them for the same quality of meal." She believed that an important factor in the delinquency of the girls was that parents and others had treated them as equals. Part of the "treatment" of the "home" was to make them realize they were "only children"—and that they therefore deserved less (*Illinois Crime Survey*, 702).

49. The careful and imaginative work of David Tanenhaus reconciles both perspectives (*Juvenile Justice in the Making*). He reveals how unresolved the legal issues about the juvenile court were, even in its early Progressive heyday. The social-control perspective was given its strongest form by Anthony Platt. See, along with reconsiderations and a survey of the literature that followed him, the 2009 edition of his work *The Child Savers*. One can read Platt as articulating a perspective that Jack Robbins might have shared. Much of the second perspective (the anti-social-control understanding) was written in the shadow of In re Gault, 387 U.S. 1 (1967), the Supreme Court case that marked the constitutional failure of the juvenile court to offer justice and due process to juveniles, in large part because of its informality. Behind that judicial conclusion lay the known reality that juvenile courts had long been overcrowded and underfunded. The "justice" they offered was neither caring nor protective of the children who fell into it. The juvenile court and the structures of policing and probation and parole and the reform schools and other placements that revolved around it constituted a bureaucratic system that enveloped the "delinquent." For many of those scholars, the question remained whether a well-funded juvenile court that did what it promised to do, that is, one that provided individual attention and care to the errant child, might have passed scrutiny as a legal institution; see Ryerson, *Best Laid Plans*. The conflict between the two perspectives also has much to do with changing evaluations of the agency and the motives of the mostly female reformers and settlement workers. Platt's first edition, published in the late 1960s, could be read as reducing them to the values of their fathers and husbands and of sharing in a general upper-class consciousness. Later writers, like Ryerson, incorporated new understandings of women's agency and of the distinctiveness of female thought. They were influenced by the rise of feminist legal thought and women's history, and also by reevaluations of Progressivism.

50. Steven Schlossman, *Transforming Juvenile Justice: Reform Ideals and Institutional Realities, 1825–1920* (DeKalb: Northern Illinois University Press, 2005), 58, 60. Or, as one prominent commentator put it: "Juvenile delinquency is a by-product of parental delinquency" (H. W. Gibson, *Boyology, or Boy Analysis* [New York: Association Press, 1922], 207). The centrality of parents to the concerns of the managers of the juvenile court and its attendant institutions is well illustrated in the work of Naama Maor ("Delinquent Parents"). The absence of parents or the need to create substitute parents was often reframed as the need for "home rehabilitation" (see Ryerson, *Best Laid Plans*, 41)—itself an ambiguous term.

51. Jack Robbins, though distinctive, was not the only one to see that what "youth" needed was more and different than simply the provision of more and better parental care. Both Jane Addams and W. E. B. Du Bois voiced understandings that childhood and the recognition of children's freedoms transcended the refiguring of parental responsibilities. So, Addams wrote: "Unless we mean to go back to these Old World customs which are already hopelessly broken, there would seem to be but one path open to us in America. That path implies freedom for the young people made safe only through their own self-control" (*Spirit of Youth and the City Streets*). And for Du Bois, it was important to challenge white pathologizations of Black childhoods: "while he recognized parents' duty to influence their children's lives, he stressed that the power of the soul of the child could transcend, or transfigure, the nation" (Webster, "'Transfiguring the Soul of Childhood,'" 358).

It is worth considering whether the continuing focus on parental failure, in the legislation and the policy pronouncements of the reformers and court personnel, and also in the judgments of historians and social scientists and other later observers, may not represent a misreading of immigrant-parent understandings of family duties and obligations. Were such parents responsible for their adolescent children, particularly adolescent boys? As Daniel Richman noted in conversation, many of these parents had themselves left families as young people. Their migratory experiences may have distanced them from familial obligations. They may have understood separation of adolescents from the family as less abnormal or deviant than we might think. (One wonders if a similar reconsideration would be appropriate for those involved in the Great Migration that brought African Americans to northern cities.) All of which suggests that Jack Robbins's reframing of what boys needed might have been consistent with the shared understandings of the families from which he drew those who became the citizens of the Boys' Brotherhood Republic.

52. Gordon, *Pitied but Not Entitled*; Gordon, *Heroes of Their Own Lives*; Willrich, *City of Courts*.

53. Breckenridge and Abbott, *Delinquent Child and the Home*, 33–35; Thrasher, *Gang*; Suzie Guth, *Les Gangs de Jeunes Italo-Americains: Les Forty Two de Chicago* (Paris: L'Harmattan, 2017), 141–268.

54. Gail Bederman, *Manliness and Civilization: A Cultural History of Gender and Race in the United States, 1880–1917* (Chicago: University of Chicago Press, 1995), 77–120; John Demos and Virginia Demos, "Adolescence in Historical Perspective," *Journal of Marriage and Family* 31, no. 4 (November 1969): 632–39; William Byron Forbush, *Boy Problem: A Study in Social Pedagogy*. There was a more positive interpretation of what gang membership could mean. Part of what the discovery of adolescence offered was a kind of naturalization or domestication of "the gang." See G. Stanley Hall, "Introduction," in Joseph Adams Puffer, *The Boy and His Gang* (Boston, MA: Houghton Mifflin, 1912), https://www.gutenberg.org/cache/epub/57927/pg57927-images.html. Before he began the George Junior Republics, William R. George tried to create a "Law and Order Gang" (Holl, *Juvenile Reform in the Progressive Era*, 72–73). For a complex reading of Stanley Hall and of the longer history of the term "adolescence," see Gabrielle Owen, *A Queer History of Adolescence: Developmental Pasts, Relational Futures* (Athens: University of Georgia Press, 2020), 30–62.

55. Paula Fass helpfully reduces those mainstream programs and policies to "mandatory schooling, citizenship training, and anti-child labor laws." Foreword, in Marten, *Children and Youth during the Gilded Age and Progressive Era*, vii.

56. This letter, found in the Jack London papers at the Huntington Library, is the only extant copy of that letterhead that I have found. It may be that the letterhead for the Boys' Brotherhood Republic, which always identified Jack Robbins as "founder and supervisor," soon replaced it. See box 359, folder 38, JL 17239, Jack London Papers, Huntington Library, San Marino, CA.

57. Jane Whitaker had noticed the same letterhead in a column ("Who Will Gave [*sic*] a Fair Chance to 'Nobody's Boy'?" *Day Book*, December 26, 1914, 24–25). The phrase "nobody's boy" appeared regularly in Christian religious stories for children over the second half of the nineteenth century, identifying a child without caring or surviving parents. See, for one of several examples, Parthene Ballard, *Nic at the Tavern, or Nobody's Boy* (Philadelphia, PA: American Sunday-School Union, 1865). Harriet Beecher Stowe used the phrase in the opening story, on Little Fred, in *Tales and Sketches of New England Life* (London: Sampson, Low, and Company, 1855). The phrase was also identified with a popular French children's novel by Hector Malot, first published in France in 1878, as *Sans Famille*, translated in 1916 as *Nobody's Boy (New York: Cupples and Leon)*. I am grateful to Bill Gleason for illuminating the publishing history. As we will see, Robbins continued to use the phrase throughout the rest of his life.

58. See box 359, folder 38, JL 17239, Jack London Papers, Huntington Library, San Marino, CA.

59. Minow, *Making All the Difference*, 258; "Conservation of the Boy Crop," *Perth Amboy Evening News*, May 3, 1918, 18.

CHAPTER THREE

1. His first appearance in the *Chicago Tribune* (March 15, 1913, 14) was in a paragraph notice. The paragraph already identified him as "big brother to the friendless and homeless boys of Chicago." It claimed he was negotiating for a home for such boys in Milwaukee after having already "organized" a home for them in Chicago. "As in Chicago, the boys will support them selves. Robbins intends to find work for them and they will pay $2.40 a week for board, lodging, washing, 'motherly care,' and brotherly advice." On Glenwood's alumni association, see *Fifty Years of Boy-Building, 1887–1937: Where the Needy, Dependent, Not Delinquent, Boy Is Given a Chance to Become the Right Sort of Man* (Glenwood, IL: Glenwood Manual Training School, 1937).

2. I am grateful to Judith Resnik, Farah Peterson, Craig Green, and Nancy Hartog for helping with this formulation. For further reflections on these themes, see chapter 5.

How did newspaper readers understand the flood of stories about Robbins? Again, the fragmentary evidence makes it difficult to come to any conclusions. One can imagine him as a Peter Pan, as a man who could not grow up. Or, worse yet, as a kind of Pied Piper, seducing children away from home and community. Both Peter Pan and the Pied Piper suggested a core parental and community fear that might have resonated with many of the newspaper readers who read about him. Both readings would have qualified and complicated his self-presentation as an innocent man who cared for adolescent boys. J. M. Barrie's character, Peter Pan, first appeared in an adult novel, *The Little White Bird*, in 1902. His play, *Peter Pan, or the Boy Who Wouldn't Grow Up*, opened in London in 1904 and was such a success that it led his publishers to extract the sections of the earlier novel about Peter and Wendy and the lost boys and publish them with illustrations in 1906. And then Barrie expanded the storyline in a second novel, *Peter and Wendy*, published in 1911 to enormous international success. The Pied Piper image, rooted in medieval Europe, came into the culture both by way of Grimm's fairy tales and in a poetic version by Robert Browning. Both were extraordinarily popular cultural images in the second decade of the twentieth century. See "Pied Piper, Peter Pan," Google Books Ngram Viewer, 1800–2019, accessed August 16, 2023, https://books .google.com/ngrams/graph?content=Pied+Piper%2CPeter+Pan&year_start=1800& year_end=2019&corpus=26&smoothing=3&direct_url=t1%3B%2CPied%20Piper%3B %2Cc0%3B.t1%3B%2CPeter%20Pan%3B%2Cc0#t1%3B%2CPied%20Piper%3B%2Cc0 %3B.t1%3B%2CPeter%20Pan%3B%2Cc0.

3. One is reminded, once again, of Meredith Willson's 1957 musical *The Music Man*, but also of Melville's 1857 novel *The Confidence-Man*.

4. *Geyserville Gazette* 13, no. 46 (December 12, 1913): 2, available at California Newspaper Project, UC-Riverside.

5. "Sinclair's 'Worst' Boy Colony 'Lost' in Nevada," *Inter Ocean*, February 21, 1914, 5. There is a Derby Dam on the Truckee River, about twenty miles east of Reno, constructed between 1903 and 1905, that blocked the Pyramid Lake fishery located on the

Pyramid Lake Paiute Indian Reservation. There is no town of Derbuy or Derby, and there seems never to have been one. On the other hand, there was a Derby station on the Southern Pacific Railroad line, and there remains a Nevada Historical Marker (no. 43). Derby Dam takes its name from that station. See "Nevada: Derby Diversion Dam," National Park Service, accessed August 17, 2023, https://www.nps.gov/articles/ nevada-derby-diversion-dam.htm; and "Derby Diversion Dam," Waymarking.com, June 7, 2008, https://www.waymarking.com/waymarks/wm3YXB_Derby_Diversion _Dam. While challenging Jack Robbins's veracity, it is important not to take the words of others as if they were gospel truth tellers. Were there really thirty letters sitting in the post office in Reno? Or had the journalist at the *Inter Ocean* made that up? If there never was a Last Chance Ranch, who would have written to its fictional residents?

6. *Colusa Daily Sun* 66, March 18, 1914, 2, available at California Newspaper Project, UC-Riverside, https://cdnc.ucr.edu/?a=d&d=DCS19140318.2.1&e=-------en--20--1 --txt-txIN--------.

7. *Colusa Daily Sun* 66, March 18, 1914, 2.

8. *Colusa Daily Sun* 66, March 18, 1914, 2. Upton Sinclair retold the story in 1920, as part of his critique of journalism. See Upton Sinclair, *The Brass Check: A Study of American Journalism* (Champaign: University of Illinois Press, 2003), 142–43. His version made no mention of Jack Robbins.

On the other hand, Sinclair did quote from Jack Robbins extensively in his report on the protest march in Chicago after the Ludlow massacre ("Colorado War Spreads to All Sections of U.S.," *Appeal to Reason*, June 13, 1914, 2). And in that article he wrote as follows about Robbins: "The first person I met in Chicago was Jack Robbins, 'Big brother' of a number of orphan street-waifs of that city. Jack has organized half a dozen clubs; also he has what he calls the 'Last Chance Farm' in Nevada, where he has taken a dozen of the worst boys the police of our cities could find. These boys are working on a farm in Nevada and having a grand time. What is more, they are almost paying for their own keep, and soon will be doing it entirely." The mystery may be why Sinclair removed any mention of Robbins elsewhere. Why did he hide his connections with Robbins?

9. See, for examples, "May Be 'Peck's Bad Boy' Is Cause," *Portage Daily Register*, January 15, 1915, 4; "Buffalo's Worst Boy Not as Bad as Brooklyn Lad," *Buffalo Courier*, December 19, 1913, 7.

10. Jack Robbins, "Boy Scouts Evil," *Day Book*, December 20, 1915, 26–27. See "Letter," *Our Dumb Animals 55*, no. 5 (1922–23): 68, where Robbins wrote that he was most anxious to join the "Jack London Club," so "that I may be of some help in stopping cruelty to dumb creatures such as I have just witnessed at a County Fair." See also the 1919 Victor Berger hearings, where Robbins is quoted as having offered to finance the printing of a pamphlet for boys that would tell the truth about the war (United States Congress House Special Committee on Victor L. Berger Investigation, *Victor L. Berger: Hearings before the Special Committee Appointed . . . Concerning the Right of Victor L. Berger to Be Sworn In as a Member of the Sixty-Sixth Congress*, vol. 2 [Washington,

DC: Government Printing Office, 1919], 439). Prior to World War I, Robbins's socialism would not have made him anathema to much more conventional public opinion. See Christopher Lasch, *The New Radicalism in America 1889–1963: The Intellectual as a Social Type* (New York: Norton, 1965).

11. Jack Robbins, *Day Book*, October 12, 1915, 23–24. See also a short piece where he critiques the administration of charities, saying: "Remember also that less than 4c of your dime goes where you meant for it to go" (*Day Book*, November 12, 1915, 25).

12. It is not clear for whom Seman wrote the report in 1921. It appears and is discussed in the Rosenwald Papers, as part of a general investigation of whether to give money to the BBR. See box 4, folder 10, Julius Rosenwald Papers, Hanna Holborn Gray Special Collections Research Center, University of Chicago Library; see also chapter 5. On the Jewish People's Institute, see Beryl Satter, *Family Properties: Race, Real Estate, and the Exploitation of Black Urban America* (New York: Metropolitan Books, 2009), 17–36. Seman's papers can be found at "A Finding Aid to the Philip L. Seman Papers: Manuscript Collection no. 578," American Jewish Archives, 1999, http://collections.americanjewisharchives.org/ms/ms0578/ms0578.html.

13. All the quotations in this paragraph are drawn from the inquiries conducted by the Rosenwald Fund prior to agreeing to provide support to the BBR in the second half of the 1920s. See "Guide to the Julius Rosenwald Papers 1905–1963," University of Chicago Library, 2009, https://www.lib.uchicago.edu/e/scrc/findingaids/view.php?eadid=ICU.SPCL.ROSENWALDJ. For more on these, see chapter 5.

14. "Orphan Home Boys Go Out into World and Make Finest Sort of Criminals," *Day Book*, December 1, 1916, 32. Robbins was implicitly suggesting the need for an institution like the Boys' Brotherhood Republic. In this situation Robbins was willing to argue the virtues of the "home" over the institutions, even if his more normal stance was one of criticism of the private family.

15. In February 1915, Lonston had played King Ahasuerus, the lead, in a Purim play, "Haman's Conspiracy," at the Marks Nathan Home, where he was still a student. In 1916, he had twice contributed letters to the *Day Book*, one critiquing New York's willingness to have girls hired as newsboys when the boys went out on strike and one challenging the popularity of what he regarded as unprogressive socialism. A. E. Lonston, "Is This a Great Hope?" *Day Book*, November 7, 1916, 22–23; "Does Socialism of Today Promote or Demote Progress?" *Day Book*, November 11, 1916, 23–24; "At the Orphan Homes," *Sentinel*, February 26, 1915, 17.

16. A. E. Lonston, "Answers Jack Robbins," *Day Book*, December 7, 1916, 24–25. In 1927, Lonston would run for alderman in the 49th ward, identifying himself as a former resident of the Marks Nathan Home. *Jewish Sentinel*, February 27, 1927, 16.

17. Sam A. Dwork, "Answers Lonston," *Day Book*, December 13, 1916, 24; A. R., "Job Holders," December 14, 1916, 22; Irving De-Hol, "Invitation to Lonston," December 16, 1916, 24–25.

18. I think of the BBR as exemplifying what Sally Falk Moore called "a semi-autonomous social field" (*Law as Process: An Anthropological Approach* [London:

Routledge and K. Paul, 1978]). As we will see, boys were "turned over" to the BBR. What that meant legally is unclear. As far as I have been able to tell, boys could always walk away, and the institution depended on their voluntary participation. In this regard it resembles the lodging houses for newsboys that Charles Loring Brace opened in the second third of the nineteenth century in New York City. See Karen M. Staller, *New York's Newsboys: Charles Loring Brace and the Founding of the Children's Aid Society* (New York: Oxford University Press, 2020), xvi.

19. Lewis G. Stevenson, Biennial Report of Secretary of State of the State of Illinois: Fiscal Years Beginning October 1, 1914, and Ending September 30, 1916 (London: Forgotten Books, 2022 [repr.]), 110: chartered as a nonprofit corporation, July 2, 1915. See also Bulletin of the Department of Public Welfare, City of Chicago 1, no. 2 (September 1916): 37–38, https://books.google.td/books?id=hbCO6KBIjIYC&hl=fr&source =gbs_book_other_versions_r&cad=4.

20. Charles S. Winslow, *Historical Events of Chicago* (Chicago: Soderland Printing Service, 1937), 72; "6 Day Festival in Lawndale to Mark Jubilee," *Chicago Tribune*, April 28, 1946, w1; *The WPA Guide to Illinois: The Federal Writers' Project Guide to 1930s Illinois* (New York: Pantheon, 1939), 271–72; W.O.S., "Wanted–The Worst Boy," *National Humane Review* 6 (July 1918): 130. Beginning publication in 1913, the *National Humane Review* was the journal of the American Humane Association, which by then had become a federation "for the prevention of cruelty" both to children and animals. On the growth of the BBR, and the need to move to larger quarters, see "Boys' Brotherhood Secures Larger Quarters," *Day Book*, September 26, 1916, 12.

21. Clara E. Laughlin, "The 'Boy Problem' and How It Has Been Solved—by Boys!" *Chamberlin's* (December 1919): 14–16.

22. See "Children's Home and Aid Society of Illinois Records," University of Illinois Chicago Library Special Collections, accessed August 17, 2023, https://findingaids .library.uic.edu/sc/MSCHAS75.xml.

23. Several early readers asked whether the isolation of the boys from the adult world created a "Lord of the Flies" situation. So far as I have been able to tell, the answer is no. There was a fair amount of political conflict within the BBR, but the boys never turned on one another.

24. Reynolds, whom we will see more of in chapter 4, long remained a prominent figure in Chicago's social reform community. In 1933, he was the executive secretary of the Illinois Emergency Relief Commission. See Wilfred S. Reynolds, "Organizing Governmental Agencies for Unemployment Relief," *Social Service Review* 7, no. 3 (September 1933): 365–74, and "Public Welfare Administration: A Patchwork in Illinois," *Social Service Review* 11, no. 1 (March 1937): 1–8. On the Home and Aid Society, see Elizabeth White, "The History and Development of the Illinois Children's Home and Aid Society" (MA thesis, University of Chicago, 1934), https://www.proquest.com/docview/ 301782118?pq-origsite=gscholar&fromopenview=true.

25. Children's Home and Aid Society records, box 48, folder 570, University of Illinois, Chicago, Special Collections. On Minnie Low, see Shelly Tenenbaum, "Minnie

Low," *Shalvi/Hyman Encyclopedia of Jewish Women*, December 31, 1999, https://jwa
.org/encyclopedia/article/low-minnie.

26. See the Children's Home and Aid Society letter to Joel D. Hunter, Chief Probation officer of the Cook County Juvenile Court, asking him to serve as chairman and
listing the names of the other members of the "subcommittee" (January 5, 1917), as
well a reply from Hunter agreeing to serve as chairman of the new committee (January
9, 1917). An undated handwritten note from F. A. Crosby, the head of the YMCA, and
a member of the committee, includes an ambiguous paragraph asking "how about
Robbins[?] is he to take up with Hulbert's proposition? or will you keep him on for a
while[?]" A receipt in the archive, dated January 31, 1917, from the owner of the Ashland
house where the BBR was located at the time, shows that forty-five dollars was received
from W. S. Reynolds and from Jack Robbins, for one month's rent. All the aforemen-
tioned documents are housed in the Children's Home and Aid Society records, box 48,
folder 570, University of Illinois, Chicago, Special Collections.

27. Jack M. Holl, *Juvenile Reform in the Progressive Era: William R. George and
the Junior Republic Movement* (Ithaca, NY: Cornell University Press, 1971); Jennifer S.
Light, *States of Childhood: From the Junior Republic to the American Republic, 1895–
1945* (Cambridge, MA: MIT Press, 2020). Early documents published by the BBR always
also marked his identity as the "founder." See for example the cover of the published
"Constitution of the Boys' Brotherhood Republic" (Sheldon Glueck, Social Ethics
course teaching notes, in the Sheldon Glueck Papers, Historical and Special Collections, Harvard Law School Library, Cambridge, MA, https://hollisarchives.lib.harvard
.edu/repositories/5/archival_objects/1200979). One might say that the George Republics and the BBR modeled two very different ways adults thought about children (adolescents) performing adolescence. See Robin Bernstein, *Racial Innocence: Performing
American Childhood from Slavery to Civil Rights* (New York: New York University Press,
2011).

28. Children's Home and Aid Society to Minnie F. Low, January 25, 1917, Children's Home and Aid Society records, box 48, folder 570, University of Illinois, Chicago, Special Collections. The folder includes a "Financial Statement" of the Chicago
Women's Club and the "Northwest Branch of the Boys' Brotherhood Republic," dated
November 18, 1918 (at that time, there was no other branch.). In October 1918, the BBR
had received as "income" $433.94 from the Chicago Women's Club. Its expenses had
come to $475.56 for September through November, though by that time Carpenter's
and Robbins's salaries were not counted (probably salaries were being paid by the
banker Hulbert). In 1922, the financial statement of the BBR (included with the 1923
pamphlet) reveals "disbursements" of $6,077 for "salaries, supervisors, assistants[,]
and janitors"—But offers no breakdown beyond that. The expenses of the BBR that
year also included $2,340 for rents and $5,789.63 for "general running expenses." Those
expenses were paid for with $13,000 in contributions and a balance of $1,200 brought
forward from the previous year (Glueck, Social Ethics Course teaching notes). In 1937,
there were still few adults involved. See M. M. Chambers, *Youth-Serving Organizations:*

National Non-Governmental Associations; an Introductory Survey and Descriptive Directory (Washington, DC: American Council on Education, 1937), 27–28. Chambers reported that in 1937 the Chicago BBR served 1,100 boys (the New York City BBR at that time served 410). The Chicago BBR had two full-time paid employees, two part-time employees, and one part-time unpaid worker. It had an operating income of just under $11,000, from nineteen private donors. At that time, the salary of the NYC supervisor (Slonaker) was $2,400. The Chicago BBR did not reveal its salaries.

29. Clara Laughlin, who had written many articles in Chicago's *Evening American* on the unacknowledged labor of women, particularly wives, devoted several paragraphs in her manuscript autobiography to Myrtle Carpenter. After describing Jack Robbins's qualities as a big brother, Laughlin continued:

> Then, as if his own singularly fine qualifications were not enough, Jack had the rare fortune to meet a woman who has [a] clearer vision of social and educational problems than almost any other individual I [have] ever known. Her name is Myrtle Carpenter, and she studied sociology in the university in Chicago, and then went forth to study it at first hand. . . . She never has any money; sometimes I marvel how she supplies even her exceedingly modest wants. And she devalues herself [devotes herself?] . . . without recompense, year in and year out, wholeheartedly to various kinds of social service, always in a stage of development where it most needs understanding and guidance and nursing. . . . enthusiasm that never lags? Neither recompence nor glory seems to enter into her scheme of things; her joy which is abundant, comes through doing things whose need of being done she feels; and in the gratitude of those who realize that but for her they could not have pulled through. . . . What she has been to various fine pieces of constructive social work, can never be estimated, because she never lets it become apparent. "Credit" means nothing to her; anyone who yearns for it may have it. But if I ever get where "all things are known," I expect to find Myrtle Carpenter in the seats of the mighty; and if bragging isn't unthinkable there I shall brag that "I knew her when—" . . . Very early in the existence of Jack's "grain of mustard seed," she felt its possibilities. ("Traveling through Life," unpublished manuscript, 1934, 348-51, Clara E. Laughlin Papers, box 5, Sophia Smith Collection, Smith College, Northampton, MA, https://findingaids.smith.edu/repositories/2/archival_objects/122455).

It is worth adding that neither Jack Robbins nor Myrtle Carpenter plays any part in Laughlin's eventually published autobiography (*Traveling through Life, Being the Autobiography of Clara E. Laughlin* [Boston, MA: Houghton Mifflin, 1934]).

Myrtle L. Carpenter was born in 1868 in Iowa, and she died in Chicago in 1947. An obituary noted her devotion to volunteer work. In 1946 she was chair of the Civil Service Department of the Cook County Federation of Women's Clubs. See "Myrtle Luella Carpenter," *Find a Grave*, November 24, 2002, https://www.findagrave.com/memorial/6948372/myrtle-luella-carpenter?_gl=1*btz36m*_ga*NjE5MDgxMjUzLjE2MzQxMzc2MDY.*_ga_4QT8FMEX30*MTY10TgwMTAyOC44LjEuMTY10TgwMTIyMS4w; see also Ancestry.com. Carpenter was evidently a member of the women's Cordon Club, which Laughlin headed. At least, in 1925, she was reported to have served dinner there to seventeen members of the Federation of Women's Clubs (see Proquest.com). In the 1940 census, she was identified as the head of a household of single men and women. She gave her occupation as "writer." At her death, seven years later, she was identified as a "social worker." See Ancestrylibrary.com.

30. *Final Report and Testimony of Industrial Relations Commission*, 11 vols. (Washington, DC: Government Printing Office, 1916) (S. Doc. No. 415, at 9470–71). In the same report, Robbins also described the BBR as existing "for the sole purpose of taking the boys who have been turned out of institutions with instructions to go out and make a living. We have a boy committee whose business it is to secure such boys positions and find homes for them if possible."

31. Constitution of the BBR, from Glueck, Social Ethics Course teaching notes. Note that this printed constitution might not be the actual original one, though it is dated May 1914. In the Children's Home and Aid Society folder there is a typescript of what may be an earlier constitution, undated, along with a copy of the May 1914 printed constitution. That possibly earlier typescript constitution did not contain an article devoted to the duties of the supervisor. Reynolds, the head of the Home and Aid Society, received both versions of the constitution from S. A. Black (otherwise unidentified). Black added a note: "What is new in the organization? Robbins + the boys are understandably very happy in having secured considerable publicity. They grow fat + sassy in such stuff" (Children's Home and Aid Society records, box 48, folder 570, University of Illinois, Chicago, Special Collections).

32. One example of their learned skill in promotion, from a later period: Harry Slonaker, who had been an early member or citizen of Chicago's BBR, would later on become the first supervisor of the New York BBR, which began in the early 1930s. In 1935, he and his new organization were invited to testify at a New York Crime Commission hearing in Albany. He brought along one officer; the mayor, Mack Williams; and another boy, George Count, who wrote a brief account forty-five years later, in 1981, of the experience as he remembered it. According to Count, the problem was how to make sure the news media understood that Williams was a sixteen-year-old, not just another person testifying before the commission. They drove up from New York City in Slonaker's car. On the way, Slonaker told Count to wear old pants and a torn BBR sweater. Count was put up in a flophouse, while Slonaker and Williams went to a nice hotel. Around midnight, George Count was supposed to go to the local newspaper and describe how he had hitchhiked to Albany. "Look hungry," Slonaker told him. He should tell the paper he had done so because he thought Mack needed company, and there would be "strength in unity." Count did as he was directed. He gave an "Oscar performance." The newspaper editor ordered coffee and sandwiches for him, and they got him a chocolate bar. And the next day the story about their testimony appeared across the national wire services. See George Count, personal reminiscence, probably to Harry Slonaker, April 1, 1981, in Harry E. Slonaker Papers, History San Jose Research Library, San Jose, CA.

33. On alumni celebrations, see chapter 5. In contrast to Jack Robbins's identity as "big brother" and as "supervisor," William George was usually referred to as "Daddy." See Holl, *Juvenile Reform in the Progressive Era*, 146.

34. William Welling to Richard Welling, undated (Harry E. Slonaker Papers, History San Jose Research Library, San Jose, CA) correcting his mistakes in draft of what later became William Welling, *East Side Story: The Boys Brotherhood Republic's First Fifty Years on New York's Lower East Side* (New York: Boys' Brotherhood Republic of New York, Inc., 1982). Herbert K. Abrams, "Practicing Social Medicine: Memoirs from the Neighborhood" (unpublished manuscript in possession of Alan Derickson), 2–3. Slonaker 's memories were of the BBR in the 1910s. Abrams's would have been from 1929 or 1930.

35. Later letterheads included a quotation from Theodore Roosevelt—"The B.B.R. is the heart of American boyhood"—as well as other quotes from dignitaries. Above the masthead, it read, "When you think of Chicago think of the . . . Boys' Brotherhood Republic." Letter dated January 8, 1920 (Children's Home and Aid Society records, box 48, folder 570, University of Illinois, Chicago, Special Collections). See also letterheads (1907, 1946, and undated) found in the Van Lieu Minor Papers, folder 24, box 2, Clarke Historical Library, Central Michigan University, Mt. Pleasant, MI. Van Lieu was teaching at University High School and taking classes at the University of Chicago. He had apparently offered to have several of his students come to teach night classes in civics at the BBR. Copies of the constitution can be found in the Glueck lecture notes and in the University of Illinois, Chicago, Special Collections, as well as in the Van Lieu Minor Papers.

36. *Final Report and Testimony of Industrial Relations Commission*, 9470–71; M. M. Chambers, *Youth-Serving Organizations*, 27–28. There is a buried gender story that goes beyond the silent presence of the mostly unacknowledged Myrtle Carpenter. What did it mean that the BBR was an all-boy institution, with only a single male "supervisor"? If one imagined the BBR as a prison or reform school substitute, it would not have seemed surprising that women were absent. Such sites—filled with potentially violent young men and built to control and to disarm—were not thought to be suitable sites for women. On the other hand, the early child savers thought women were especially suited for working with the delinquent young, male and female. Anthony M. Platt quoted Lucy Sickels from Michigan's State Industrial School for Girls: "A reformatory without a woman" was "like a home without a mother—a place of desolation" (*The Child Savers: The Invention of Delinquency*, introduction by Miroslava Chavez-Garcia

[New Brunswick, NJ: Rutgers University Press, 2009], 79). What then did it mean that the BBR was imagined as a place without the presence of women? And to make it still more complicated, what did it mean that there were a number of prominent women who were strong supporters of Robbins and of his vision of the BBR? In a culture that still assumed that women/mothers provided a necessary softening to the harshness of the life poor boys confronted, what did it mean that such women were mostly absent?

37. Neil M. Clark, "'When a Feller Needs a Friend,'" *American Magazine* 98 (1924): 52–53, 138–42; *Final Report and Testimony of Industrial Relations Commission*, 9470. In 1937, a report by M. M. Chambers reported that the Chicago BBR served 1100 boys (the New York City BBR at that time served 410). The Chicago BBR then had two full-time paid employees, two part-time employees, and one part-time unpaid worker. It had an operating income of just under $11,000, from nineteen private donors. At that time, the salary of the NYC supervisor (Slonaker) was $2400. The Chicago BBR did not reveal its salaries. M. M. Chambers, *Youth-Serving Organizations: National Non-Governmental Associations; an Introductory Survey and Descriptive Directory* (Washington, DC: American Council on Education, 1937), 27–28. By contrast, after around 1910, the George Junior Republics became increasingly dependent on full-time adult employees (Holl, *Juvenile Reform in the Progressive Era*, 161).

38. Clara E. Laughlin, "Where Boys Rule," *Red Cross Magazine* 16 (August 1920): 74–75. She wrote two articles with that title; see also Clara E. Laughlin, "Where Boys Rule," *National Magazine* 49 (August 1920): 223–24, 238. The BBR did soon create a form of "junior" citizenship.

39. Citizenship application and membership card, Chicago Home and Aid Society records, box 48, folder 570, University of Illinois, Chicago, Special Collections. There are copies of citizenship applications in the Glueck lecture notes and many completed applications in the Harry E. Slonaker Papers at the History San Jose Research Library in San Jose, CA.

40. *Life of the Boys' Brotherhood Republic* (Chicago: Boys' Brotherhood Republic, 1938); Philip Seman letter, box 4, folder 10, Julius Rosenwald Papers, Hanna Holborn Gray Special Collections Research Center, University of Chicago; "News of the Day," *Day Book*, November 15, 1916, 6. The *Jewish Sentinel* (December 24, 1915, 8) wrote that Robbins as a Jew and a former "incorrigible" was "spiritualizing the gang." He offered "sociology in the best sense."

41. "Facts about the Boys' Brotherhood Republic," (first page), circa 1916, Van Lieu Minor Papers, box 2, folder 24, Clarke Historical Library, Central Michigan University, Mount Pleasant, MI. By the 1920s, the letterhead of the BBR included Teddy Roosevelt's endorsement. On October 2, 1915, included in a series of announcements for various socialist meetings, the BBR announced that it was holding a debate on whether "labor unions are detrimental to society" (*Day Book*, 32). Homer Lane, the director of the Ford Republic, an alternative institution for delinquent children outside of Detroit, talked and wrote in ways somewhat similar to Jack Robbins, as did Judge Ben Lindsey. See LeRoy Ashby, *Saving the Waifs: Reformers and Dependent Children, 1890–1917* (Philadelphia, PA: Temple University Press, 1984), 139–49; Ben B. Lindsey, "The Boy and the Court: The Colorado Law and Its Administration," *Charities* 13 (1905): 350–57.

42. Glueck lecture notes (I am guessing the pamphlet was produced in 1923 because it includes 1922 budget figures); *Life of the Boys' Brotherhood Republic*. In the 1938 book, the quotation is located on a page that also contrasted the George Junior Republic. It imagined the George Junior Republic as a substitute for reform school, unlike the BBR, which prevented engagement with the courts. On the other hand, some donors and supporters understood the BBR as drawing on a common impulse with the George Junior Republics. See Richard Welling, *As the Twig Is Bent* (New York: G. P. Putnam, 1942), 147–57. The wealthy reformer and member of the New York BBR's board of directors Caroline Bayard Colgate described the constitution of the BBR as providing a "game of self-government" that made the boys feel as if they were running the show themselves. Read thusly, this game does exhibit the performative qualities that Light identifies as central to the George Junior Republics. See Light, *States of Childhood*; Caroline Bayard Dod Colgate, *Off the Straight and Narrow* (New York: Lee Furman, 1937), 232. Colgate may have construed the organization as more conventional and familiar than it was, although it may be that Colgate's understanding was correct for the New York BBR by the time it was organized in 1932.

43. Constitution of the BBR, article 1, section 2. By contrast, the George Junior Republic mantra was "Nothing without Labor." That mantra meant "learning by earning" when the republic added schooling. And that meant paying wages for doing schoolwork (Holl, *Juvenile Reform in the Progressive Era*, 94–95, 179).

44. I draw the notion of a horizontal structure of authority from the work of Camille Robcis, *Disalienation: Politics, Philosophy, and Radical Psychiatry in Postwar France* (Chicago: University of Chicago Press, 2021). On the role of charity: the members of the BBR reflected Robbins's hostility, even as the BBR also depended on contributions from wealthy adults. See the 1922 financial statement in the Glueck lecture notes.

45. "Facts About the Boys' Brotherhood Republic," (first page), circa 1916, Van Lieu Minor Papers, box 2, folder 24, Clarke Historical Library, Central Michigan University, Mount Pleasant, MI.

46. "Facts About the Boys' Brotherhood Republic," (first page); "Boys' Brotherhood Plans to Put Chicago on Trial," *Day Book*, December 28, 1916, 12.

47. The 1923 pamphlet, *The Boys' Brotherhood Republic, Organized May 8, 1914, Jack Robbins . . . Founder, Its Work and Aims*, can be found in the Glueck lecture notes, https://hollisarchives.lib.harvard.edu/repositories/5/archival_objects/1200979.

On the continuing distrust of charities, consider this anecdote from a 1916 article: The BBR had an extra bed, unneeded, and they wanted to give it to a poor family, so that a "boy too young to work" would not have to sleep on the floor. But the BBR had no way to move the large bed. Robbins suggested that a boy use the pay phone to call local charities to see if they would move the bed. The boy used one coin to call United Charities. After several efforts to describe what was needed, he was told that "this was not their line of work," but he might try Jewish charities, as the name of the family sounded Jewish. He then called the Red Cross, which after several attempts told him that it was not a charity institution. He then called the Charity Alliance, which eventually told him that they didn't do business on the west side of Chicago. Then he called the Chicago Industrial League, where he was told that if the BBR was so generous, why not pay for the hauling as well? But the BBR had no money for that. In the end "five or six of us boys will have to carry that bed if it breaks our back." And the boy was out five nickels ("The Public Forum: Charity That Gives Not," *Day Book*, March 4, 1916, 22).

48. The comparison is unclear since most George Junior Republics did not serve as reform schools or as places to which delinquents were diverted, though they were often understood as "extensions" of the reformatory principle (Holl, *Juvenile Reform in the Progressive Era*, 237, 295). A closer comparison to the Chicago BBR may be found with the Ford Republic outside Detroit, which took in boys put on probation by the juvenile court. The Ford Republic was a "private" reform school to which delinquents were sent, though early on most residents were apparently "dependent" youths, not accused of crime. The Ford Republic, not connected to Henry Ford, copied some features of the George Junior Republics, though William George was critical of its practices. It took from George the focus on work and schooling, and making the boys pay for the services provided. Although the language of a "republic" was used, for the most part boys did not stay long enough to identify with self-governance of the institution. Work was required and paid for using an internal currency. Boys were charged for their board, clothes, and other essentials. They could buy "luxuries" (candy) if they had money left. And they would be fined when they committed "misdemeanors." Recognition of private property was central. One result was that there was "a considerable range of wealth" within the institution: rich citizens and poor citizens, and envy and some thievery within. It should be added that the structure of self-government at the Ford Republic went along with a quantity of corporal punishment, unlike that of the BBR, which forbade corporal punishment. Until 1930, such punishments included "blows with a leather strap ordered by the boy judge and inflicted by the boy sheriff." Also, a miscreant could be ordered to walk a circular path in the front yard for a stated period of time. And the most severe punishment, for having run away and getting caught, consisted in a spank from each of the other boys in the same building. See Ashby, *Saving the Waifs*, 133–69; Courtlandt Churchill Van Vechten Jr., "A Study of Success and Failure of One Thousand Delinquents Committed to a Boys' Republic" (PhD diss., University of Chicago, 1935), ProQuest dissertation no. T-04690; Light, *States of Childhood*, 102. William George, in contrast, abandoned corporal punishment in Freeville (see Holl, *Juvenile Reform in the Progressive Era*, 97).

49. 1916 pamphlet, Van Lieu Minor Papers, box 2, folder 24, Clarke Historical Library, Central Michigan University, Mount Pleasant, MI. The relationship of the BBR to gangs was complex, and it was noted in Frederic M. Thrasher's study of Chicago's gangs, who drew on what he identified as "Jack Robbins' Scrapbook" (not found), perhaps compiled by Clara Laughlin. The BBR offered space for neighborhood gangs to meet and to parley and to have symbolic battles. Later on, they may have colonized and "incorporated" the Boundary Gang, which operated along Twelfth Street, and other gangs, into their civic structure. Thrasher regarded the BBR as distinctively successful in dealing with gangs. See *The Gang: A Study of 1,313 Gangs in Chicago* (Chicago: University of Chicago Press, 1927), 182–83, 282–84, 323, 517–18. By 1941, they had opened a formal "court of arbitration," where rival gangs could negotiate their conflicts ("Boys Know How to End Wars in Incident Stage," *Chicago Daily Tribune*, November 30, 1941, sw7).

50. Jane Whitaker, "'And a Bunch of Boys Shall Lead Us'–Or at Least We Can Get Some Pointers," *Day Book*, November 8, 1915, 30–31. Four days later, perhaps responding to Whitaker's column, Robbins wrote a short critique of "organized charity" for its waste of resources (Jack Robbins, "Charity," *Day Book*, November 12, 1915, 25). Robbins's invocation of the need for pals was, of course, not original. Ben Lindsey argued that the juvenile court judge should play that role. See David B. Wolcott, *Cops and Kids: Policing Juvenile Delinquency in Urban America, 1890–1940* (Columbus: Ohio State University Press, 2005), 19; Lindsey, "The Boy and the Court," 350–57.

51. The red typescript was in the Slonaker papers, prepared in the early 1930s for the New York BBR, almost certainly copied from a text in the Chicago BBR (as almost all the early 1930s New York materials were). By the later 1920s, newspapers noticed that a boy might be awarded a prize as an "ideal pal." See headline "500 Boys Name Ideal Pals; 300 Pick Same One," undated, but probably 1927, in Julius Rosenwald Papers, box 4, folder 10, Hanna Holborn Gray Special Collections Research Center, University of Chicago Library. It seems unlikely that such a competitive designation occurred in the early years of the BBR.

52. In another of the origin stories told about its beginnings, Jack Robbins began the BBR after having discovered that the boys he wanted to save from the juvenile court were already members of boys' clubs. What was the matter with these clubs? "These clubs," Robbins recalled, "were organized, ruled and run entirely by grownups. Belonging to a boys' club meant obeying rules the kids had no part in making. I made up my mind to start a new boys' club with everything turned upside down." See Webb Waldron, "B.B.R.—Of, by, and for Boys," *Rotarian* 48 (April 1936): 21–23, https:// flashbak.com/the-boys-brotherhood-republic-tear-up-new-york-city-1955-50824/; Light, *States of Childhood*, 10; Holl, *Juvenile Reform in the Progressive Era*, 225 (on the complexities and confusions in defining what the George Republic "was"). See also William Welling on the New York BBR's history, which begins with a chapter devoted to the George Junior Republics (*East Side Story*, 21, quoting Arnold Grossman, *The Launching Pad* [New York: BBR, 1967, ii]). Note that the classic origin story for Father Flanagan's Boy's Town has the boys paroled into the care of Father Flanagan. There is no suggestion that the boys took an active role in the creation of the relationship or of the organization. See Kenneth B. Kidd, *Making American Boys: Boyology and the Feral Tale* (Minneapolis: University of Minnesota Press, 2004), 116–17.

53. "Boys' Brotherhood Police Hunt for Robbers of Club," *Chicago Examiner*, January 28, 1917, 2–3; "Hint Pool Men Seek to Wreck Boy Fraternity," *Chicago Tribune*, February 10, 1917, 12. The fact that one of the few African American boys in the BBR would be working as a "caretaker" suggests that the BBR was not immune from the racism of the time.

54. "Health Official Has Tiff with Mother Jones," *Chicago Tribune*, January 23, 1916, 3. On Fischer, see Michael Willrich, *City of Courts: Socializing Justice in Progressive Era Chicago* (New York: Cambridge University Press, 2003), 186, 188.

55. Whitaker, "'And a Bunch of Boys Shall Lead Us'–Or At Least We Can Get Some Pointers," *Day Book*, November 8, 1915, 30. A *Day Book* article in April 1916 quantified the work all the BBR committees did. See "Boys Can Help Boys Is Good Plan to Work On," April 29, 1916, 8.

56. "Announcement," *Day Book*, June 6, 1916, 32. On Marks and Abrams, see chapters 6 and 7.

57. Moore, *Law as Process*. On the other hand, the BBR did not fetishize "work" as intrinsic to life in the BBR, as William George did.

58. Copies of the Job Day materials can be found in the Glueck lecture notes and in the Chicago Home and Aid Society Papers, University of Illinois, Chicago, Special Collections.

59. Ralph Lee Goodman, "Solving Chicago's Boy Problem," *Sentinel* 23, no. 6 (September 1916): 11, 20, "Boys Job Day," *Clarksburg Sunday Telegram*, April 2, 1916, 4. "All Help Find Jobs for Boys in Chicago," *Topeka Daily State Journal*, April 10, 1916, 5, noted that "large institutions" expected to place two or three boys apiece. The paper identified those boys as "embryo J.P. Morgans." See advertisement for Jobs Day in the Glueck lecture notes; similar ad, *Day Book*, October 13, 1915, 7. "Bits of News," *Day Book*, April 11, 1916, 8, reported that the first "Job Day" was a success, with more than five hundred boys getting jobs at salaries up to ten dollars a week. On Job Day, see "Boys' Job Day," *Day Book*, April 10, 1916, 28; "Chicago Plans Boys' Job Day," *Grand Forks Daily Herald*, March 21, 1916, 9; "This Is 'Boys' Job Day' in Chicago," *Wisconsin State Journal*, April 10, 1916, 8, and "Boys' Job Day in Chicago," *Boise Evening Capital News*, April 10, 1916, 1. The pamphlet produced by the BBR in 1916 reported that the "Employment Committee and the Boys' Free Employment Office had found 712 jobs on Boys' Job Day." The pamphlet claimed that the committee had found 1,500 jobs since the beginning of 1916. In October, fifty-three boys were placed in after school jobs, seventeen jobs were changed for boys "where they were most fitted," and thirty-six "Saturday only" jobs were given out. See Van Lieu Minor Papers, box 2, folder 24, Clarke Historical Library, Central Michigan University, Mount Pleasant, MI. See also "They Want a Thousand Boys for a Thousand Jobs in Chicago April 10," *Commonwealth* (NC), March 27, 1917, 5; "Plan Big Work For April 10–Boys' Job Day," *Day Book*, April 9, 1917, 29.

60. There were a variety of ways that those who had once been in the BBR remained involved, including serving as judges in the court structure that the BBR created and, later on, helping establish new BBRs in other cities and elsewhere in Chicago. See Application for Citizenship, in 1923 pamphlet. There are many filled-in New

York citizenship forms, probably from 1932, in the Harry E. Slonaker Papers, History San Jose Research Library, San Jose, CA. The form was unchanged from that used in Chicago. For an example of the form, see figure 6.

61. Jack Robbins, "Give Them a Chance," *Day Book*, October 16, 1915, 26. What happened to those boys who joined the BBR but did later on find themselves in trouble with the law? I have found remarkably little evidence about those boys, although they undoubtedly existed.

62. 1916 pamphlet, Van Lieu Minor Papers, Clarke Historical Library, Central Michigan University, Mount Pleasant, MI. See also *Life of the Boys' Brotherhood Republic* (1938), 12, 18; and BBR constitution, article 11, section 10.

63. Ralph Lee Goodman, "Solving Chicago's Boy Problem," *Sentinel* 23, no. 6 (1916): 11, 20; "Protest Listing Innocents as Criminals," *Day Book*, October 15, 1915, 7; "Boys Win Fight against Finger-Print Plan," *Day Book*, October 22, 1915, 7. On Pinckney, see Frank T. Flynn, "Merritt W. Pinckney and the Early Days of the Juvenile Court in Chicago," *Social Service Review* 28, no. 1 (March 1954): 20–30. On Olson, see Willrich, *City of Courts*, 47–50, and passim. Chicago's Legal Aid Society had been established in 1905; see "Legal Aid Society Offices, c. 1910," *Electronic Encyclopedia of Chicago*, 2005, http://www.encyclopedia.chicagohistory.org/pages/11196.html.

64. "Boys' 'Mayor' Protests to Olson on Fingerprints," *Chicago Tribune*, October 22, 1915, 7. When Goodman, with Mother Jones and Jack Robbins, went to call on the Chicago mayor to get him to support an anti-fingerprinting policy, they could not get past his secretary's desk—an experience quite unlike the success the boys had achieved with Olson. On Olson, see Michael A. Rembis, *Defining Deviance: Sex, Science, and Delinquent Girls, 1890–1960* (Urbana: University of Illinois Press, 2011). See also Elliott J. Gorn and Rosemary Feurer, "Commentary: Chicago Played a Big Role in Mother Jones' Life: Why No Statue of Her," *Chicago Daily Tribune*, July 14, 2020 (includes photograph of Mother Jones with boys); and "Mother Mary Harris Jones," Daily Kos, accessed September 16, 2023, https://www.dailykos.com/blog/Mother%20Mary%20Harris%20Jones.

65. "Chicago Briefs," *Day Book*, December 13, 1916, 30; "VENGEANCE? The Slain Youth, His Slayer, and His Playmates Who Tell Jury Unshaken Story," *Chicago Daily Tribune*, December 14, 1916, 3. According to Moga, a "Roumanian," the boys had thrown stones at him, and he hurled the shears as the result of "reflux action." A physician also testified that the wound would not have caused death if it had been properly treated. See "Doctor Says Boy Killed by Shears Might Have Lived," *Day Book*, December 14, 1916, 32.

66. "Boys' Republic Would Convict Club Gardener," *Chicago Daily Tribune*, July 26, 1916, 13; J. Dwork, "Answers Charges Against B.B.R.," *Day Book*, December 20, 1916, 23; "Boys Seek Punishment for Slayer," *Chicago Examiner*, July 26, 1916, 1; "Boys Ready to Fight Slayer," July 27, 1916, 7; "Silk Stocking Club Defends Killing of Young Boy," *Day Book*, July 25, 1916, 3; "Boys Republic Takes Stand against Rich Men's Club," July 26, 1916, 3.

67. "Boys' Republic Would Convict Club Gardener," *Chicago Daily Tribune*, July 26, 1916, 13; J. Dwork, A B.B.R. Member, "Answers Charges against B.B.R.," *Day Book*, December 20, 1916, 23; "Ulrey's Father Hints Mystery in Club's Stand," *Chicago Daily Tribune*, December 15, 1916, 9. In the end, the jury deadlocked eight to four on conviction of Ulrey for manslaughter. And it appears that there was never a retrial. See "Court Releases Moga Jury When Locked, 8 to 4," *Chicago Daily Tribune*, December 18, 1916, 1. Robbins quotation is from an unidentified newspaper in Children's Home and Aid Society records, box 48, folder 570, University of Illinois, Chicago, Special Collections.

68. "Doctor Says Boys Killed by Shears Might Have Lived," *Day Book*, December 14, 1916, 32; "Exclusive Rights of Saddle Club to Be Tested," July 27, 1916, 6; "Lake Shore Fenced In," *Chicago Eagle*, August 5, 1916, 1; "Lake Shore Fenced In," September 30, 1916, 3. On Branovitz as one mayor negotiating with another mayor (Chicago's), see "Two Mayors and Boys," *Modern View* (St. Louis), March 31, 1916, 7.

69. "'You Mustn't Touch' Spirit of Saddle and Cycle Club Halts Much Good Bathing," *Day Book*, July 31, 1916, 30. Fyffe was a Democrat, and he had emigrated from Ireland. He had been the lawyer for the Chicago Motor Coach Company, and he was the vice president of the Illinois Manufacturers' Mutual Casualty Association. See "Fultz to Fyvie," PoliticalGraveyard.com, accessed August 18, 2023, https://politicalgraveyard.com/bio/fulwood-fyke.html.

70. "Wilmette Rich Face Fight against Private Beaches," *Day Book*, August 8, 1916, 8. I'm not sure the attorney meant to imply that the BBR possessed the right to condemn the property of the country club. See "To Fight for Right to Use Saddle and Cycle Beach," *Day Book*, August 1, 1916, 29; "State Law Holds S. and S. [*sic*] Club Is Wrong in Holding Beach from Public," August 3, 1916, 28–29. Needless to say, the Saddle and Cycle Club disputed the existence of that right. According to the "silk-stocking directorate of the club," no one but members of the club had any right to set foot on the beach. See "Exclusive Rights of Saddle Club to Be Tested," *Day Book*, July 27, 1916, 6. On the later history of the club's negotiations over its beach, see Joseph D. Kearney and Thomas W. Merrill, *Lakefront: Public Trust and Private Rights in Chicago* (Ithaca, NY: Cornell University Press, 2021), 210, 215–16 (including a map of the site of the club and a 1915 photograph).

71. "What the Boys Brotherhood Republic Might Profitably Tackle Next," *Sentinel* 23, no. 5 (August 4, 1916), 8.

72. "Boys Blank File at Saddle Club, March through Grounds in Memory of Lost Member," *Chicago Daily Tribune*, August 6, 1917, 1, 3 (with pictures).

73. A few examples: "Meanest Boy to Be Made Model if Chicago Society Finds Him," *Muskogee Times-Democrat*, January 4, 1918, 1; "Seek 100 Percent Bad Boy," *Courier*, January 6, 1918, 5; "Want Meanest Boy in Country," *Record-Journal*, January 5, 1918, 15; "Would Grow Wings on Prize Bad Boy," *Pittsburgh Post*, January 7, 1918, 4; "Chicago Society Wants the Very Worstest Boy," *Pratt Daily Tribune*, January 8, 1918, 4; "Fine Chance for Meanest Boy in the United States," *Fort Wayne Sentinel*, January 4, 1918, 20; "Looking for a Real Bad Boy to Convert into Angelic Child," *New Castle Herald*, January

4, 1918, 6; "Meanest Boy Will Be Lad Who Lacks Mother to Defend," *Drumright Weekly Derrick*, January 5, 1918, 8.

74. A search in Newspapers.com for "Boys' Brotherhood Republic" and "bad boys" or "worst boy" generated more than sixty almost-identical articles between January 4 and January 20, 1918. See for one example, "Country's Worst Boy in Perth Amboy?" *Perth Amboy Evening News*, January 18, 1918, 17.

75. Under the headline: "Wanted—The Worst of All," *Work with Boys: A Magazine of Methods* 18 (1918): 208.

76. "Would Grow Wings on Prize Bad Boy," *Pittsburgh Daily Post*, January 7, 1918, 4.

77. "Country's Worst Boy in Perth Amboy?" *Perth Amboy Evening News*, January 18, 1918, 17.

78. "Country's Worst Boy in Perth Amboy?" *Perth Amboy Evening News*, January 18, 1918, 17.

79. The visitors ignored the fact that those the Perth Amboy paper had interviewed back in January had "vehemently denied that the worst boy in the country" lived in the New Jersey town. See "The Conservation of the Boy Crop," *Perth Amboy Evening News*, May 2, 1918, 4; "Seek Country's Worst Boy Here," May 20, 1918, 5; "Seeking Worst Boy in U.S. Here," May 24, 1918, 1.

80. E. C. Rodgers, "How Boys Are Going to Reform America's Worst Boy," *Arkansas City Daily News*, May 4, 1918, 3. See, also, many other papers: "Alleghany Boys Not Bad Enough, Conclusion of 'Jack' Robbins," *Pittsburgh Daily Post*, May 12, 1918, 10; "Worst Boy in Town Being Sought Here by 'Jack" Robbins," May 11, 1918, 7; "Robbins Wants Bad Boy Here; Can't Have Him, Says Black," June 5, 1918, 3.

81. E. C. Rodgers, "How Boys Are Going to Reform America's Worst Boy," *Arkansas City Daily News*, May 4, 1918, 3.

82. See "Worst Boy in the Country Found; Is to Be Reformed," *El Paso Herald*, June 6, 1918, 7. On the other hand, the story had what one might call moral legs. A Sunday school teacher used it as an opportunity. When he read that the citizens of the BBR wanted to become "brothers to the meanest boy and melt his meanness out of him by kindness," and that "they don't believe that he can quit his meanness until a new somebody else comes to his help with friendliness," he realized that their "method" was "too good to be used by them alone." He asked his Sunday school class: "Who is the meanest boy in your . . . class?" He had probably dropped out of the class. But "what is to become of him? Is it not time a relief party of brothers and friends went in search of—the meanest boy?" See *Frank R. Shipman, "The Meanest Boy," Congregationalist and Advance, March 7, 1918, 308.*

83. Charles C. Keith, "Boys' Work Conference," *Work with Boys: A Magazine of Methods* 18 (1918): 162–64, 190–196. A program schedule for the conference, published earlier, did not show Robbins or the BBR as speaking. See *Boys Workers' Round Table: A Magazine of Applied Ideals in Boy Craft* 1, no. 1 (March 1918): 26–27. Of the conference itself, the magazine editorialized: "Were there not differences of opinion? Yes! Were there not caustic remarks and keen rejoinders? Yes, of a verity, but no discord, because all were attune[d]. Whether bass or tenor, alto or soprano, they were true to the keynote of the Conference—the Boy" (*Boys Workers' Round Table* 2 [June 1918]: 3).

84. "Jack Robbins' Republic," *Work with Boys: A Magazine of Methods* 18 (1918): 190–96.

85. "Jack Robbins' Republic," *Work with Boys: A Magazine of Methods* 18 (1918): 190–96.

86. "Jack Robbins' Republic," *Work with Boys: A Magazine of Methods* 18 (1918): 190–96.

87. "Jack Robbins' Republic," *Work with Boys: A Magazine of Methods* 18 (1918): 190–96.

88. "Jack Robbins' Republic," *Work with Boys: A Magazine of Methods* 18 (1918): 190–96.

89. "Jack Robbins' Republic," *Work with Boys: A Magazine of Methods* 18 (1918): 190–96.

90. "Jack Robbins' Republic," *Work with Boys: A Magazine of Methods* 18 (1918): 190–96.

91. "Jack Robbins' Republic," *Work with Boys: A Magazine of Methods* 18 (1918): 190–96.

92. "Jack Robbins' Republic," *Work with Boys: A Magazine of Methods* 18 (1918): 190–96.

93. "Jack Robbins' Republic," *Work with Boys: A Magazine of Methods* 18 (1918): 190–96.

94. "Jack Robbins' Republic," *Work with Boys: A Magazine of Methods* 18 (1918): 190–96.

95. "Jack Robbins' Republic," *Work with Boys: A Magazine of Methods* 18 (1918): 190–96.

CHAPTER FOUR

1. "Seek to Save Slayer," *New York Tribune*, May 22, 1918, 8; "Chicago Boys Here to Plead for Life of 16-Year-Old Slayer," May 28, 1918, 16. When the BBR had advocated for Chapman earlier that year, it was "no breach of confidence," the paper said, to report that the governor's heart had been touched and that he had promised them "every possible aid" ("Youths Ask Whitman to Save Choir Boy Slayer," February 24, 1918, 7).

2. "Seek to Save Slayer," *New York Tribune*, May 22, 1918, 8; "Chicago Boys Here to Plead for Life of 16-Year-Old Slayer," May 28, 1918, 16.

3. "Seek to Save Slayer," *New York Tribune*, May 22, 1918, 8; "Chicago Boys Here to Plead for Life of 16-Year-Old Slayer," May 28, 1918, 16.

4. "Boys Advise Chapman to Demand Liberty or Death," *New York Tribune*, December 18, 1918, 11. The BBR would continue to advocate against executions of boys. See *American Hebrew* (May 8, 1925, 844), which noted that two representatives of the BBR were elected to intercede for the life of Willie Cavalier. And see the case of Roy

Wolff, a seventeen-year-old, condemned to death in California ("Boys Take Up Fight for Condemned Boy," *Decatur Daily Review*, August 26, 1920, 1; "Boys' Republic Appeals," *Bakersfield Morning Echo*, August 27, 1920, 1; and more). The Chapman Case continued to resonate for the BBR. In the notes for an opening meeting of the NYC BBR in May 1932, Jack Robbins, who was visiting from Chicago, told of his "future plans" and then described the "strange case" of Paul Chapmen [*sic*]. See handwritten notes, May 20, 1932, in the Harry E. Slonaker Papers, History San Jose Research Library, San Jose, CA.

5. "So-Called 'Bad' Boys Now Help Lick Kaiser," *Evening Missourian*, August 31, 1918, 1; "Many Youths Are Reclaimed from Vicious Environment," *Daily Ardmoreite*, September 4, 1918, 4.

6. "Conservation of the Boy Crop," *Perth Amboy Evening News*, May 3, 1918, 18.

7. "Penny Campaign Is Started by Boys of U.S. to Pay Lindsey's Fine," *Omaha Daily Bee*, August 31, 1919, 4; (and others). The story of the case is summarized in the "Boys Give Pennies to Save Judge Lindsey from Jail," *Washington Herald*, October 8, 1919, 5. (and others). Lindsey decided to serve the jail sentence rather than pay the fine, if the US Supreme Court would not reverse the decision of the criminal court judge. The Colorado Supreme Court had upheld the lower court decision by a 4–3 vote. One of the dissenters wrote that it would be "opposed to public policy, decency and justice for Lindsey to have violated" the boy's confidence. See Lindsey v. People, 66 Colo 343, 181 P. 531 (1919) (Bailey, J. dissenting). See also Jackson Springer, "'Against the Order of Nature': Creating a Gay Identity under the Law in Colorado, 1880–1914" (BA thesis, Princeton University, 2018), https://catalog.princeton.edu/catalog/dsp012227ms385, and Naama Maor, "Delinquent Parents: Punitive Welfare and the Creation of Juvenile Justice, 1899–1927" (PhD diss., University of Chicago, 2020), ProQuest dissertation no. 28026706

8. "Scheme to Oust Juvenile Court Judge Exposed," *Chicago Daily Tribune*, October 1, 1919, 10. When he died in 1929, Victor Arnold would be remembered as "the greatest friend" of delinquent boys (Obituary, *New York Times*, May 4, 1929, 12). Jack Dwork would later on become the president of the Decalogue Society of Lawyers, an organization for Jewish lawyers in Chicago; see the society letterhead on Michael Levin to Albert B. Sabin, May 2, 1966, online via Digital Resource Commons at https://drc.libraries.uc.edu/server/api/core/bitstreams/274712d9-43b2-4aeb-ae24-52c615362783/content; and elsewhere.

9. On horizontal constitutionalism, see Camille Robcis, *Disalienation: Politics, Philosophy, and Radical Psychiatry in Postwar France* (Chicago: University of Chicago Press, 2021).

10. "Jack Robbins Here to Organize Boys," *Perth Amboy Evening News*, May 7, 1920, 19; *Buffalo Enquirer*, April 14, 1920, 9; *Boston Globe*, April 27, 1920, 4; *Fort Wayne Journal-Gazette*, April 12, 1920, 10; April 13, 1920, 7; *Times Tribune* (Altoona, PA), April 7, 1920, 13.(and many more); "Newsboys Ask U.S. Boy Board," *Washington Herald*, May 10, 1920, 2; "Newsboy 'Statesmen' in Capital to Urge 'U.S. Boy Commission,'" May 10, 1920,

7; "Chicago Newsies Breakfasting in Bed as Part of 'Millionairies [*sic*] Day in New York," *Brainerd Daily Dispatch*, May 12, 1920, 1: "We are the only bunch of self-governed boys in existence." One of the two boys, Max Swiren, would become a prominent attorney in Chicago, specializing in public utility regulation, arguing cases before the Supreme Court, and, during World War II, serving as legal counsel to the office of price stabilization. In 1921, an article about him ("A Millionaire for a Day," *Sioux City Journal*, July 3, 1921, 8) reimagined him (by then sixteen years of age and taking law classes at the University of Chicago, and visiting relatives in South Dakota), as the creator of the Boys' Brotherhood Republic, without any mention of Jack Robbins. According to the paper, Swiren had once been a member of a gang "under the direction of elders" in a Chicago settlement house. "The boys' rights, as he called them, were imposed upon." They were subjected to "autocratic government." Swiren gathered companions together, and they organized a "walk out" on the settlement. They met in the basement of his father's home and founded an "organization." According to his version of their time at the Waldorf-Astoria, they kept trying to spend their money but were stopped by a trailing press agent.

11. Sumner Keene, "Get to the Point," *American Magazine* 89 (1920): 266. On Hulbert paying Robbins a salary, see chapter 5.

12. James Franklin Page, *Socializing for the New Order or Educational Values of the Juvenile Organization* (Rockland, IL: Augustana College, 1919), 90–92.

13. Wilfred S. Reynolds to Joseph P. Murphy, chief probation officer, Erie County Court, December 29, 1920; and also Wilfred S. Reynolds to Harriet Townsend, lecturer in social science, Teachers College, Columbia University, February 2, 1921. Both letters are housed in the Children's Home and Aid Society Records, box 48, folder 570, University of Illinois, Chicago, Special Collections.

14. Reynolds to Murphy, December 29, 1920; Reynolds to Townsend, February 2, 1921.

15. Reynolds to Murphy, December 29, 1920; Reynolds to Townsend, February 2, 1921.

16. Reynolds to Murphy, December 29, 1920; Reynolds to Townsend, February 2, 1921.

17. Reynolds to Murphy, December 29, 1920; Reynolds to Townsend, February 2, 1921.

18. . Reynolds to Murphy, December 29, 1920; Reynolds to Townsend, February 2, 1921.

19. Laughlin would later on open a travel service, and she wrote many books that advised unaccompanied women about how to travel in foreign places. In 1917 and 1918, she was also writing an almost-daily column for a Chicago paper, the *Chicago Evening American*. The column usually went by the heading "Somewhere in Chicago," always with her name in the heading. At least one such column she devoted to the Boys' Brotherhood Republic. See "Clara E. Laughlin's Article: A Meeting of the Boys' Brotherhood Republic Reveals the Nourishing Sap of Clean Ideals Surging through the Roots of Democracy—A Waif Who Joined 'to Get a Chance' and Died for Fair Play" (undated, but probably from 1917 or 1918; see the Clara E. Laughlin Papers, box 2, folder 2, Sophia Smith Collection, Smith College, Northampton, MA). See also Judith Raftery, "Chicago Settlement Women in Fact and Fiction: Hobart Chatfield Chatfield-Taylor, Clara Elizabeth Laughlin, and Elia Wilkinson Peattie Portray the New Woman," *Illinois Historical Journal* 88, no. 1 (Spring 1995): 37–58. Clara E. Laughlin, "The Worst Boy in the United States: Two Chicago Boys Go Traveling to 27 Cities for Him and Find Him," *Ladies' Home Journal* 36 (October 1919): 7–8, 191–92; Clara E. Laughlin, "The 'Boy Problem' and How It Has Been Solved—by Boys!" *Chamberlin's* (December 1919): 14–16; Clara E. Laughlin, "Where Boys Rule," *Red Cross Magazine* 16 (August 1920): 74–75; Clara E. Laughlin, "Where Boys Rule," *National Magazine* 49 (August 1920): 223–24, 238; Clara E. Laughlin, "Here's a Real Boys' Club, in Which There Are No Grown Folks, but Just Boys," *Ladies' Home Journal* 36 (October 1919): 83. (These articles can all be found in the Clara E. Laughlin Papers, Sophia Smith Collection, Smith College, Northampton, MA.) She also apparently interviewed Robbins; Frederic M. Thrasher, in *The Gang: A Study of 1,313 Gangs in Chicago* (Chicago: University of Chicago Press, 1927), cites a "scrapbook" Laughlin kept on Jack Robbins, which I have not been able to find.

20. Laughlin, "Here's a Real Boys' Club"; Laughlin, "Worst Boy." The short editorial had the title "Talk about Americanization! Here Is the Real Thing," *Ladies' Home Journal* 36 (October 1919): 7. It continued a theme that the journal had developed in a longer editorial at the front of the issue, on the need to focus on Americanization and domestic politics now that the war was won. "Now Our Own: An Editorial," *Ladies Home Journal* 36 (October 1919): 1.

21. For a typical expression of the anxiety, see "Boy Delinquency in America, and the War: Discussing the Rumors of Its Increase. Drawing Conclusions from the Facts," *Boys' Workers Round Table* 1, no. 1 (1918): 12–13.

22. Clara E. Laughlin, "The Worst Boy in the United States: Two Chicago Boys Go Traveling to 27 Cities for Him and Find Him," *Ladies' Home Journal* 36 (October 1919): 7–8, 191–92.

23. Laughlin, "Worst Boy in the United States."

24. Laughlin, "Worst Boy in the United States."

25. Laughlin, "Worst Boy in the United States."

26. Laughlin, "Worst Boy in the United States."

27. Laughlin, "Worst Boy in the United States."

28. Laughlin, "Worst Boy in the United States."

29. Laughlin, "Worst Boy in the United States."

30. Laughlin, "Worst Boy in the United States."

31. Laughlin, "Worst Boy in the United States."

32. Laughlin, "Worst Boy in the United States." On the reality that tenement homes had little space for children, that children "only got in the way," during the day, see Pamela Riney-Kehrberg, *The Nature of Childhood: An Environmental History of Growing Up in America since 1865* (Lawrence: University Press of Kansas, 2014), 48–49.

Boys, but not girls, would be "turned out into the streets to play." The presence of two boy citizens, along with Jack Robbins, as "delegates," is noted in *Proceedings of the National Housing Association* (New York: National Housing Association, 1918), 428, 432, 438, https://www.google.com/books/edition/Proceedings_of_the_National_Housing _Asso/mgxLAAAAYAAJ?hl=en&kptab=getbook&gbpv=1.

33. Laughlin, "Worst Boy in the United States."

34. Laughlin, "Worst Boy in the United States."

35. Laughlin, "Worst Boy in the United States."

36. Laughlin, "Worst Boy in the United States."

37. Laughlin, "Worst Boy in the United States."

38. Laughlin, "Worst Boy in the United States."

39. Laughlin, "Here's a Real Boys' Club."

40. Laughlin, "'Boy Problem' and How It Has Been Solved." She also published two more pieces, later in 1920, that restated many of the themes of the earlier articles. Both were entitled "Where Boys Rule." See Laughlin, "Where Boys Rule," *Red Cross Magazine*; and Laughlin, "Where Boys Rule," *National Magazine*. See also Laughlin, "Clara E. Laughlin's Article: A Meeting of the Boys' Brotherhood Republic," *Chicago Evening News*, undated (see Clara E. Laughlin Papers, Sophia Smith Collection, Smith College, Northampton, MA, https://findingaids.smith.edu/repositories/2/archival _objects/122437). This last piece concluded with a proposal to make a movie of life in the Boys' Brotherhood Republic. Laughlin, it should be added, wrote scripts (based on novels she had previously published) for at least two early movies. See "Clara E. Laughlin," IMDB, accessed September 16, 2023, https://www.imdb.com/name/ nm0490847/?ref_=fn_al_nm_1. In her manuscript autobiography, "Traveling through Life," she restated her belief in the "innate sense of justice" she found in the BBR. Her associations with them "cheered" her. See "Traveling Through Life," unpublished manuscript, c. 1934, around p. 348, in the Clara E. Laughlin Papers, box 5, Sophia Smith Collection, Smith College, Northampton, MA. Nothing about the BBR or Jack Robbins appeared in her published autobiography; see Clara E. Laughlin, *Traveling through Life, Being the Autobiography of Clara E. Laughlin (Boston, MA: Houghton Mifflin, 1934).*

41. "Give Boys a Chance," *Day Book*, November 5, 1915, 24; Jane Addams, *The Spirit of Youth and the City Streets* (New York: Macmillan, 1909), https://www.gutenberg.org/ files/16221/16221-h/16221-h.htm. On social reformers of the era traveling to Europe to investigate circumstances, including subways and socialized housing, see Daniel T. Rodgers, *Atlantic Crossings: Social Politics in a Progressive Age* (Cambridge, MA: Harvard University Press, 1998).

42. For a description of the institutions that "treated" delinquency, see the *Illinois Crime Survey,* in association with the Chicago Crime Commission Illinois Association for Criminal Justice (Chicago: Illinois Association for Criminal Justice, 1929), 677–706. I have sometimes wondered, and others have asked me, whether I ought to treat Robbins as a carceral or prison abolitionist. The historian in me bridles at this suggestion.

What radical fantasies he contemplated in private, I know not. But his public life and words took the institutions of the law as a given and a continuing presence.

43. The converse was the case as well. According to the BBR, and for Jack Robbins, criminality or "bad boys" were produced by state institutions. The state made boys bad. One might suspect that for Jack Robbins, the socialist, capitalism lurked in the background as a cause. And yet that paradigm was never articulated.

44. Luke Billingham and Keir Irwin-Rogers, "The Terrifying Abyss of Insignificance: Marginalisation, Mattering and Violence Between Young People," *Onati Socio-Legal Series* 11, no. 5 (2021): 1222–49. This second notion of freedom resembles the notions of institutional psychotherapy identified in France with the work of François Tosquelles; see Robcis, *Disalienation.* One might add that the freedom they sought was inevitably enmeshed with the situations in which they found themselves, including the looming presence of a carceral state. Or, to quote the philosopher, Brian Massumi, "Freedom is not about breaking or escaping constraints. It's about flipping them over into degrees of freedom. You can't really escape the constraints. No body can escape gravity. . . . Freedom always arises from constraint—it's a creative conversion of it, not some utopian escape from it" (quoted in Maggie Nelson, *On Freedom: Four Songs of Care and Constraint* [Minneapolis, MN: Greywolf Press, 2021], 155–56).

45. Randolph S. Bourne, *Youth and Life* (Boston, MA: Houghton Mifflin, 1913), 86. I have been helped here by Judith Resnik, "Iconographies of Punishment in Polities Democratic and Not," reflections for the Workshop on the Iconography of Democracy, Princeton University, April 2022, Princeton, NJ. Like the prisoners whose letters Resnik mobilizes, Robbins and they "sought to end a three-hundred-year tradition of state power whose only fetters were its own choices" ("Iconographies," 10). Karen Staller describes the nineteenth-century newsboys' lodging houses, as well as more recent shelters in New York influenced by 1960s counterculture, as shaped by similar values; see Staller, *New York's Newsboys: Charles Loring Brace and the Founding of the Children's Aid Society* (New York: Oxford University Press, 2020).

46. Saidiya V. Hartman, *Wayward Lives, Beautiful Experiments: Intimate Histories of Riotous Black Girls, Troublesome Women, and Queer Radicals* (New York: Norton, 2019).

47. Alexandra Cox, *Trapped in a Vice: The Consequences of Confinement for Young People* (New Brunswick, NJ: Rutgers University Press, 2018), 161.

48. Hartman, *Wayward Lives*, 227–28.

CHAPTER FIVE

1. "Boys' Republic Chief Gives Up Wife for 'Pals,'" *Chicago Daily Tribune*, October 28, 1920, 17.

2. "Boys' Republic Chief Gives Up Wife for 'Pals,'" *Chicago Daily Tribune*, October 28, 1920, 17. According to the *Tribune* article, the marriage occurred on October 19, 1919. In the 1920 census, Jack Robins and Cora Robins were living as tenants in the household of Ignatz Zillner; see Ancestry.com. On her marriage to Maysels, see "Marriages," *Philadelphia Inquirer*, March 2, 1919, 20. Her parents were both born in Russia. Her father owned a cigar factory. Maysels' native language was Yiddish. They lived in Bethlehem, Pennsylvania. She died in 1955. After her death, Alexander Maysels established a scholarship fund in her honor at Lehigh University. See "Lehigh Course Catalog (1964–1965)," Internet Archive, accessed September 17, 2023, https://archive .org/stream/lehighcoursecata1964/lehighcoursecata1964_djvu.txt.

3. On the other hand, the *Tribune* article could have been largely fictional, but strategic, placed to deflect or counter criticism or rumors about Robbins's sexual life. If so, I have not been able to find evidence of that criticism or such rumors. Throughout the rest of his life, Robbins would identify himself as "divorced."

4. Clara Laughlin, "Traveling Through Life," unpublished manuscript, c. 1934, p. 349, box 5, in the Clara E. Laughlin Papers, Sophia Smith Collection, Smith College, Northampton, MA, https://findingaids.smith.edu/repositories/2/archival_objects/ 122455. None of her discussion of Jack Robbins appears in the published version of her autobiography; see Clara E. Laughlin, *Traveling Through Life, Being the Autobiography of Clara E. Laughlin* (Boston, MA: Houghton Mifflin, 1934).

In some ways, Robbins lived relationships with boys that paralleled common Victorian descriptions by and about adult men of their intense relationships with children. See Lewis Perry, *Childhood, Marriage and Reform: Henry Clarke Wright, 1797–1870* (Chicago: University of Chicago Press, 1980), 183–86.

For an example of how the possibly abusive behavior of a boy worker, that is, a man who worked with boys, might be articulated, see a 1918 article surveying the qualifications for workers with boys: "I also want to object to the term 'handler of boys.' The worker had better keep his hands off the boys." To which came the ambiguous response: "The term 'handling boys' was undoubtedly used to mean the disciplining, managing, or dealing with boys. We do not believe that our friend . . . pins his faith to a cure by laying on of hands" ("Around the Table: Qualifications for Workers with Boys," *Boys' Workers Round Table* 1, no. 1 [1918]: 13–14).

For a discussion of the repression of sexualities in the early criminological literature, see Roger A. Salerno, *Boyhood and Delinquency in 1920s Chicago: A Sociological Study of Juvenile Jack-Rollers and Gender* (Jefferson, NC: McFarland, 2017), 43–51.

5. In one announcement for such an event, Reitman described the boys as "delightful" and as a "howling group of healthy, happy playful boys." See Martha Lynn Reis, "Hidden Histories: Ben Reitman and the 'Outcast' Women behind 'Sister of the Road: The Autobiography of Box-Car Bertha'" (PhD diss., University of Minnesota, 2000), 58, ProQuest dissertation no. 9983595. On the memorial event for him at the BBR after his death, see "Reitman, a Friend of Boys, Dead," *Southtown Economist* (Chicago), November 22, 1942, 1, 23. Reitman, an abortionist and a doctor to "hoboes," opened the first venereal disease clinic at Cook County Jail.

6. Ben Reitman to Jack Robbins, undated (summer 1942), Ben Lewis Reitman Papers, box 7, folders 122–37, University of Illinois, Chicago, Special Collections.

7. Reitman to Robbins, undated (summer 1942).

8. Reitman to Robbins, undated (summer 1942). Reitman also wrote Rodney Brandon, the director of the Illinois Department of Public Welfare in a similarly dyspeptic voice (undated, circa summer 1942, Ben Lewis Reitman Papers, box 7, folders 122–37, University of Illinois, Chicago, Special Collections). He told Brandon about Betty Martin, and he invited Brandon to attend a lecture he would give to the boys at the BBR, with a movie, about venereal disease. He obviously found it annoying that Brandon could "earn a living, be important and have the power to refuse to employ talented men." (Evidently, he had been refused a job.) The phrase "generation of vipers" comes from Philip Wylie's popular book of the same name, published in early 1942 (New York: Rinehart).

9. Girls' basketball teams apparently used the gymnasium of the BBR in the 1920s. See "Tri Chi Girls Win 159 Games; Lose Only 4," *Chicago Daily Tribune*, January 1, 1927, 15; Frederic M. Thrasher, *The Gang: A Study of 1,313 Gangs in Chicago* (Chicago: University of Chicago Press, 1927), 222–32; Caroline Bayard Dod Colgate, *Off the Straight and Narrow* (New York: Lee Furman, 1937), 246–47. See also Laughlin's undated daily columns in the *Chicago Evening American*. Historians Mary Odem and Estelle Freedman, in particular, have devoted attention to delinquent girls, though with greater attention to the post-1920 period. See Mary Odem, *Delinquent Daughters* (Chapel Hill: University of North Carolina Press, 1995); and Estelle B. Freedman, *Maternal Justice: Miriam Van Waters and the Female Reform Tradition* (Chicago: University of Chicago Press, 1996). In 1998, the New York Boys' Brotherhood Republic became the Boys and Girls Republic. A similar name change occurred organizationally in Chicago sometime in the 1940s. See Jennifer S. Light, "Building Virtual Cities, 1895–1945," *Journal of Urban History* 38, no. 2 (March 2012): 336–71. At least one anti-suffrage critique of the BBR's search for the worst of the worst boys argued that it substituted a male institutional solution for what should have been the responsibility of mothers: "It proves that the woman is failing in her calling . . . If the boy is falling short of being a good citizen, then there is none to blame but the mother of that boy." See W. G. Canion, *The Truth of the Hour, Not the Truth of Yesterday, Not the Truth of Tomorrow, but the Truth of Today* (Baltimore, MD: W. G. Canion, 1919), 100–02.

10. See Beryl Satter, *Family Properties: Race, Real Estate, and the Exploitation of Black Urban America* (New York: Metropolitan Books, 2009), for a portrait of postwar Lawndale and the transition from Jewish to African American. For a study of the long-term isolation of African Americans in Chicago, see John R. Logan, Weiwei Zhang, and Miao David Chunyu, "Emergent Ghettos: Black Neighborhoods in New York and Chicago, 1880–1940," *American Journal of Sociology* 120, no. 4 (January 2015): 1055–94.

11. Clara E. Laughlin, "The 'Boy Problem' and How It Has Been Solved—by Boys!" *Chamberlin's* (December 1919): 14–16; James Davis to Alfred Stern, April 27, 1927, in the Julius Rosenwald Papers, box 4, folder 10, Hanna Holborn Gray Special Collections Research Center, University of Chicago Library. On Jewish Lawndale, in addition to Satter, *Family Properties*, see Peri E. Arnold, "What Bonded Immigrants to Urban Machines?

The Case of Jacob Arvey and Chicago's 24th Ward," *Journal of Policy History* 25, no. 4 (2013): 463–88; and Erich Rosenthal, "This Was North Lawndale: The Transplantation of a Jewish Community," *Jewish Social Studies* 22, no. 2 (April 1960): 67–82. See also Meyer Levin, *The Old Bunch* (New York: Waking Lion Press, 2012). It may be that the BBR appealed to a distinctive subgroup of poor Jewish boys. I see no direct evidence of any interest in Labor Zionism on the part of the boys. See J. J. Goldberg and Elliot King, eds., *Builders and Dreamers: Habonim Labor Zionist Youth in North America* (New York: Herzl Press, 1993). Saul Alinsky went to the same public high school as did many of the members of the BBR in the 1930s, but he grew up in an Orthodox family and so far as I can tell never had contact with Robbins or the citizens. See Sanford D. Horwitt, *Let Them Call Me Rebel: Saul Alinsky—His Life and Legacy* (New York: Knopf, 1989).

12. On the other hand, the BBR was not identified as one of the multitude of strictly ethnically defined youth organizations. See Lizabeth Cohen, *Making a New Deal: Industrial Workers in Chicago, 1919–1930* (New York: Cambridge University Press, 1990), 143–47.

13. Eugene Kinckle Jones, "Problems of the Colored Child," *Annals of the American Academy of Political and Social Science* 98 (November 1921): 142–47; "Do Chicago Boys Want a Boys' Republic?" *Chicago Defender*, October 15, 1921, 5; "Chicago Mayor Greets Big Brothers at Mass Meeting," February 11, 1939, 12; "First Boys Republic Is Founded," October 4, 1939, 24. See also "Boys' Brotherhood Opens First Colored Republic," *Chicago Daily Tribune*, October 5, 1939, 28; "Boys' Republic in Chicago," *California Eagle*, October 19, 1939, 3; "Uncle Greggy's Question Box," *Pittsburgh Courier*, October 28, 1939, 19 (where knowing about the opening of the new "colored republic" in Chicago answered question 3 of a weekly quiz on current events). The articles noted that a building at 3140 Indiana Avenue, in Hyde Park, the former home of a Swedish choral society, was donated by a white attorney, Daniel M. Schuyler.

There is no mention of the BBR in the reports on the Chicago race riot of 1919, probably because the violence occurred on the South Side, which was where most African Americans lived at the time. See Oenone Kubie, "The Swarm: Children in Chicago, 1890–1933" (PhD diss., Brasenose College, University of Oxford, 2018), http://ora.ox.ac.uk/objects/uuid:faa166c5-612f-4de4-b5ff-ec3f62f68745; and Tera Eva Agyepong, *The Criminalization of Black Children: Race, Gender, and Delinquency in Chicago's Juvenile Justice System, 1899–1945* (Chapel Hill: University of North Carolina Press, 2018).

On the other hand, New York's version of the BBR, which came into existence on the Lower East Side in the early 1930s, with the support of the Chicago mothership, was racially integrated from its inception. In 1942, Richard Welling, a member of his board, wrote Harry Slonaker, the supervisor of the New York BBR, at the instigation of Judge Jackson of New York's Juvenile Court. Judge Jackson wondered about starting a BBR "among the Harlem Negroes." The crime problem there was, he thought, much more serious than that on the Lower East Side, where the New York BBR was located. See Richard Welling to Harry Slonaker, April 6, 1942, in the Harry E. Slonaker papers, History San Jose Research Library, San Jose, CA.

14. James Davis to Julius Rosenwald, October 13, 1925; and Spencer Williams to Julius Rosenwald, December 31, 1926, Julius E. Rosenwald Papers, box 4, folder 10, Hanna Holborn Gray Special Collections Research Center, University of Chicago Library. See also various articles in "Scrapbook Relating to Edmund Daniel Hulbert," Chicago Historical Society—for example, "Erect a Memorial to Mr. Hulbert" (undated and unsourced). After his death, Hulbert's widow continued to pay Robbins the same amount, although it is not clear how long she did so. In 1951, papers around the country reported that the will of Emily S. Hulbert included a $5,000 bequest to feed pigeons three times a week on two downtown street corners. She also set aside $10,000 of her estimated $550,000 estate to care for and eventually bury her mixed-breed terrier, Judy. The widow left her chauffeur, George Cooper, $20,000 to buy a home, $3,600 a year for life and $10,000 to his family upon his death. She left nothing for Robbins. See "Ex-Winoan Leaves $5000 for Pigeons," *Winona Republic-Herald*, May 11, 1951, 1; "Life's Little Whims, Whirls," *Siskiyou Daily News*, May 8, 1951, 5.

15. "Plan Boys' Clubhouse as Hulbert Memorial," *Chicago Tribune*, November 21, 1923, 6.

16. Julius E. Rosenwald Papers, box 4, folder 10, Hanna Holborn Gray Special Collections Research Center, University of Chicago Library. Mary Barbour Blair was the divorced wife of a coal company executive. Her Boston millionaire father gave her as a dowry her weight in gold. Since she weighed 132 pounds at that time, at the then-gold price, her dowry amounted to $32,558. See Mary Barbour Blair obituary, *New York Daily News*, April 27, 1954, 114. See also "Ex-Wife Wants 'Weight in Gold' Dowry Returned," *Chicago Daily Tribune*, April 17, 1917, 13.

17. James P. Soper to W. J. Parker, March 30, 1927; James P. Soper to Alfred Stern, May 25, 1927; James P. Soper to Frank D. Loomis, November 2, 1927, and November 9, 1927; memorandum with "Offer," April 13, 1927; and "Notes on Boys Brotherhood Republic" (undated), Julius E. Rosenwald Papers, box 4, folder 10; Edwin R. Embree, *Julius Rosenwald Fund: Review of Two Decades, 1917–1936* (Chicago: n.p., 1936); Edwin Rogers Embree and Julia Waxman, *Investment in People: The Story of the Julius Rosenwald Fund* (New York: Harper and Brothers, 1947). On the Chicago Community Trust, see "Our Beginning," Chicago Community Trust and Affiliates, accessed August 20, 2023, https://web.archive.org/web/20161007031158/http://cctfiles.cct.org/about/history. On the end of the story: a table shows that when the Boys' Brotherhood Republic shut down in the early 1960s, $50,000, presumably in the form of real estate, was transferred to the Community Trust from this "expiring institution." See Frank Denman Loomis, *The Chicago Community Trust: A History of Its Development, 1915–1962* (Chicago: Chicago Community Trust, 1962), 43.

18. Julius E. Rosenwald Papers, box 4, folder 10. This gift was one of a very small number of "miscellaneous" gifts made by the Fund. See Embree, *Julius Rosenwald Fund*, 48–49.

19. On the National Information Bureau, see S. M. Cutlip, *Fund Raising in the United States: Its Role in America's Philanthropy* (New Brunswick, NJ: Rutgers University Press, 1965); Clinton Rogers Woodruff, "Making the World Safe for Generosity," *National Municipal Review* 9 (1920): 151–56; Anne L. New, *Service for Givers: The Story of the National Information Bureau* (New York: National Information Bureau, Inc., 1982).

20. Philip Seman to Henry Stewart, March 24, 1921; Spencer Williams, National Information Bureau report, June 13, 1921; William C. Parker to William C. Graves, November 19, 1925; Alfred Stern to "Mother and Dad," January 28, 1927, all in Julius E. Rosenwald Papers, box 4, folder 10, Hanna Holborn Gray Special Collections Research Center, University of Chicago Library.

21. Seman report, 1921, Julius E. Rosenwald Papers, box 4, folder 10; Jack Robbins to W. S. Reynolds, January 8, 1920, 75–107, Children's Home and Aid Society records, box 48, folder 570, University of Illinois, Chicago, Special Collections. Robbins continued: "I am not at all surprised at Mr Seman's statements, knowing that a bigger liar never lived, but I am worried because you allow him to use your name to back up his lies." Reynolds sent a copy of the letter to Myrtle Carpenter. He tried to smooth things over with Jack Robbins, and he evidently hoped that Carpenter would do the same. On the creation of the American Boys' Commonwealth, see James Davis to Alfred Stern, April 15, 1927, in the Julius E. Rosenwald Papers, box 4, folder 10, Hanna Holborn Gray Special Collections Research Center, University of Chicago Library. In postwar Lawndale, after it had become a mostly African American community, the two were merged together in the Chicago Youth Centers. See Johnathon E. Briggs and *Tribune* staff reporter, "Commitment to Needy Kids Spans 50 Years," *Chicago Tribune*, July 3, 2006, https://www.chicagotribune.com/news/ct-xpm-2006-07-03-0607030112 -story.html.

22. Maurice J. Karpf, 1890–1964, was director of Chicago Jewish Charities, president of and professor at the Graduate School of Jewish Social Work, executive director of the Federation of Jewish Welfare Organizations of Los Angeles, and president of the International Conference of Jewish Social Work. See his "Sociologists and Social Workers Meet," *Families in Society* 9, no. 2 (April 1, 1928): 39–45, https://doi.org/10 .1177/104438942800900202; and "The Demoralized Family," *Social Forces* 1, no. 4 (May 1923): 417 (about families profiting from the 1918 influenza). See also "Dr. Maurice J. Karpf, Noted Jewish Social Work Leader, Dies at 73," *Jewish Telegraphic Agency*, April 13, 1964, https://www.jta.org/archive/dr-maurice-j-karpf-noted-jewish-social-work -leader-dies-at-73. Luba Robin Goldsmith mostly practiced in Pittsburgh. She served as national chair of the US Public Health Advisory Committee and was active in public health movements. See Corinne Azen Krause, "Luba Robin Goldsmith," *Shalvi/Hyman Encyclopedia of Jewish Women*, December 31, 1999, https://jwa.org/encyclopedia/ article/goldsmith-luba-robin.

23. See William Forbath, "A Jewish Constitutional Moment," Law and Public Affairs Seminar, Princeton University, April 1, 2019, Princeton, NJ; and Laura Weinrib, "Law, History, and the Interwar ACLU's Jewish Lawyers," draft, forthcoming.

24. Seman's memory seems confused. The *Los Angeles Times* bombing had occurred several years earlier, and the McNamara brothers had confessed and been convicted in 1911. There were, however, related trials of anarchists and labor leaders in Indianapolis and elsewhere in 1914 and 1915.

25. Seman report, 1921.

26. Seman report, 1921.

27. Seman report, 1921.

28. Seman report, 1921.

29. Spencer Williams, National Information Bureau report, June 13, 1921.

30. Spencer Williams, National Information Bureau report, June 13, 1921. At the time, Myrtle Carpenter was the vice president of the Woman's Protective Association, which worked with Chicago's courts. "Women's Protective Club Picks Chiefs," *Chicago Daily Tribune*, April 23, 1921, 19.

31. Parker, who held the office of general secretary in Chicago from 1923 to 1939, had continuing relations with Rosenwald and the Rosenwald fund. He played a central role in the construction of African American YMCAs in Chicago and elsewhere in the United States, with Rosenwald's support. See Mary Janzen, Christopher Ann Paton, Richard Popp, and Anthony Ochoa, eds., "YMCA of Metropolitan Chicago records, 1853–1980: Descriptive Inventory for the Collection at Chicago History Museum, Research Center," Chicago Historical Society, 2013, http://chsmedia.org/media/fa/fa/M -XYZ/YMCA-inv.htm.

32. Spencer Williams, National Information Bureau report, 1921.

33. William C. Parker to William C. Graves, November 19, 1925. The list of people he interviewed included the head at that time of the Glenwood Manual Training School. See Julius E. Rosenwald Papers, box 4, folder 10, Hanna Holborn Gray Special Collections Research Center, University of Chicago Library.

34. William C. Parker to William C. Graves, November 19, 1925.

35. William C. Parker to William C. Graves, November 19, 1925.

36. William C. Parker to William C. Graves, November 19, 1925.

37. Alfred Stern to "Mother and Dad," January 28, 1927, in Julius E. Rosenwald Papers, box 4, folder 10. The Rosenwald papers also include Stern's notes on his 1926 interview with Otto Wander, another boy worker. Wander had worked in 1921 as an "assistant" to Robbins, while managing the short-lived Hyde Park branch of the BBR and also being a student at the University of Chicago. In 1926, Wander recalled that there was much "misconduct" at Hyde Park, because it was "undersupervised." Robbins spent little of his time there. Wander then turned to Robbins and the practices of self-government. Robbins, he thought, continually acted in an advisory role, although he tried to stay in the background. Wander thought the boys that Robbins brought in were "of the very lowest type and toughest gangs." Robbins didn't try to break up the gang organization. Instead, he "adapted" the BBR. Wander shared Parker's sense that Robbins was carrying out "constructive" work, even though "professional social workers would discredit it." Alfred Stern, notes on "Interview with Otto Wander," undated, in Julius E. Rosenwald Papers, box 4, folder 10.

In the 1960s, Wander was a board member of the Chicago Committee to Defend the Bill of Rights, identified as a Communist front organization. In January 1968, he wrote a letter to the *Tribune* critiquing the policy in the city jail barring Christmas presents to prisoners. The letter identified him as a former parole officer and social worker. See Otto Wander, letter to the editor, *Chicago Tribune*, January 7, 1968, 28.

38. Associated Press, "Alfred K. Stern, Spy Suspect; Fled to Prague over Charges," *New York Times*, June 24, 1986, http://www.nytimes.com/1986/06/24/obituaries/ alfred-k-stern-spy-suspect-fled-to-prague-over-charges.html; see "Ex-Chicagoans Red Spies! How Stern and Wife Operated in U.S. Told," *Chicago Tribune*, August 23, 1957, 1.

39. Alfred Stern to "Mother and Dad," January 28, 1927.

40. Alfred Stern to "Mother and Dad," January 28, 1927. The BBR also received funds from other foundations. The Wieboldt Foundation regularly donated $100. One year it gave $300. See "Report and List of Donations 1921–1945," Wieboldt Foundation, accessed August 21, 2023,https://www.google.com/books/edition/ Report/ZWksAQAAMAAJ?hl=en&gbpv=1&dq=wieboldt+foundation+%22boys%27 +brotherhood+republic%22&pg=RA9-PA11&printsec=frontcover.

41. John Higham, *Strangers in the Land: Patterns of American Nativism, 1860–1925* (Newark, NJ: Rutgers University Press, 2002); Katherine Benton-Cohen, *Inventing the Immigration Problem: The Dillingham Commission and Its Legacy* (Cambridge, MA: Harvard University Press, 2018); James R. Grossman, "Great Migration," *Electronic Encyclopedia of Chicago*, 2005, http://www.encyclopedia.chicagohistory.org/pages/545 .html; Claudia Goldin, "America's Graduation from High School: The Evolution and Spread of Secondary Schooling in the Twentieth Century," *Journal of Economic History* 58, no. 2 (1998): 345–74.

42. *Way-Bill* 14–15 (1923–1924): 3; "Doings of the Traffic Clubs," *Traffic World* 33, no. 11 (March 15, 1924): 687 https://archive.org/details/sim_traffic-world_1924-03-15 _33_11/page/686/mode/2up.

43. William Welling, *East Side Story: The Boys Brotherhood Republic's First Fifty Years on New York's Lower East Side* (New York: Boys' Brotherhood Republic of New York, Inc., 1982), 29–37. I have not found the report that Robbins drafted.

44. Welling, *East Side Story*. See also letters and notes from Harry Slonaker to William Welling, undated, in Harry E. Slonaker Papers, History San Jose Research Library, San Jose, CA. Welling's response is dated March 21, 1983. The same story about Slonaker playing craps with a group of boys also appears in Mack Williams, "Johnny Went to Prison," *Washington Evening Star Magazine*, September 20, 1936, 2, 13 (reprinted in *St. Louis Globe-Democrat*, September 20, 1936, 87; *Buffalo Times*, September 20, 1936, 1).

45. Welling, *East Side Story*, 28–35; letters and Notes, Slonaker to Welling, undated. Note that the chronology in Welling's book does not entirely make sense. And Slonaker challenged it in his letters and notes. The influence of the Chicago BBR model apparently extended to the creation of an integrated Boys' Club in Brownsville, in Brooklyn. See Gerald Sorin, *Nurturing Neighborhood: The Brownsville Boys' Club and Jewish Community in Urban America, 1940–1990* (New York: New York University Press, 1990), 112–14.

46. See Alfred Eisenstaedt, photograph of Harry Slonaker, circa 1932, in the Harry E. Slonaker Papers, History San Jose Research Library, San Jose, CA.

47. Mack Williams, "Johnny Went to Prison," *St. Louis Globe-Democrat*, September 20, 1936, 2, 87 (also printed in *Washington Evening Star* and *Buffalo Times*). The contrast between boys (often siblings), one of whom is saved and the other of whom falls to a life of crime and imprisonment, was a standard theatrical and cinematic trope. See Norman Taureg, dir., *Boys Town* (Hollywood: MGM, 1938), https://www.imdb.com/title/tt0029942/; see also Kenneth B. Kidd, *Making American Boys: Boyology and the Feral Tale* (Minneapolis: University of Minnesota Press, 2004), 117–23. The relatively greater success of the New York BBR has continued to the near present. It joined to the Henry Street Settlement, and it has several famous alumni, including the actor and comedian Jerry Stiller and the cartoonist Jack Kirby. See photographs from 1955 in Paul Sorene, "The Boys Brotherhood Republic Tear Up New York City (1955)," *Flashbak*, January 7, 2016, https://flashbak.com/the-boys-brotherhood-republic-tear-up-new-york-city-1955-50824/.

48. Salerno, *Boyhood and Delinquency*; James Bennett, *Oral History and Delinquency: The Rhetoric of Criminology* (Chicago: University of Chicago Press, 1981); Miriam Van Waters, "Juvenile Delinquency and Juvenile Courts," in *Encyclopaedia of the Social Sciences*, vol. 7, edited by Edwin Robert Anderson Seligman (New York: Macmillan, 1932), 528–33; Suzie Guth, *Les Gangs de Jeunes Italo-Americains: Les Forty Two de Chicago* (Paris: L'Harmattan, 2017), 9–140. See generally, Andrew V. Papachristos and James F. Short, "The Chicago School's Contribution to Criminological Theory and Methods," in *The Encyclopedia of Research Methods in Criminology and Criminal Justice, eds. J. C. Barnes and David R. Forde* (Hoboken, NJ: Wiley, 2021), 169–78. I have not been able to find any connection between Saul Alinsky and the BBR, although he graduated from Marshall High School, which was also the school that many of the BBR alumni from the 1930s graduated from. (I wonder if his absence may have resulted from the fact that Alinsky grew up in an Orthodox Jewish family.) See Horwitt, *Let Them Call Me Rebel*. Nor have I found connections between the research of Clifford Shaw and the Institute for Juvenile Research and the BBR. The Chicago Area Project, which succeeded the Institute for Juvenile Research, focused on an area of South Chicago, Russell Square, far away from Lawndale. See Steven Schlossman and Michael Sedlak, "The Chicago Project Revisited," *Crime and Delinquency* 29, no. 3 (July 1983): 398–462. The notion of the distinctiveness of the young criminal and of his trajectory as not particularly defined by the law and the state would be challenged by heterodox sociologists and criminologists a generation later, in the 1960s. See David Matza, *Delinquency and Drift* (London: Routledge, 2017); and Thomas G. Blomberg, Francis T. Cullen, Christoffer Carlsson, and Cheryl Lero Jonson, eds., *Delinquency and Drift Revisited: The Criminology of David Matza and Beyond* (London: Routledge, 2018).

49. See Sheldon Glueck, Social Ethics course teaching notes, 36 (p. 3 of lecture "Prevention of Crime"), in the Sheldon Glueck Papers, Historical and Special Collections, Harvard Law School Library, Cambridge, MA.

50. See "Outward Passenger Lists" (on Bremen, 1930); "Arriving Passenger and Crew Lists," (from Genoa, 1933); same (from LeHavre, 1936), all at Ancestry.com.

51. "Contempt for Law Is Responsible for Crime among Boys," *Omaha Daily Bee*, February 28, 1921, 2. The rest of the article included quotations by Judge Olson, the eugenicist, and by a social worker who blamed crime on the poolrooms.

52. "Appeal to Chicago Jews to Aid in Emigration of German Boys," *Sentinel* 102, no. 9, May 29, 1936, 11.

53. "Boys' Brotherhood Will Extend Helping Hand to Wayward Youths of L.A.," *Los Angeles Evening Post-Record*, May 18, 1925, 2. On Van Waters, see Freedman, *Maternal Justice*, 108–46.

54. A 1938 article in the local Stockton paper crowed that it and Modesto were the only towns outside of New York City and Chicago with operating BBRs. See "Modestans to Form Boys' Brotherhood," *Stockton Evening and Sunday Record*, May 20, 1937, 1; Boys' Brotherhood Republics Are Described at Club Meeting," May 21, 1937, 5; "Plans For Boys' Brotherhood Unit to Be Outlined at Meeting of Exchange Club," *Stockton Independent*, May 20, 1937, 1; May 21, 1937, 3; Irving Martin, "Boys' Brotherhood Republic, *Stockton Evening and Sunday Record*, January 6, 1938, 24; and Irving Martin, "Chest Accepts Boys' Brotherhood Republic," *Stockton Evening and Sunday Record*, February 10, 1943, 16. The BBR "council" in Modesto was successful in having two boys who had been arrested for burglary released to them on probation in September 1937. See *Stockton Evening and Sunday Record*, September 13, 1937, 11; February 9, 1940, 13 (Jack Wherry given an award for organizing.). Other than a request for tools in the Stockton paper (*Stockton Evening and Sunday Record* , November 12, 1938, 6) and the announcement of a magic show at the local high school (*Stockton Evening and Sunday Record*, May 25, 1940, 6), the only other surviving evidence of Modesto activities may be a newspaper article describing an overnight hike that the boys took in May 1938, referenced in Lillian Creisler, "Little Oklahoma: A Study of the Social and Economic Adjustment of Refugees in the Beard Tract, Modesto, Stanislaus County, California" (MA thesis, University of California, Berkeley, 1940), 72, 105. Robbins also visited Los Angeles, shortly after speaking at Stockton; see "Founder of 'Republic' for Boys Visits L.A," *Los Angeles Evening Citizen News*, May 24, 1937, 16.

55. "Boys' Republic to Expand," *Christian Science Monitor*, May 18, 1937, 1. This article, unchanged, found its way to New Zealand; see the *Evening Star* (Dunedin, New Zealand), July 21, 1937, 1.

56. Colgate, *Off the Straight and Narrow*, 245. See also Colgate's obituary, *New York Times*, October 6, 1940, 51, which emphasized her involvement with the New York BBR.

57. *Proceedings of the Attorney General's Conference on Crime Held December 10–13, 1934, in Memorial Continental Hall, Washington, D.C.* (Washington, DC: US Bureau of Prisons, Department of Justice, 1934), 198, 250, https://www.google.com/books/edition/Proceedings_of_the_Attorney_General_s_Co/H3MEAAAAMAAJ?hl=en.

58. I. M. P., "Turns with a Bookworm," *New York Herald Tribune*, February 9, 1930,

L23. The list can be found in the *Napa Valley Register* (February 8, 1930), where Robbins was described as a friend of Jack London and the BBR was said to have branches in other cities in the US and also in Hong Kong. The *Lima Morning Star and Republican Gazette* ran a longer article under the heading "Chicago Now Involved in Controversy over List of Books for Boys' Reading," (January 15, 1930, 3). See Julia F. Carter, "Some Thoughts on Boys' Reading," *Elementary English Review* 7, no. 7 (September 1930): 175–78.

59. "Boys Hear Sleuth," *Chicago Daily Tribune*, January 20, 1923, 7; "'Obey Parents' to Keep Out of Jail, Weil Tells Boys," January 27, 1923, 3; "Marching as Kids in Loyalty Parade," May 25, 1924, 7. On Camp Freedom, see *Life of the Boys' Brotherhood Republic* (Chicago: Boys' Brotherhood Republic, 1938); and "Boys' Republic Will Require Military Drill," *Chicago Daily Tribune*, August 4, 1940, w1.

60. "Drive to Find Boys' Jobs Opens Today in Chicago," *Chicago Daily Tribune*, January 14, 1940, 13; "13 Youths Apply for Every Job in Boys Drive," February 11, 1940, w4.

61. "Dr. Cook Is Given Director's Post by Boys' Republic," *Chicago Daily Tribune*, March 21, 1930, 6. See Cook's obituary, *New York Herald Tribune*, August 6, 1940, 15.

62. "Swing Music Harmless, Police Chiefs Contend," *Toronto Globe and Mail*, August 31, 1938, 4.

63. *Life of the Boys' Brotherhood Republic.*

64. *Life of the Boys' Brotherhood Republic.*

65. Ernest Thompson Seton, *Two Little Savages* (New York: Doubleday, 1903). See Jack Robbins, "Boy Scouts Evil," *Day Book*, December 20, 1915, 27. In his attack on the Boy Scouts, Robbins had used the fact that Seton had apparently quit the organization because of its inculcation of militaristic practices. Implicitly, if even Seton rejected its militarism, that rejection reinforced Robbins's argument. The same quotation was also on the wall at the New York BBR.

66. *Life of the Boys' Brotherhood Republic.*

67. *Life of the Boys' Brotherhood Republic.*

68. *Life of the Boys' Brotherhood Republic.*

69. "Boys' Republic Will Require Military Drill," *Chicago Daily Tribune*, August 4, 1940, w1; "Anti-Conscript Mayor to Head Boys' Republic," October 27, 1940, w1.

70. "Boys' Republic Pushes $25,000 Fund Campaign," *Chicago Daily Tribune*, April 17, 1943, 16 (by then the campaign was directed by an advertising executive); "Plan Memorial for Judge Lindsey," *Daily Herald*, April 16, 1943, 3; "Boys' Group Plan Judge Lindsey Memorial Ranch," *Oakland Tribune*, April 16, 1943, 7; "Boys Launch Penny Drive to Build Judge Lindsey Memorial," *Ventura County Star*, April 16, 1943, 13; and others.

71. In his draft card, Millman also listed Hamlin Avenue as his home. At the time of his enlistment, he was employed as a "huckster and peddler" (see Ancestrylibrary .com). He became a successful jeweler after the war. See Caroline Stanley, "From Downtown to Freestanding: The Evolution of Shellé Jewelers," November 12, 2014,

https://news.centurionjewelry.com/articles/detail/from-downtown-to-freestanding
-the-evolution-of-shelle-jewelers.

72. "Jewish Council Boys Programs Open This Week," *Chicago Daily Tribune*,
June 29, 1950, W_A2; "Boys Leader Will Address Penn PTA Unit," September 16, 1951,
w3; "Boys' Republic Names New Executive Head," September 19, 1954, w3; "Simmons
Heads Boys Republic," *Chicago Defender*, September 11, 1954, 12; photo of Nat King
Cole and Ruth Brown at Boys' Brotherhood Republic, *Chicago Defender*, June 4, 1955,
22; "Chicagoan Leaves $40,000 for Bias Victims," *Jet* 15, no. 10 (January 8, 1959): 20. On
the postwar history of Lawndale, see Satter, *Family Properties*. In November 1968, the
BBR remained on a list of "community serving organizations" in the Lawndale area.
See "List of Lawndale Community Organizations," Chicago Urban League Records,
University of Illinois, Chicago, Special Collections.

73. "Boys Brotherhood Republic Sets Up Quarters in L.A.," *Los Angeles Daily
News*, October 6, 1943, 10; "Boys' Leader Talks on Delinquency," *Los Angeles Evening
Citizen News*, October 6, 1943, 11; "Goodman Will Aid Costello Youth Foundation
Plan," January 28, 1947, 5; "Youths Win Their Way to Bud, Lou," *Valley Times*, January
18, 1947, 2; "Costello Youth Project to Have 3400 'Citizens,'" January 30, 1947, 16. . Also
in October 1943, San Fernando Valley social agencies held a debate on the radio on
the question whether parents should be held liable for the crimes committed by their
children. Two former "citizens" of the BBR, one by then an attorney, took the negative
side. A police captain and a local civic leader took the positive side. See *Van Nuys Valley Times*, October 1, 1943, 5; "Negro Child Fund Upheld by Court," *New York Times*,
May 12, 1962, 67.

74. Clara Laughlin had suggested back in 1917 or 1918 that a movie be made of the
BBR. "Some day, when we have found a moving picture man able to think of pictures
apart from 'Her Costly Sin, or the Cloak Model's Temptation,'" she said, "the boys and
I are going to work together with any one who can and will help us to put the vital
drama and tremendous principles of the B.B.R. into a film for showing not here in this
country alone, but for export to Russia and other countries which sorely need to know
what ideals of government we have in these United States and how—when they are
properly understood—they fire the idealism of boys like those of the B.B.R." See Clara
E. Laughlin, "Clara E. Laughlin's Article: A Meeting of the Boys' Brotherhood Republic
Reveals the Nourishing Sap of Clean Ideals Surging Through the Roots of Democracy—A Waif Who Joined 'to Get a Chance' and Died for Fair Play," in *Chicago Evening
American* (undated, but probably from 1917 or 1918); see the Clara E. Laughlin Papers,
box 2, folder 2, Sophia Smith Collection, Northampton, MA).

75. *Loretta Young Show*, season 1, episode 25, "Nobody's Boy," directed by Robert
Florey, screenplay by Gene Levitt, aired March 7, 1954, on NBC, https://www.youtube
.com/watch?v=Gugf4Su6mTk; and season 2, episode 16, "Big Jim," written and directed
by Richard Morris, aired December 5, 1954, on NBC, https://www.youtube.com/watch
?v=KZmgMfwgRD4&list=PLeCx1fxAQ3ZvMyHkeIhysEZVz-k9509TQ&index=52.

76. *Loretta Young Show*, season 3, episode 3, "Reunion," directed by Harry Keller, written by Gene Levitt (teleplay) and Jack Robbins (story), aired September 11, 1955, on NBC. The script can be found in box 7 of the Levitt Papers, American Heritage Center of the University of Wyoming, Laramie, Wyoming. On the front, it reads: "Loretta Young Show, Reunion, By Gene Levitt (Prod. #8003 (B-3), 7-7-55." There is, so far as I know, no surviving copy of the televised production. The cast and crew are listed at "The Loretta Young Show: Reunion: Full Cast and Crew," IMDB, accessed September 17, 2023, https://www.imdb.com/title/tt0630938/fullcredits?ref_=tt_ov_st_sm.

77. *Loretta Young Show*, season 3, episode 3, "Reunion."

78. *Loretta Young Show*, season 3, episode 3, "Reunion."

79. *Loretta Young Show*, season 3, episode 3, "Reunion."

80. Jack Robbins to Harry E. Slonaker, February 15, 1954; Harry E. Slonaker to Jack Robbins, March 8, 1954, congratulating him on looking so well on television. Both letters are housed in the Harry E. Slonaker Papers, History San Jose Research Library, San Jose, CA.

81. "Boys Brotherhood Republic Founder Will Be Honored," *Chicago Daily Tribune*, September 28, 1953, b11; "Happy Reunion," September 30, 1953, 5; May 23, 1955, a6; "Honor Boys Brotherhood Founder," May 21, 1956, 18; "Boys' Leader Is Honored at Reunion Fete," December 9, 1957, a6. There had been earlier celebrations. In 1927 and in 1935, parties were held to celebrate the successes of the BBR's original members, those who first met with Jack Robbins in 1914. See "Boys' Republic to Honor Its Original 16 Members," *Chicago Daily Tribune*, January 27, 1935, 5; "Past Day Gang Members Meet," *Los Angeles Times*, February 21, 1927, 11.

82. Nicholas Ray, dir., *Rebel without a Cause* (Hollywood: Warner Brothers, 1955); https://www.imdb.com/title/tt0048545/?ref_=tt_mv_close; Jack Robbins to Harry Slonaker, January 21, 1956, Harry E. Slonaker Papers, History San Jose Research Library, San Jose, CA. Sol "Bulldog" Feldman was a Chicago gangster in the 1930s. On Feldman's girlfriends and wives, see C. V. R. Thompson, *I Lost My English Accent* (New York: Putnam, 1939), 130–32.

83. Jack Robbins to Harry Slonaker, January 21, 1956.

84. "Obituary," *Chicago Daily Tribune*, October 15, 1958, b4.

CHAPTER SIX

1. Like the three trustees, Resnick graduated from Marshall High School. So he almost certainly lived in the same neighborhood as other boys in the BBR. I can find no evidence that he was in the BBR, but it is possible that he too had been a citizen. Resnick served for many years as the "collector" of revenues for the city of Cicero, just to the west of Lawndale. In 1999–2000, when he was around seventy, he was accused and convicted of bribe taking. See "Ex-Town Official Accused of Bribe Taking," *Chicago Daily Tribune*, June 4, 1999, C_A1; "2 from Cicero File Guilty Pleas," March 17, 2000, C_B2. There is another name at the bottom of the will text, just above that of Resnick. The first name is Seymour; the rest of the name is illegible. This Seymour may also have been an attorney, and he gave 6636 N. Washington in Chicago as his address. There were three witnesses to the will, two of whom have names that the lawyers writing the briefs found legible: Irving Slutsky and Allan W. Daird. The third had an illegible name, but lived at 5036 N. Springfield, in Chicago. Jack Robbins's will was appended to Hugh R. Manes's brief to the California Supreme Court, "Petition for Hearing in the Supreme Court of the State of California, in the Matter of the Estate of Jack Robbins . . . ," November 24, 1961 (2d civil no. 25273) (found at the Los Angeles Law Library; also available through the California State Archives).

2. Those parcels are not identified in the will, nor in any of the briefs or opinions in the case. In the 1950 census, Jack Robbins was living at 1133 Mountain View, in San Fernando, California, in the San Fernando Valley. In his January 21, 1956, letter to Harry Slonaker, the letterhead identifies him as living at 2138 Vine Street in Hollywood (Harry E. Slonaker Papers, History San Jose Research Library, San Jose, CA). According to Zillow, the online real estate database, the San Fernando house was built in 1927, and the Hollywood house was built in 1949. Today, the former is valued at $649,000, and the latter is worth almost $1.3 million.

3. Will as appended to Hugh R. Manes's brief to the California Supreme Court, "Petition for Hearing in the Supreme Court of the State of California, in the Matter of the Estate of Jack Robbins . . . ," November 24, 1961 (2d civil no. 25273).

4. "Boys' Brotherhood Republic to Elect New Mayor," *Chicago Tribune*, October 10, 1931, 6. On Herbert K. Abrams, see Alan Derickson, "Inventing the Right to Know: Herbert Abrams's Efforts to Democratize Access to Workplace Health Hazard Information in the 1950s," *American Journal of Public Health* 106, no. 2 (February 2016): 237–45; and Herbert K. Abrams, "Practicing Social Medicine: Memoirs from the Neighborhoods," ca. 2003, unpublished manuscript in Abrams family papers (copy in Alan Derickson's possession). I'm grateful that Professor Derickson shared it with me. See also "Herbert K. Abrams," "Obituary," *New York Times*, July 30, 2006, sec 1, 16; Julius B. Richmond, "Herbert K. Abrams, in Memoriam," *Journal of Public Health Policy 27, no. 4 (January* 2006): 323–26. Albert Soglin, a mathematics teacher, was the lead plaintiff in a suit to challenge Illinois's Broyles Act, which required all state employees to sign a loyalty oath that they were not members of the Communist Party. See "3 Chicagoans Balk at Taking Loyalty Oaths," *Mt. Vernon Register-News*, November 3, 1955, 1, and other papers; for the appeal, see "File Appeal against Decision Upholding Broyles Loyalty Oath Law," *Daily Register* (Harrisburg, IL), June 15, 1956, 8. The challenge failed. The Albert Soglin/Thomas McBride Scholarship was established in memory of Albert Soglin, at Harold Washington College in Chicago, and Thomas McBride, a former HWC student. Albert Soglin's son, Paul Soglin, became a long-serving mayor of Madison, Wisconsin. On Abert Marks, see the obituary in the *Chicago Daily Tribune*, January 13, 1987, A13.

5. Will as appended to Hugh R. Manes's brief to the California Supreme Court, "Petition for Hearing in the Supreme Court of the State of California, in the Matter of the Estate of Jack Robbins . . . ," November 24, 1961 (2d civil no. 25273).

CHAPTER SEVEN

1. O. J. N. Jr., "Right of a Non-Resident to Qualify and Serve in Fiduciary Capacities—An Analysis," *Virginia Law Review* 37, no. 8 (1951): 1137. I am grateful to conversations with John Langbein and Howard Erlanger for helping me with the technical questions involved in determining how and whether a nonresident of a state could serve as an executor or trustee in the state.

2. In 1948, Jack Robbins was listed as one of the survivors after Irvine Robbins's father's death in Los Angeles. See Aaron Robbins obituary, *Los Angeles Times*, April 20, 1948, 15. If Manes was hired by Irvine, it becomes an even greater mystery how Irvine Robbins came into the case. For more on Irvine Robbins, see chapter 8.

3. This interpretation is all inference, because the Los Angeles Superior Court Archives have been unable to find any records or transcripts.

4. There might be answers in a document labelled "Statement of Claim of Interest in Estate" that Mishkin filed on May 4, 1960 with the Superior Court of California and that is referenced in Hugh R. Manes, "Appellant's Opening Brief," *In the Matter of the Estate of Jack Robbins, Deceased*, in the District Court of Appeal, Second Appellate District, filed May 1, 1961, 4 (2d civil no. 25273). But that document has not been found in the archives of the Superior Court in Los Angeles or anywhere else.

5. Manes, "Appellant's Opening Brief." Mishkin's father's mother was born Rabinovitch or Rabinovitz. If Ancestry.com is correct, Manes was wrong; Mishkin's mother was still alive at the time of the litigation. See note 7 below.

6. His career is summarized in IMDB. See "Lee Mishkin," IMDB, accessed August 22, 2023, https://www.imdb.com/name/nm0592767/.

7. Manes, "Appellant's Opening Brief," notes the existence of ten collateral heirs. I am not sure that is correct. There may have been more. On California's rules for intestate succession at the time of the litigation, see Succession Probate Code of 1947, division II, chapter 2: Separate Property, section 225.1, in *Chase California Codes: Containing Civil, Probate, Penal Codes and Code of Civil Procedure, with Multiple Index*, 9th biennial ed. (n.p.: n.p., 1947), 25. Given the absence of issue and of spouse and of parents, as would be the case with Jack Robbins's estate, the property would go to brothers and sisters in equal shares, "and to the descendants of deceased brothers and sisters by right of representation."

Since I have not been able fully to reconstruct the degrees of separation of the collateral heirs to Robbins's estate or how many fit into which category, I can't put a number on what Mishkin would have gotten, if anything, by right of representation, if he'd won the case. From Ancestry.com, I worked out the following: Jack Robbins had at least one sister living, Anna Wigdor. His brother (Irvine's father) had died. I don't know if he had other living siblings. But I suspect not, certainly not any living in North America. So, under California intestacy law, Anna Wigdor would get 50 percent of the trust fund, if it went by intestacy. That might have been worth around $11,000, before subtracting the costs of litigation. (She still had three living children, one of whom benefited in the other part of Robbins's will.) Irvine Robbins had two sisters, Shirley, who married Baskin, and Elka, who married Weiner. Both were alive in 1960. (Indeed, Shirley Baskin was still alive, at 99, in 2019.) I have not been able to determine with certainty who Lee Mishkin's mother's parents were. But she was born a Rabinovitch, and she is identified as the child of Jack Robbins's sister. So, there must have been at least four collateral heirs who were nieces and nephews of Jack Robbins: Irvine Robbins, Shirley Baskin, Elka Weiner, and Mishkin's mother. Each would be perhaps entitled to one-fourth of the remaining 50 percent, by right of representation, after Anna Wigdor, the sister, took her share. The brief notes that Mishkin was one of three children of the child of Robbins's sister. So, whatever he was entitled to could not be more than one-third of what his mother would have inherited, assuming that she could not take (because she had died). But, so far as I can tell from Ancestry.com, his mother was still alive at the time of Robbins's will litigation. So, really, would Lee Mishkin be entitled to anything then? How many others there were, similarly situated (other grandnieces and grandnephews), I don't know.

8. "Military Graduates," *Chicago Daily Tribune*, June 28, 1942, S5. See Fred Okrand, interviewed by Michael Balter, "Forty Years Defending the Constitution," oral history transcript, completed under the auspices of the UCLA Oral History Program, 1984, 373–74, Department of Special Collections, Charles E. Young Research Library, UCLA, Los Angeles, CA, http://content.cdlib.org/view?docId=ft258003n2&brand=oac4. See also Mike Davis and Jon Weiner, *Set the Night on Fire: L.A. in the Sixties* (New York: Verso, 2020), 73–74. He ran for municipal court judge around the time of the Robbins litigation. He was quoted regularly by the newspapers. Note that there is nothing on the Robbins case in the archived Manes papers at UCLA, although he kept meticulous records of the cases of his legal practice. See "Finding Aid for the Hugh R. Manes papers, 1940–2009," Department of Special Collections, Charles E. Young Research Library, UCLA, Los Angeles, CA, accessed August 22, 2023, https://oac.cdlib.org/findaid/ark: /13030/kt6l99s3dp/entire_text/.

9. As a member of the executive committee of the Southern California ACLU, Clore Warne appears regularly in the online ACLU Papers ("The Making of Modern Law: American Civil Liberties Union Papers, Part I: 1912-1990," Gale.com, accessed September 18, 2023, https://www.gale.com/c/making-of-modern-law-american-civil -liberties-union-papers-part-i).

It should be added that the names on all the briefs challenging the trust include Harvey M. Grossman and Ira E. Bilson, along with Clore Warne. Both Bilson and Grossman were young attorneys at the time of the litigation who had recently joined Warne's firm. Grossman had graduated as the top student in his class at UCLA Law School, and he had just finished clerking for Justice William O. Douglas on the US Supreme Court. Bilson had moved from Stanford Law School, where he taught for a time after serving in the JAG corps. He would become a prominent tax attorney. Grossman would later on become the legal director of the ACLU of Illinois.

10. A small selection of Warne's early activities: In 1916, in an article about his opposition to military training in the St. Louis schools, Warne was identified as a "socialist." He participated in the St. Louis branch of the People's Council of America, an organization affiliated with the IWW and other radical groups, formed to carry on pacifist propaganda and to aid conscientious objectors to the draft. Around the same time, he was part of another St. Louis group that met with Roger Baldwin, soon to become a founder of the national American Civil Liberties Union, about starting a local civil liberties bureau. In December 1916 he spoke, as a member of the bar and as a prominent socialist, to a St. Louis Jewish group, on the "socialist perspective" on the World War. In February 1918, when twenty-three IWW members were arrested for advocating sabotage, he represented them. See "Peoples' Council in St. Louis Is Disbanded," *St. Louis Post Dispatch*, August 4, 1918, 4, 18; "Not Trying to Hamper Army Raising, Baldwin Declares," August 26, 1917, 44. In 1919, shortly after having moved to California, he wrote a critique of a critique of Bolshevism, in a letter to the *Santa Ana Register* (May 5, 1919, 5). See also People v. Steelik, 187 Cal. 361, 203 P. 78 (1921). A memoir described Warne as a "hillbilly" member of the National Lawyers' Guild in the 1920s. See Elmer Gertz, *To Life: The Story of a Chicago Lawyer* (New York: McGraw-Hill Book Company, 1974), 97.

11. Both of these reminiscences, by McWilliams and by Monroe, were from the 1970s. See Joel Gardner's interview with Carey McWilliams, dated July 19, 1978:

```
Well, Clore was a very dear friend of mine and a wonderful person,
wonderful person. And he had had—I think fortunately—he had had an
involvement with the socialist movement in St. Louis just preceding
World War I. I think this was very good for him because it gave him
that kind of perspective. He had to come to Los Angeles for reasons
of health. Then when he began to practice law, he became inter-
ested—he was always interested in civil liberties—but he always
had this carry-over of interest, a political interest which he never
lost. And it's to me interesting that people who have been involved,
or who were involved, in the socialist movement in that period
usually retain their interest. It was not something that they
altogether abandoned; they kept [it] up. Through Clore I met Louis
Boudin and other people of this kind, and it was very interesting, a
very valuable experience for me. And we were neighbors of the Warnes
for many years. As a matter of fact, the home that we still own in
Los Angeles was purchased from Clore originally. So he was a neigh-
bor. And we used to discuss everything under the sun every Sunday
morning.

    (Carey McWilliams, interviewed by Joel Gardner, "Honorable in
All Things," oral history transcript, completed under the auspices
of the Oral History Program, 1982, Department of Special Collec-
tions, Charles E. Young Research Library, UCLA, Los Angeles, CA,
https://oac.cdlib.org/view?query=Warne&docId=ft2m3nb08v&chunk.id=0
&toc.depth=1&toc.id=0&brand=oac4&x=18&y=12)
```

See also Eason Monroe, interviewed by Joel Gardner, "Safeguarding Civil Liberties," oral history transcript, completed under the auspices of the Oral History Program, 1974, Department of Special Collections, Charles E. Young Research Library, UCLA, Los Angeles, CA, https://oac.cdlib.org/search?query=Eason%20Monroe;group=Items ;idT=UCb112325361.

12. He also represented the mobster Bugsy Siegel (including Siegel's suit when Loretta Young tried to get out of the purchase of Siegel's house when she realized that it had termites), as well as several in the movie business, including Shirley Temple's divorcing husband and the African American actress Hattie McDaniel, who had won an academy award for *Gone with the Wind*, as well as a union of technical craft workers. See, for a selection: "Police Win Court Fight to Block Red Speaker," *Los Angeles Times*, June 26, 1932, A1; "Screen Union Quiz Launched," November 9, 1937, 1; "Spy Suspects Near Break," December 28, 1938, A1; "Convicted Spy for Russia Freed on Bond of $50,000," March 14, 1939, A1; "Siegel Wins Freedom on Bond of $25,000," April 18, 1941, 3; "Siegel Will Fight Return to Face Brooklyn Indictment," May 13, 1941, 11; "Loretta Young Tells of Hate for Termites," December 14, 1944, A3; "Divorce Granted to Shirley Temple," December 6, 1949, 2; and "Chapter News: Los Angeles and San Francisco," Lawyers Guild Review 1, no. 1 (October 1940): 26–28. Ben Margolis described Warne as a "social democrat"; see Margolis, "Law and Social Conscience," interviewed by Michael S. Balter, 1984–1985, p. 138–39, UCLA Library, Center for Oral History Research, University of California, Los Angeles. Margolis, who helped draft the United Nations charter and who represented many of the Hollywood 10, was recruited by Warne to head the Sleepy Lagoon litigation team. At the time, Margolis was practicing law in northern California but was planning to move to Los Angeles. Margolis was also the law partner of John T. McTernan. On the Sleepy Lagoon case, see Eduardo Obregon Pagan, *Murder at the Sleepy Lagoon: Zoot Suits, Race, and Riot in Wartime L.A.* (Chapel Hill, University of North Carolina Press, 2003). On the other hand, Monroe's reminiscence remarked on Warne's apparently growing anti-communism (see Monroe, "Safeguarding Civil Liberties," 111–12).

13. John T. McTernan was, with Ben Margolis, a constant presence in anti-communist prosecutions. He is the lawyer in several of the most notorious such prosecutions. At one point, he was himself forced to testify before HUAC. See McTernan, "The Role of the Communist Lawyer," testimony before the House Un-American Activities Committee [HUAC], House of Representatives, 86th Congress, February 14, 1959, 55; Davis and Weiner, *Set the Night on Fire*, 474; David Caute, *The Great Fear: The Anti-Communist Purge under Truman and Eisenhower* (New York: Simon and Schuster, 1978), 135; Ellen Schrecker, *Many Are the Crimes: McCarthyism in America* (Boston, MA: Little, Brown, 1998), 348–49; Barbara Enloe Hadsell, "Celebration of a Radical Life: John McTernan (1910–2005)," *Guild Practitioner 62* (2005): 53–64; Scott L. Cummings, "Privatizing Public Interest Law," *Georgetown Journal of Legal Ethics* 25, no. 1 (Winter 2012): 1–90.

14. Evidently, the FBI had an informer within the ACLU of Southern California. See "FOIA: ACLU Los Angeles 14," Federal Bureau of Investigation, January 4, 2012, at:

https://archive.org/stream/foia_ACLU-Los_Angeles-14/ACLU-Los_Angeles-14_djvu
.txt. The informer, unfortunately, reported nothing about the internal deliberations.

15. On the activism and relative radicalism of the southern California ACLU (certainly as compared to the national office in the 1950s and early 1960s), see Davis and Weiner, *Set the Night on Fire*, 5. For a general history of the national ACLU, see Laura Weinrib, *The Taming of Free Speech: America's Civil Liberties Compromise* (Cambridge, MA: Harvard University Press, 2016).

16. The official history of the Southern California ACLU emphasizes that it had always identified civil rights and "minority rights" as central features of its mission. Beginning in 1926, it had made as its motto: "A threat to any minority is a threat to all minorities." And it had long participated in challenges to Japanese internment and anti-Japanese discrimination, to Mexican American school segregation, and to racially restrictive covenants. See "From 1941–1960," ACLU Southern California, accessed August 23, 2023m https://www.aclusocal.org/en/1941-1960.

17. On the history of the Southern California ACLU, which famously began with the arrest of Upton Sinclair in 1923 for reading the Declaration of Independence and the First Amendment on the docks of San Pedro during a strike (after his arrest, he decided to fund the office), see Judy Kutulas, "Matters of Principle," ACLU, July 23, 2019, https://www.aclu.org/issues/free-speech/matters-principle; and Martin Zanger, "Politics of Confrontation: Upton Sinclair and the Launching of the ACLU," *Pacific Historical Review* 38, no. 4 (November 1969): 383–406. One argument for imagining this case as a setup, or as a constructed test case involving lawyers on both sides who shared the same goals, might be that if one looked at the case in terms of its material stakes, no one would be hurt one way or another. The case could be treated as a law-school examination hypothetical, one without harsh consequences. If the will were enforced, a Negro child or two would benefit in a small but perhaps life-changing way. If the will were not enforced, no one's life would be changed for the worse. But for the lawyers in the ACLU, victory could mean a new frame of analysis and an opportunity to establish the significance of the Southern California ACLU for race relations, at least in California.

18. Throughout the rest of this chapter, I will be using the language that the lawyers used: "Negro" and "Negro children." The word "Negro" is archaic and awkward, but an inevitable presence in that historical moment.

19. The Southern California ACLU was much involved in the case of Caryl Chessman, which led them toward the position that the death penalty constituted cruel and unusual punishment under the Eighth Amendment. See Okrand, "Forty Years Defending the Constitution," 357–63. On the broader history of "conditions of imprisonment," see Judith Resnik, *Impermissible Punishments: The Problem Prison Poses in Democracies* (Chicago: University of Chicago Press, forthcoming 2025). On the history of civil disobedience as a cultural and intellectual stance, see Lewis Perry, *Civil Disobedience: An American Tradition* (New Haven, CT: Yale University Press, 2013). On its contested legal status as a practice, see Abe Fortas, *Concerning Dissent and Disobedience* (New York: World Publishing, 1968).

20. All the briefs are available through the Los Angeles Law Library. There are also copies in the California State Archives. The following briefs appear in chronological order: "In The Matter of the Estate of Jack Robbins, Deceased," appeal from Superior Court of Los Angeles County to District Court of Appeal, Second Appellate District; Hugh R. Manes, "Appellant's Opening Brief," filed May 1, 1961; Pacht, Ross, Warne, and Bernhard, "Respondent's Brief," filed [no date listed]; [Manes], "Petition for Rehearing," filed May 1, 1961; Pacht, Ross, Warne, and Bernhard, "Answer to Petition for Rehearing," filed November 3, 1961; Hugh R. Manes, "Appellant's Reply Brief," filed June 26, 1961. Then, in the Supreme Court of the State of California: Hugh R Manes, "Petition for Hearing," filed November 24, 1961; John T. McTernan, "Application for Permission to File Brief Amicus Curiae and Brief Amicus Curiae," filed [no date]; Pacht, Ross, Warne, and Bernhard, "Answer to Petition for Hearing and Answer to Brief Amicus Curiae," filed December 5, 1961. The published cases are found at In Re Estate of Robbins, 16 Cal. Rptr. 412 (District Court of Appeal, 2d District, 1961) and In Re Robbins' Estate, 57 Cal. Rep. 2d 765, 371 P2d 573 (1962) (reversing16 Cal. Rptr. 412).

21. The earlier procedural history is summarized in Manes's brief to the California District Court of Appeal (see Manes, "Appellant's Opening Brief"). On the Field case, see Albert E. Kahn, "The Crime against Jean Field," in United States Senate, *Communist Activity in Mass Communications: Hearing before the Subcommittee to Investigate the Administration of the Internal Security Act, . . . of the Committee on the Judiciary, United States Senate, Eighty-Fifth Congress, Second Session*, 3 vols. (Washington, DC: Government Printing Office, 1958), 286–88. John T. McTernan served as Jean Field's attorney; see "Committee Aids Woman Fighting Children's Loss," *Los Angeles Times*, March 13, 1951, 16; "'Treason' Laid to Mother in Battle for Children," December 14, 1950, 18. Once, when asked if he knew any Mexicans, Schweitzer replied that he knew the gardeners who worked around the courthouse. See Ian F. Haney Lopez, *Racism on Trial: The Chicano Fight for Justice* (Cambridge, MA: Harvard University Press, 2003), 98.

22. Manes, "Appellant's Opening Brief." Cy pres is the judicial practice that allows a will, invalid for one or another reason, to be reconstructed, effectively redrafted, in a way that is true to its underlying purposes while not violating law.

23. Jackson v. Phillips, 14 Allen 539, 96 Mass. 539 (1867). The only notice given to the second trust in Jackson that I have found is in "Trusts—Charitable Trusts: Illegal Purpose—In Re Robbins' Estate, 57 Cal. Rep.2d 765, 371 P.2d 573 (1962) 57 Cal. Rep.2d 765, 371 P.2d 573 (1962)," *DePaul Law Review* 12, no. 2 (Spring–Summer 1963): 364–68.

24. N.A.A.C.P. v. Alabama ex rel. Patterson, 357 U.S. 449 (1958), reversing 265 Ala. 349 (1956). See Thomas I. Emerson, *The System of Freedom of Expression* (New York: Random House, 1970), 425–34; and Taylor Branch, *Parting the Waters: America in the King Years, 1954–1963* (New York: Simon and Schuster, 1988), 186–87. On the case as emblematic of the right to anonymity and freedom of association, see Norman Dorson, Paul Bender, and Bert Neuborne, *Emerson, Haber, and Dorson's Political and Civil Rights in the United States, 4th ed., vol. 1* (Boston, MA: Little, Brown, 1977), 301, 739, 931–35; and Anita L. Allen, "Associational Privacy and the First Amendment: NAACP v.

Alabama, Privacy and Data Protection," *Alabama Civil Rights and Civil Liberties Law Review* 1, no. 1 (2011): 1–13.

25. Beilan v. Board of Public Education, 357 U.S. 399 (1958); Communist Party of the United States v. Subversive Activities Control Board, 367 U.S. 1 (1961).

26. "Respondent's Brief," *In the Matter of the Estate of Jack Robbins*, in the District Court of Appeal, Second Appellate District, filed May 26, 1961 (2d civil no. 25273).

27. "Appellant's Reply Brief," *In the Matter of the Estate of Jack Robbins*, in the District Court of Appeal, Second Appellate District, filed June 26, 1961 (2d civil no. 25273).

28. The rest of the reply brief answered more of the claims that Warne had made. The cases did not support the notion that beneficiaries had to be needy. He acknowledged that early California cases invalidated trusts if there were "a mere possibility of a non-charitable use." A later case pointed out that although "no charitable trust is ever free" from the possibility that it might be used by private individuals for private gain, courts retained powers to discipline and to stop such misuse, and the Attorney General had overarching responsibility in that regard. The earlier cases on which Warne relied were decided in a period of public antagonism to charitable dispositions. More recent cases moved "gradually but perceptively" in the direction of "greater liberality toward interpretation in favor of charitable intention" (referencing Moore's Estate, 190 Cal. App. 2d 833, 12 Cal. Rptr. 436 (District Court of Appeal, 4th, 1961)). And a charitable "although political" intention was certainly disclosed by the terms of the Robbins trust.

29. In re Estate of Robbins, 16 Cal. Rptr. 412 (District Court of Appeal, 2d District, 1961). John Joseph Ford taught at Loyola Law School, where his father had been the founding dean.

30. The treatises were Austin Wakeman Scott, *The Law of Trusts*, 2nd ed. (Boston, MA: Little Brown, 1956), 4: section 377; American Law Institute, *Restatement of the Law, Second: Trusts*, 2nd ed. (St. Paul, MN: American Law Institute Publishers, 1959), § 377 b.

31. [Manes], "Petition for Rehearing," filed May 1, 1961, to the District Court of Appeal; Pacht, Ross, Warne, and Bernhard, "Answer to Petition for Rehearing," filed November 3, 1961, to the District Court of Appeal.

32. Manes, "Petition for Hearing," filed November 24, 1961, to the California Supreme Court.

33. Manes, "Petition for Hearing," filed November 24, 1961, 10–11, 13, 15, 19.

34. Manes, "Petition for Hearing," filed November 24, 1961, 26.

35. Bailey v. Patterson, 369 U.S. 31 (1962); vacating, 199 F. Supp. 595 (S.D. Miss, 1961), which included the appendix. John T. McTernan to Miss Constance Baker Motley, January 18, 1962, in ACLU of Southern California Papers, collection 900, box 973, 67, UCLA Special Collections, Los Angeles, CA.

36. John T. McTernan to Congress of Racial Equality, December 20, 1961; and John T. McTernan to Robert L. Carter, Esquire, December 15, 1961, both in ACLU of Southern California Papers, collection 900, box 973, 67, UCLA Special Collections, Los Angeles, CA; John T. McTernan, David B. Finkel, A. L. Wirin, and Fred B. Okrand, "Application for Permission to File Brief Amicus Curiae in Support of Petition for Hearing and Brief

Amicus Curiae in Support of Petition for Hearing, of American Civil Liberties Union, Southern California Branch," undated, available through the Los Angeles Law Library and the California State Archives. The exchange of letters makes it apparent that Mc-Ternan drafted the brief, but it was also signed by David B. Finkel, A. L. Wirin, and Fred Okrand.

37. John T. McTernan to Congress of Racial Equality, December 20, 1961, John T. McTernan to Robert L. Carter, Esquire, December 15, 1961.

38. Melvin Wulf to Fred Okrand, January 4, 1962, ACLU of Southern California Papers, collection 900, box 973, 67, UCLA Special Collections, Los Angeles, CA. See Jack Greenberg, *Race Relations and American Law* (New York: Columbia University Press, 1959). Maria Marcus, the assistant counsel working with Robert Carter of the NAACP, made the same suggestion. If the book were not available in Los Angeles, he could send to the Crisis Book Shop in New York City. On January 4, 1962, she also sent him a list of cases. See also NAACP Papers, Robert L. Carter general correspondence, Re-Ri, folder 001475-004-0581, part 22: Legal Department Administrative Files, 1956–1965.

39. McTernan et al., "Application for Permission to File Brief Amicus Curiae in Support of Petition for Hearing and Brief Amicus Curiae in Support of Petition for Hearing, of American Civil Liberties Union, Southern California Branch."

40. McTernan et al., "Application for Permission to File Brief Amicus Curiae in Support of Petition for Hearing and Brief Amicus Curiae in Support of Petition for Hearing, of American Civil Liberties Union, Southern California Branch."

41. McTernan et al., "Application for Permission to File Brief Amicus Curiae in Support of Petition for Hearing and Brief Amicus Curiae in Support of Petition for Hearing, of American Civil Liberties Union, Southern California Branch." The cases are Shelley v. Kraemer, 334 U.S. 1 (1948); Brown v. Board of Education of Topeka, 347 U.S. 483 (1954); Yick Wo v. Hopkins, 118 U.S. 356 (1886).

42. Andrea Gibbons, *City of Segregation: 100 Years of Struggle for Housing in Los Angeles* (New York: Verso, 2018); Davis and Weiner, *Set the Night on Fire.*

43. McTernan et al., "Application for Permission to File Brief Amicus Curiae in Support of Petition for Hearing and Brief Amicus Curiae in Support of Petition for Hearing, of American Civil Liberties Union, Southern California Branch."

44. Pacht, Ross, Warne, and Bernhard, "Answer to Petition for Hearing and Answer to Brief Amicus Curiae in support of Petition for Hearing . . . ," filed December 5, 1961, on appeal to California Supreme Court.

45. Pacht, Ross, Warne, and Bernhard, "Answer to Petition for Hearing and Answer to Brief Amicus Curiae in support of Petition for Hearing . . . ," filed December 5, 1961, on appeal to California Supreme Court.

46. 57 Cal. Rep. 2d 765, 371 P2d 573 (1962). One of the few comments on the case in the law-review literature criticizes the decision for not attending to the identification of the children as "Negro." The author suggested that the trust might be suspect because of its limitation by race. See James R. Bridges, "Note: Charitable Trusts: The Liberal Construction Rule and Public Policy—*In the Matter of Estate of Robbins* (Cal. 1962)," *California Law Review* 50, no. 5 (December 1962): 885–90. On Traynor's significance as a policy-oriented judge, see Stewart Macaulay, "Justice Traynor and the Law of Contracts," *Stanford Law Review* 13 (July 1961): 812–64.

47. 57 Cal. Rep. 2d 765, 371 P2d 573 (1962).

48. 57 Cal. Rep. 2d 765, 371 P2d 573 (1962). The Mississippi case is Westbrook v. Mobile & O.R. Co., 66 Miss. 560 (1889). I'm guessing this case would not be found on the list of Mississippi cases and laws that McTernan wanted to present to the court.

49. 57 Cal. Rep. 2d 765, 371 P2d 573 (1962). One might imagine that Traynor was also implicitly drawing parallels between illegitimate children (bastards) and the Negro children who were to benefit from the trust. Just as once it had been law that illegitimates should not inherit, so as not to reward the sexual misconduct of parents, so it might have been for the imagined beneficiaries of Robbins's trust. In both instances, "innocent childhood" served as a solvent, made the parents' conduct irrelevant. See In re Garcia's Estate, 34 Cal. 2d 419, 210 P.2d 841 (1949); and Estate of Lund, 26 Cal. 2d 472, 159 P.2d 643 (1945) (Traynor dissented on other grounds). In *Levy v. Louisiana*, the exclusion of illegitimate children from inheritance rights was declared unconstitutional (391 U.S. 68 (1968)).

50. I am grateful to Judith Resnik and to Michael Grossberg for helping me toward this formulation of Traynor's purposes. For his later work as a carceral reformer and as a defender of prisoner rights, see chapter 20 of Resnik's *Impermissible Punishments*. On his pragmatic methods of decision-making, see John W. Poulos, "The Judicial Philosophy of Roger Traynor," *Hastings Law Review* 46, no. 6 (August 1995): 1643–722, at 1697:

```
[The judge] cannot remain disoriented forever, his mind suspended
between alternative passable solutions. Rather than to take the easy
way out via one or the other, he can strive to deepen his inquiry and
his reflection enough to arrive at last at a value judgment as to
what the law ought to be and to spell out why. In the course of doing
so he channels his interest in a rational outcome into an interest
in a particular result. In that limited sense he becomes result-
oriented, an honest term to describe the stubbornly rational search
for the optimum decision. Would we have it otherwise?
```

On his concern for and engagement with young lawbreakers, see Roger J. Traynor, "Lawbreakers, Courts, and Law-Abiders," *Missouri Law Review* 31, no. 2 (Spring 1966): 181–208. G. Edward White, in *The American Judicial Tradition*, explores the ways that Traynor's rhetoric of restraint and process gave an impression of inevitability and common sense to transformative rulings (3rd ed. [New York: Oxford University Press, 2007], 243–66).

CHAPTER EIGHT

1. Associated Negro Press (ANP) press releases, April 23, 1962, and May 30, 1962; "Negro Child Fund Upheld by Court," *New York Times*, May 27, 1962, 67. The ANP served African American newspapers, and it was located in Chicago. On the ANP, see

Lawrence Daniel Hogan, "Associated Negro Press," *Electronic Encyclopedia of Chicago*, 2005, http://www.encyclopedia.chicagohistory.org/pages/1734.html.

2. ANP press release, May 30, 1962.

3. "Chicagoan Leaves $40,000 for Bias Victims, *Jet*, January 8, 1959, 20; "Heir Contests $22,500 Will for Bias Victims," May 10, 1962, 20; "Uphold $22,250 Trust Fund for Negro Children," June 7, 1962, 4; "Attacks Will Fund for Negro Children of 'Political Victims,'" *Oklahoma City Daily Law Journal-Record*, April 21, 1962, 1, and "California Supreme Court Upholds Trust Fund for Negro Children," June 28, 1962, 1; "Court Upholds Right to Differ," *Oakland Tribune*, May 22, 1962, 6." See also "Legacy to 'Political Victims' Defended," *Open Forum, Newsletter of the ACLU of Southern California* 39, no. 1 (January 1962): 1; "Unique Legacy Held 'Benefit to Society,'" *Open Forum, Newsletter of the ACLU of Southern California* 39, no. 6 (June 1962): 1.

4. I have written to some of the children of the trustees. The California State Archives (secretary of state records) and the LA Superior Court Archives have found nothing. The search continues.

5. California then and now places no restriction on the capacity of nonresidents to serve as trustees. But it did then require a nonresident trustee to come to the state and submit to the jurisdiction of the court. See O. J. N. Jr., "Right of a Non-Resident to Qualify and Serve in Fiduciary Capacities—An Analysis," *Virginia Law Review* 37, no. 8 (1951): 1137.

6. Scott Cohen, *Meet the Makers: The People behind the Product* (New York: St. Martin's Press, 1979), 56–63; "Ice Cream Store Owners Fined," *Metropolitan Pasadena Star-News*, December 5, 1947, 11; "New Businesses on File in Various Valley Locations," *Van Nuys News*, May 12, 1949, 8; "PTA Activities," *Los Angeles Evening Citizen News*, May 7, 1953, 4; and elsewhere. Irving Robbins was the head of the Honor Lodge of the Encino B'nai B'rith in 1966 and 1967. Apparently he and his brother-in-law and business partner, Burton Baskin, were also charter members of the organization. See "Rites Slated Today for Ice Cream Store Founder," *Valley News* (Van Nuys, California), December 26, 1967, 13. Later on he served as the Honor Lodge's program chairman. See "B'Nai B'Rith Honor Lodge Elects New Officers' Slate," *Van Nuys News*, June 8, 1972, 127. In 1970, he and his wife established the Irvine and Irma Robbins Foundation, although it may not have been funded (around one million dollars) until after his death in 2008. See "Private Foundations Release for March," IRS, 2010, https://archive.org/stream/IRS990–2010_03_PF/manifest.2010_03_PF.txt. In 2012–2014, under the direction of his daughter, D. Veit, it made a large contribution to the Braille Institute and later to the International Rescue Foundation. See Braille Institute, *Imagining the Future*, annual report (Los Angeles, CA: Braille Institute, 2014), https://www.brailleinstitute.org/wp-content/uploads/2014/01/Light-2014.pdf; and Population Media Center, *Storytelling for Good: Improving the Health and Well-Being of People*, annual report (South Burlington, VT: Population Media Center, 2012), https://issuu.com/globalpopulationspeakout/docs/2012-annual-report-final.

7. On the founding of the Boys' Club, see "Club History," Boys and Girls Club of

San Fernando Valley, accessed August 24, 2023, https://www.bgcsfv.org/club-history; Crystal Jackson, *The Entrance: Pacoima's Story* (Los Angeles, CA: BAIT-CAL, 2019), 228–32; *Van Nuys Valley News*, March 16, 1973, 15; Irvine Robbins obituary, *Desert Sun*, May 7, 2008; "Lodge Commended," *Los Angeles Times*, September 26, 1968, SF10 (noting that the Boys' Club was sponsored by the Honor Lodge).

8. Sandy Banks, "Black Middle Class: Getting Used to Isolation," *Los Angeles Times*, August 25, 1982, B1. Joe Louis, the boxer, lent his name to the project. As of 1950, a two-bedroom house sold for $7400; see "Joe Louis' New Village Opened," *Los Angeles Times*, March 19, 1950, D2; "Pacoima Area Revamped by Awakened Citizenry: Los Angeles Program for Slum Clearance," May 18, 1955, 1. A later column emphasized the complexity of the community; see "Pacoima Striving to Erase Racial Feeling: Negroes, Mexican-Americans and Whites Stress Harmony Existing in Community," *Los Angeles Times*, February 13, 1966, sf-1. For a short survey of Pacoima's history, emphasizing environmental issues, see Stacy Warren, Robert Sauders, and Anna Dvorak, "For Anna: After Critical GIS, What Next?" *Canadian Geographer* 64, no. 4 (Winter 2020): 529–42; and Laura R. Barraclough, *Making the San Fernando Valley* (Athens: University of Georgia Press, 2011), 131–33.

9. Jackson, *Entrance*, 274–90; Mike Davis and Jon Weiner, *Set the Night on Fire: L.A. in the Sixties* (New York: Verso, 2020), 520–23; Earl Anthony, *The Time of the Furnaces* (New York: Dial, 1971), 47.

10. Personal communication with Nicole Chase, director of the Boys and Girls Club of the San Fernando Valley, September 26, 2022.

11. "Press Releases –03/22/1973-03/31/1973," box P14, in collection "Reagan, Ronald: Gubernatorial Papers, 1966-74: Press Unit," Ronald Reagan Presidential Library Digital Collections, https://www.reaganlibrary.gov/public/digitallibrary/gubernatorial/pressunit/p14/40-840-7408623-p14-009-2017.pdf; "B'Nai B'Rith Lodge Sponsors Boys Club," *Los Angeles Times*, April 2, 1967, sf_a9; "Lodge Commended," September 26, 1968, sf10. 113 Cong. Rec. S30684 (October 31, 1967) (remarks of the Hon. James C. Corman, on the service of the Honor Lodge of B'nai B'rith). According to Corman, the Honor Lodge was contributing $16,000–17,000 a year, the majority of its needs, to the annual budget of the Boys Club of Pacoima. One obituary mentioned that Robbins was "instrumental in starting and funding a Boys Club in Pacoima (now the Boys and Girls Club of the San Fernando Valley), positively impacting thousands of young people." See "Irvine Robbins," obituary, *Desert Sun*, May 7, 2008, https://m.legacy.com/ns/obituary.aspx?n=irvine-robbins&pid=109159880. (One should add that Southern California postwar newspapers covered Irvine Robbins's attendance at several charitable events as he became a wealthy man. But none of those charities involved juvenile delinquency or boys' clubs or anything similar. "Bad boys" were not connected to his charitable practice until the later 1960s, until the years after he became the administrator of his uncle's estate.)

12. The closest I can get to an articulation of commitment on Irvine Robbins's part to carry out his uncle's wishes may be found in a column from the African American newspaper, the *Los Angeles Sentinel*, written after Burton Baskin's death. The article gets almost everything wrong, except, perhaps, for the notion that Irvine Robbins believed that the will should be carried out to the letter. "After World War II, Baskin teamed with his brother-in-law, Irvine Robbins, and opened their first ice cream shop in Glendale. Success grew for both men. Then Robbins died [wrong Robbins]. In his will he stipulated that certain portions of his bequeathed interests should be placed in a special fund—to aid poverty-stricken Negroes in fighting their civil rights cases in the nation's courts. A big legal fight shaped up in Chicago [?] over the will, but finally it was decided that Robbins' will should be carried out to the letter." And so it was. See Bill Lane, "The Inside Story," *Los Angeles Sentinel*, January 11, 1968, C9.

13. "Shaken Valley State Seeks Peace Formula," *Los Angeles Times*, December 8, 1968, sf_a1; "Secret Talk Brings Valley State Peace," January 11, 1969, a1; "Minority Pair Head Program at Valley State," January 21, 1969, e1; "How Valley State Moved to 'New Kind of Education,'" February 2, 1969, b1. The leaders of the Valley State 19 were paroled after a few months in state prison, including time in a maximum-security penitentiary. On Earl Anthony's life both as a Black Panther Party member and an FBI informant, see M. Keith Claybrook, Jr., "Earl Anthony and the Black Panther Party," *Black Perspectives*, August 11, 2022, https://www.aaihs.org/earl-anthony-and-the-black-panther-party/. See also "Students Oppose, Support Valley State Administration," *Valley News* (Van Nuys, California), November 17, 1968, 18; Jackson, *Entrance*, 265–88; Davis and Weiner, *Set the Night on Fire*, 520–23; Anthony, *Time of the Furnaces*. After the mid-1970s, as the community became increasingly Latino, it suffered first from drugs and then from gang-related violence. See Stefano Bloch and Susan A. Phillips, "Mapping and Making Gangland: A Legacy of Redlining and Enjoining Gang Neighbourhoods in Los Angeles," *Urban Studies* 59, no. 4 (2022): 750–70.

14. In the 1980s it became the Boys and Girls Club of the San Fernando Valley.

15. Judy Kutulas, "Matters of Principle," ACLU, July 23, 2019, https://www.aclu .org/issues/free-speech/matters-principle; "History," ACLU Southern California, accessed August 24, 2023, https://www.aclusocal.org/en/about/history. See also Davis and Weiner, *Set the Night on Fire*; Risa Goluboff, *Vagrant Nation: Police Power, Constitutional Change, and the Making of the 1960s* (New York: Oxford University Press, 2016).

16. Dorothy Healey and Maurice Isserman, *Dorothy Healey Remembers: A Life in the American Communist Party* (New York: Oxford, 1990), 214–16; Davis and Weiner, *Set the Night on Fire*, 474–75; Dale E. Hanst, "Presentation of the Loren Miller Legal Services Award to John T. McTernan," *Guild Practitioner* 41, no. 3 (Summer 1984): 95–96.

17. . Clore Warne, "Book Review," *Law in Transition* 23, no. 1 (Spring 1963): 81–90. The right of association would be used for contradictory purposes, in those years. For its use as a challenge to equality and civil rights, see Herbert Wechsler, "Toward Neutral Principles of Constitutional Law," *Harvard Law Review* 73, no. 1 (November 1959): 1–35.

18. Eason Monroe, interviewed by Joel Gardner, "Safeguarding Civil Liberties," oral history transcript, 111–12, completed under the auspices of the Oral History Program, 1974, Department of Special Collections, Charles E. Young Research Library, UCLA, Los Angeles, CA, https://oac.cdlib.org/search?query=Eason%20Monroe;group =Items;idT=UCb112325361.

19. Elaine Woo, "Hugh R. Manes Dies at 84; Lawyer Fought for Victims of Police Misconduct," *Los Angeles Times*, June 18, 2009, https://www.latimes.com/local/ obituaries/la-me-hugh-manes18-2009jun18-story.html.

20. Note the sale of Baskin-Robbins to United Fruit in the late 1960s, though Irvine continued to be involved, even after the death of Baskin; see "Baskin, Burton, and Robbins, Irvine," *Encyclopedia.com*, accessed August 24, 2023, https://www.encyclopedia .com/education/economics-magazines/baskin-burton-robbins-irvine; *Metropolitan Pasadena Star-News*, December 5, 1947, 11; Joseph J. Fucini and Suzy Fucini, *Entrepreneurs: The Men and Women behind Famous Brand Names and How They Made It* (Boston: G. K. Hall, 1985), 32–34.

21. Dennis Hevesi, "Irvine Robbins, Ice Cream Entrepreneur and a Maestro of 31 Flavors, Dies at 90," *New York Times*, May 7, 2008, https://www.nytimes.com/2008/05/ 07/business/07robbins.html. See also "Ocean Robbins," Oceanrobbins.com, accessed August 24, 2023, https://www.oceanrobbins.com/; "John Robbins," Johnrobbins .info, accessed August 24, 2023, https://www.johnrobbins.info/; "About Ocean," Oceanrobbins.com, accessed August 24, 2023, https://www.oceanrobbins.com/bio/; *Santa Cruz Sentinel*, March 29, 1989, 34–35. John Robbins lost a fortune by investing with Bernie Madoff. He regained wealth after writing another best-selling book. See Jerry Oppenheimer, *Madoff with the Money (Hoboken, NJ: John* Wiley and Sons, 2009), 224–29.

22. "Lee Mishkin," IMDB.com, accessed August 24, 2023, https://www.imdb.com/ name/nm0592767/; Dan Sarto, "Academy Award Winning Animator Lee Mishkin Passes Away," *Animation World Network*, June 26, 2001, https://www.awn.com/news/ academy-award-winning-animator-lee-mishkin-passes-away; "About Us," Vancouver Institute of Media Arts, accessed August 24, 2023, https://www.vanarts.com/about -us/; obituary, *Los Angeles Times*, July 1, 2001.

23. "Lee Mishkin," IMDB.com; Lee Mishkin, dir., *Is It Always Right to Be Right?* (Stephen Bosustow Productions: n.p., 1970), short animated film, 7:50, uploaded to YouTube by Jérôme Labbé, May 26, 2013, https://www.youtube.com/watch?v= NM2KvijwlNE. I have not found viewable copies of the other 1970 cartoons. Schmidt taught at UCLA. The film was produced by Steven Bosustow.

CONCLUSION

1. "Boy Republic Chapter Is Plan of L.A. Visitor," *Los Angeles Evening Express*, June 9, 1925, 9; "Boys' Brotherhood Will Extend Helping Hand to Wayward Youths of L.A.," *Los Angeles Evening Post-Record*, May 18, 1925, 2. The *Post-Record* article described Robbins as an "intimate" of Jack London.

2. Ancestry.com, 1930 census, 1920 census.

3. For a selection of coverage by California papers: "On the Air," *Los Angeles Evening Citizen News*, February 25, 1936, 13; "Forum on Juvenile Crime Prevention Presented Friday," *Wilmington Daily Press Journal*, October 21, 1937, 7; "California Attorneys Try to Educate Youth to Observe Law," *Desert Sun*, June 30, 1939, 3; "State Bar Campaign Acclaimed," *Highland Park News-Herald*, July 3, 1939, 1; "Bar Will Aid Campaign on Crime Futility," *Long Beach Sun*, August 5, 1939, 12; "Anti-Crime Program Starts in L.A. Schools This Week," *Daily News*, September 11, 1939, 18; "Lawyers Open Campaign against Juvenile Crime by Education of Youth," *Independent*, September 26, 1939, 5; "Harold H. Krowech Will Address Bar at Noon Gathering," *Long Beach Sun*, October 17, 1939, 3.

4. Harold H. Krowech, "Legal Guidance in Crime Prevention," *Federal Probation* 6, no. 2 (1942): 33-37.

5. "Legal Guidance in Crime Prevention" identifies Krowech as also the director of the Southern California Academy of Criminology, the founder of "Legal Guidance in Crime Prevention," and the author of the crime prevention digest of the state bar. This document was a report prepared for the Western Probation and Parole Conference in Reno, Nevada, in June 1942. See also "Juvenile Crime and Its Prevention [Notes]," *Los Angeles Bar Bulletin* 20, no. 7 (March 1944-45): 215-21; and *Los Angeles Times*, July 25, 1942, A3.

6. His and his family's occasional appearances at society events, as recorded in the *Los Angeles Times*, suggest that he was a successful lawyer. He died in May 1974 while living in Beverly Hills. See Ancestrylibrary.com.

7. Harold H, Krowech, *Poems . . . Based upon the Writer's Experiences and Feelings of Children While Presiding as Referee as Needed, Juvenile Court, Los Angeles County, State of California. Dedicated to Children Everywhere* (Los Angeles, CA: Harold Krowech, 1965)

8. Barry C. Feld, *The Evolution of the Juvenile Court: Race, Politics, and the Criminalizing of Juvenile Justice* (New York: New York University Press, 2017). In other ways, the judge was as different from Jack Robbins as two "reformers" could be. After mentioning the founding of the juvenile court in Illinois in 1899, the judge, William B. McKesson, then asked, "What gave rise to this movement of separate courts" for children? He continued: "I think it is the common denominator of parenthood. Whether a person were a lawyer, judge, teacher, doctor, merchant, legislator, minister or industrialist—when it came to his own children he was a parent first and a leader or follower in his profession or business second" ("Enlightened Juvenile Justice," *Juvenile Court Judges Journal* 4 [1953]: 36-41). Like Jack Robbins, McKesson got involved in the movie business, and he made two shorts that involved juvenile justice. In one, *The Terrible Truth* (1951), he revealed that the availability of marijuana for the young was a plot by Soviet Communists. In the second, *Name Unknown* (1951), he described how he proceeded as a judge in the case of Edie, a young girl who had run away from home with a boy who had promised to marry her. In court, he told her about what happened to teenagers who didn't listen to their parents or other authority figures. The answer: assault, rape, and murder. And all because parents were too permissive "and let them have jobs outside the home, or the girls were too defiant." Edie was reduced to a wreck by those words. But the good judge (at least in the movie) finished by throwing her into juvenile detention for three months to give her time to think about "whether showing off is worth a lifetime of regrets." That was his version of crime prevention. See Sid Davis, dir., *The Terrible Truth* (United States: Sid Davis Productions, 1951); Sid Davis, dir., *Name Unknown* (United States: Sid Davis Productions, 1951); "Name Unknown Plot," IMDB.com, accessed August 25, 2023, https://www.imdb.com/title/tt0260220/plotsummary?ref_=tt_ov_pl.

9. Tamara Gene Myers, *Youth Squad: Policing Children in the Twentieth Century (Montreal: McGill-Queens University Press, 2019)*, 9, 28.

10. See John Griffiths, "Ideology in Criminal Procedure or a Third 'Model' of the Criminal Process," *Yale Law Journal* 79, no. 3 (January 1970): 359–417; David B. Wolcott, *Cops and Kids: Policing Juvenile Delinquency in Urban America, 1890–1940* (Columbus: Ohio State University Press, 2005), 126–32; Myers, *Youth Squad*; Thomas G. Blomberg, Francis T. Cullen, Christoffer Carlsson, and Cheryl Lero Jonson, eds., *Delinquency and Drift Revisited: The Criminology of David Matza and Beyond* (London: Routledge, 2018), 15.

11. Krowech, "Legal Guidance in Crime Prevention."

12. James Forman, "The Superpredator Myth Did a Lot of Damage. Courts Are Beginning to See the Light," *New York Times*, April 24, 2022, Sunday opinion, SR3.

13. There is today a rich philosophical debate over how to justify giving the young criminal a "break" in terms of punishment. The debate revolves around what counts in mitigation of the wrongfulness of criminal acts by the young, whether nature, nurture, culture, or the absence of political capacity; see Gideon Yaffe, *The Age of Culpability: Children and the Nature of Criminal Responsibility* (New York: Oxford University Press, 2018). To a nonexpert, to a nonphilosopher, what seems most striking about the debate is the work it takes today to distinguish adult criminals from young criminals, the flimsiness of the categories mobilized to distinguish one from the other. By the mid-1970s, the successors to the Chicago criminologists who had created a criminology of juvenile delinquency acknowledged that they were relatively uninterested in juvenile delinquency, which they folded in with a broader notion of "deviance." See William Simon, Joseph E. Puntil, and Emil Peluso, "Continuities in Delinquency Research," in *Delinquency, Crim, and Society*, ed. James F. Short Jr. (Chicago: University of Chicago Press, 1976), 56. It should be added that a predominant version of the recent history denies the "innocence" of children accused of crimes, insists on their likeness to adult criminals. Often the recent history begins with the decision in In Re Gault (387 U.S. 1 [1967]) that granted constitutional rights to children subjected to the juvenile court. In the last few years, though, there has been a countermovement. As Martha Minow reminded me, the Massachusetts Supreme Judicial Court has used brain science to reject sentences of life without parole for minors. And the US Supreme Court in 2012 abolished sentences of life without parole for youthful offenders, emphasizing the capacity of the child to change. 567 U.S. 460 (2012).

14. We know *The Wire* is about an enclosed world of career criminals because its imagined Baltimore is a largely African American world. By contrast, the multiracial adolescents of Inglewood, in Los Angeles, on the series *On Our Block*, have a more contingent and less determinate relationship to crime and to adult criminals (gang members). They can be understood as children and as adolescents. In the now largely African American neighborhood of North Lawndale, the effects of what Wacquant calls hyperpenalization are particularly shocking. He estimates that over 80 percent of the adult males living there have a criminal conviction, either as juveniles or as adults. In 2000, the population was over 59 percent females, because so many of the men and boys were serving time in carceral institutions. See Loïc Wacquant, *Bourdieu in the City: Challenging Urban Theory* (Hoboken, NJ: Polity, 2023), 141–42, relying on Lisa McKean and Jody Raphael, *Drugs, Crime, and Consequences: Arrests and Incarceration in North Lawndale* (Chicago: Center for Employment Research / North Lawndale Employment Network, October 2002).

15. There is a huge literature to choose from on the failures of juvenile justice. See, for a selection, Alexandra Cox, *Trapped in a Vice: The Consequences of Confinement for Young People* (New Brunswick, NJ: Rutgers University Press, 2018); Mark Dostert, *Up in Here: Jailing Kids on Chicago's Other Side (Iowa City: University of Iowa Press, 2014)*; James Forman Jr., *Locking Up Our Own: Crime and Punishment in Black America* (New York: Farrar, Straus, and Giroux, 2018); Jyiti Nanda, "Set Up to Fail: Youth Probation Conditions as a Driver of Incarceration," *Lewis and Clark Law Review* 26, no. 3 (2022): 677–747.

16. That said, one could also imagine, as several readers have mentioned, that his notion of a republic and of a society of "pals" connects to a variety of more recent countercultural practices, like those in schools like Summerhill and the work of radical psychiatry and radical education. And some of the same impulses may still be found in sites as varied as Alcoholics Anonymous and nonhierarchical workplaces.

A 1992 documentary about the New York Boys' Brotherhood Republic was appreciatively reviewed in the *New York Times* (December 22, 1992, C20). On the other hand, in the *School Library Journal*, the film was seen as an exploration of a once successful experiment that did not keep pace with a changing environment (*School Library Journal* 39, no. 7 [July 1, 1993]: 51). See Frederick Rendina, dir., *A Gang for Good*, aired 1992 on PBS, https://www.imdb.com/title/tt0905335/.

Bibliography

Abrams, Herbert K. "Practicing Social Medicine: Memoirs from the Neighborhood." Unpublished manuscript, n.d. In possession of Alan Derickson.

Adams, Jane. *The Transformation of Rural Life: Southern Illinois, 1890–1990*. Chapel Hill: University of North Carolina Press, 1994.

Addams, Jane. *The Spirit of Youth and the City Streets*. New York: Macmillan, 1909. https://www.gutenberg.org/files/16221/16221-h/16221-h.htm.

Agyepong, Tera Eva. *The Criminalization of Black Children: Race, Gender, and Delinquency in Chicago's Juvenile Justice System, 1899–1945*. Chapel Hill: University of North Carolina Press, 2018.

———. "Who Gets a Girlhood? Constructing Race and Gendered Delinquency in the Juvenile Justice System." Prepared for a workshop on Children and the Law at the American Society for Legal History conference, November 2022, Chicago, IL.

Allen, Anita L. "Associational Privacy and the First Amendment: NAACP v. Alabama, Privacy and Data Protection." *Alabama Civil Rights and Civil Liberties Law Review* 1, no. 1 (2011): 1–13.

Amenta, Edwin, and Neal Caren. *Rough Draft of History: A Century of US Social Movements in the News*. Princeton, NJ: Princeton University Press, 2022.

Andrews, Thomas G. *Killing for Coal*. Cambridge, MA: Harvard University Press, 2010.

Anthony, Earl. *The Time of the Furnaces*. New York: Dial, 1971.

Argo, Grace. "Survived and Punished: Incest Victims' Treatment in Progressive-Era Chicago." *Journal of the History of Childhood and Youth* 16, no. 1 (Winter 2023): 28–49.

Arnold, Peri E. "What Bonded Immigrants to Urban Machines? The Case of Jacob Arvey and Chicago's 24th Ward." *Journal of Policy History* 25, no. 4 (2013): 463–88.

Arthur, Anthony. *Radical Innocent: Upton Sinclair*. New York: Random House, 2006.

Ashby, LeRoy. *Saving the Waifs: Reformers and Dependent Children, 1890–1917*. Philadelphia, PA: Temple University Press, 1984.

Ballard, Parthene. *Nic at the Tavern, or Nobody's Boy*. Philadelphia, PA: American Sunday-School Union, 1865.

Barraclough, Laura R. *Making the San Fernando Valley*. Athens: University of Georgia Press, 2011.

Barton, Robert. "Citizens, Present and Future." *Advance* 68 (March 1916): 773–77.

Bederman, Gail. *Manliness and Civilization: A Cultural History of Gender and Race in the United States, 1880–1917*. Chicago: University of Chicago Press, 1995.

Bennett, James. *Oral History and Delinquency: The Rhetoric of Criminology*. Chicago: University of Chicago Press, 1981.

Benton-Cohen, Katherine. *Inventing the Immigration Problem: The Dillingham Commission and Its Legacy*. Cambridge, MA: Harvard University Press, 2018.

Bernstein, Robin. *Racial Innocence: Performing American Childhood from Slavery to Civil Rights*. New York: New York University Press, 2011.

Billingham, Luke, and Keir Irwin-Rogers. "The Terrifying Abyss of Insignificance: Marginalisation, Mattering and Violence Between Young People." *Onati Socio-Legal Series* 11, no. 5 (2021): 1222–49.

Bloch, Stefano, and Susan A. Phillips. "Mapping and Making Gangland: A Legacy of Redlining and Enjoining Gang Neighbourhoods in Los Angeles." *Urban Studies* 59, no. 4 (2022): 750–70.

Blomberg, Thomas G., Francis T. Cullen, Christoffer Carlsson, and Cheryl Lero Jonson, eds. *Delinquency and Drift Revisited: The Criminology of David Matza and Beyond*. London and New York: Routledge, 2018.

Bourne, Randolph S. *Youth and Life*. Boston, MA: Houghton Mifflin, 1913.

Boyer, Paul S. *Urban Masses and Moral Order in America, 1820–1920*. Cambridge, MA: Harvard University Press, 1978.

Boys Workers' Round Table: A Magazine of Applied Ideals in Boy Craft 1, no. 1 (March 1918). New York: Boys' Club Federation, Inc.

Braille Institute. *Imagining the Future*. Annual report. Los Angeles, CA: Braille Institute, 2014. https://www.brailleinstitute.org/wp-content/uploads/2014/01/Light-2014.pdf.

Branch, Taylor. *Parting the Waters: America in the King Years, 1954–1963*. New York: Simon and Schuster, 1988.

Breckenridge, Sophonisba P., and Edith Abbott. *The Delinquent Child and the Home: A Study of the Delinquent Wards of the Juvenile Court of Chicago*. New York: Survey Associates, Inc., 1916.

Brewer, Holly, and Omohundro Institute of Early American History and Culture. *By Birth or Consent: Children, Law, and the Anglo-American Revolution in Authority*. Chapel Hill: Published for the Omohundro Institute of Early American History and Culture, Williamsburg, Virginia, by the University of North Carolina Press, 2005.

Bridges, James R. "Note: Charitable Trusts: The Liberal Construction Rule and Public Policy—*In the Matter of Estate of Robbins* (Cal. 1962)." *California Law Review* 50, no. 5 (December 1962): 885–90.

Canion, W. G. *The Truth of the Hour, Not the Truth of Yesterday, Not the Truth of Tomorrow, but the Truth of Today*. Baltimore, MD: W. G. Canion, 1919.

Carter, Julia F. "Some Thoughts on Boys' Reading." *Elementary English Review* 7, no. 7 (September 1930): 175–78.

Caute, David. *The Great Fear: The Anti-Communist Purge under Truman and Eisenhower*. New York: Simon and Schuster, 1978.

Chambers, M. M. *Youth-Serving Organizations: National Non-Governmental Associations; an Introductory Survey and Descriptive Directory.* Washington, DC: American Council on Education, 1937.

Chinn, Sarah E. *Inventing Modern Adolescence: The Children of Immigrants in Turn-of-the-Century America.* New Brunswick, NJ: Rutgers University Press, 2009.

Clark, Neil M. "'When a Feller Needs a Friend.'" *American Magazine* 98 (December 1924): 52–53, 138–42.

Cohen, Lizabeth. *Making a New Deal: Industrial Workers in Chicago, 1919–1930.* New York: Cambridge University Press, 1990.

Cohen, Scott. *Meet the Makers: The People behind the Product.* New York: St. Martin's Press, 1979.

Colgate, Caroline Bayard Dod. *Off the Straight and Narrow.* New York: Lee Furman, 1937.

Colley, Linda. "Part of the Punishment: Convict Flows." *London Review of Books* 45, no. 1 (January 5, 2023). https://www.lrb.co.uk/the-paper/v45/n01/linda-colley/part-of -the-punishment.

Cox, Alexandra. *Trapped in a Vice: The Consequences of Confinement for Young People.* New Brunswick, NJ: Rutgers University Press, 2018.

Creisler, Lillian. "Little Oklahoma: A Study of the Social and Economic Adjustment of Refugees in the Beard Tract, Modesto, Stanislaus County, California." MA thesis, University of California, Berkeley, 1940.

Cummings, Scott L. "Privatizing Public Interest Law." *Georgetown Journal of Legal Ethics* 25, no. 1 (Winter 2012): 1–90.

Cutlip, S. M. *Fund Raising in the United States: Its Role in America's Philanthropy.* New Brunswick, NJ: Rutgers University Press, 1965.

Dapping, William Osborne. *The Muckers: A Narrative of the Crapshooters Club.* Edited by Woody Register. Syracuse, NY: Syracuse University Press, 2016.

Davis, Mike, and Jon Weiner. *Set the Night on Fire: L.A. in the Sixties.* New York: Verso, 2020.

Davis, Sid, dir. *Name Unknown.* United States: Sid Davis Productions, 1951.

———. *The Terrible Truth.* United States: Sid Davis Productions, 1951.

Demos, John, and Virginia Demos. "Adolescence in Historical Perspective." *Journal of Marriage and Family* 31, no. 4 (November 1969): 632–39.

Derickson, Alan. "Inventing the Right to Know: Herbert Abrams's Efforts to Democratize Access to Workplace Health Hazard Information in the 1950s." *American Journal of Public Health* 106, no. 2 (February 2016): 237–45.

DiGirolamo, Vincent. *Crying the News: A History of America's Newsboys.* New York: Oxford University Press, 2019.

Dimitriadis, Greg. "The Situation Complex: Revisiting Frederic Thrasher's *The Gang*: A Study of 1,313 Gangs in Chicago." *Cultural Studies, Critical Methodologies* 6, no. 3 (August 2006): 335–53.

Dorson, Norman, Paul Bender, and Bert Neuborne. *Emerson, Haber, and Dorson's Political and Civil Rights in the United States.* 4th ed. Vol. 1. Boston, MA: Little, Brown, 1977.

Dostert, Mark. *Up in Here: Jailing Kids on Chicago's Other Side.* Iowa City: University of Iowa Press, 2014.

Edelman, Murray. *Constructing the Political Spectacle.* Chicago: University of Chicago Press, 1988.

"Editorial Comment." *Work with Boys: A Magazine of Methods* 15, no. 10 (1915–16): 365.

"Editorial Comment." *Work with Boys: A Magazine of Methods* 17, no. 1 (1917): 1–3.

Embree, Edwin R. *Julius Rosenwald Fund: Review of Two Decades, 1917–1936.* Chicago: n.p., 1936.

Embree, Edwin Rogers, and Julia Waxman. *Investment in People: The Story of the Julius Rosenwald Fund.* New York: Harper and Brothers, 1947.

Emerson, Thomas I. *The System of Freedom of Expression.* New York: Random House, 1970.

Feld, Barry C. *The Evolution of the Juvenile Court: Race, Politics, and the Criminalizing of Juvenile Justice.* New York: New York University Press, 2017.

Fifty Years of Boy-Building, 1887–1937: Where the Needy, Dependent, Not Delinquent, Boy Is Given a Chance to Become the Right Sort of Man. Glenwood, IL: Glenwood Manual Training School, 1937.

Fliegelman, Jay. *Prodigals and Pilgrims.* Cambridge, MA: Harvard University Press, 1984.

Florey, Robert, dir. *Loretta Young Show.* Season 1, episode 25, "Nobody's Boy." Screenplay by Gene Levitt. Aired March 7, 1954, on NBC. https://www.youtube.com/watch?v=Gugf4Su6mTk.

Flynn, Frank T. "Merritt W. Pinckney and the Early Days of the Juvenile Court in Chicago." *Social Service Review* 28, no. 1 (March 1954): 20–30.

Forbath, William. "A Jewish Constitutional Moment." Law and Public Affairs Seminar, Princeton University, April 1, 2019, Princeton, NJ.

Forbush, William Byron. *The Boy Problem: A Study in Social Pedagogy; with an Introduction by G. Stanley Hall.* Cambridge, MA: Pilgrim Press, 1901.

———. *The Boy Problem in the Home.* Boston, MA: Pilgrim Press, 1915.

———. "A New Apostle's Creed." *How to Help Boys* 2, no. 4 (October 1902): 173.

Forman, James, Jr. *Locking Up Our Own: Crime and Punishment in Black America.* New York: Farrar, Straus, and Giroux, 2018.

Fortas, Abe. *Concerning Dissent and Disobedience.* New York: World Publishing, 1968.

Fox, Sanford J. "Juvenile Justice Reform: An Historical Perspective." *Stanford Law Review* 22, no. 6 (June 1970): 1187–239.

Fraser, Nancy, and Linda Gordon. "A Genealogy of Dependency: Tracing a Keyword of the U.S. Welfare State." *Signs* 19, no. 2 (Winter 1994): 309–36.

Freedman, Estelle B. *Maternal Justice: Miriam Van Waters and the Female Reform Tradition.* Chicago: University of Chicago Press, 1996.

Friedman, Daniel. *The King of Chicago: The Incredible True Story of a Jewish Orphan's Rise from Despair to Triumph in 1920s Chicago.* New York: Carrel Books, 2017.

Friedman, Lawrence J. *Crime and Punishment in American History: The Price of Freedom in the History of American Criminal Justice.* New York: Basic Books, 1993.

Fucini, Joseph J., and Suzy Fucini. *Entrepreneurs: The Men and Women behind Famous Brand Names and How They Made It.* Boston: G. K. Hall, 1985.

Fukuyama, Francis. "The Latin American Experience." *Journal of Democracy* 19, no. 4 (2008): 69–79.

Ganz, Melissa J. "'A Kind of Insanity in My Spirits': *Frankenstein,* Childhood, *and* Criminal Intent." *Eighteenth Century Studies* 56, no. 1 (Fall 2022): 53–74.

Gertz, Elmer. *To Life: The Story of a Chicago Lawyer*. New York: McGraw-Hill Book Company, 1974.

Gibbons, Andrea. *City of Segregation: 100 Years of Struggle for Housing in Los Angeles*. New York: Verso, 2018.

Gibson, H. W. *Boyology, or Boy Analysis*. New York: Association Press, 1922.

Goldberg, J. J., and Elliot King, eds. *Builders and Dreamers: Habonim Labor Zionist Youth in North America*. New York: Herzl Press, 1993.

Goldin, Claudia. "America's Graduation from High School: The Evolution and Spread of Secondary Schooling in the Twentieth Century." *Journal of Economic History* 58, no. 2 (1998): 345–74.

Goluboff, Risa. *Vagrant Nation: Police Power, Constitutional Change, and the Making of the 1960s*. New York: Oxford University Press, 2016.

Gordon, Linda. *The Great Arizona Orphan Abduction*. Cambridge, MA: Harvard University Press, 1999.

———. *Heroes of Their Own Lives*. New York: Vintage, 1988.

———. *Pitied but Not Entitled: Single Mothers and the History of Welfare*. New York: Free Press, 1994.

Grant, Julia. *The Boy Problem: Educating Boys in Urban America, 1870–1970*. Baltimore, MD: Johns Hopkins University Press, 2014.

Green, Thomas A. *Freedom and Responsibility in American Legal Thought*. New York: Cambridge University Press, 2015.

Greenberg, Jack. *Race Relations and American Law*. New York: Columbia University Press, 1959.

Griffiths, John. "Ideology in Criminal Procedure or a Third 'Model' of the Criminal Process." *Yale Law Journal* 79, no. 3 (January 1970): 359–417.

Grossberg, Michael. *Governing the Hearth: Law and the Family in Nineteenth-Century America*. Chapel Hill: University of North Carolina, 1985.

———. "Legal Rights for Children? A Historical Look at a Continuing Legal Paradox." In *Children at Risk in America, edited by Roberta Wollens*. Albany: State University of New York Press, 1992.

———. "A Protected Childhood: The Emergence of Child Protection in America." In *American Public Life and the Historical Imagination*, edited by Wendy Gamber, Michael Grossberg, and Hendrik Hartog, 213–39. Notre Dame, IN: University of Notre Dame Press, 2003.

Gruenberg, Aaron, project coordinator, Marks Nathan Oral History Project. *Home Kids Memories of the Marks Nathan Jewish Orphan Home*. Chicago: Jewish Children's Bureau of Chicago: n.d. https://jgs.jgsi.org/cmn/documents/MN-Oral-History-Memories.pdf.

Guth, Suzie. *Les Gangs de Jeunes Italo-Americains: Les Forty Two de Chicago*. Paris: L'Harmattan, 2017.

Hadsell, Barbara Enloe. "Celebration of a Radical Life: John McTernan (1910–2005)." *Guild Practitioner* 62 (2005): 53–64.

Hall, G. Stanley. "Introduction." In Joseph Adams Puffer, *The Boy and His Gang*. Boston, MA: Houghton Mifflin, 1912. https://www.gutenberg.org/cache/epub/57927/pg57927-images.html.

Haney Lopez, Ian F. *Racism on Trial: The Chicano Fight for Justice*. Cambridge, MA: Harvard University Press, 2003.

Hanst, Dale E. "Presentation of the Loren Miller Legal Services Award to John T. McTernan." *Guild Practitioner* 41, no. 3 (Summer 1984): 95–96.

Hartman, Saidiya V. *Wayward Lives, Beautiful Experiments: Intimate Histories of Riotous Black Girls, Troublesome Women, and Queer Radicals*. New York: Norton, 2019.

Hartog, Hendrik. "The Constitution of Aspiration and 'The Rights That Belong to Us All.'" *Journal of American History* 74, no. 3 (December 1987): 1013–34.

———. "Four Fragments on Doing Legal History, or Thinking with and against Willard Hurst." *Law and History Review* 39, no. 4 (November 2021): 835–66.

Healey, Dorothy, and Maurice Isserman. *Dorothy Healey Remembers: A Life in the American Communist Party*. New York: Oxford, 1990.

Hiatt, James S. *The Truant Problem and the Parental School*. US Bureau of Education Bulletin 1915, no. 29. Washington, DC: Government Printing Office, 1915.

Hickson, William J. "The Defective Delinquent." *Journal of Criminal Law and Criminology* 5, no. 3 (September 1914): 397–403.

Higham, John. *Strangers in the Land: Patterns of American Nativism, 1860–1925*. Newark, NJ: Rutgers University Press, 2002.

Holl, Jack M. *Juvenile Reform in the Progressive Era: William R. George and the Junior Republic Movement*. Ithaca, NY: Cornell University Press, 1971.

Holt, Marilyn Irvin. *Orphan Trains: Placing Out in America*. Lincoln: University of Nebraska Press, 1992.

Horwitt, Sanford D. *Let Them Call Me Rebel: Saul Alinsky—His Life and Legacy*. New York: Knopf, 1989.

Horwitz, Morton. *The Transformation of American Law, 1780–1860*. Cambridge, MA: Harvard University Press, 1977.

Hurley, T. D. *Origin of the Juvenile Court Law*. 3rd edition. Chicago: Visitation and Aid Society, 1907.

Hurst, J. Willard. *Law and the Conditions of Freedom in the Nineteenth Century United States*. Madison: University of Wisconsin Press, 1956.

Illinois Blue Book, 1953–54. Springfield: Illinois Secretary of State, 1953.

Illinois Crime Survey. In association with the Chicago Crime Commission Illinois Association for Criminal Justice. Chicago: Illinois Association for Criminal Justice, 1929.

Industrial Relations Commission. *Final Report and Testimony of Industrial Relations Commission*. 11 vols. Washington, DC: Government Printing Office, 1916.

Jackson, Crystal. *The Entrance: Pacoima's Story*. Los Angeles, CA: BAIT-CAL, 2019.

Jeter, Helen Rankin. "The Chicago Juvenile Court" (Washington, DC: US Department of Labor, Children's Bureau, 1922). Reprinted in *The Juvenile Court*, edited and compiled by Robert M. Mennel, 18–19 (New York: Arno Press, 1974).

Jones, Eugene Kinckle. "Problems of the Colored Child." *Annals of the American Academy of Political and Social Science* 98 (November 1921): 142–47.

Jones, Jacqueline. *Goddess of Anarchy: The Life and Times of Lucy Parsons, American Radical*. New York: Basic Books, 2017.

"Juvenile Crime and Its Prevention [Notes]." *Los Angeles Bar Bulletin* 20, no. 7 (March 1944–45): 215–21.

Karpf, Maurice J. "The Demoralized Family." *Social Forces* 1, no. 4 (May 1923): 417.

———. "Sociologists and Social Workers Meet." *Families in Society 9, no. 2* (April 1, 1928): 39–45. https://doi.org/10.1177/104438942800900202.

Kearney, Joseph D., and Thomas W. Merrill. *Lakefront: Public Trust and Private Rights in Chicago.* Ithaca, NY: Cornell University Press, 2021.

Keene, Sumner. "Get to the Point." *American Magazine* 89 (1920): 62–63, 266.

Keller, Harry, dir. *Loretta Young Show.* Season 3, episode 3, "Reunion." Written by Gene Levitt (teleplay) and Jack Robbins (story). Aired September 11, 1955, on NBC.

Kidd, Kenneth B. *Making American Boys: Boyology and the Feral Tale.* Minneapolis: University of Minnesota Press, 2004.

Kirtley, James S. *That Boy of Yours: Sympathetic Studies of Boyhood.* New York: Hodder and Stoughton, 1912.

Krowech, Harold H. "Legal Guidance in Crime Prevention." *Federal Probation* 6, no. 2 (1942): 33–37.

———. *Poems . . . Based upon the Writer's Experiences and Feelings of Children While Presiding as Referee as Needed, Juvenile Court, Los Angeles County, State of California. Dedicated to Children Everywhere.* Los Angeles, CA: privately published, 1965.

Kubie, Oenone. "Reading Lewis Hine's Photography of Child Street Labour, 1906–1918." *Journal of American Studies* 50, no. 4 (2016): 873–97.

———. "The Swarm: Children in Chicago, 1890–1933." PhD diss., Brasenose College, University of Oxford, 2018. http://ora.ox.ac.uk/objects/uuid:faa166c5-612f-4de4-b5ff-ec3f62f68745.

Lasch, Christopher. *The New Radicalism in America 1889–1963: The Intellectual as a Social Type.* New York: Norton, 1965.

Lassonde, Stephen. *Learning to Forget: Schooling and Family Life in New Haven's Working Class, 1870–1940.* New Haven, CT: Yale University Press, 2005.

Laughlin, Clara E. "The 'Boy Problem' and How It Has Been Solved—by Boys!" *Chamberlin's* (December 1919): 14–16.

———. "Here's a Real Boys' Club, in Which There Are No Grown Folks, but Just Boys." *Ladies' Home Journal* 36 (October 1919): 83.

———. *Traveling through Life, Being the Autobiography of Clara E. Laughlin.* Boston, MA: Houghton Mifflin, 1934.

———. "Where Boys Rule." *National Magazine* 49 (August 1920): 223–24, 238.

———. "Where Boys Rule." *Red Cross Magazine* 16 (August 1920): 29–33, 74.

———. "The Worst Boy in the United States: Two Chicago Boys Go Traveling to 27 Cities for Him and Find Him." *Ladies' Home Journal* 36 (October 1919): 7–8, 191–92.

"Legacy to 'Political Victims' Defended." *Open Forum, Newsletter of the ACLU of Southern California* 39, no. 1 (January 1962): 1.

Levin, Meyer. *The Old Bunch.* New York: Waking Lion Press, 2012.

Life of the Boys' Brotherhood Republic. Chicago: Boys' Brotherhood Republic, 1938.

Light, Jennifer S. "Building Virtual Cities, 1895–1945." *Journal of Urban History* 38, no. 2 (March 2012): 336–71.

———. *States of Childhood: From the Junior Republic to the American Republic, 1895–1945.* Cambridge, MA: MIT Press, 2020.

Lindsey, Ben B. "The Boy and the Court: The Colorado Law and Its Administration." *Charities* 13 (1905): 350–57.

Logan, John R., Weiwei Zhang, and Miao David Chunyu. "Emergent Ghettos: Black Neighborhoods in New York and Chicago, 1880–1940." *American Journal of Sociology* 120, no. 4 (January 2015): 1055–94.

Loomis, Frank Denman. *The Chicago Community Trust: A History of Its Development, 1915–1962.* Chicago: Chicago Community Trust, 1962.

Macaulay, Stewart. "Justice Traynor and the Law of Contracts." *Stanford Law Review* 13 (July 1961): 812–64.

Mack, Julian W. "The Juvenile Court." *Harvard Law Review* 23, no. 2 (December 1909): 104–22.

Malot, Hector. *Nobody's Boy.* New York: Cupples and Leon, 1916.

Maor, Naama. "Delinquent Parents: Punitive Welfare and the Creation of Juvenile Justice, 1899–1927." PhD diss., University of Chicago, 2020. ProQuest dissertation no. 28026706.

———. "'We Cannot Be Hoodwinked into Making Paroles': Delinquent Children, State Institutions, and the Boundaries of Juvenile Justice." Prepared for Children and the Law: A Conference in Honor of Michael Grossberg, American Society for Legal History Pre-Conference, November 10, 2022, Chicago, IL.

Mari, Will. *The American Newsroom: A History, 1920–1960.* Columbia: University of Missouri Press, 2021.

Marten, James, ed. *Children and Youth During the Gilded Age and Progressive Era.* New York: New York University Press, 2014.

Mattson, Kevin. *Upton Sinclair and the Other American Century.* New York: Wiley, 2006.

Matza, David. *Delinquency and Drift.* London: Routledge, 2017.

Maza, Sarah. "AHR Exchange: The Kids Aren't All Right: Historians and the Problem of Childhood." *American Historical Review* 125, no. 4 (December 2020): 1261–85.

McDougal, Luther L., III, and Myres S. McDougal. *Property, Wealth, Land: Allocation, Planning and Development.* 2nd ed. Indianapolis: Michie Company; Bobbs-Merrill Company, 1981.

McDougal, Myres Smith. *Property, Wealth, Land: Allocation, Planning, and Development; Selected Cases and Other Materials on the Law of Real Property.* Charlottesville, VA: Michie Casebook Corp., 1948.

McKean, Lisa, and Jody Raphael. *Drugs, Crime, and Consequences: Arrests and Incarceration in North Lawndale.* Chicago: Center for Employment Research / North Lawndale Employment Network, October 2002.

McQueary, T. H. "Schools for Dependent, Delinquent, and Truant Children in Illinois." *American Journal of Sociology* 9, no. 1 (July 1903): 1–23.

Mennel, Robert M., ed. and comp. *The Juvenile Court.* New York: Arno Press, 1974.

———. *Thorns and Thistles: Juvenile Delinquents in the United States, 1825–1940.* Hanover: University of New Hampshire by the University Press of New England, 1973.

Minow, Martha. *Making All the Difference: Inclusion, Exclusion, and American Law.* Ithaca, NY: Cornell University Press, 1990.

———. "We, the Family: Constitutional Rights and American Families." *Journal of American History* 74, no. 3 (December 1987): 959–83.

Mintz, Steven. *Huck's Raft: A History of American Childhood*. Cambridge, MA: Belknap Press of Harvard University Press, 2004.

Mishkin, Lee, dir. *Is It Always Right to Be Right?* Stephen Bosustow Productions: n.p., 1970. Short animated film, 7:50. Uploaded to YouTube by Jérôme Labbé, May 26, 2013. https://www.youtube.com/watch?v=NM2KvijwlNE.

Moore, Sally Falk. *Law as Process: An Anthropological Approach*. London: Routledge and K. Paul, 1978.

Morris, Richard, dir. *Loretta Young Show*. Season 2, episode 16, "Big Jim." Written by Richard Morris. Aired December 5, 1954, on NBC. https://www.youtube.com/watch?v=KZmgMfwgRD4&list=PLeCx1fxAQ3ZvMyHkeIhysEZVz-k9509TQ&index=52.

Myers, Tamara Gene. *Youth Squad: Policing Children in the Twentieth Century*. Montreal: McGill-Queens University Press, 2019.

N., O. J., Jr. "Right of a Non-Resident to Qualify and Serve in Fiduciary Capacities—An Analysis." *Virginia Law Review* 37, no. 8 (1951): 1119–44.

Nanda, Jyiti. "Set Up to Fail: Youth Probation Conditions as a Driver of Incarceration." *Lewis and Clark Law Review* 26, no. 3 (2022): 677–747.

National Housing Association. *Proceedings of the National Housing Association*. New York: National Housing Association, 1918.

Nelson, Maggie. *On Freedom: Four Songs of Care and Constraint*. Minneapolis, MN: Greywolf Press, 2021.

New, Anne L. *Service for Givers: The Story of the National Information Bureau*. New York: National Information Bureau, Inc., 1982.

Newcomb, Arthur W. "Making the Man of Tomorrow out of the Glenwood Boy." *Business Philosopher 6, no. 8* (August 1910): 456–65.

Nord, David Paul. *Communities of Journalism: A History of American Journalism and Their Readers*. Urbana and Chicago: University of Illinois Press, 2001.

Odem, Mary. *Delinquent Daughters*. Chapel Hill: University of North Carolina Press, 1995.

Okrand, Fred. "Forty Years Defending the Constitution." Interview by Michael Balter. Oral history transcript. Completed under the auspices of the UCLA Oral History Program, 1984, 373–74, Department of Special Collections, Charles E. Young Research Library, UCLA, Los Angeles, CA. http://content.cdlib.org/view?docId=ft258003n2&brand=oac4.

Oppenheimer, Jerry. *Madoff with the Money*. Hoboken, NJ: John Wiley and Sons, 2009.

Owen, Gabrielle. *A Queer History of Adolescence: Developmental Pasts, Relational Futures*. Athens: University of Georgia Press, 2020.

Pagan, Eduardo Obregon. *Murder at the Sleepy Lagoon: Zoot Suits, Race, and Riot in Wartime L.A.* Chapel Hill, University of North Carolina Press, 2003.

Page, James Franklin. *Socializing for the New Order or Educational Values of the Juvenile Organization*. Rockland, IL: Augustana College, 1919.

Papachristos, Andrew V., and James F. Short. "The Chicago School's Contribution to Criminological Theory and Methods." In *The Encyclopedia of Research Methods in Criminology and Criminal Justice*, edited by J. C. Barnes and David R. Forde, 169–78. Hoboken, NJ: Wiley, 2021.

Park, Robert Ezra, and Herbert Adolphus Miller. *Old World Traits Transplanted*. New York: Harper, 1921.

Penningroth, Dylan C. *The Claims of Kinfolk: African American Property and Community in the Nineteenth-Century South*. Chapel Hill: University of North Carolina Press, 2003.

Perry, Lewis. *Childhood, Marriage and Reform: Henry Clarke Wright, 1797–1870*. Chicago: University of Chicago Press, 1980.

———. *Civil Disobedience: An American Tradition*. New Haven, CT: Yale University Press, 2013.

Philips, Leo A. "The Institutional Care of the Normal Dependent Child." *Institution Quarterly* 5, no. 1 (March 1914): 78–83.

Pifferi, Michele. *Reinventing Punishment: A Comparative History of Criminology and Penology in the Nineteenth and Twentieth Centuries*. Oxford: Oxford University Press, 2016.

Platt, Anthony M. *The Child Savers: The Invention of Delinquency*. Introduction by Miroslava Chavez-Garcia. New Brunswick, NJ: Rutgers University Press, 2009.

Population Media Center. *Storytelling for Good: Improving the Health and Well-Being of People*. Annual report. South Burlington, VT: Population Media Center, 2012. https://issuu.com/globalpopulationspeakout/docs/2012-annual-report-final.

Poulos, John W. "The Judicial Philosophy of Roger Traynor." *Hastings Law Review* 46, no. 6 (August 1995): 1643–722.

Proceedings of the Attorney General's Conference on Crime Held December 10–13, 1934, in Memorial Continental Hall, Washington, D.C. Washington, DC: US Bureau of Prisons, Department of Justice, 1934. https://www.google.com/books/edition/Proceedings_of_the_Attorney_General_s_Co/H3MEAAAAMAAJ?hl=en.

Puffer, Joseph Adams. *The Boy and His Gang*. Boston, MA: Houghton Mifflin, 1912. https://www.gutenberg.org/cache/epub/57927/pg57927-images.html.

Rabban, David M. *Free Speech in Its Forgotten Years, 1870–1920*. Cambridge and New York: Cambridge University Press, 1997.

Raftery, Judith. "Chicago Settlement Women in Fact and Fiction: Hobart Chatfield Chatfield-Taylor, Clara Elizabeth Laughlin, and Elia Wilkinson Peattie Portray the New Woman." *Illinois Historical Journal* 88, no. 1 (Spring 1995): 37–58.

Ray, Nicholas, dir. *Rebel without a Cause*. Hollywood: Warner Brothers, 1955. https://www.imdb.com/title/tt0048545/?ref_=tt_mv_close.

Redfield, Isaac. Commentary on *People v. Turner*. *American Law Register (N.S.)* 10 (June 1871): 366–73.

Register, Woody. "Introduction: The Charm That Truth Never Lacks: A Brief History of William Osborne Dapping and his Crapshooters Club." In William Osborne Dapping, *The Muckers: A Narrative of the Crapshooters Club*, edited by Woody Register. Syracuse, NY: Syracuse University Press, 2016, 3–48.

Reis, Martha Lynn. "Hidden Histories: Ben Reitman and the 'Outcast' Women behind 'Sister of the Road: The Autobiography of Box-Car Bertha.'" PhD diss., University of Minnesota, 2000. ProQuest dissertation no. 9983595.

Rembis, Michael A. *Defining Deviance: Sex, Science, and Delinquent Girls, 1890–1960*. Urbana: University of Illinois Press, 2011.

Rendina, Frederick, dir. *A Gang for Good*. Aired 1992 on PBS. https://www.imdb.com/title/tt0905335/.

Report of the City Council Committee on Crime of the City of Chicago. Chicago: H. G. Adair, 1915.

Resnik, Judith. "Iconographies of Punishment in Polities Democratic and Not." Reflections for the Workshop on the Iconography of Democracy, Princeton University, April 2022, Princeton, NJ.

———. *Impermissible Punishments: The Problem Prison Poses in Democracies*. Chicago: University of Chicago Press, forthcoming 2025.

Reynolds, Wilfred S. "Organizing Governmental Agencies for Unemployment Relief." *Social Service Review* 7, no. 3 (September 1933): 365–74.

———. "Public Welfare Administration: A Patchwork in Illinois." *Social Service Review* 11, no. 1 (March 1937): 1–8.

Richmond, Julius B. "Herbert K. Abrams, in Memoriam." *Journal of Public Health Policy* 27, no. 4 (January 2006): 323–26.

Riis, Jacob A. *Children of the Poor*. New York: Scribner, 1908. https://www.gutenberg.org/files/32609/32609-h/32609-h.htm#:~:text=If%20the%20question%20were%20put,society%20and%20the%20%E2%80%9CSunday%2Dschool.

Riney-Kehrberg, Pamela. *The Nature of Childhood: An Environmental History of Growing Up in America since 1865*. Lawrence: University Press of Kansas, 2014.

Robcis, Camille. *Disalienation: Politics, Philosophy, and Radical Psychiatry in Postwar France*. Chicago: University of Chicago Press, 2021.

Rodgers, Daniel T. *Atlantic Crossings: Social Politics in a Progressive Age*. Cambridge, MA: Harvard University Press, 1998.

Rosenthal, Erich. "This Was North Lawndale: The Transplantation of a Jewish Community." *Jewish Social Studies* 22, no. 2 (April 1960): 67–82.

Rothschild, Emma. *An Infinite History: The Story of a French Family over Three Centuries*. Princeton, NJ: Princeton University Press, 2021.

Ryerson, Ellen. *The Best Laid Plans: America's Juvenile Court Experiment*. New York: Hill and Wang, 1978.

Salerno, Roger A. *Boyhood and Delinquency in 1920s Chicago: A Sociological Study of Juvenile Jack-Rollers and Gender*. Jefferson, NC: McFarland, 2017.

Satter, Beryl. *Family Properties: Race, Real Estate, and the Exploitation of Black Urban America*. New York: Metropolitan Books, 2009.

Schlossman, Steven. *Transforming Juvenile Justice: Reform Ideals and Institutional Realities, 1825–1920*. DeKalb: Northern Illinois University Press, 2005.

Schlossman, Steven, and Michael Sedlak. "The Chicago Project Revisited." *Crime and Delinquency* 29, no. 3 (July 1983): 398–462.

Schmidt, James D. "'Restless Movements Characteristic of Childhood': The Legal Construction of Child Labor in Nineteenth-Century Massachusetts." *Law and History Review* 23, no. 2 (Summer 2006): 315–50.

Schrecker, Ellen. *Many Are the Crimes: McCarthyism in America*. Boston, MA: Little, Brown, 1998.

Schuman, Michael. "History of Child Labor in the United States—Part One: Little Children Working." *Monthly Labor Review* (January 2017). https://www.bls.gov/opub/mlr/2017/article/history-of-child-labor-in-the-united-states-part-1.htm.

———. "History of Child Labor in the United States—Part Two: The Reform Movement." *Monthly Labor Review* (January 2017). https://www.bls.gov/opub/mlr/2017/article/history-of-child-labor-in-the-united-states-part-2-the-reform-movement.htm.

Scott, Austin Wakeman. *The Law of Trusts*. 2nd ed. Boston, MA: Little Brown, 1956.

Seton, Ernest Thompson. *Two Little Savages*. New York: Doubleday, 1903.

Shaw, Clifford R. *The Jack-Roller: A Delinquent Boy's Own Story*. Mansfield Centre, CT: Martino Publishing, 2013.

Shaw, Clifford R., and Frederick M. Zorbaugh, with the collaboration of Henry D. McKay and Leonard S. Cottrell. *Delinquency Areas: A Study of the Geographic Distribution of School Truants, Juvenile Delinquents, and Adult Offenders in Chicago*. Chicago: University of Chicago Press, 1929.

Sigal, Clancy. *A Woman of Uncertain Character: The Amorous and Radical Adventures of My Mother Jennie (Who Always Wanted to Be a Respectable Jewish Mom)*. New York: Carroll and Graf, 2006.

Silberstein-Loeb, Jonathan. *The International Distribution of News: The Associated Press, Press Association, and Reuters, 1848–1947*. New York: Cambridge University Press, 2014.

Simon, Jonathan. "Visions of Self-Control: Fashioning a Liberal Approach to Crime and Punishment in the Twentieth Century." In *Looking Back at Law's Century*, edited by Bryant Garth and Austin Sarat, 109–59. Ithaca, NY: Cornell University Press, 2002.

Simon, William, Joseph E. Puntil, and Emil Peluso. "Continuities in Delinquency Research." In *Delinquency, Crime, and Society*, edited by James F. Short Jr. Chicago: University of Chicago Press, 1976.

Sinclair, Upton. *The Brass Check: A Study of American Journalism*. Champaign: University of Illinois Press, 2003.

Soifer, Aviam. "The Paradox of Paternalism and Laissez-Faire Constitutionalism: United States Supreme Court, 1888–1921." *Law and History Review* 5, no. 1 (Spring 1987): 249–79.

Sorin, Gerald. *Nurturing Neighborhood: The Brownsville Boys' Club and Jewish Community in Urban America, 1940–1990*. New York: New York University Press, 1990.

Springer, Jackson. "'Against the Order of Nature': Creating a Gay Identity under the Law in Colorado, 1880–1914." BA thesis, Princeton University, 2018. https://catalog.princeton.edu/catalog/dsp012227ms385.

Staller, Karen M. *New York's Newsboys: Charles Loring Brace and the Founding of the Children's Aid Society*. New York: Oxford University Press, 2020.

Steedman, Carolyn. *Strange Dislocations: Childhood and the Idea of Human Interiority, 1780–1930*. London: Virago Press, 1995.

Steidinger, Amy. *Joliet Prison Blues: A Century of Stories*. Arcadia, SC: Arcadia Publishing, 2021.

Stevenson, Lewis G. *Biennial Report of Secretary of State of the State of Illinois: Fiscal Years Beginning October 1, 1914, and Ending September 30, 1916*. London: Forgotten Books, 2022 (repr.).

Stolzius, Duane C. S. *Freedom from Advertising: E. W. Scripps's Chicago Experiment*. New Brunswick, NJ: Rutgers University Press, 2007.

Stowe, Harriet Beecher. *Tales and Sketches of New England Life*. London: Sampson, Low, and Company, 1855.

Tanenhaus, David S. "Creating the Child, Constructing the State: *People v. Turner*, 1870." In *Children as Equals: Exploring the Rights of the Child*, edited by Kathleen Alaimo and Brian Klug. Lanham, MD: University Press of America, 2002.

———. *Juvenile Justice in the Making*. New York: Oxford University Press, 2004.

Taureg, Norman, dir. *Boys Town*. Hollywood: MGM, 1938. https://www.imdb.com/title/tt0029942/.

Thompson, C. V. R. *I Lost My English Accent*. New York: Putnam, 1939.

Thrasher, Frederic M. *The Gang: A Study of 1,313 Gangs in Chicago*. Chicago: University of Chicago Press, 1927.

Traynor, Roger J. "Lawbreakers, Courts, and Law-Abiders." *Missouri Law Review* 31, no. 2 (Spring 1966): 181–208.

"Trusts—Charitable Trusts: Illegal Purpose—In Re Robbins' Estate, 57 Cal. Rep.2d 765, 371 P.2d 573 (1962) 57 Cal. Rep.2d 765, 371 P.2d 573 (1962)." *DePaul Law Review* 12, no. 2 (Spring–Summer 1963): 364–68.

United States Bureau of the Census. *Fourteenth Census of the United States: State Compendium, Illinois*. Washington, DC: Government Printing Office, 1924.

United States Congress House Special Committee on Victor L. Berger Investigation. *Victor L. Berger: Hearings before the Special Committee Appointed . . . Concerning the Right of Victor L. Berger to Be Sworn In as a Member of the Sixty-Sixth Congress*. Vol. 2. Washington, DC: Government Printing Office, 1919.

United States Senate. *Communist Activity in Mass Communications: Hearing before the Subcommittee to Investigate the Administration of the Internal Security Act, . . . of the Committee on the Judiciary, United States Senate, Eighty-Fifth Congress, Second Session*. 3 vols. Washington, DC: Government Printing Office, 1958.

"Unique Legacy Held 'Benefit to Society.'" *Open Forum, Newsletter of the ACLU of Southern California* 39, no. 6 (June 1962): 1.

Van Vechten, Courtlandt Churchill, Jr. "A Study of Success and Failure of One Thousand Delinquents Committed to a Boys' Republic." PhD diss., University of Chicago, 1935. ProQuest dissertation no. T-04690.

Van Waters, Miriam. "Juvenile Delinquency and Juvenile Courts." In *Encyclopaedia of the Social Sciences*, vol. 7, edited by Edwin Robert Anderson Seligman, 528–33. New York: Macmillan, 1932.

Veal, Ronald Tuttle, J. T. Bowne, and G. E. Carr. *Classified Bibliography of Boy Life and Organized Work with Boys*. New York: Association Press, 1919.

Voorhees, Daniel S. *Report of the Joint Committee on Treasurer's Accounts, and of the State Treasurer, to the Legislature of New Jersey, with the Treasurer's Report to the Governor on the Finances of the State, for the Fiscal Year Ending October 31, 1908*. Trenton, NJ: State Gazette Publishing Company, 1908. https://dspace.njstatelib.org/handle/10929/47018.

Wacquant, Loic. *Bourdieu in the City: Challenging Urban Theory*. Hoboken, NJ: Polity, 2023.

Waldron, Webb. "B.B.R.—Of, by, and for Boys." *Rotarian* 48 (April 1936): 21–23.

Warne, Clore. "Book Review." *Law in Transition* 23, no. 1 (Spring 1963): 81–90.

Warren, Stacy, Robert Sauders, and Anna Dvorak. "For Anna: After Critical GIS, What Next?" *Canadian Geographer* 64, no. 4 (Winter 2020): 529–42.

Webb, Harold Lew. "A Program for Employed Boys' Clubs and Its Use." Bachelor of Associated Science thesis, Young Men's Christian Association College, 1923. https://openlibrary.org/books/OL25487900M/A_program_for_employed_boys'_clubs_and_its_use.

Webster, Crystal Lynn. "'Transfiguring the Soul of Childhood': Du Bois's Private Vision and Public Activism for Black Children." *Journal of the History of Childhood and Youth* 14, no. 3 (Fall 2021): 347–66.

Wechsler, Herbert. "Toward Neutral Principles of Constitutional Law." *Harvard Law Review* 73, no. 1 (November 1959): 1–35.

Weinrib, Laura. "Law, History, and the Interwar ACLU's Jewish Lawyers." Draft, forthcoming.

———. *The Taming of Free Speech: America's Civil Liberties Compromise.* Cambridge, MA: Harvard University Press, 2016.

Welke, Barbara. *Law and the Borders of Belonging.* New York: Cambridge University Press, 2010.

Welling, Richard. *As the Twig Is Bent.* New York: G. P. Putnam, 1942.

Welling, William. *East Side Story: The Boys Brotherhood Republic's First Fifty Years on New York's Lower East Side.* New York: Boys' Brotherhood Republic of New York, Inc., 1982.

Wertheimer, John William. "Free-Speech Fights: The Roots of Modern Free-Expression Litigation in the United States." PhD diss., Princeton University, 1992. https://www.google.com/books/edition/Free_speech_Fights/uU-fAAAAMAAJ?hl=en.

White, Elizabeth. "The History and Development of the Illinois Children's Home and Aid Society." MA thesis, University of Chicago, 1934. https://www.proquest.com/docview/301782118?pq-origsite=gscholar&fromopenview=true.

White, G. Edward. *The American Judicial Tradition. 3rd ed.* New York: Oxford University Press, 2007.

Wiley, Philip. *Generation of Vipers.* New York: Rinehart, 1942.

Willrich, Michael. *City of Courts: Socializing Justice in Progressive Era Chicago.* New York: Cambridge University Press, 2003.

Wines, E. C. *The State of Prisons and of Child-Saving Institutions in the Civilized World.* Cambridge, MA: John Silson and Sons, 1880.

Winslow, Charles S. *Historical Events of Chicago.* Chicago: Soderland Printing Service, 1937.

Wolcott, David B. *Cops and Kids: Policing Juvenile Delinquency in Urban America, 1890–1940.* Columbus: Ohio State University Press, 2005.

Wood, Betsy. *Upon the Altar of Work: Child Labor and the Rise of a New American Sectionalism.* Champaign: University of Illinois Press, 2020.

Woodruff, Clinton Rogers. "Making the World Safe for Generosity." *National Municipal Review* 9 (1920): 151–56.

Work with Boys: A Magazine of Methods 18 (1918). Reading, PA: William McCormick.

The WPA Guide to Illinois: The Federal Writers' Project Guide to 1930s Illinois. New York: Pantheon, 1939.

Wright, Danaya C. *From Feudalism to Family Law: Inter-Spousal Custody Disputes and Repudiation of Mother's Rights*. PhD diss., Johns Hopkins University, 1998. ProQuest dissertation no. 9920805.

Wright, Helen R. "Dependency." In *Encyclopaedia of the Social Sciences*, vol. 7, edited by Edwin Robert Anderson Seligman, 94–95. New York: Macmillan, 1932.

Yaffe, Gideon. *The Age of Culpability: Children and the Nature of Criminal Responsibility*. New York: Oxford University Press, 2018.

Yates, Seymour. "A City of Boys: Where Leadership and Obedience Are Taught." *Rotarian* (October 1927), 25–26, 45.

Zanger, Martin. "Politics of Confrontation: Upton Sinclair and the Launching of the ACLU." *Pacific Historical Review* 38, no. 4 (November 1969): 383–406.

Zelizer, Viviana A. *Pricing the Priceless Child*. Princeton, NJ: Princeton University Press, 1994.

Zinn, Howard. *The Politics of History*. Boston, MA: Beacon Press, 1970.